TAX PLANNING HANDBOOK

STRATEGIES AND APPLICATIONS

Robert D. Gordon C.P.A.

New York Institute of Finance
A Prentice-Hall Company

Library of Congress Cataloging in Publication Data

Gordon, Robert D.
Tax planning handbook.

Includes index.
1. Tax planning—United States. I. Title.

KF6297.G64	343.7304	81-14167
ISBN 0-13-885111-1	347.3034	AACR2

This publication is designed to provide accurate and authoritative information in regard to the subject matter covered. It is sold with the understanding that the publisher is not engaged in rendering legal, accounting, or other professional service. If legal advice or other expert assistance is required, the services of a competent professional person should be sought.

—From a Declaration of Principles jointly adopted by a Committee of the American Bar Association and a Committee of Publishers and Associations

Printed in the United States of America
10 9 8 7 6 5 4 3 2 1

PREFACE

As both a practitioner and an instuctor, I have often been faced with explaining the tax structure of our business world. I am sure that all those in my profession have heard, "Why can't the government just say it in English?"

The fact that the Internal Revenue Code is not written in plain English (and, in deference to the lawyers, probably could not be) causes many to avoid even trying to understand the tax consequences of their activities. This is a luxury that few can afford. For those of us lucky enough to make a few dollars, Uncle Sam is waiting for his share.

While one's business and social decisions cannot be based solely on giving the government the least amount possible, most often a proper knowledge of the tax system and the "right way" can save significant taxes without altering the objectives and needs of the taxpayer.

Every practicing accountant and tax attorney has uttered the words, "Why didn't you call me first?" In most cases it is because the taxpayer has always been afraid of taxes. Occasionally, even the taxpayer's investment advisor is one of those who wishes "it were written in English."

This book is written for those who need to know when to call. The purpose is to reduce to plain English the concepts of the Internal Revenue Code and the planning techniques that are most often used to reduce taxes.

Chapter 1 is designed for those who know nothing of the tax structure. It introduces the novice to the concepts and thereby begins the process of tax planning. The remaining chapters discuss specific areas. Readers with some familiarity of taxation may wish to go directly to areas of particular interest to them. Others may wish to proceed in the order I believe the easiest to build a solid foundation for tax planning and therefore tax avoidance.

Once the book has been read, the index will provide

a quick reference for a refresher as subjects come up. One of the reasons I enjoy being an instructor of tax planning is that I am never afraid to say, "I don't know." No one can possibly know or remember the entire Internal Revenue Code, the related regulations and rulings, and the relevant court cases. As subjects come up, we all need to look back and refresh our thoughts.

The appendix (just before the index) cites my sources for each paragraph. In law, one must always have a source. This appendix also provides the reader with the next step if additional, more detailed, information is required. It will also be helpful for the student of taxation as he or she first enters the profession of tax advisor.

My thanks to William (Bill) Rini, the teachers' teacher. Bill has tried his best to make a teacher out of a CPA. To the extent that the book is really written to be understood by those who want to learn more, Bill deserves the credit. Thanks must also go to the editor, Fred Dahl. Fred's concepts of how to organize and present my ideas were invaluable.

ROBERT D. GORDON

CONTENTS

For general reference purposes, use the following table of contents. For more specific referencing, go to the index at the back of this book. For additional research on particular sections, regulations, rulings, decisions, and reports, make use of the Appendix on page 507

2
GROSS INCOME: TOTAL AND PARTIAL EXCLUSIONS

3
GROSS INCOME: INCLUSIONS

4
RECOGNITION OF GAIN AND LOSS

5
CAPITAL GAINS AND LOSSES

6
BUSINESS-RELATED DEDUCTIONS AND EXPENSES

06-01 DEDUCTIONS FOR ADJUSTED GROSS INCOME

06-02 EXPENDITURES NOT ALLOWED AS DEDUCTIONS

06-03 DEDUCTIONS ALLOWED IN GENERAL

06-04 "NONBUSINESS" DEDUCTIONS

06-05 NONDEDUCTIBLE BUSINESS EXPENDITURES

06-06 PENSIONS

06-07 EXPENDITURES FOR REAL AND PERSONAL PROPERTY

06-08 INSURANCE PREMIUMS

06-09 TRAVEL AND TRANSPORTATION EXPENSES

06-10 ENTERTAINMENT EXPENSES

06-11 MOVING EXPENSE ADJUSTMENT

06-12 EDUCATION EXPENSES

06-13 NET OPERATING LOSS (NOL)

7
PERSONAL DEDUCTIONS— INDIVIDUAL TAXPAYERS

07-01 INTEREST EXPENSE

07-02 NONDEDUCTIBLE INTEREST EXPENSE

07-03 TAXES

07-04 CHARITABLE CONTRIBUTIONS

07-05 LIMITATION ON CONTRIBUTION DEDUCTIONS

07-06 CARRY-OVER OF UNUSED CONTRIBUTION DEDUCTIONS

07-07 MEDICAL EXPENSE

07-08 CASUALTY LOSSES

07-09 MISCELLANEOUS DEDUCTION

07-10 DEDUCTION FOR TWO EARNER MARRIED COUPLES

8
INVESTMENT-RELATED DEDUCTIONS

9
SPECIAL TAX COMPUTATIONS AND CREDITS

10
TAXES AND ACCOUNTING

11
PARTNERSHIPS

12
CORPORATIONS

13
GIFT TAXES

14
ESTATE TAXES

APPENDIX

INDEX

1
THE BASIC STRUCTURE

01-01 OBJECTIVES OF THE BOOK

This book is designed to be a plain language, concise explanation of the federal income, gift, and estate taxes. The topics covered meet the needs of financial planners, securities and insurance salespersons, and others serving in the financial industries. So they also serve the needs of individuals by addressing their personal tax problems and planning situations.

Each subject is first explained in "lay" English, and the explanation is followed by an example for further clarity. Where appropriate, "Tax Hints" and "Tax Warnings" are included to present tax planning ideas and to warn readers of tax pitfalls.

To put readers at ease with the "experts," the "buzz" words of taxation are explained. Further, when they are used in the text, they are cross-referenced to the paragraphs where they were first introduced. The notation (01-06), for example, means, "See paragraph 01-06." The same notation may also mean, "See paragraph 01-06 for greater detail." This system allows you to use the book as a quick reference when a particular subject comes up in practice.

In many cases the final word on any subject is to "seek competent tax advice." Taxation is a subject that no one knows completely. After covering the basics of a subject, readers are given a brief idea of the potential variations from the "general rule," so they may be knowledgeable enough to ask the right questions.

THE SOURCE 01-02

The 16th Amendment 01-02.1

Who said Congress can impose all these taxes? Is the income tax constitutional?

It is! In 1913 the 16th Amendment to the Constitution did away with any questions. The amendment, specifically designed to allow the income tax laws as we now have them, reads:

> The Congress shall have power to lay and collect taxes on incomes, from whatever source derived, without apportionment among the several States, and without regard to any census or enumeration.

A number of income tax laws were passed between 1913 and 1939, when the Internal Revenue Code of 1939 combined them into one law.

The Internal Revenue Code of 1954 01-02.2

We still find court decisions under the 1939 Code that apply to the Internal Revenue Code of 1954, which is the current law. The *Code,* as the 1954 Code is called, is the *law.* It is based on the authority of the 16th Amendment. So to violate the Code intentionally is a criminal offense, referred to as *tax evasion.*

The Code has been modified many times, the last major modifications coming in the form of the Tax Reform Act of 1976, Revenue Act of 1978 and the Economic Recovery Tax Act of 1981.

The Code is divided into numbered sections, each section dealing with a specific subject. As an example, Code Section 1245 (Sec. 1245) deals with certain assets and transactions relating to them. Since the list of assets covered under Sec. 1245 is rather long, such assets are often referred to simply as "Section 1245 assets." This is the beginning of tax buzz words.

01-02.3 Internal Revenue Service Regulations

The Code itself is often short and to the point. It generally does not try to cover in complete detail every last point of what constitutes compliance. Often the Code requires that the Treasurer of the United States, through the Internal Revenue Service (IRS), issue regulations to expand on and to interpret the law. The *Regs*, as they are called, are the IRS' opinion as to what constitutes compliance with the Code. The Regs can, in some ways, be considered "semi-law." A taxpayer has the right to challenge the Regs on the assumptions that they do not reflect Congressional intent and that they therefore do not truly reflect the law. Such a challenge must be made in the court system.

The Regs are numbered by cross-reference to the Code.

> *Example:* Sec. 48 deals with the Investment Tax Credit. Reg 1.48-8 addresses the Investment Tax Credit as it relates to certain educational and entertainment movies and video tapes. Here's what the numbers mean:
>
> 1. means this is an income tax Regulation.
>
> 48 means it covers Sec. 48.
>
> -8 means this is the eighth regulation under Section 48.

Revenue Procedures and Revenue Rulings 01-02.4

Revenue Procedures are the IRS' "how-to" book. They cover the mechanical procedures of compliance such as which forms to file, what information should be in the forms, as well as where and when to file them. Revenue Procedures are numbered consecutively by the year in which they are published.

> *Example:* Rev. Proc. 77-35 was the 35th procedure published in 1977.

Following the Procedures is very important. Many court cases have been based on the taxpayer's failure to follow these procedures properly, and the IRS has often been sustained in their position due to such a failure.

Revenue Rulings deal with specific situations presented by taxpayers. As taxpayers notify the IRS that they have done—or intend to do—certain things, the IRS may issue rulings on the tax consequences of those particular actions. Revenue Rulings come in two classes: public and private.

1. *Public* Rulings are numbered in a manner similar to Revenue Procedures, and taxpayers may rely on them if their situations are exactly the same as those addressed in the Rulings.
2. More often, in such cases, the IRS issues *private Rulings,* or what are called *private letters.* While the contents of such a Ruling are available to the public, only the taxpayer to whom the letter is addressed may rely on it. Others may use the Ruling only as a guide to how the IRS *might* rule on their own particular cases.

The Courts 01-02.5

If the IRS and a taxpayer cannot agree either on the intent of the law in a specific case or on the facts of a particular case, the case then goes to the courts. Of the various levels of courts, the Supreme Court, in the final analysis, determines what Congress meant when it wrote the Code and how it is to be applied.

01-03 OBJECTIVES OF THE LAW

You must understand the objectives of Congress in passing these laws, because it is impossible for you to know all the laws, Regulations, and court decisions on every subject. Very often, you can reach a "reasonable" presumption on a tax question just by keeping in mind what Congress is, or was, trying to accomplish. The Code really has three major objectives:

1. raising revenue;
2. promoting social reform; and,
3. encouraging economic development.

Keep the last two objectives in mind. They can be of great help if you use the incentives that the Code tries to provide for those who follow the path that Congress desires.

01-03.1 Raising Revenue

Taxation of any kind must have as its prime objective the support of government functions. To that end, the income tax is the single largest source of revenue to the federal government. Also, through a myriad of revenue- and cost-sharing programs, it is a major source of revenue for the state and local governments.

01-03.2 Social Objectives

When accomplishing what Congress perceives to be socially desirable goals, the Code is truly a two-edged sword. Through numerous and complicated directions, the Code encourages giving to charities, promoting the use of renewable energy sources, reconstructing the inner cities, hiring the disadvantaged, and so on. Not only does the Code encourage "Good," but it punishes what Congress sees as "Bad." For example, gambling losses are not deductible; entertainment expenses involve special record-keeping requirements; conventions in foreign countries are discouraged; and, of course, bribery and traffic ticket expenses are not deductible. The list goes on and on.

Sometimes the socially desirable goals change. Prior to 1971 the tax rates were weighted heavily in favor of married couples; so being married was socially desirable. But due to extreme pressure from singles, this orientation was changed. In changing the tax structure Congress—intentionally or not—created an additional burden on married couples, and the present tax structure actually contains a penalty for being married, the so-called "marriage tax" (01-06.1A).

The major social objective, the redistribution of money from the wealthy to the poor, is clear from the graduated income tax rates: that is, the more money you earn, the greater your rate of tax.

> *Example:* Examining Figure 1–1, we see that a single taxpayer with taxable income of $10,800 pays $1,203, an effective rate of just over 11%. But the same person with taxable income of $28,800 pays $5,705, an effective rate of almost 20%. The same person would pay 50% of all taxable income over $81,800.

Economic Objectives 01-03.3

The Code uses incentives to promote industries that Congress feels need "indirect" government subsidies. Special incentives exist for the capital goods industries, real estate development, farming, the extraction of natural resources, and others. Many of these incentives form the backbone of tax shelters, which exist, with the blessing of Congress, in those industries in need of capital formation incentives. To funnel the needed funds from the private sector of the economy, Congress finds it easier (and probably cheaper) to employ tax incentives rather than tax-collection and fund-appropriation mechanisms.

01-04 WHO MUST FILE TAX RETURNS

Whether a person must file a tax return is based on his or her filing status (01-06) and gross income. (Generally, *gross income* means all income less exclusions, as we shall see in the next section and in Chapter 2.) The general rule is: if a person's Gross Income is greater than the total of his/her Zero Bracket Amount (01-05.2c) plus the exemptions to which he/she is automatically entitled (01-07), then that person must file. The income levels required for filing are:

Single	$3,300
Married, filing jointly	$5,400
Surviving spouse	$4,400
Single, over 65	$4,300
Married, filing jointly, one over 65	$6,400
Married, filing jointly, both over 65	$7,400
Surviving spouse, over 65	$5,400

> *Example:* In the chart, the minimum required Gross Income for a married couple, both over 65 and filing jointly, is $7,400. This amount is computed as $3,400 for their Zero Bracket Amount plus $4,000, the exemptions to which they are automatically entitled.

Exceptions 01-04.1

There are two exceptions to the filing rule with regard to the *self-employed.* First, self-employed persons must file returns if their net income from business is $400 or more, because they are subject to self-employment tax (Social Security) at that level. Additionally, for those in the business of selling products, as opposed to services, Gross Income is defined as Sales less Cost of Sales. So self-employed persons with sales of $20,000 and cost of sales of $19,000 would not be required to file unless their net income was $400 or more.

Persons who have *passive income* (interest, dividends, and the like) of $1,000 or more and who can be claimed as someone else's dependents (01-08) must file. They are so required because the child (the class of taxpayer most likely to be involved) is probably not able to claim the normal zero bracket amount of $2,300 allowed to other singles.

Persons who received *advanced earned income credits* (09-08.11) must file, regardless of their income levels or filing status.

Tax *Warning* 01-04.2

When in doubt, *file!* Failure to file is a serious offense, and it could be construed as tax evasion. More important, the statute of limitations does not start to run until a return has been filed. Normally, the IRS has only three years to audit a return, although certain exceptions can extend this limitation to five years. But, if no return is filed, the IRS can come back anytime and question the validity of the decision.

Remember: Just because a taxpayer has no tax liability, he or she is not relieved from the responsibility of filing a return.

01-05 FRAMEWORK OF THE INDIVIDUAL TAX COMPUTATION

01-05.1 Gross Income and Exclusions

Since we are dealing with an income tax, we should start with the *total* amounts received by the taxpayer, something I call Gross Amounts Received, a term you will not find in the Code. Then we can proceed to Gross Income, which is a term that *is* in the Code. So the first step in the tax computation is:

Gross income = Gross amounts received − Exclusions

Hence the actual computation of an individual's tax liability begins with Gross Income and with the exclusions from Gross Income. (Chapter 2 deals with those exclusions in detail. Some of them, such as interest on tax-exempt municipal bonds, never even appear on the individual's tax return. Others, such as Social Security payments received, are not included in Gross Income, but they may come into play when the tax liability has to be computed.)

01-05.1A Example

If an individual has Gross Amounts Received of $100,000, but $45,000 of that is excluded, then:

Gross Amounts Received	$100,000
Less: Exclusions	− 45,000
Gross Income (the first figure to appear in the tax computation)	$ 55,000

01-05.1B Tax ***Warning***

Gross Income includes not only cash, but also the fair market value of any property received. That means if you perform a service for someone and they pay you for that service by giving you property—let's say a color TV set—then you have Gross Income equal to the fair market value of that TV set.

In recent years, so-called barter associations have become very popular. These organizations bring together professionals from different fields who exchange services. A lawyer may exchange a "free" will for a root canal. In such a case, both the dentist and the lawyer have Gross Income to the extent of the fair market value of the services they received. (See paragraph 13-06 for a further discussion of how fair market value is computed.)

Adjusted Gross Income (AGI) 01-05.2

Deductions *for* AGI 01-05.2A

From Gross Income, you then deduct certain expenses to arrive at Adjusted Gross Income (AGI). Expenses that are deductible *for* AGI generally relate directly to a taxpayer's business; expenses such as advertising or wages paid to employees are typical deductions. But there are many exceptions; as an example, alimony paid is a deduction for AGI. So it is always wise to check each expense to see if it is deductible for AGI.

Example 01-05.2A-1

A taxpayer who has wages of $50,000 and pays alimony of $12,000 to her ex-husband. Her Adjusted Gross Income is:

Gross Income (wages)	$50,000
Deduction for AGI (alimony)	−12,000
AGI	$38,000

Deductions *from* AGI 01-05.2B

Taxpayers may also deduct from AGI certain "personal" expenses. Items such as most contributions to recognized charities, real estate taxes on a personal residence, and interest on a mortgage against a personal residence all fall into this category. Again, there are some exceptions. Business items, such as stock transfer taxes and union dues, are also deductions from AGI.

01-05.2C **Zero bracket amount**

Deductions from AGI are generally called *itemized deductions.* The Code gives each taxpayer a minimum amount of itemized deductions, whether he or she has any or not. This minimum amount, called the Zero Bracket Amount or formerly the Standard Deduction, is determined by the filing status of the taxpayer. The Zero Bracket Amounts are:

Married filing jointly	$3,400
Qualified widow(er)	$3,400
Single	$2,300
Head of household	$2,300
Married filing separate returns	$1,700

For itemized deductions to be of any tax benefit, they must exceed the Zero Bracket Amount.

Since the Zero Bracket Amount depends on the filing status, the IRS has included the Zero Bracket Amount in the Tax Rate Schedules.

Examine Tax Rate Schedule 1 (single taxpayers) in Figure 1-1. Note that when Taxable Income is less than $2,300, no tax is due. Since the Zero Bracket Amount for singles is $2,300, that amount is automatically deducted from Taxable Income.

For 1985 and subsequent years the zero bracket amount will be increased by indexing (01:05.4).

Examples 01-05.2C-1

Samuel Morse and his wife have itemized deductions amounting to $2,900. So their deduction from AGI is zero, since more than that amount ($3,400) is already built into the tables.

Andrew Jackson, a single taxpayer, has itemized deductions of $2,900. But his deduction from AGI is $600. This is the amount his itemized deductions exceed his Zero Bracket Amount, which is $2,300.

Tax Rate Schedules 01-05.3

Since the Tax Rate Schedules do not include the number of exemptions (01-07), you have an additional step in figuring what is called Taxable Income.

Example 01.05.3A-1

A husband and wife filing a joint return have the following:

Gross Income		$200,000
Deductions for AGI		− 250
AGI		$199,750
Total itemized deductions	$17,400	
Zero Bracket Amount	− 3,400	14,000
Taxable income before exemptions		$185,750
Exemptions (01-07)		− 2,000
Taxable Income		$183,750

Using Tax Rate Schedule 2, married filing jointly:

Tax on $162,400	$ 62,600
Tax on excess @ 50% ($183,750 less $162,400 times 0.50)	+ 10,675
Total tax	$ 73,275

01-05.4 Ever Changing Tax Rate Schedules

The Economic Recovery Act of 1981 added a new term to taxation: Indexing. For each year until 1984 Section 1 of the Code lists the tax rates for each filing status. For each year, 1981 to 1984, the tax rates are reduced from those prevailing in the previous year.

Beginning in 1985, the tax rate schedules, the Zero Bracket Amount and amount for each exemption (currently $1,000) will be adjusted to reflect inflation.

In measuring inflation, the base year will be the 12 months ended September 30, 1983, and the Consumer Price Index (CPI) is the measuring stick. The adjustment for each year will reflect the CPI for the 12 months ended on the previous September 30th.

01-05.4A Example

If the average CPI for the 12 months ended September 30, 1983 were 100, and the average CPI for the 12 months ended September 30, 1984 were 110, then for 1985:

1. the tax rates would be reduced by 10%; and
2. exemptions would be increased by 10%; and
3. the Zero Bracket Amount would be increased by 10%.

01-05.5 Pick a Table

For illustration purposes we will use the tax rates in effect for 1984. This will not change any of our tax planning strategies, *but—*

Tax Hint 01-05.6

Since the tax rates are declining from year to year, the basic tax planning strategy is to accelerate deductions and delay income. This will serve two purposes:

1. The income will be reported in a year with lower tax rates, and the deductions will be taken in a year with higher tax rates; and
2. tax payments delayed mean interest income earned. Better you have the money earning interest than Uncle Sam.

Be careful! This can be overdone. Since the tax rates are progressive, too much shifting could cause very low rates on one year and very high rates in another.

FILING STATUS 01-06

Each taxpayer falls into one of five filing statuses:

Single
Married filing joint return
Married filing separately
Head of household
Qualifying widow(er)

Since the tax rates are based on filing status, it is extremely important to choose the correct status.

Married or Single? 01-06.1

Married taxpayers may fall into one of two categories:

married filing separately or married filing jointly. If a taxpayer is married, it is almost always better to file jointly, since the tax rate schedule presumes the most unfavorable distribution of earnings between the parties.

Single taxpayers have three possible filing statuses. In order of the most favorable first, they are:

Qualifying widow(er) (01-06.2A)

Head of household (01-06.2B)

Single

Note that married people cannot elect one of the statuses reserved for singles, and that two single people cannot elect to file as married.

Marital status is determined as of the last day of the tax year, generally December 31. A person who is single on the last day of the year is considered to be single for the entire year. And if a couple is married on the last day of the year, they are considered married for the entire year. They are considered married if they fall into any one of the following situations:

1. They are married and living as husband and wife, *unless* the marriage is subsequently annulled.
2. They are living together in common-law marriage recognized by state law.
3. They are married and living apart, but not legally separated under a decree of divorce or separate maintenance.
4. They are married and living apart under an interlocutory decree of divorce.

Courts have held that a couple is still married if they merely obtain a divorce at the end of the year and then remarry at the beginning of the following year. Occasionally couples have employed this tactic to avoid the so-called marriage tax.

Update page for Gordon, Tax Planning Handbook, pg. 17

FIGURE 1-1.

The Tax Rate Schedules

For taxable years beginning after 1983.—

SCHEDULE 1: UNMARRIED INDIVIDUALS (OTHER THAN SURVIVING SPOUSES AND HEADS OF HOUSEHOLDS)

If taxable income is:	*The tax is:*
Not over $2,300	No tax.
Over $2,300 but not over $3,400	11% of the excess over $3,400.
Over $3,400 but not over $4,400	$121, plus 12% of the excess over $3,400.
Over $4,400 but not over $6,500	$241, plus 14% of the excess over $4,400.
Over $6,500 but not over $8,500	$535, plus 15% of the excess over $6,500.
Over $8,500 but not over $10,800	$835, plus 16% of the excess over $8,500.
Over $10,800 but not over $12,900	$1,203, plus 18% of the excess over $10,800.
Over $12,900 but not over $15,000	$1,581, plus 20% of the excess over $12,900.
Over $15,000 but not over $18,200	$2,001, plus 23% of the excess over $15,000.
Over $18,200 but not over $23,500	$2,737, plus 26% of the excess over $18,200.
Over $23,500 but not over $28,800	$4,115, plus 30% of the excess over $23,500.
Over $28,800 but not over $34,100	$5,705, plus 34% of the excess over $28,800.
Over $34,100 but not over $41,500	$7,057, plus 38% of the excess over $34,100.
Over $41,500 but not over $55,300	$10,319, plus 42% of the excess over $41,500.
Over $55,300 but not over $81,800	$16,115, plus 48% of the excess over $55,300.
Over $81,800	$28,835, plus 50% of the excess over $81,800.

SCHEDULE 2: MARRIED INDIVIDUALS FILING JOINT RETURNS AND SURVIVING SPOUSES

If taxable income is:	*The tax is:*
Not over $3,400	No tax.
Over $3,400 but not over $5,500	11% of the excess over $3,400.
Over $5,500 but not over $7,600	$231, plus 12% of the excess over $5,500.
Over $7,600 but not over $11,900	$483, plus 14% of the excess over $7,600.
Over $11,900 but not over $16,000	$1,085, plus 16% of the excess over $11,900.
Over $16,000 but not over $20,200	$1,741, plus 18% of the excess over $16,000.
Over $20,200 but not over $24,600	$2,497, plus 22% of the excess over $20,200.
Over $24,600 but not over $29,900	$3,465, plus 25% of the excess over $24,600.
Over $29,900 but not over $35,200	$4,790, plus 28% of the excess over $29,900.
Over $35,200 but not over $45,800	$6,274, plus 33% of the excess over $35,200.
Over $45,800 but not over $60,000	$9,772, plus 38% of the excess over $45,800.
Over $60,000 but not over $85,600	$15,168, plus 42% of the excess over $60,000.
Over $85,600 but not over $109,400	$25,920, plus 45% of the excess over $85,600.
Over $109,400 but not over $162,400	$36,630, plus 49% of the excess over $109,400.
Over $162,400	$62,600, plus 50% of the excess over $162,400.

SCHEDULE 3: MARRIED INDIVIDUALS FILING SEPARATE RETURNS

If taxable income is:	*The tax is:*
Not over $1,700	No tax.
Over $1,700 but not over $2,750	11% of the excess over $1,700.
Over $2,750 but not over $3,800	$115, plus 12% of the excess over $2,750.
Over $3,800 but not over $5,950	$241, plus 14% of the excess over $3,800.
Over $5,950 but not over $8,000	$542, plus 16% of the excess over $5,950.
Over $8,000 but not over $10,100	$870, plus 18% of the excess over $8,000.
Over $10,100 but not over $12,300	$1,248, plus 22% of the excess over $10,100.
Over $12,300 but not over $14,950	$1,732, plus 25% of the excess over $12,300.
Over $14,950 but not over $17,600	$2,395, plus 28% of the excess over $14,950.
Over $17,600 but not over $22,900	$3,137, plus 33% of the excess over $17,600.
Over $22,900 but not over $30,000	$4,886, plus 38% of the excess over $22,900.
Over $30,000 but not over $42,800	$7,584, plus 42% of the excess over $30,000.
Over $42,800 but not over $54,700	$12,960, plus 45% of the excess over $42,800.
Over $54,700 but not over $81,200	$18,315, plus 49% of the excess over $54,700.
Over $81,200	$31,300, plus 50% of the excess over $81,200.

SCHEDULE 4: HEADS OF HOUSEHOLDS

If taxable income is:	*The tax is:*
Not over $2,300	No tax.
Over $2,300 but not over $4,400	11% of the excess over $2,300.
Over $4,400 but not over $6,500	$231, plus 12% of the excess over $4,400.
Over $6,500 but not over $8,700	$483, plus 14% of the excess over $6,500.
Over $8,700 but not over $11,800	$791, plus 17% of the excess over $8,700.
Over $11,800 but not over $15,000	$1,318, plus 18% of the excess over $11,800.
Over $15,000 but not over $18,200	$1,894, plus 20% of the excess over $15,000.
Over $18,200 but not over $23,500	$2,534, plus 24% of the excess over $18,200.
Over $23,500 but not over $28,800	$3,806, plus 28% of the excess over $23,500.
Over $28,800 but not over $34,100	$5,290, plus 32% of the excess over $28,800.
Over $34,100 but not over $44,700	$6,986, plus 35% of the excess over $34,100.
Over $44,700 but not over $60,600	$10,696, plus 42% of the excess over $44,700.
Over $60,600 but not over $81,800	$17,374, plus 45% of the excess over $60,600.
Over $81,800 but not over $108,300	$26,914, plus 48% of the excess over $81,800.
Over $108,300	$39,634, plus 50% of the excess over $108,300.

SCHEDULE 5: ESTATES AND TRUSTS

If taxable income is:	*The tax is:*
Not over $1,050	11% of taxable income.
Over $1,050 but not over $2,100	$115, plus 12% of the excess over $1,050.
Over $2,100 but not over $4,250	$241, plus 14% of the excess over $2,100
Over $4,250 but not over $6,300	$542, plus 16% of the excess over $4,250.
Over $6,300 but not over $8,400	$870, plus 18% of the excess over $6,300.
Over $8,400 but not over $10,600	$1,248, plus 22% of the excess over $8,400.
Over $10,600 but not over $13,250	$1,732, plus 25% of the excess over $10,600.
Over $13,250 but not over $15,000	$2,395, plus 28% of the excess over $13,250.
Over $15,900 but not over $21,200	$3,137, plus 33% of the excess over $15,900.
Over $21,200 but not over $28,300	$4,886, plus 38% of the excess over $21,200.
Over $28,300 but not over $41,100	$7,584, plus 42% of the excess over $28,300.
Over $41,100 but not over $53,000	$12,960, plus 45% of the excess over $41,100.
Over $53,000 but not over $79,500	$18,315, plus 49% of the excess over $53,000.
Over $79,500	$31,300, plus 50% of the excess over $79,500.

If one spouse dies during the year the surviving spouse, if he or she does not remarry, may file a joint return and benefit from the exemptions of the deceased spouse.

A taxpayer married to a *nonresident alien* is categorized as married. The taxpayer must file either as married filing separately or as married filing jointly. But when filing jointly with a non-resident alien spouse, the taxpayer must include all the world-wide income of both spouses.

A person may be considered an *abandoned spouse* and therefore single under certain conditions. The most important of these conditions is that the person lived apart from his or her spouse for the *entire* year and provided the household for a dependent child for at least six months.

01-06.1A **Tax hint: the marriage tax**

When both parties to a "husband-and-wife" relationship are equal income producers, it is often better to be single than to be married.

01-06.1A-1 ***Example***

Mr. M and Ms. W had a combined taxable income of $100,000 last year, If each had $50,000 of taxable income, then:

Joint Return (Schedule 2)	
Tax on first $85,600	$25,920
Tax on excess ($100,000 less $85,600 times 0.45)	+ 6,480
Total tax	$32,400
Single Returns (Schedule 1)	
Tax on first $41,500	$10,319
Tax on excess ($50,000 less $41,500 times 0.42)	+3,570
Tax on one single taxpayer	$13,889
$13,889 times 2 (combined tax)	$27,778
Savings by filing single	$ 4,622

See paragraph 07-10 for a deduction for married couples where both have "qualified" income. This deduction can reduce the effects of the marriage tax.

On the other hand, when only one party to the relationship is an income-producer it is often better to be married.

What if the distribution of the income had been different? Suppose Ms. W had $90,000 of taxable income and Mr. M had $10,000 of taxable income:

Single Returns

Tax on single return with $90,000 of taxable income	$32,935
Tax on single return with $10,000 of taxable income	+ 1,075
Total tax filing as singles	$34,010
Tax on joint return	− 32,400
Savings by filing jointly	$ 1,610

Obviously, it may be better to be married or single, depending on the situation. You have the opportunity for tax planning with regard to the timing of both marriages and divorces.

Somewhere in Between Married and Single 01-06.2

Congress provides some relief for single taxpayers with family responsibilities. This relief is provided in the form of reduced rates for those who qualify.

Qualifying Widow(er) 01-06.2A

Taxpayers may continue to use the rate schedules for married filing jointly (the lowest rates) for the first two years following the death of their spouses, if they meet *all* of the following requirements:

1. They were eligible to file a joint return in the year the spouse died and have not subsequently remarried.
2. They live with their dependent children the entire year and are entitled to claim the dependency exemption (**01-08**).
3. They provide over half the household costs.

01-06.2B **Head of household**

The head of household tax rates are lower than the single rate but higher than married filing jointly. Single taxpayers may qualify for these lower rates if:

1. Their households are the principal places of residence for a relative for the *entire* year (see the exception for parents below).
2. And they contribute over half the costs of maintaining the household.

01-06.2C **Special nonresident alien rules**

For the purposes of determining head of household status, persons who are married to nonresident aliens qualify as singles. But nonresident aliens cannot quality as heads of household.

01-06.2D **Special rule for parent care**

If taxpayers are entitled to claim either or both of their parents as dependent (**01-08**), there is no requirement that the parent live with the taxpayer as there is for other relatives. This special rule is aimed specifically at giving tax relief to those taxpayers who support their parents, even if the parents are in homes or health care centers.

01-06.2E **Tax hint: parent care**

Taxpayers may be able to claim a parent or parents as dependent (as discussed further in 01-08). Normally this merely provides the taxpayer with an additional exemption equal to a $1,000 deduction. But if the taxpayer is single, it may also qualify him or her to use the more favorable head of household rate—which could be worth a lot more than just a $1,000 deduction.

So when possible, make the extra effort to obtain that dependent status. As an example, if several people contribute to the support of a taxpayer's parent, the group could make tax-exempt gifts to the taxpayer in question rather than give the funds to the parent directly. Another approach might be to arrange the parent's financial position to meet the Gross Income test described in paragraph 01-08.3

Tax hint: dependent status 01-06.2F

Except for parents not living with the taxpayer, relatives do not have to qualify as the taxpayer's dependents. This hint is especially important for a woman who has custody of her children but who has given the husband the right to claim them as his dependents. This is a typical divorce arrangement.

Tax *warning* 01-06.2G

Divorce and custody agreements must be carefully worded as well as intended. A split-custody agreement could make it impossible for either parent to claim the head of household status, since the relative must live with the taxpayer for the entire year.

EXEMPTIONS FOR THE TAXPAYER 01-07

Individual Exemption 01-07.1

Each taxpayer is entitled to a $1,000 exemption as an individual from federal income tax. For a husband and wife filing a joint return, each is entitled to one such exemption, or $2,000. See paragraph 01-05.3D-1 for an example of how the exemption is used to reduce taxable income.

01-07.2 Additional Exemptions for Age

An additional exemption of $1,000 is allowed for a taxpayer who attains the age of 65 by January 1 of the following year. For example, a taxpayer whose 65th birthday is January 1, 1981 is considered to be 65 for the tax year ending December 31, 1980.

On a joint return, both spouses are entitled to claim the additional exemption if it applies to both. So on a joint return where one spouse is over 65, the total exemptions are three, or $3,000. If both spouses have attained the age of 65, the total exemptions are four, or $4,000.

No additional exemption is allowed if a dependent is over 65.

01-07.3 Additional Exemption for Blindness

A taxpayer may claim an additional exemption if "blind," as defined by the code. The blindness exemption may be claimed in addition to any other exemption. On a joint return, either or both spouses may claim the additional exemption, if it applies. As an example, a taxpayer whose wife is blind would be entitled to three exemptions: one for himself, one for his wife, and one for his wife's blindness. Or, on a joint return, if both spouses were over 65 and both were blind, the total exemptions would be six, or $6,000.

No additional exemption is allowed for the blindness of a dependent.

Blindness is determined as of the last day of the tax year. In the case of a deceased person, it is determined as of the date of death.

01-07.3A Definition of blindness

Blindness means that:

1. the central visual acuity does not exceed 20/200 in the better eye with correcting lenses; *or*

2. the widest diameter of the visual field subtends an angle no greater than 20 degrees.

Tax hint 01-07.3B

To qualify for the additional exemption, the condition does not have to be irreversible, nor does the blindness have to be total. This exemption is often overlooked on the returns of the elderly and infirmed.

EXEMPTIONS FOR THE TAXPAYER'S DEPENDENTS 01-08

Taxpayers are entitled to an exemption of $1,000 for each of their "dependents," as defined in the Code. To quality as a dependent, and therefore to entitle the taxpayer to the exemption, the person in question must meet five tests:

1. a support test (01-08.1),
2. a relationship test (01-08.2),
3. a Gross Income test (01-08.3),
4. a type of return filed test (01-08.4), *and*
5. a citizenship or residency test (01-08.5).

As long as a person meets all these tests, the taxpayer is entitled to the full $1,000 exemption, even if the dependent is born or dies during the year. No exemption, however, is allowed for a stillborn child.

The Support Test 01-08.1

The taxpayer must provide *more than* one-half of the support of the dependent (with certain exceptions). *Support* is defined in the broadest sense, and it is not limited to expenses that constitute minimum support under state laws. Such items as wedding apparel and church contributions have been held to be part of support. If support is provided in kind (such as lodging, food, and the like), the fair market value of the goods is counted. But one major item that does not count as support is the value of services provided by the taxpayer to the dependent. Any questions as to whether an expenditure counts as support should be referred to competent tax counsel.

01-08.1A **Example**

Robert and Deborah provide the entire support of their father. Robert contributed $4,000 for the year and Deborah $3,000. Robert is entitled to the full $1,000 exemption.

01-08.1B **Use of Funds**

If dependents have income of their own, it need not be counted toward support if it was not spent for support.

01-08.1B-1 ***Example***

If Robert and Deborah's father received $5,000 in Social Security and put the entire amount into the bank, Robert would still be entitled to claim the dependency exemption.

01-08.1C **Tax hint**

Since Robert and Deborah are the beneficiaries under their father's will, the arrangement is not really costing them any money in the long run. Moreover, they enjoy two additional benefits! Robert may claim his father's medical expenses as *his* deduction (07-07). And, if Robert is single, he is entitled to claim head of household status and the related lower income tax rate.

If taxpayers support both parents, they are considered to be one unit. That is, if they provide more than half the support of both combined, they are entitled to two exemptions.

Multiple support agreements 01-08.1D

What happens when a number of people take the responsibility for the support of another, but no one person contributes more than one-half of that support? They can enter into a *multiple support agreement,* which gives the exemption to one of the group. The only considerations are that the person chosen to claim the exemption must contribute more than 10% of the support, and that all the other persons who contribute more than 10% agree to designate the one person to claim the exemption. Form 2120 should be signed by all those not claiming the exemption to evidence their written agreement not to claim the exemption themselves.

Students 01-08.1E

Most scholarships do *not* count towards the test of support. But if a parent or guardian pays for a college education, it does count.

Example. Mr. Taxpayer pays $4,000 toward the support of his child, and Mrs. Taxpayer pays $1,000. The child has a scholarship worth $6,000. In such a case, Mr. Taxpayer can claim the exemption. But competent tax counsel should be sought, to insure that both the scholarship and the educational institution qualify for this treatment. 01-08.1E-1

The Relationship Test 01-08.2

To be a taxpayer's dependent, a person must be either a relative or a member of the household.

Relatives 01-08.2A

For the purpose of claiming dependency exemptions, relatives include:

1. children, grandchildren and great grandchildren,

2. parents, grandparents, and great grandparents,
3. siblings,
4. nephews and nieces,
5. uncles and aunts,
6. inlaws (son, daughter, father, mother, brother, or sister), and
7. stepchildren, stepparents.

Adopted children have the same status as natural-born children, but foster children do *not* qualify.

Cousins are not relatives for the dependency test.

01-08.2B Member of the Taxpayer's Household

Persons who do not meet the "relative" test may still qualify if they are members of the taxpayer's household for the *entire* year—including cousins and foster children. The only exception is that the relationship must not be an illegal one.

01-08.3 Gross Income Test

The dependent's gross income must not exceed $1,000 for the year in question. (See the exception below for taxpayers' children.)

01-08.3A Gross income defined

In determining Gross Income for the dependency test, all exempt income is excluded, such as Social Security payments, state disability, interest on municipal bonds, and the like.

01-08.3A-1 ***Tax hint.*** If tax-exempt income is not used for support—that is, if it is reinvested or put in the bank—it does not count towards the support test. Some rearranging of investments for the elderly could easily avoid losing the exemption for those who would otherwise qualify (01-08.1B).

Exceptions for taxpayer's children 01-08.3B

Taxpayer's children do not have to meet the gross income test, if they fall into *either* of two categories:

1. They have not reached the age of 19 by the end of the tax year, or
2. they are full-time students.

A *full-time student* is one who during any five calendar months was enrolled full-time at a regular educational institution. Students must be taking enough credits to graduate or to complete their studies in the regular time established by the educational institution. So a night student *might* qualify. A regular educational institution must have facilities and a faculty; so correspondence schools do *not* qualify.

Tax hint. In only one instance may a person generate exemptions on two tax returns: Dependent children can be taken as exemptions on their parents' tax returns, *and* they can claim their own exemptions on their own returns. 01-08.3B-1

***Tax* warning.** Persons who may be claimed as dependents on their parents' returns may lose some or all of their Zero Bracket Amounts. This rule does not come into effect unless the dependent has more than $1,000 of unearned income, such as dividends or interest. This somewhat involved rule can best be described in the following example: 01-08.3B-2

> Colin Gordon, a single individual, can be claimed as a dependent on his parent's return. His adjusted gross income was:

Wages from a summer job	$1,500
Interest income	+$2,500
AGI	$4,000

Normally, his AGI ($4,000), less his $1,000 exemption would be his Taxable Income ($3,000), if he did not have any itemized deductions. But in this case he loses $800 of his Zero Bracket Amount, and his Taxable Income is $3,800, computed as follows:

AGI		$4,000
Zero Bracket Amount	$2,300	
Less the greater of itemized deductions *or* earned income	−1,500	+ 800
Taxable Income before exemption		$4,800
Exemption		−1,000
Taxable Income		$3,800

When either earned income *or* itemized deductions exceed the Zero Bracket Amount, the adjustment is zero, and the "penalty" no longer comes in play.

01-08.4 The Type of Return Test

If a person who would otherwise qualify as a dependent files a joint return, the dependency exemption is lost. The only exception is that if *neither* the dependent *nor* the dependent's spouse is required to file a return, but if they file a joint return for the sole purpose of obtaining a refund, then the dependency exemption is not lost.

01-08.5 Citizenship or Residency Test

To qualify as a dependent, the person in question must be *either*:

1. a U.S. citizen, or
2. a resident of the U.S., Canada, or Mexico *some* time during the year.

An exception is made for U.S. citizens living abroad who adopt a child and who have the child live with them for the *entire* year.

INDIVIDUAL TAX RATE SCHEDULES 01-09

Figure 1-1 shows the tax rates in effect as of 1984. There are four schedules:

Schedule 1, Single Taxpayers

Schedule 2, Married Taxpayers Filing Jointly and Qualifying Widow(er)

Schedule 3, Married Filing Separately, and

Schedule 4, Head of Household.

In paragraph 01-06.1A, you saw how to compare the tax consequences of being single to those of being married. So we have covered the first two applications.

Married Filing Separately 01-09.1

Almost never does filing separately reduce taxes. As an example of how the Code tries to prevent this effect, the rule is that, if one spouse itemizes deductions, the other spouse must do so also. This rule prevents one spouse from taking the Zero Bracket Amount while the other itemizes. In all cases where expense or loss deductions are limited, the limitation is reduced to one-half of normal so that no additional deductions can be obtained. As an example, note in paragraph 05-05 that the deductibility of capital losses is limited to $3,000 per year, *except* for married taxpayers filing separately for whom the limit is $1,500 per year.

Schedule 3 shows the tax rates for married

persons filing separately. This table assumes that *exactly* one-half of the taxable income is attributed to each spouse. To the extent that this assumption represents the actual case, such as in a community property state, there is no difference between filing jointly and filing separately. But if the distribution is not even, then the total tax will be higher when separate returns are filed.

01-09.1A **Example**

Mr. and Mrs. Taxpayer have $100,000 of Taxable Income. See Figure 1-1. If they elect to file jointly, the tax would be:

Tax on $85,600	$25,920
Tax on excess ($100,000 − $85,600) × 0.45	+ 6,480
Total tax	$32,400

If the $100,000 were equally divided, the tax would be exactly the same if they elected to file separately:

Tax on $42,800	$12,960
Tax on excess ($50,000 − $42,800) × 0.45	+ 3,240
Tax *each* would pay	$16,200
Combined tax for both (2 × $16,200)	$32,400

But if they elected to file separately, and if Mrs. Taxpayer had Taxable Income of $90,000 and Mr. Taxpayer only had $10,000, their taxes would be:

Mrs. Taxpayer:	
Tax on $81,200	$31,300
Tax on excess ($90,000 − $81,200) × 0.50	+ 4,400
Total tax	$35,700
Mr. Taxpayer:	
Tax on $8,000	$ 870
Tax on excess ($10,000 − $8,000) × 0.18	+ 360
Total tax	$ 1,230
Combined tax	$36,930

Increase in tax due to filing separately ($36,930 − $32,400)	$ 4,530

Head of Household 01-09.2

Head of household rates are lower than single rates, to provide some relief for single taxpayers with family responsibilities.

Example 01-09.2A

Mr. Likekids is single and has taxable income of $100,000. His tax, based on the single rates, would be:

Tax on $81,800	$28,835
Tax on excess ($100,000 − $81,800) × 0.50	+9,100
Total tax (single)	$37,935
Filing as Head of Household, his taxes would be:	
Tax on $81,800	$26,914
Tax on excess ($100,000 − $81,800) × 0.48	+ 8,736
Total tax (head of household)	$35,650
Tax saved by filing as head of household ($37,935 − $35,650)	$ 2,285

Tax Tables 01-09.3

Figure 1-2 shows one page from the Tax Tables for 1980. Taxpayers who may use the Tax Tables, *must* use the tax tables. A taxpayer may *not* figure whether the Tables or the Schedules result in a lower tax and then choose the one more favorable. To use the Tax Tables, you must:

1. Find the table to use based on the taxpayer's filing status:
   a. Table A, Single

b. Table B, Married Filing Jointly and Qualifying Widow(er)
c. Table C, Married Filing Separately
d. Table D, Head of Household

2. find the Tax Table Income (which is Taxable Income before exemptions) on the table; and
3. read across to find the correct number of exemptions.
4. The figure shown is the taxpayer's tax liability.

The Tables provide what the tax liability would be if Taxable Income were the midpoint. Working out the taxes both ways and choosing the lower amount—even if you were allowed to do so—wouldn't make much difference.

01-09.3A **Example**

Mr. Taxpayer files jointly with $15,160 in Tax Table Income. Using Figure 1-2, he reads across the line for "$15,150 to $15,200." If he has nine exemptions, his tax would be $402. If the taxpayer had more than nine exemptions, he would have to use the Tax Schedules.

01-10 THE "MARGINAL" OR "INCREMENTAL" TAX BRACKET

With regard to tax-exempt or tax-sheltered investment opportunities, presentations are often made "for those in the 50% tax bracket," for those "with an incremental tax rate of 50%," and so on. The "incremental" or "marginal" tax rate refers to the *next* dollar of income or to the *next* dollar of deduction. Since the tax rates are graduated, taxpayers normally have much higher incremental or marginal tax rates then their overall tax rates.

You should also understand that the marginal tax rate does not remain constant as additional income is added or subtracted from Taxable Income. As taxpayers

IGURE 1-2. A Tax Table

979 Tax Table B—MARRIED FILING JOINT RETURN (Filing Status Box 2) and QUALIFYING WIDOW(ER)S (Filing Status Box 5)

ontinued)

your income or exemptions are not covered, use Schedule TC (Form 1040), Part I to figure your tax)

line 34, Form 040, or line 11, orm 1040A, is—		And the total number of exemptions claimed is—							
ver	But not over	2	3	4	5	6	7	8	9
		Your tax is—							
1,200	11,250	923	743	570	410	256	116	0	0
1,250	11,300	932	752	578	418	263	123	0	0
1,300	11,350	941	761	586	426	270	130	0	0
1,350	11,400	950	770	594	434	277	137	0	0
1,400	11,450	959	779	602	442	284	144	4	0
1,450	11,500	968	788	610	450	291	151	11	0
1,500	11,550	977	797	618	458	298	158	18	0
1,550	11,600	986	806	626	466	306	165	25	0
1,600	11,650	995	815	635	474	314	172	32	0
1,650	11,700	1,004	824	644	482	322	179	39	0
1,700	11,750	1,013	833	653	490	330	186	46	0
1,750	11,800	1,022	842	662	498	338	193	53	0
1,800	11,850	1,031	851	671	506	346	200	60	0
1,850	11,900	1,040	860	680	514	354	207	67	0
1,900	11,950	1,049	869	689	522	362	214	74	0
1,950	12,000	1,058	878	698	530	370	221	81	0
2,000	12,050	1,067	887	707	538	378	228	88	0
2,050	12,100	1,076	896	716	546	386	235	95	0
2,100	12,150	1,085	905	725	554	394	242	102	0
2,150	12,200	1,094	914	734	562	402	249	109	0
2,200	12,250	1,103	923	743	570	410	256	116	0
2,250	12,300	1,112	932	752	578	418	263	123	0
2,300	12,350	1,121	941	761	586	426	270	130	0
2,350	12,400	1,130	950	770	594	434	277	137	0
2,400	12,450	1,139	959	779	602	442	284	144	4
2,450	12,500	1,148	968	788	610	450	291	151	11
2,500	12,550	1,157	977	797	618	458	298	158	18
2,550	12,600	1,166	986	806	626	466	306	165	25
2,600	12,650	1,175	995	815	635	474	314	172	32
2,650	12,700	1,184	1,004	824	644	482	322	179	39
2,700	12,750	1,193	1,013	833	653	490	330	186	46
2,750	12,800	1,202	1,022	842	662	498	338	193	53
2,800	12,850	1,211	1,031	851	671	506	346	200	60
2,850	12,900	1,220	1,040	860	680	514	354	207	67
2,900	12,950	1,229	1,049	869	689	522	362	214	74
2,950	13,000	1,238	1,058	878	698	530	370	221	81
3,000	13,050	1,247	1,067	887	707	538	378	228	88
3,050	13,100	1,256	1,076	896	716	546	386	235	95
3,100	13,150	1,265	1,085	905	725	554	394	242	102
3,150	13,200	1,274	1,094	914	734	562	402	249	109
3,200	13,250	1,283	1,103	923	743	570	410	256	116
3,250	13,300	1,292	1,112	932	752	578	418	263	123
3,300	13,350	1,301	1,121	941	761	586	426	270	130
3,350	13,400	1,310	1,130	950	770	594	434	277	137
3,400	13,450	1,319	1,139	959	779	602	442	284	144
3,450	13,500	1,328	1,148	968	788	610	450	291	151
3,500	13,550	1,337	1,157	977	797	618	458	298	158
3,550	13,600	1,346	1,166	986	806	626	466	306	165
3,600	13,650	1,355	1,175	995	815	635	474	314	172
3,650	13,700	1,364	1,184	1,004	824	644	482	322	179
3,700	13,750	1,373	1,193	1,013	833	653	490	330	186
3,750	13,800	1,382	1,202	1,022	842	662	498	338	193
3,800	13,850	1,391	1,211	1,031	851	671	506	346	200
3,850	13,900	1,400	1,220	1,040	860	680	514	354	207
3,900	13,950	1,409	1,229	1,049	869	689	522	362	214
3,950	14,000	1,420	1,238	1,058	878	698	530	370	221
4,000	14,050	1,430	1,247	1,067	887	707	538	378	228
4,050	14,100	1,441	1,256	1,076	896	716	546	386	235
4,100	14,150	1,451	1,265	1,085	905	725	554	394	242
4,150	14,200	1,462	1,274	1,094	914	734	562	402	249
4,200	14,250	1,472	1,283	1,103	923	743	570	410	256
4,250	14,300	1,483	1,292	1,112	932	752	578	418	263
4,300	14,350	1,493	1,301	1,121	941	761	586	426	270
4,350	14,400	1,504	1,310	1,130	950	770	594	434	277
4,400	14,450	1,514	1,319	1,139	959	779	602	442	284
4,450	14,500	1,525	1,328	1,148	968	788	610	450	291
4,500	14,550	1,535	1,337	1,157	977	797	618	458	298
4,550	14,600	1,546	1,346	1,166	986	806	626	466	306
4,600	14,650	1,556	1,355	1,175	995	815	635	474	314
4,650	14,700	1,567	1,364	1,184	1,004	824	644	482	322
4,700	14,750	1,577	1,373	1,193	1,013	833	653	490	330
4,750	14,800	1,588	1,382	1,202	1,022	842	662	498	338

n' nued next column

If line 34, Form 1040, or line 11, Form 1040A, is—		And the total number of exemptions claimed is—							
Over	But not over	2	3	4	5	6	7	8	9
		Your tax is—							
14,800	14,850	1,598	1,391	1,211	1,031	851	671	506	346
14,850	14,900	1,609	1,400	1,220	1,040	860	680	514	354
14,900	14,950	1,619	1,409	1,229	1,049	869	689	522	362
14,950	15,000	1,630	1,420	1,238	1,058	878	698	530	370
15,000	15,050	1,640	1,430	1,247	1,067	887	707	538	378
15,050	15,100	1,651	1,441	1,256	1,076	896	716	546	386
15,100	15,150	1,661	1,451	1,265	1,085	905	725	554	394
15,150	15,200	1,672	1,462	1,274	1,094	914	734	562	402
15,200	15,250	1,682	1,472	1,283	1,103	923	743	570	410
15,250	15,300	1,693	1,483	1,292	1,112	932	752	578	418
15,300	15,350	1,703	1,493	1,301	1,121	941	761	586	426
15,350	15,400	1,714	1,504	1,310	1,130	950	770	594	434
15,400	15,450	1,724	1,514	1,319	1,139	959	779	602	442
15,450	15,500	1,735	1,525	1,328	1,148	968	788	610	450
15,500	15,550	1,745	1,535	1,337	1,157	977	797	618	458
15,550	15,600	1,756	1,546	1,346	1,166	986	806	626	466
15,600	15,650	1,766	1,556	1,355	1,175	995	815	635	474
15,650	15,700	1,777	1,567	1,364	1,184	1,004	824	644	482
15,700	15,750	1,787	1,577	1,373	1,193	1,013	833	653	490
15,750	15,800	1,798	1,588	1,382	1,202	1,022	842	662	498
15,800	15,850	1,808	1,598	1,391	1,211	1,031	851	671	506
15,850	15,900	1,819	1,609	1,400	1,220	1,040	860	680	514
15,900	15,950	1,829	1,619	1,409	1,229	1,049	869	689	522
15,950	16,000	1,840	1,630	1,420	1,238	1,058	878	698	530
16,000	16,050	1,850	1,640	1,430	1,247	1,067	887	707	538
16,050	16,100	1,861	1,651	1,441	1,256	1,076	896	716	546
16,100	16,150	1,871	1,661	1,451	1,265	1,085	905	725	554
16,150	16,200	1,882	1,672	1,462	1,274	1,094	914	734	562
16,200	16,250	1,892	1,682	1,472	1,283	1,103	923	743	570
16,250	16,300	1,903	1,693	1,483	1,292	1,112	932	752	578
16,300	16,350	1,913	1,703	1,493	1,301	1,121	941	761	586
16,350	16,400	1,924	1,714	1,504	1,310	1,130	950	770	594
16,400	16,450	1,934	1,724	1,514	1,319	1,139	959	779	602
16,450	16,500	1,945	1,735	1,525	1,328	1,148	968	788	610
16,500	16,550	1,955	1,745	1,535	1,337	1,157	977	797	618
16,550	16,600	1,966	1,756	1,546	1,346	1,166	986	806	626
16,600	16,650	1,976	1,766	1,556	1,355	1,175	995	815	635
16,650	16,700	1,987	1,777	1,567	1,364	1,184	1,004	824	644
16,700	16,750	1,997	1,787	1,577	1,373	1,193	1,013	833	653
16,750	16,800	2,008	1,798	1,588	1,382	1,202	1,022	842	662
16,800	16,850	2,018	1,808	1,598	1,391	1,211	1,031	851	671
16,850	16,900	2,029	1,819	1,609	1,400	1,220	1,040	860	680
16,900	16,950	2,039	1,829	1,619	1,409	1,229	1,049	869	689
16,950	17,000	2,050	1,840	1,630	1,420	1,238	1,058	878	698
17,000	17,050	2,060	1,850	1,640	1,430	1,247	1,067	887	707
17,050	17,100	2,071	1,861	1,651	1,441	1,256	1,076	896	716
17,100	17,150	2,081	1,871	1,661	1,451	1,265	1,085	905	725
17,150	17,200	2,092	1,882	1,672	1,462	1,274	1,094	914	734
17,200	17,250	2,102	1,892	1,682	1,472	1,283	1,103	923	743
17,250	17,300	2,113	1,903	1,693	1,483	1,292	1,112	932	752
17,300	17,350	2,123	1,913	1,703	1,493	1,301	1,121	941	761
17,350	17,400	2,134	1,924	1,714	1,504	1,310	1,130	950	770
17,400	17,450	2,144	1,934	1,724	1,514	1,319	1,139	959	779
17,450	17,500	2,155	1,945	1,735	1,525	1,328	1,148	968	788
17,500	17,550	2,165	1,955	1,745	1,535	1,337	1,157	977	797
17,550	17,600	2,176	1,966	1,756	1,546	1,346	1,166	986	806
17,600	17,650	2,186	1,976	1,766	1,556	1,355	1,175	995	815
17,650	17,700	2,197	1,987	1,777	1,567	1,364	1,184	1,004	824
17,700	17,750	2,207	1,997	1,787	1,577	1,373	1,193	1,013	833
17,750	17,800	2,218	2,008	1,798	1,588	1,382	1,202	1,022	842
17,800	17,850	2,228	2,018	1,808	1,598	1,391	1,211	1,031	851
17,850	17,900	2,239	2,029	1,819	1,609	1,400	1,220	1,040	860
17,900	17,950	2,249	2,039	1,829	1,619	1,409	1,229	1,049	869
17,950	18,000	2,260	2,050	1,840	1,630	1,420	1,238	1,058	878
18,000	18,050	2,271	2,060	1,850	1,640	1,430	1,247	1,067	887
18,050	18,100	2,283	2,071	1,861	1,651	1,441	1,256	1,076	896
18,100	18,150	2,295	2,081	1,871	1,661	1,451	1,265	1,085	905
18,150	18,200	2,307	2,092	1,882	1,672	1,462	1,274	1,094	914
18,200	18,250	2,319	2,102	1,892	1,682	1,472	1,283	1,103	923
18,250	18,300	2,331	2,113	1,903	1,693	1,483	1,292	1,112	932
18,300	18,350	2,343	2,123	1,913	1,703	1,493	1,301	1,121	941
18,350	18,400	2,355	2,134	1,924	1,714	1,504	1,310	1,130	950

Continued on next page

obtain more deductions from taxable income, each additional deduction is worth fewer "net dollars." On the other side of the coin, as taxpayers accumulate more taxable income, the tax rate on each "new" dollar added becomes greater and so each dollar is worth less "net after tax."

01-10.1 Example

Sam and Sarah Investor file jointly and have $100,000 of taxable incqme. Their investment advisor has told them that they are in the 45% incremental tax bracket. She explains this by taking their tax computation as follows:

Tax on $85,600	$25,920
Tax on excess ($100,000 − $85,600) × 0.45	+ 6,480
Total income tax	$32,400

She notes that, although their "overall" tax rate is only 32.4% ($32,400/$100,000), the following things can happen:

1. *Additional deductions will be worth fewer net dollars.* The *next* $14,400 ($100,000 − $85,600) of deductions will reduce their taxes at an effective rate of 45%. Examining Figure 1-1, we see that any deductions in addition to the $14,400 will reduce income tax at the rate of 42%, or 42¢ of reduced taxes for each dollar of deductions.
2. *Additional taxable income will result in less net after tax.* The *next* $9,400 of taxable income will then be taxed at the rate of 45%, generating only 55¢ net after taxes for each dollar of income. Examining Figure 1-1, we see that any income above the $9,400 will be taxed at the rate of 49%, generating only 51¢ of net income after taxes.

Sam and Sarah ask the investment advisor what the net cash value of a $20,000 deduction would be and what the net cash flow of a $20,000 income item would be. In response, the investment advisor presents the following:

Tax deduction of $20,000	
First $14,400 @ 45%	$6,480
Next $5,600 @ 42%	+2,352
Total cash value	$8,832
Incremental tax rate ($8,832/$20,000)	44%
Additional Taxable Income of $20,000	
First $9,400 @ 45%	$4,230
Next $10,600 @ 49%	+5,194
Total taxes	$9,424
Incremental tax rate ($9,424/$20,000)	47%

Effect of Incremental Tax Rate on Credits 01-10.2

Many tax-shelter plans generate credits in addition to deductions. A *credit* is a direct reduction of taxes (09-06), so that each dollar of credit reduces taxes by a full dollar.

Often the "value" of the credit is restated in terms of the amount of deductions needed to generate the same reduction in taxes. To restate this "deduction" value of a credit, you must know the incremental tax bracket of the investor. For example, the simplest conversion is for an investor in the 50% incremental tax bracket. Obviously, this investor needs $2 of deductions to generate $1 of tax reduction. So each dollar of credit is worth $2 as a deduction. The conclusion is that, in relation to a deduction, a credit has more value in the lower incremental tax brackets and less value in the higher brackets.

Example 01-10.2A

Robert Investor is in the 49% incremental tax bracket. What is the equivalent deduction for a $1,000 credit? To obtain the answer, divide the credit by the tax bracket: **$1,000 ÷ 49% = $2,041. Investor needs $2,041 in deductions** to reduce his taxes as much as a $1,000 credit would.

John Investor is in the 30% incremental tax bracket. What is the equivalent deduction for a $1,000 credit? The answer: $1,000 ÷ 30% = $3,333.

01-10.2B **Example: Tax shelter presentation**

"Wild-Man Tax Shelter" announces that it is providing the equivalent of a 4-to-1 write-off for investors in the 50% tax bracket. That is, for every $10,000 invested, investors get "deductions" equivalent to $40,000. The write-off is a big 4¾-to-1 for investors in the 40% bracket. Here is how "Wild Man" computes these figures:

50% tax bracket:	
$10,000 deduction	$10,000
$15,000 credit ÷ 0.50	+30,000
Equivalent deduction	$40,000
40% tax bracket:	
$10,000 deduction	$10,000
$15,000 credit ÷ 0.40	+37,500
Equivalent deduction	$47,500

01-11 TAX AVOIDANCE VERSUS TAX EVASION

With a basic understanding of the structure of the income tax, you would be wise to consider some tax planning comments before looking at specific ideas and subjects. . . .

The income tax is not a voluntary payment to the government. It is a tax imposed—an obligation to pay—that is enforced by the government. Penalties for noncompliance can run from relatively small financial penalties for simple negligence, to five years in jail for each count of certain types of fraud.

Tax evasion is the intentional disregard of the law. This can take many forms: failure to report transactions, reporting transactions incorrectly, creating fictitious situations without economic substance, and simply failing to pay taxes. The American Institute of Certified Public Accountants, the American Bar Association, the Treasury, and others have established standards of ethical conduct that tax practitioners should follow. Yet there is no strict definition of what constitutes evasion. In the end, the courts will decide.

On the other hand, the Code is so structured that the "same" transaction may be taxed differently based on minor changes of form or inconsequential substance. No requirement obliges taxpayers to structure their finances so as to pay the maximum tax. Hence tax planning is the avoidance of taxes by structuring taxpayers' finances so as to incur the minimum taxes consistent with the "realities" of the situation.

Proper tax planning—proper tax avoidance—requires practitioners to cite substantial authority for the positions they recommend or take. From the many cases discussed in this book, several different interpretations of the same facts may emerge. It is not unusual for different courts to hold differently on the same set of facts. If that were not true, there would be no need for an appeals process.

So plan! And avoid! But don't evade!

2

GROSS INCOME: TOTAL AND PARTIAL EXCLUSIONS

EXCLUSIONS AND THE REASONS FOR THEM 02-01

The starting point for computing income tax liability is Gross Income (01-05). And we arrive at Gross Income by subtracting all Exclusions from what we're calling Gross Amounts Received. Many types of "Gross Amounts Received"—the receipt of cash, property, or some asset—are either totally or partially excluded from Gross Income, for three basic reasons:

1. The asset is not income, but rather capital that is being returned.
2. Taxation of the receipt, such as interest as certain municipal bonds, is prohibited by the United States Constitution.
3. The item in question is excluded from Gross Income by statute, such as certain death payments under a life insurance policy.

These, then, are the grounds for Exclusions from Gross Income.

02-01.1 **Tax Hint**

Since any items excluded from Gross Income are *not* subject to taxation, such exclusions should obviously be a taxpayer's first step in avoiding unnecessary taxes. Looking for exclusions constitutes tax avoidance from step one—an important step for investors and their financial advisors. For example:

- In catastrophe planning, such items as life insurance proceeds, Social Security benefits, disability insurance, and workers' compensation provide tax-free dollars to taxpayers and their families.
- In estate planning and current management of income-producing property, the tax-exempt municipal bond and the tax-exempt receipt of gifts form the core of many strategies. But keep in mind that while the receipt of a gift is tax-free, the *donor* may be subject to taxation (see Chapter 13).

02-02 EXCLUDIBLE INTEREST INCOME

As a general rule, interest income is fully taxable, ordinary income, including:

- interest that is specifically stated as such in a bond or a contract,
- interest that may be imputed based on the terms of a contract (10-12.2), and
- discount earned on such instruments as U.S. government Treasury bills (05-11), commercial paper, and bankers' acceptances.

So to exclude interest income from Gross Income, taxpayers must find a specific statute to cite.

02-02.1 Qualified Savings Certificates

Banks and other thrift institutions may issue Qualified Savings Certificates as described in Section 128 of the Code. The Code requires that the issuer use the funds to finance residential housing, but this is of little concern to the taxpayer. What is of concern to the taxpayer is that these certificates:

1. are issued between October 1, 1981 and December 31, 1982;
2. have a maturity of 1 year;
3. must yield 70% of the average yield of the most recently issued 52-week Treasury Bill; and
4. are in denominations of $500 each.

The law provides for individuals and the estates of individuals a once-in-a-lifetime exclusion for the first $1,000 of interest income earned on these certificates. The exclusion is increased to $2,000 on a joint return, regardless of which spouse earned the interest.

The exclusion is lost if the certificate is prematurely redeemed.

Tax Hint 02-02.1A

For any taxpayer with an incremental tax bracket of 30% or more, these certificates are an excellent first step in tax planning. These certificates are insured by an agency of the U.S. government, so they are safe. Since the interest is based on an instrument of similar maturity and nearly the same safety, the taxpayer is receiving a competitive interest rate.

How much to buy? That depends on the interest rate to be earned. Simply divide $1,000 ($2,000 for a joint return) by the interest rate. Of course, you will have to round off to the nearest $500.

As an example, if the interest rate were 14%, then $2,000 divided by 14% is $14,286, rounded to $14,500. Checking our math, 14% of $14,500 for one year is $2,030. The first $2,000 would be excluded from Gross Income, and the $30 would be taxable interest income.

General Interest Exclusion 02-02.2

Beginning in 1985, taxpayers may exclude 15% of their *net* interest income. The maximum exclusion is $450 ($900 on a joint return regardless of which spouse earned the interest).

Net interest income means gross interest income less interest expense (07-01) except interest expense on the taxpayer's home mortgage and interest expense in connection with a trade or business.

02-02.2A **Tax Hint**

Borrow against the house, or even the summer house, rather than take a personal unsecured loan. However, once gross interest income exceeds by $3,000 ($6,000 on a joint return) deductible interest expense, it no longer matters since 15% of $3,000 is $450, the maximum exclusion.

02-02.3 Interest on Municipal Bonds

The so-called "municipal" bonds are bonds issued by states and by their political subdivisions. The term "political subdivisions" includes cities and counties, as well as special authorities such as the New Jersey Turnpike Authority and the Port Authority of New York and New Jersey.

The courts of the United States have repeatedly held that the Constitution bars the federal government from taxing the interest paid on the debts of states or their political subdivisions. The rationale behind these decisions is simply that the power to tax is the power to control—a condition prohibited by the Constitution.

Yet although the exempt status of interest on municipal bonds is recognized in the Code, it is not absolute. For the interest to be exempt, the obligation must be issued for the "normal" operations of the issuing authority. Since the tax-exempt status is not automatic, all municipal bonds carry a "legal opinion." This is an opinion of bond counsel that:

1. the bonds are a legal obligation of the issuer, and
2. the interest is exempt from present federal income taxes.

The Code prohibits an issuer from "misusing" its tax-exempt status. Two examples of these prohibitions are the so-called "arbitrage" bonds and "industrial revenue" bonds.

02-02.3A **Arbitrage bonds**

An arbitrage bond is one whose proceeds are invested in higher-yielding bonds, thus causing net interest income to the issuer.

02-02.3A-1 ***Example***

The State of New Jersey issues $100,000,000 of bonds

bearing interest at 8%. This rate would cost the state $8,000,000 in interest expense per year. Now the state invests that money in U.S. government direct obligations yielding 11½%. That would generate $11,500,000 in interest income. The $3,500,000 difference is profit to the State. In such a case, the New Jersey bond interest would probably be classified as taxable interest to the holder.

Industrial revenue bonds 02-02.3B

An industrial revenue bond is one whose issuer borrows money for the direct or indirect use by a commercial enterprise. Since investors normally accept a lower yield on tax-exempt bonds than on taxable corporate bonds, the effect is that the commercial enterprise is borrowing at a lower rate. Generally, these bonds are guaranteed by the corporation—not by the issuing authority. The Code restricts the use of such a "corporate" bond both as to the amount of money that may be raised and as to the use of the funds raised. One of the legal purposes for such a bond is pollution control.

Tax *warning* 02-02.3C

Interest paid by municipalities on such items as condemnation awards and income tax refunds is *taxable,* and it must be included in Gross Income.

Interest on U.S. Possession Bonds 02-02.4

Interest on the debt of the U.S. government or its instrumentalities issued on or after March 1, 1941 is fully taxable for federal purposes. But interest on bonds issued by possessions, such as Puerto Rico and the Virgin Islands, is exempt from *both* federal and state income taxes.

Original Issue Discount 02-02.5

While the interest on municipal bonds may be exempt from federal taxes, trading profits are not; the gain realized from the appreciation in value of a bond is normally taxable (05-04). The one exception to this rule involves municipal bonds that are originally issued at a discount from face value. If a bond is an "original issue" discount bond, the Official Statement (similar to a prospectus) will give that information. See also 05-11.

02-02.5A **Example**

Sam Investor purchases a $10,000 bond from the City of Hoboken for $8,000 and holds it to maturity. He realizes a $2,000 profit since the bond is redeemed at face value. In this case, the increase in value is considered tax-exempt interest income.

The holder of the bond earns the interest (or discount from face) pro rata over the life of the bond.

02-02.5B **Example**

Sam's bond has ten years to maturity, but he sells it for $9,000 after holding it for only three years. He computes his gain as:

Selling price		$9,000
Less: Cost	$8,000	
Pro rata share of discount		
$2,000 × (3 years ÷ 10 years)		
$2,000 × 30%	+ 600	−8,600
Taxable gain		$ 400

The $600 would be tax-exempt interest.

02-02.5C **Tax *warning***

Many municipal bonds can be purchased in the secondary market at a discount from face value. In most cases, these are *not* considered original issue discount bonds, and the appreciation *is* considered taxable income (05-04).

02-02.6 State Income Tax Considerations

Just as municipal bond interest is exempt from federal income tax, so is interest on the direct obligations of the U.S. and its possessions exempt from state income taxes.

EXCLUDIBLE INTEREST INCOME

Interest on the obligations of agencies of the U.S. government is usually taxable for state income tax purposes. However, the following agency bonds are exempt from state income tax:

1. Federal Home Loan Bank,
2. Banks for Cooperatives,
3. Federal Land Banks, and
4. Federal Intermediate Credit Banks.

Further, most states do not tax their residents on the interest on their own bonds, but they do tax their residents on interest earned on other states' bonds. So you must examine each issue and each state law to determine the tax liability in a particular situation.

Taxable Equivalent Yield 02-02.7

One of the major attractions of a tax-exempt bond is that each dollar received is a full dollar. But you must have objective criteria for comparing the impacts of a tax-exempt yield versus a taxable yield. The method most widely used is to convert the tax-exempt yield to a taxable equivalent. To do so, divide the tax-exempt yield by the reciprocal of the taxpayer's incremental tax rate. (The reciprocal is equal to 1 minus the decimal equivalent of the investor's tax rate.)

Example 02-02.7A

Sam Investor has $100,000 to invest in bonds. He is offered two bonds of equal credit quality and maturity. One is a tax-exempt bond with a yield of 8%, and the other is a taxable bond with a yield of 14%. Which one should he choose?

First, let's assume he is in the 30% incremental tax bracket. So the taxable equivalent of the 8% bond is: .08 (from 8%) ÷ 0.70 (1 − 0.30) = 0.1143. What does the 0.1143 or

11.43% mean? It means that Sam has to earn \$11.43 in taxable dollars on every \$100 to pocket \$8 after taxes. Checking our math:

He would have to earn	\$11.43
Less: Taxes (\$11.43 × 0.30 tax rate)	3.43
Net after taxes	\$ 8.00

Since the tax-exempt bond is equivalent to only 11.43%, and since the taxable bond yields 14%, he should choose the taxable bond, all other things being equal.

But now let's assume he is in the 49% incremental tax bracket: $0.08 \div 0.51\ (1 - .49) = 0.1569$, or 15.69%. Again checking our math:

He would have to earn	\$15.69
Less taxes (\$15.69 × 0.49)	7.69
Net after taxes	\$ 8.00

Obviously, Sam would now opt for the tax-exempt bond since he would have to earn a 15.69% yield on a taxable bond.

02-03 LIFE INSURANCE PROCEEDS

As a general rule, the proceeds of a life insurance policy paid upon the death of the insured is exempt from income taxes.

02-03.1 Tax *Warning*

If a policy is sold, a taxpayer *may* convert tax-exempt life insurance payments into *taxable* proceeds. If the sale is not structured properly, the proceeds may become taxable. Section 101A and Regulation 1.101-1(b) deal with the subject of selling life insurance policies.

Example 02-03.1A

Sarah Almostrich buys an insurance policy on the life of her husband with a death benefit of $100,000. She pays the first annual premium of $1,000. So far, so good: The $100,000 payment on death will be exempt from income taxes.

A year later she sells the policy to her son for $1,500. He then pays the second premium of $1,000. Boom! The proceeds on death now have to be included in the son's Gross Income as follows:

Proceeds		$100,000
Less: Cost of policy	$1,500	
Subsequent premium	+1,000	− 2,500
Taxable amount		$ 97,500

If she had given the policy to her son, instead of selling it to him, it would have fallen under one of the exceptions in Section 101A. Another exception would be if she had sold the policy to her husband's business corporation. The point is to seek competent tax counsel if a policy is to be transferred.

Tax *Warning* 02-03.2

When a corporation owns a life insurance policy, and when the premiums are paid out of corporate earnings, and when the proceeds are payable to the shareholders, the proceeds *may* be taxed as a dividend to the shareholders (02-09).

Interest on Life Insurance Proceeds 02-03.3

When a beneficiary elects to receive payments over a period of time, rather than in a lump sum, the interest payments are taxable.

02-03.3A **Example**

Sarah Mourning is entitled to collect $100,000 on account of her husband's death, but she elects to take 10 payments of $12,000 instead. So $2,000 of each payment received will be interest income. But if the policy *required* Sarah to take the payments over a fixed period of time, then the proceeds would not generally include any interest factor.

If she elects to take the payments over the life of the beneficiary, the interest portion is computed by reference to the mortality tables. If Sarah's life expectancy were 15 years, and if the insurance company agreed to pay her $11,000 per year, then:

$100,000 divided by 15 years	$6,667
Total payment	$11,000
Less: Excluded amount	− 6,667
Interest portion	$ 4,333

02-03.3B **Exclusions for widow(er)s**

Widow(er)s constitute an exception to this rule. The surviving spouse is entitled to exclude from Gross Income the first $1,000 of interest income received on account of the periodic payments made under a payment schedule. To qualify the recipient for this exclusion, some of the insurance proceeds must be paid out each year, and so the schedule cannot consist only of interest payments.

02-03.3C **Tax hint**

First, check the interest rates that the insurance company is paying on life insurance proceeds payout plans. Usually, these rates are lower than you could obtain by investing in taxable corporate or government bonds, but they are higher than you could obtain by a similar investment in tax-exempt bonds. This is particularly true since the credit-worthiness of an insurance carrier is generally higher than that of a tax-exempt bond issuer.

If the proceeds are to be invested partially in tax-exempt bonds anyway, it is normally better to leave some portion of the proceeds with the insurance company and take the payments in the form of an annuity.

Surrender of Policy Before Death 02-03.4

Policy holders who surrender their policies are taxed on the amount received to the extent that it exceeds the premiums paid. Conversely, if the amount received is less than the premiums paid, they cannot deduct the loss. But an insurance policy may be "traded-in" for another insurance policy, for an endowment contract (02-04), or for an annuity contract (02-05) in a tax-free exchange.

ENDOWMENT CONTRACTS 02-04

An *endowment contract* is a contract with a life insurance company that depends in part on the life expectancy of the insured. Although it may be payable in full in a single payment during the life of the insured, such contracts normally call for a single payment of a fixed sum, either on the death of the insured or at a fixed date, whichever occurs first.

One objective of purchasing an endowment contract is to defer realizing taxable income. If the proceeds are received in a lump sum, at maturity or at surrender, the difference between the amount paid for the contract and the amount received is fully taxable ordinary income.

Example 02-04.1

John Taxpayer purchases an endowment contract for $10,000 that matures in five years. Five years later, the life insurance company pays him $14,693, the agreed-upon amount. John has taxable income of $4,693 in year five

($14,693 − $10,000). Had he invested the $10,000 in an interest-bearing vehicle, he would probably have had interest income during *each* of the five years.

02-04.2 Option to Receive an Annuity

Even *after* the maturity date of an endowment contract, a taxpayer has 60 days to "trade it in" for an annuity contract and thereby delay paying the tax on the accumulated earnings even further. If John Taxpayer from the preceding example makes this election, the basis of the annuity (02-05) is $10,000, although he obviously obtains an annuity worth $14,693.

02-04.3 Tax *Warning*

If taxpayers want to make this tax-free exchange, they must *not* receive the proceeds of the endowment and then purchase an annuity. Also, if they don't make the election within the 60-day period, the appreciation in value will be taxable even if they do not actually receive the funds.

02-04.4 Additional Points

Although an insurance policy may be exchanged tax-free for an endowment (02-03), an endowment may *not* be exchanged tax-free for an insurance policy. But an endowment contract may be exchanged tax-free for another endowment contract, *provided* the starting date of the payments is not extended beyond the original contract. (See Figure 2-1.)

FIGURE 2-1. Summary of Tax-Free Exchanges

- An annuity may be exchanged for another annuity without tax consequences.
- Insurance policies and endowment contracts may be exchanged for an annuity tax-free.
- An annuity can*not* be exchanged for either an endowment contract or an insurance policy in a tax-free exchange.

ANNUITIES 02-05

An *annuity* is a contract under which the annuitant receives periodic payments. The number of payments to be received may be either fixed in the annuity contract or based on the life of the annuitant. Most of the time the writer of an annuity contract is an insurance company, but this need not be the case.

To determine the taxability of annuity payments received, taxpayers must determine the "cost" of the contract and the number of payments to be received. Each payment is then taxed based on the formula:

$$\text{Taxable portion} = \frac{\text{Total portion earned}}{\text{Total proceeds}} \times \text{Payment amount}$$

Example 02-05.1

Sarah Taxpayer purchases an annuity for $100,000, which is her cost. Under the terms of the contract, she is to receive $1,000 per month for 15 years. The total amount she will receive is therefore $180,000 ($1,000 × 12 months in a year × 15 years); that constitutes her total proceeds. The difference between the cost and the total proceeds represents the total portion earned: $80,000 = $180,000 − $100,000. Each payment then represents a partial return of her cost ($100,000), along with part of the income she will earn over the life of the contract ($80,000). So:

The taxable portion of each payment is:	
$80,000/$180,000 × $1,000	$ 444
The tax-free portion is:	
$100,000/$180,000 × $1,000	+ 556
Total payment	$1,000

02-05.2 Life Annuity

Many annuity contracts guarantee payments for the life of the annuitant. Some contracts, called *joint* and *survivor annuities,* guarantee payments for as long as either of two people live. How do you determine how many payments will be received? Regulation 1.72-9 gives the taxpayer mortality tables that must be used to compute the expected number of payments. These tables cover almost every conceivable contract.

02-05.2A Example

Sam and Sarah Investor purchase an annuity for $250,000. The contract guarantees to pay them $1,000 per month for as long as *either* shall live. He is 41 years old, she is 39. Looking at Reg. 1.72-9, Table II, we find that the *return multiple* is 44.2. This multiple means that the total return must be figured on the assumption that the last to die will live 44.2 years more. In other words, the annuity will pay $1,000 a month for an anticipated 44.2 years. So the total return is $530,400: $1,000 per month × 12 months in a year × 44.2. And the income part of the total proceeds is $280,400 ($530,400 − $250,000). We can now compute:

The taxable portion of each payment to be:	
$280,400/$530,400 × $1,000	$ 529
The tax-free portion:	
$250,000/$530,400 × $1,000 or	471
Total payment	$1,000

This exclusion ratio does not change regardless of the actual life span of the annuitants. If Sam should suddenly die, Sarah's life expectancy would be 34.7 years. Yet the exclusion ratio would still be based on the original computation. Even if they both live to be 100, the excludible amount for each year would still be $471.

In practice, the insurance company computes the excludible amount and reports it to the annuitant, normally as a percentage: "47.13% excludible." In this example, this percentage is simply another way of expressing $250,000/ $530,400.

"Cost" 02-05.3

When an annuity is acquired in exchange for an insurance policy or for an endowment contract, the cost to the taxpayer is the net cost of the policy or contract. *Net cost* is equal to the total premiums paid *less* any dividends.

Dividends on insurance policies are considered to be merely a return of premiums to the extent that they do not exceed the premiums paid. If dividends on an insurance policy exceed the premiums paid, then the excess is taxable income to the insured. In such a situation, the annuitant's cost would be zero.

Employee Annuities 02-05.4

When an employer contributes to the annuity of an employee, the question of "cost" must be addressed. The general rule is: if the employee pays income tax on the amounts contributed by the employer, the amounts are included in the employee's "cost." But if the amounts are not taxable income to the employee, then the contributions do not count towards the employee's "cost."

COLLECTIONS FOR INJURY AND ILL HEALTH 02-06

The taxability or excludibility of payments received for injury or ill health depends on two factors:

1. the source of the payments and
2. the type of illness or injury.

02-06.1 Purchased Insurance

All payments received for illness and injury from insurance purchased and paid for by taxpayers are excluded from their Gross Income. Yet if taxpayers deduct the medical expenses for which they are being reimbursed (07-07), then the reimbursement is taxable to the extent that the deduction reduces taxable income.

02-06.2 State Payments for Employees

Most states have state funds established to care for employees who are injured or taken ill in a job-related incident. Similarly, many states require that employers carry workers' compensation insurance to accomplish this task. It is not unusual for states to have both a state fund and mandatory workers' compensation. All payments received under such programs are excluded from Gross Income.

02-06.3 Payments from an Employer

Here is where tax planning makes a difference. If payments are received from an employer under a *nonqualified* plan, they are taxable compensation to the employee. If the payments are received from a *qualified* plan, then:

1. the medical expense reimbursement is 100% excludible,
2. payments for the loss of limbs or other bodily functions are 100% excludible, and
3. disability payments are partially excludible (02-06.4).

Employer-qualified plan 02-06.3A

For a plan to be *qualified,* it must:

1. be in writing and
2. not discriminate in favor of officers or highly paid employees.

Note that it does *not* have to be insured, which means the company can make the payments directly.

Tax hint 02-06.3B

Medical expenses are deductible, but with severe limitations (07-07). Many taxpayers lose all or most of their medical deductions due to the Zero Bracket Amount or the 3% of AGI limitation. So for taxpayers whose business is a closely held corporation, have the corporation pay all medical expenses under a written plan. The corporation gets to deduct fully the medical expenses and/or the insurance premiums on a health insurance policy. The amount of these payments are then not included in the taxpayers' Gross Income. Partnerships (Chapter 11) and Subchapter S corporations (12-09) cannot avail themselves of such a program since the owners are not considered "employees" for this purpose.

Disability (Sick Pay) Payments 02-06.4

Disability payments may be fully or partially excludible from Gross Income. Yet since the restrictions and limitations are so tight, few taxpayers qualify for the exclusion, and so such an exclusion is never part of tax or financial planning strategies. For the payments to be excluded, the taxpayer must meet both a "status" test and a Gross Income test. Even if both tests are met, the exclusion is limited to a maximum of $100 per week, for a maximum annual exclusion of $5,200 ($100 per week × 52 weeks). The amount of the $5,200 exclusion is reduced dollar for dollar for Gross Income (including the disability pay) over $15,000. So a taxpayer with $20,200 of Gross Income ($15,000 plus $5,200 maximum disability exclusion for one year) gets *no* exclusion.

To meet the "status" test, *all* of the following conditions must exist:

1. The taxpayer must neither be 65 or older nor reach mandatory retirement age by the end of the year.
2. The taxpayer must be permanently and totally disabled.
3. The taxpayer must not elect to treat the payments as a pension or an annuity (02-06.4B).

Lastly, if married, the taxpayer must file a joint return to claim the exclusion.

02-06.4A **Example**

Sarah Sickly met all these "status" conditions and received $6,000 of disability payments from a qualified plan. She also earned $10,000 in taxable interest income. Her disability income exclusion would be:

Total disability received		$ 6,000
Amount received above maximum (maximum is $100 per week for 52 weeks)		− 800
Exclusion before Gross Income limitation		$5,200
Gross Income:		
Disability payments	$ 6,000	
Taxable interest income	10,000	
	$16,000	
Less: Gross Income limitation	−15,000	− 1,000
Amount of exclusion		$ 4,200
Gross Income		$16,000
Less: Disability exclusion		− 4,200
Adjusted Gross Income		$11,800

Tax Hint 02-06.4B

Taxpayer may elect to treat disability payments as an annuity or as a pension. In some cases, this election results in lower taxes than claiming the disability income exclusion. Figure Adjusted Gross Income *both* ways, and select the election producing the lower AGI.

GIFTS AND OTHER UNSOLICITED RECEIPTS 02-07

Gifts and other unsolicited receipts are not income to the recipient and are therefore excluded from Gross Income. The *donor,* however, may be subject to gift tax (Chapter 13). Often gifts are part of estate planning (Chapter 14). So it is important to the *donor* that title to the property is properly conveyed and that enjoyment of the property is relinquished. But to the *donee* these "fine points" are not relevant, because gifts are not included in Gross Income!

Gifts Defined 02-07.1

Gifts comprise one of those comfortable areas where the Code and English are the same. When the donor gives property to a donee without compensation, there has been a gift.

Income from Gifted Property 02-07.2

Although the gift itself is not included in Gross Income, any subsequent earnings from the property are.

Example 02-07.2A

Sam's father gave him 50 shares of American Telephone and Telegraph common stock valued at $2,500. During the year, Sam received $250 in dividends on the stock. Sam must report the $250 dividend income to the extent that it exceeds the dividend income exclusion (02-09), but he does not have to include the $2,500 value of the stock.

02-07.3 Gifts Versus Compensation

Compensation (03-02) is includible in Gross Income. Normally, when an employer pays money to an employee, it is compensation—even if the employer attaches no legal liability. Classically, year-end bonuses, special awards, and trips for high-production salespersons fall into the category of compensation. Face it, the employer expects to get *something* in return for such payments (employee loyalty, dedication, and so on).

Awards and *prizes* are generally taxable as compensation since the taxpayer usually does something to merit the payment. But awards given for outstanding literary, civic, or other such deeds—where the taxpayer did not solicit the award—are not included in Gross Income. The Nobel Prize is an example, but any similar award also qualifies.

Scholarships are generally not included in Gross Income since the student is not performing any services. But examine the terms both of the scholarship or fellowship and of the grantor carefully. The rules are rather complicated, but get to the heart of the matter. If the recipient is performing services, then part or all of a so-called scholarship may be classified as compensation. Many factors enter into the determination of whether a scholarship is included in, or excluded from, Gross Income: Is the recipient a candidate for a degree? Is the grantor "approved"?

02-07.3A Exceptions

Section 274(b) provides two exceptions where the employer can make a gift to an employee *and* take a deduction for the gift. Since it is a gift, the employee does not have to include the amount received in Gross Income.

1. The employer may award an item of tangible personal property that cost $400 or less for length of service, productivity, or safety achievement.
2. An employer may set up a "Qualified Plan Award." The plan must be in writing and must not discriminate in favor of officers, shareholders, or highly paid employees. Under such a plan an award for length of service, productivity, or safety achievement may be tangible personal property that cost $1,600 or less. However, under a qualified plan, the average cost of all awards may not exceed $400.

GOVERNMENT TRANSFER PAYMENTS 02-08

Social Security benefits (including those for Medicare), as well as welfare and other public assistance payments, are fully excludible from Gross Income.

Unemployment compensation may be includible or excludible, depending on the taxpayer's income from other sources. The basic rule is twofold: Unemployment compensation is excludible, but the exclusion is reduced 50¢ for each $1 that the taxpayer's "income" exceeds the taxpayer's "base."

1. *Income*, for this computation only, is defined as Adjusted Gross Income, plus Unemployment Insurance, plus Excluded Disability Insurance.
2. And the *base* is $25,000 for married taxpayers filing jointly, zero for married taxpayers filing separately, and $20,000 for all other taxpayers.

Example 02-08.1

Sarah Inandoutofwork collected $2,000 in state unemployment benefits and earned $8,000 in salary. Her husband collected $16,000 in salary. Their Adjusted Gross Income would be:

Computation of Excludible Unemployment:	
Her salary	$ 8,000
His salary	16,000
Unemployment compensation	+ 2,000

"Income"	$26,000
"Base"	−25,000
"Income" in excess of "base"	$ 1,000
Unemployment collected	$ 2,000
50% of amount "income" exceeds "base" ($1,000 × 0.50)	− 500
Excludible Unemployment Benefits	$ 1,500
Salaries	$24,000
Taxable Unemployment Benefits ($2,000 − $1,500)	+ 500
Adjusted Gross Income	$24,500

02-09

CASH DIVIDENDS

The so-called dividends paid by savings institutions on deposit balances are not really dividends, but rather interest. (See 03-08 for the discussion of taxable interest.) And the "dividends" received from insurance companies are essentially a return of premiums. To the extent that the premiums were deductible, the return of those premiums is included in Gross Income. But to the extent that the premiums were not deductible, the premium is excluded from Gross Income, unless the dividends received exceed the total premiums paid. In that event, the excess would be included in Gross Income.

For income tax purposes, *dividends* are amounts received from corporations as a distribution of the corporation's "earnings and profits." Assuming that dividends represent a distribution of income, the corporation must have income to distribute; the Code refers to this distributable income as "earnings and profits," or simply E&P. Hence these "real" dividends are fully taxable ordinary income to the extent that:

1. they exceed the exclusions discussed in paragraphs 02-09.3, 02-11 and 02-14, and
2. they are paid out of "earnings and profits."

Dividends received from *regulated investment companies* (mutual funds) are reported by the stockholder either as dividends, interest or as long-term capital gains (12-13).

Dividends received from *personal holding corporations* (12-12) and from Subchapter S corporations (12-09) receive special treatment.

Constructive Dividends 02-09.1

Dividends are taxable to the shareholder, but they are not deductible by the corporation. Even when no dividend is declared by the corporation, the IRS has sometimes held that there was a *constructive* dividend. This sort of dividend normally occurs when a closely held or controlled corporation pays amounts to, or for, the controlling shareholders. Items such as excessive salaries paid to a controlling shareholder, withdrawals from the corporation for personal use, and similar items may cause the IRS to take such a position. When the IRS takes such a position, it is punitive in nature, and it normally results from what the IRS perceives to be an abuse of the shareholders' ability to control the corporation.

Dividends in Kind 02-09.2

Dividends received in *kind*—that is, in the form of property rather than of cash—are considered to be received at their fair market value. (However, see 02-11 for stock dividends and stock splits.)

Example 02-09.2A

Colin Gordon receives a dividend of 100 shares of AT&T common stock from the PinA Corporation. The market value of the stock is $50 per share. Colin must report dividend income of $5,000. His basis in the stock is also $50 per share (04-02).

Individual Dividend Exclusion 02-09.3

Under Section 116(a), each individual taxpayer is entitled to exclude from Gross Income the first $100 of dividends received from a domestic corporation. This amount is increased to $200 on a joint return regardless of which spouse earned the dividend.

Dividends received from foreign corporations do not qualify for this exclusion.

02-09.4 Reinvestment of Dividends in Public Utilities

Many public corporations have dividend reinvestment plans. Under these plans the stockholder may reinvest the dividends received in newly issued stock of the corporation. These plans work well for both the corporation obtaining fresh capital and stockholder loyalty; the stockholder buys more shares without paying commission, and under some plans at a price slightly below the current market value.

As a general rule, dividends reinvested are taxable to the shareholder in the same manner as if they had not been reinvested.

Code Section 305(e) allows for an exception for certain qualified public utilities. To qualify the stock must be issued at a price between 95% and 105% of market value, and the public utility must follow certain rules set out in the Code, but these are of little importance to the taxpayer.

What is important is that each taxpayer may reinvest up to $750 per year ($1,500 on a joint return without regard to which spouse earned the dividend) and avoid the income tax on the dividend paid by the utility.

To take advantage of this the taxpayer must:

1. make a positive election on the tax return upon which the dividend would have been reported; and
2. not sell any of the stock in that utility for a period of one year.

If any stock of the utility is sold within one year, it is presumed to be the stock purchased by reinvestment, and the proceeds of sale are reported as ordinary income.

The basis of such stock is zero (04-03), and the holding period begins on the day the dividend would have been collected (05-02).

Taxable dividends, by definition, constitute a distribution of "income," or more correctly of E&P. What happens if a corporation has no E&P but declares and pays a "dividend" anyway? The general rule is that the stockholders have simply recovered their investments, and that the dividend is excluded from income.

Nice and easy? Wrong! Probably one of the most complicated areas in both income and estate taxation is the "liquidation" of a taxpayer's interest in a corporation. Except with a "public" corporation that is at "arm's length," all the general rules go by the wayside. Because the "liquidation" and return of capital dividends receive such favorable tax treatment, they are often the vehicle for very sophisticated tax and estate planning. In this area, a court may overturn the IRS, only to have a "smarter" court overturn the first one.

In "general," then, the following general rule applies. When a corporation pays a dividend in excess of its E&P, the dividend is excluded from Gross Income. It simply reduces the basis of the stock, in effect returning the investment. If the amount of the dividend reduces the basis below zero, then the difference is taxable as a capital gain (Chapter 5).

Example: Distribution in Excess of E&P 02-10.1

Brynne Gordon purchases 100 shares of New Jersey Public Service Electric and Gas for $18 per share. Her basis is therefore $1,800 (04-02). During the year she receives $232 in dividends. The company informs her that of the dividends distributed during the year, 25% are in excess of E&P and should be considered a return of capital.

1. For federal income tax purposes she should report dividend income of $174 (75% of $232).

2. The remaining $58 serves to reduce her basis, which is now $1,742 ($1,800 − $58).

If at this point she sells the stock for $1,850, her gain would be:

Proceeds of sale	$1,850
Less: Basis	1,742
Gain	$ 108

Eventually, her basis could be reduced to zero, but not to below zero. Suppose that in several years her basis is reduced to $100 by successive return-of-capital dividends and that she then receives a return of capital dividend in the amount of $150. The first $100 serves to reduce her basis to zero, and the remaining $50 is reported as a capital gain (Chapter 5).

02-10.1A **Tax hint**

Several public utility stocks repeatedly pay dividends that are partially or totally return-of-capital dividends. These can make an excellent investment vehicle for persons interested in high-yield (as most of them are), tax-deferred income. In our previous example, Brynne does not have to pay income taxes on the $58 until she sells the stock. Taxes delayed mean interest earned! More importantly, long-term capital gains receive favorable tax treatment (Chapter 5). She may have to report only 40% of the $58 as taxable income in the year of sale.

As with any tax motivated investment, seek competent advice on the safety and long-term potential of the investment.

02-10.2 Example: Liquidating Dividend

Brynne Gordon purchases 100 shares of MBS Corporation for $50 per share. Her basis is therefore $5,000. She receives a notice from the company that they are liquidating and going out of business. In 1980, she receives a $2,000 liquidating dividend, and in 1981 she receives an additional $4,000 as a final liquidation. For federal income tax purposes, the first $2,000 reduces her basis to $3,000 ($5,000 − $2,000), and she has no taxable income. The second distribution is reported as follows:

1. The first $3,000 (of the $4,000) reduces her basis to zero.
2. The remaining $1,000 is gain.

STOCK DIVIDENDS AND STOCK SPLITS 02-11

The Code recognizes stock dividends and stock splits for what they are, noneconomic events. Stockholder simply receive more pieces of paper, representing the same investment. Regardless of whether a distribution is classified as a stock dividend or as a stock split, the "proceeds" or additional shares are not included in Gross Income. The holding period (05-02) of the new shares is the same as the old shares, and the basis of the newly acquired stock is prorated from the old stock.

Example 02-11.1

Colin Gordon purchases 100 shares of MBS Corporation for $50 per share on January 2, 1980. MBS declares and pays a 10% stock dividend; that is, for every share that shareholders own they will receive an additional 1/10th share. Colin therefore receives 10 new shares. (See 02-11.2 for fractional shares.) Colin now owns 110 shares of stock, *each* with a basis of $45.4545. This new basis is computed as follows:

$$\text{New basis} = \frac{\text{Original basis}}{\text{New number of shares}}$$

$$= \frac{\$5{,}000}{110}$$

$$= \$45.4545\ldots$$

Notice that his total basis is still $5,000 (110 shares × $45.4545 each). And the holding period of the 110 shares still dates back to the original purchase: January 2, 1980.

Fractional Shares 02-11.2

Most companies do not distribute fractional shares as a result of a stock dividend. Normally, all fractional shares are sold by the company, and the stockholders receive "cash in lieu." The cash in lieu of fractional shares is considered a return of capital dividend, and it serves to reduce the basis of the stock (02-10).

02-11.2A **Example**

Colin, in the previous example, owns not 100 but 52 shares of stock. The company sends him 5 shares plus $9.50 cash in lieu of the 2/10th share to which he was entitled. His basis in the 57 shares he now owns is:

Cost of original 52 shares @ $50	$2,600.00
Less: Return of capital dividend	− 9.50
Basis of 57 shares	$2,590.50

The basis of each share is: $2,590.50 ÷ 57 shares = $45.4474.

02-11.3 Terminology

To the accountant, a stock dividend and a stock split are different; different entries are made on the books of the issuing company. To the stock exchanges, there is also a difference between a stock dividend and a stock split; the difference is in the way statistics are maintained and in the way open orders are treated. But to the investor they are *exactly* the same. In the preceding example, the company might have called its dividend a "1-for-10" split or a 10% dividend; both would be the same to the investor. Or a company could have either a 100% stock dividend or a 2-for-1 split; in either case, stockholders have twice as many shares as they had before, but no taxable income.

02-11.4 Taxable Stock Dividends

Stock dividends can become taxable if any one of the following conditions exist:

1. Some or all of the shareholders have the right to take cash or property in lieu of the stock (except for cash in lieu of fractions). (See also 02-09.4.)
2. The distribution is "disproportionate"—that is, some stockholders get more than others.
3. The distribution is in other than common stock (such as in preferred stock) and certain conditions are not met.

Most of these situations occur in closely held corporations, where an attempt is being made to frustrate the Code through preferential dividends.

STOCK AND BOND RIGHTS 02-12

A *right* is an instrument that is distributed by the issuing company to current stock or bond holders and that allows them to purchase additional stock or bonds, usually at a price below market value. Rights also have an expiration date, beyond which they are, of course, worthless. Rights may be issued either because some state laws require that current holders be allowed the opportunity to retain their current proportional ownership (preemptive rights) or because the right may be just a means of marketing the new issue.

Stock Rights 02-12.1

When stock rights are issued, federal securities law requires that one right be issued for each share. For example, if a company has 1,000,000 shares outstanding and wishes to issue an additional 100,000 shares through the use of rights, it would issue 1,000,000 rights. Holders would then need 10 rights to purchase one share.

The receipt of the rights is not a taxable event (04-01), and so no taxable income is received. But the holder of a right *must* take some action, normally within a few weeks. The three possible actions are:

1. let the rights expire worthless, or
2. exercise the rights and buy the stock, or
3. sell the rights.

02-12.2 Basis of Rights

If at the date of distribution the market value of the rights is less than 15% of the market value of the stock, then the basis is zero unless the taxpayer elects otherwise.

If the market value of the rights is 15% or more of the market value of the stock, then the taxpayer must allocate basis from the common stock to the rights.

02-12.2A Example

Sarah Investor owns 100 shares of MBS Corporation, which she acquired at $50 per share in 1978. The company announces that it will issue rights, with 10 rights required to purchase 1 share at $70. Immediately before the distribution of the rights, the stock was selling for $103 per share. Immediately after the distribution, the stock was selling for $100 per share, and the rights for $3 each. The allocation of basis between the stock and the rights is based on the relative values of the two instruments. If Sarah elects to allocate her basis, the computation would be:

Basis of each old share held ($100/$103 × $50)	$48.54
Basis of rights ($3/$103 × $50)	+ 1.46
Total	$50.00

The holding period of the rights is based on the holding period of the stock, so it dates back to 1978.

Rights Expire Worthless 02-12.3

If the stock price drops below the permitted purchase price or if the holder neglects to exercise the right before the expiration date, the right is, of course, worthless.

Example 02-12.3A

If the price of the stock drops below $70 between the date of the distribution and the expiration date, the rights would, of course, be worthless. Or if Sarah just forgot to exercise them, they would be worthless after their expiration date. Provided she elects to allocate basis, she would suffer a capital loss of $146 (100 rights × $1.46). (See 05-05 for the deductibility of capital losses.) But if Sarah fails to allocate basis and the rights therefore expire worthless, she has no loss. Her basis in the stock would remain at $50 per share.

Exercise of Rights 02-12.4

If rights are exercised, the basis of the rights is added to the exercise price to obtain the basis of the new stock. No taxable event occurs, and so no amount is included in Gross Income.

Example 02-12.4A

If Sarah exercises the rights, her basis for the new stock would be:

Exercise price	$70.00
Basis of rights (10 rights × $1.46)	+14.60
Total	$84.60

Tax *warning* 02-12.4B

The holding period for stock acquired through the exercise of rights begins on the date of exercise. The holding period that was carried over from the old stock is lost with respect to the stock acquired via the rights offering. (See 05-02 for the importance of the holding period.)

02-12.5 Sale of Rights

If rights are sold, any gain or loss is calculated on the holder's basis. And the holding period is still based on the holding period of the stock.

02-12.5A **Example**

If Sarah sells the rights, she would measure any gain or loss based on her allocated basis. If the rights were sold for $2.00, then she would have a 54¢ gain.

02-12.6 Tax Hint

In any of these three possibilities, it is *always* to the taxpayer's advantage to allocate basis.

1. In the event of *sale* or of the rights *expiring worthless,* a loss is generated or a profit is reduced.
2. In the event of *exercise,* the additional basis is added to the short-term position and subtracted from the long-term position. This switch can serve only to reduce a reportable gain and/or to increase a reportable loss (05-04 and 05-05).

02-12.7 Bond Rights

Rights to subscribe to bonds that are *convertible* into common stock are treated the same as rights to subscribe to common stock.

Rights to subscribe to *nonconvertible* bonds (straight debt) are considered to be a taxable dividend. The amount received, as well as the amount that must be included in gross dividends received, is the fair market value of the rights.

When an estate is distributed to the beneficiaries, the question is what must be included in and excluded from Gross Income? The general rule is that, if the asset in question was owned by the deceased at death, or if it was received by the estate, then the subsequent disbursement to the beneficiary is exempt from income tax. But, when a beneficiary receives an asset, and when the direct receipt of that asset *would have been* taxable to the deceased, then the amount is taxable to the beneficiary, just as if the deceased had received it. (Chapter 13 deals at length with the taxability of estates).

Example 02-13.1

Jane Nolongawithuz was a member of the State Teachers' Retirement System. She contributed $10,000 to the plan. Under the System, she was entitled to name a beneficiary to receive her vested interest in the event of her death before retirement. She named her daughter, who received $92,000, directly from the System, upon her mother's death. Since the receipt of the funds would have been taxable to the mother, and since they passed directly to the daughter without first going to the estate, the daughter must pay tax on the amount received just as her mother would have.

But two tax breaks can reduce the daughter's taxes. The first, the 10-year averaging method (09-04), is one the mother could have used herself. Second, the taxable amount is reduced by the amount of "estate tax" paid that is attributable to the funds received. The rationale is that the estate will have to pay a tax on the pension even though the estate did not receive it (Chapter 14). So let's say the estate can attribute $14,000 of estate tax to the pension value. Jane's daughter would have to report taxable income of:

Gross pension received	$92,000
Less: Jane's basis (amount contributed)	−10,000
Amount that would have been taxable to Jane	$82,000
Less: Estate tax attributable to pension	−14,000
Amount taxable to Jane's daughter	$68,000*

*See 03-03 with regard to the $5,000 death benefit exclusion, which might reduce the taxable amount even further.

02-14 EXCLUSION FOR DIVIDENDS RECEIVED BY CORPORATIONS

This so-called exclusion is really a deduction, and even then it has its limits. The general rule is that U.S. tax-paying corporations are entitled to deduct 85% of the dividends received from other U.S. tax-paying corporations. The simplistic approach—that this is an exclusion—holds up "most of the time."

02-14.1 The Classic Example

MBS Corporation of Hoboken, N.J., received $100,000 in dividends on its General Motors common stock. MBS is a profitable company, in the 46% incremental tax bracket. Its tax on this dividend would be:

General Motors dividend	$100,000
Less: 85% deduction	− 85,000
Taxable income	$ 15,000
Tax on $15,000 ($15,000 × 0.46)	$ 6,900

Many times such an investment is sold to the corporate treasurer on the theory that it is 6.9% ($6,900/$100,000) taxable. Most of the time, this presentation does represent reality, and no harm is done.

02-14.2 Tax Hint

As a corporate treasurer, you are offered the opportunity to buy 10,000 shares of *preferred* MBS stock with par value $100 and dividend 12% of par. As an alternative investment you may take $1,000,000 par value of the same company's mortgage bonds with a coupon of 12%. Since both investments cost $1,000,000 and yield 12% *logic* says, "Take the bonds!" After all, the bonds are a senior instrument that entitle you to interest. Preferred stock is far junior in liquidation preference, and the Board of Directors could pass the dividend. Interest requirements can be enforced in a court of law; dividends are at the will of the Director. But . . . the dividends are taxed at only 6.9%, while the interest is taxed at 46%. Any stockbroker will tell you why preferred stock yields are typically lower than those of the bonds of the same issuer. Interesting—how tax considerations can upset economic logic!

Limitations on the Sources of Dividends 02-14.3

The deduction for dividends received from *foreign corporations* is limited by the amounts of their income that is subject to U.S. income taxes.

The deduction for dividends received on certain *public utility* preferred stock issued before October 1, 1942 is limited to 59.13%.

Dividends received from *DISC Corporations* (Domestic International Sales Corporation, see 12-17), *affiliated corporations*, and *regulated investment companies* (12-13) come under separate rules governing the taxability of those corporations.

Taxable Income Limitation 02-14.4

The amount of the deduction is limited to *taxable income* computed *without* regard to:

1. the dividend-received deduction,
2. net operating loss carry-forward or carry-back, *or*
3. capital loss carry-back.

But the limitation does not apply if the corporation has a net loss for the year in question.

Example 02-14.4A

MBS Corporation had gross income from operation of $34,000, plus dividends from domestic corporations of $40,000. They had operating expenses of $40,000. Their taxable income, before the dividend-received deduction, would be:

Gross operating receipts	$34,000
Dividends received	+40,000
	$74,000
Business expense	−40,000
Taxable income before deduction	$34,000

The dividend-received deduction is the lower of 85% of $40,000 ($34,000) or 85% of $34,000 ($28,900). In this case, it is $28,900. This leaves taxable income of $5,100 ($34,000 − $28,900).

But let's say the gross receipts from operations were reduced to, say, $33,000, or that business expenses increased to $41,000. Then, *after* the dividend deduction, the corporation would have a net operating loss. In the first case they would have only a zero income after the dividend received deduction: 85% of $40,000 is *exactly* $34,000.

Gross operating receipts	$33,000
Dividends received	+40,000
	$73,000
Business expenses	−40,000
Taxable income, before deduction	$33,000
Deduction, 85% of 40,000	−(34,000)
Net operating loss	$ 1,000

This loss may be used to offset income of either prior or future years. Note that a $1,000 reduction in income causes a $6,100 swing in taxable income (+$5,100 to −$1,000).

02-14.5 Holding Period Limitation

In addition to holding the stock on the record date (a requirement for receiving the dividend), one of two other requirements applies:

1. *For a dividend covering 366 days or less,* the corporation must own the stock for at least 15 additional days (before or after the record date). *Or* . . .
2. *For a dividend covering more than 366 days,* the corporation must own the stock for at least 90 additional days (before or after the record date).

This rule exists to prevent corporations from buying stock just to get the partially tax-free income. It also prevents a corporation from hedging its position via short sales or other maneuvers.

02-14.6 Tax *Warning:* Short Sales

When stock is sold short, the seller must borrow the stock to make the delivery. The lender of that stock receives payments from the short seller "in lieu" of the dividends. Such payments to the *lender* are not dividends, and the dividend-received deduction is lost. The loss also holds for lenders of municipal bonds, in that the "interest" received from the borrower is not tax-exempt.

Tax *Warning:* Call Options 02-14.7

A currently popular way for investors to increase their yield on common stock investments is to buy the stock and simultaneously sell call options against the position. Corporations must be careful about this tactic. They must make sure that each stock position is "exposed" for the required 16 days. A short call option is one of the maneuvers that causes the loss of the dividends-received deduction.

DAMAGES 02-15

Damages, whether received from a court or in a settlement, are essentially a "payment in lieu" of collecting the original amount. In other words, the taxability of the amounts received for damages depend on what the payments are for.

1. If the damages are for *lost income,* then they are taxable to the extent the income would have been taxable. This rule includes treble damages under an antitrust suit.
2. If the damages are for *personal "rights,"* such as libel, personal injury, or pain, then they are excluded from Gross Income.
3. If the damages are *to an asset,* then the amount is excludible provided it does not exceed the basis of the asset (04-02). To the extent that the amount collected exceeds the basis, the difference would be included in Gross Income.

INCOME EARNED ABROAD 02-16

A citizen of the United States who is a resident of a foreign country, *or* a citizen or resident of the United States who resides in a foreign country for at least 330 days of a 12-month consecutive period, is entitled to exclude from Gross Income certain earned income. Earned income includes wages, salary, professional fees, or other amounts received for personal services. The amount that may be excluded is:

For	1982	$75,000
	1983	80,000
	1984	85,000
	1985	90,000
	1986 and thereafter	95,000

The amount excluded must be prorated on a daily basis if the taxpayer was not out of the country for the full tax year.

In addition, these taxpayers may exclude from Gross Income certain housing allowances or the value of housing provided by the employer. The amount that may be excluded is 16% of the amount earned of a U.S. employee in step 1 of grade GS-14. In 1981 this was $37,871 per year (16% of which is $6,059). This exclusion must also be prorated based on the number of days in the foreign country.

If an employer does not provide housing or a housing allowance, the expenses of housing may be taken as a deduction for AGI. The amount of the deduction is limited to the amount of foreign-earned income, which is taxable and not excluded by this provision. If a deduction is denied due to this limitation, it may be carried forward one year.

Keep in mind that under Section 119, any meals or lodging furnished by an employer for the convenience of the employer (rather than for the benefit of the employee) is excluded from Gross Income. This would include so called camps that accommodate 10 or more people.

Because of limitations in the Code, federal employees will generally not qualify for this exclusion.

3
GROSS INCOME: INCLUSIONS

TO WHOM IS GROSS INCOME TAXABLE? 03-01

Gross Income generally comes from one of two sources: It is either *earned*, as wages or as other compensation, or it results from the *ownership of property*, such as interest or dividends. Keep in mind also that "income" need not be in cash. If income is received in kind—that is, as property—it must be included in Gross Income at its fair market value. *Fair market value* is the price that a willing buyer would pay and a willing seller would accept, neither of whom is compelled to complete the transaction.

1. *Earned income is generally taxable to the person earning it.* The mere assignment of income to a third party does not transfer the tax liability. The IRS and the courts have repeatedly held that "family" companies created for the purpose of transferring income earned by the family bread-winner to lower tax bracket children will not be recognized for income tax purposes. On the other hand, community property income is attributed one-half each to the husband and wife. This separate ownership, of course, would not be of concern unless they filed separate returns. (However, see 07-10 for an exception.)

2. *Income derived from the ownership of property is attributed to the owner of the property.* State law prevails for property held as tenants by the entirety, joint tenants, and tenants in common. Transferring property ownership by gifts does transfer the income from that property to the donee. But the gift will not be recognized by the Internal Revenue Service unless it meets certain requirements. While the Code and Regulations in this area are complex, the heart of the matter is that the donor must *give up control* of the property. In some cases, the relinquishment of control does not have to be permanent, and the use of trusts to hold and manage the assets is recognized. This is one area where a lawyer is a must.

COMPENSATION 03-02

Compensation for services rendered is included in Gross Income. Whether the amounts are called salary, wages, commissions, or bonuses does not matter. Payments made in anticipation of services to be rendered are also included in Gross Income. Even if the employee can deduct the amounts paid for Adjusted Gross Income, the employer must include the payments in the computation of compensation paid; moving expenses are a good example (06-11). The *full* amount of any compensation—before any deductions for taxes, Social Security, pension contributions, and the like—must be included in Gross Income. Also, payments received under a covenant not to compete are considered to be compensation, and they too must be included.

In many cases, even payments made by an employer on behalf of an employee must be included in the employee's Gross Income as compensation. As an example, if a corporation hired a financial counselor to work with its executives on personal financial planning, the amounts paid to the counselor would be included in the executives' compensation, although they could probably deduct most of it from AGI.

(See 02-07.3 for a discussion of gifts compared to compensation.)

In general, the taxability of pensions or of other retirement benefits follows the rules set out in 02-01: The portion that is *excluded* from Gross Income is the portion that represents a return of investment, or cost. Employees' "investments" consist of:

1. the amounts they contributed to the plan for which no tax deduction was allowed (06-06); *and*
2. the amounts contributed by the employer that were previously included in the employees' Gross Income and therefore taxed; *and*
3. the employee death benefit exclusion (03-03.2).

Hence the amount *included* in Gross Income is the amount received over and above the investment.

If any amounts are received as an annuity, they are taxed as such (02-05 and 03-03.1 for an exception).

If a payment is received in a lump sum, the amount received over the investment is included in Gross Income. (See 09-05 for the availability of 10-year forward averaging.)

03-03.1 Recovery of Investment Within Three Years

If the amount that employees receive in the first three years equals or exceeds their cost, then they may elect to report all payments received as a return of investment. After the full amount of the investment has been recovered, then any additional payments are fully includible in Gross Income.

03-03.2 Employee Death Benefit Exclusion

Up to $5,000 of payments made by an employer on account of an employee's death may be excluded from Gross Income. The $5,000 may be considered as an additional cost or investment of an annuity. But that's all the exclusion you get. The *total* amount that may be excluded from Gross Income may not exceed $5,000, regardless of the number of beneficiaries or the number of employers involved (03-03.2A).

No exclusion is allowed when the deceased had a vested interest in the amounts paid, except:

1. if the amount is paid in one calendar year, *and*
2. the payment comes from a qualified annuity plan or exempt pension, profit sharing, or stock bonus plan.

In effect, to qualify for the $5,000 exclusion, a vested interest must meet the same tests as it takes to qualify for the 10-year forward averaging method (**09-04**).

Example 03-03.2A

The Board of Directors of MBS Corporation vote to give $25,000 to the widow of John Gonbyby and $5,000 to his son, "in recognition of his fine services." John taught part-time at the New York Institute of Finance, and they also voted to pay John's widow $2,000 on account of his death. All three payments (for a total of $32,000) qualify for the $5,000 exclusion, so the exclusion must be prorated. John's widow can claim $4,219 ($5,000 × $27,000/$32,000), and the son can claim $781 ($5,000 × $5,000/$32,000).

Capital Gains Treatment 03-03.3

If an employee is paid a pension in one calendar year as a lump sum, the portion of the payment that pertains to his or her participation in the plan for 1973 and prior may be treated as a long-term capital gain. The taxpayer has the choice of the 10-year forward averaging method (**09-04**) *or* the capital gains treatment. In most cases, the 10-year forward averaging method results in a lower tax, but the taxpayer should figure the tax both ways to be sure.

Rollover 03-03.4

If employees receive the distribution of a pension plan, they usually have 60 days to "roll it over" into another pension plan. If they roll the distribution into another pension plan, the amount received is excluded from Gross Income.

Tax *warning* 03-03.4A

The tax-free rollovers of pension plans constitute a highly technical area. Each "i" must be dotted, and each "t" properly crossed. Failure to follow the Code *exactly* can result in the inclusion of the entire amount in Gross Income—*plus* a penalty tax could be added on. In this area competent *written* tax opinions should be in hand.

In most cases the pension plan or the employer provides it.

03-04 COMPENSATION OTHER THAN CASH

The general rule is that compensation received in forms other than cash are included in Gross Income at its fair market value. Of course, there are some exceptions.

03-04.1 Group Term Life Insurance

As a general rule, life insurance premiums are not deductible; they are considered either a personal or capital expenditure. If an employer pays life insurance premiums on the lives of employees, and the policies are in favor of the employees, their families, or their estates, then the employer is really paying a personal expense for the employees. Following the general rule, such payments would be considered compensation to the employees and included in their Gross Incomes.

The Code contains an exception to the general rule for up to $50,000 of group term life insurance per employee. Ordinary or permanent insurance does not qualify. Multiple-purpose policies, such as those integrated with a pension plan, must clearly allocate the portion of the premium that is for group term life insurance. Otherwise the entire amount will be included in Gross Income.

When a group term policy is for more than $50,000, employees are taxed on the premium paid for the excess insurance. Regulation Section 1.79-3(b)(1) sets out the amount that the employees must include in their Gross Incomes for each additional $1,000 of group term life insurance over the first $50,000.

03-04.1A Example

Sarah Taxpayer is 42 years old. Under her employer's group term life insurance plan, she has $150,000 of coverage, for which she contributes $150 by way of withholding from her wages. The amount she must include in Gross Income is computed as follows:

Total coverage	$150,000
Excludible amount	− 50,000
Includible amount of insurance coverage	$100,000

Examining the Regulations, we find that for an employee aged 42, the amount to be included in Gross Income is 23¢ per $1,000 per month. Since Sarah was under the program for the entire year, the "compensation" to her was:

12 months × 23¢ × 100	$276
Less: The amount she contributed	−150
Amount added to her Gross Income	$126

Tax hint 03-04.1B

The conversion of a nondeductible personal expense into a deductible business expense is hard to say no to. Group term life insurance normally forms the core of any employee benefits package. For this purpose, sole proprietors, partners of partnerships, and stockholders of Subchapter S corporations are not considered to be employees.

But you can structure group term life insurance programs to benefit mainly the highly paid employee/stockholder of a Subchapter C (regular) corporation. Suppose Manny and Moe are each 50% stockholders of their plumbing company. They each take a salary of $100,000 per year, and their employees get significantly less. They could purchase group term life insurance in amounts equal to each employee's six-months' salary. In this way the owners get most of the benefits.

Split Dollar Life Insurance 03-04.2

Split dollar life insurance is really a way of transferring, sub rosa, interest income from an employer to an insurance company, for the purpose of reducing insurance premiums paid for an employee.

Here's how it's done: The employer takes out an accelerated payment life insurance policy for the benefit of its employees. The employer is the beneficiary to the extent that the policy has cash surrender value. The employees, their families, or their estates are the beneficiaries for the difference between the face of the policy and the cash surrender value. The employer pays that portion of the premium representing the increase in cash surrender value, and the employees pay the difference. Although the payments are not deductible, the employer eventually receives back all the premiums it paid. As merely a return of capital, they are not taxed to the employer.

The policy is really declining term for the employees, since the cash surrender value is increasing each year. But that is the purpose of the arrangement—to give employees more "declining term" insurance then they could otherwise afford. The cost to the employees is inevitably lower than had they purchased individual term insurance, since the insurance company is earning interest on the cash surrender value.

Employees must include in Gross Income the value of the term insurance, less the amount they had to pay (03-04.2A). The tables in Revenue Ruling 55-747 may be used to determine the value of the term insurance received by the employees and included in their Gross Incomes.

03-04.2A **Example**

MBS Corporation purchases a $200,000 accelerated payment life policy for its employee, Sam. The policy calls for 10 annual payments of $15,000 each. The first year, MBS pays $14,000, representing the increase in cash value, and Sam pays $1,000. The cost of a one-year term policy for $186,000 ($200,000 face less $14,000 cash surrender value) is $1,100. Sam must include in his Gross Income $100 ($1,100 − $1,000).

If the value of the term insurance was less than Sam paid, he would have no amount to include in Gross Income.

In future years, the amount of the term insurance declines as the cash surrender value increases.

Employer Payments for Education 03-04.3

For the average taxpayer, education expenses are normally considered a personal and therefore nondeductible expense. Educational expenses may be deducted if they are for the maintenance or the improvement of your *current* employment, but this area can be sticky.

If the employer pays for the educational expenses of employees under a qualified plan, then the employer may deduct the expense, and the employee need not include the expense in Gross Income. For a plan to qualify, it must:

1. be in writing, and
2. not discriminate in favor of highly paid employees or officers.

Expenses that qualify include: tuition, books, fees, supplies, and equipment. The eduction need not be job-related, but it cannot be related to hobbies or sports.

Tax *warning* 03-04.3A

These programs do not fit well into a closely held business situation. The Code requires that no more than 5% of the funds expended be for owners or their families.

Meals and Lodging 03-04.4

Meals provided by an employer to employees—while they are on duty and because they must remain on duty—are not included in Gross Income. What about "cash in lieu" of meals? In an Office Decision, which is similar to a Ruling, the IRS held that supper allowances were *not* income. Yet the Supreme Court has held that meal allowances to New Jersey State Policemen who were "on call" during their lunch hour were compensation and includible in Gross Income.

Lodging provided by an employer is includible in Gross Income, unless the employee must live on the business premises. Special rules exist for the clergy and for certain U.S. government employees, including members of the armed forces.

03-04.5 Notes Received

Notes received as compensation are included in Gross Income at their fair market value. If the fair market value is below face value, then the difference is included in Gross Income when collected. Notes received to evidence interest in default are *not* income, and they are not included in Gross Income.

03-05 RESTRICTED PROPERTY

Often employers compensate key employees by giving them restricted stock in the corporation or some other type of other restricted property. The restriction is usually that the employees have to forfeit the property if they leave the corporation's employ before a certain date. The general rule is that the property must be reported in Gross Income in the year that there is no longer a substantial risk of such a forfeiture.

The amount reported is the fair market value, *without* regard to any restrictions except those that never lapse. Such a permanent restriction might include the requirement that the employees sell the stock or property back to the corporation. Normally, the selling price would be on a formula basis, and that formula would be used to determine fair market value.

03-05.1 Important Election

Within 30 days after the receipt of the stock or property, employees may elect to include the amount in Gross

Income even though there is a substantial risk of forfeiture. Employees might choose to do so because they believe there is going to be a significant increase in the value of the stock or property. Perhaps by the time the restrictions are lifted, the market value might be significantly higher. Since they would rather report a lower *current* market value as fully taxable compensation, they could make such an election.

If they make such an election, the currently reported market value is the basis of the property (04-02). The increase in market value is then taxed at the more favorable capital gains rates, rather then as fully taxable compensation.

The holding period begins when the property is included in Gross Income.

Tax *Warning* 03-05.2

If the election is made, and if the property is subsequently forfeited, the taxpayer gets *no* refund of the taxes paid and *no* deduction for the loss.

Tax Hint 03-05.3

In this area taxpayers are forced to become gamblers. They must decide which way to go. Even if they make "no decision"—that is, if they put off declaring the property as Gross Income to a later year—they are still making a decision.

So what do you do? If the current fair market value is low compared to the expectations, then the "right" answer is to include the property or stock in Gross Income in the year received. If the risk of forfeiture is high, *and* if the tax that would have to be paid is high, then the "right" answer is to defer the reporting until the restrictions have substantially lapsed.

03-05.4 Deductibility by the Employer

The employer may deduct the market value of the restricted property paid as compensation only in the year that the employees include the amount in Gross Income. The amount of the deduction is the same amount as included by the employees in their Gross Income.

03-05.5 Example

MBS Corporation gave its employee, Sarah, 1,000 shares of MBS common stock. The terms of the agreement were that she would forfeit the stock if she left the employ of MBS within five years. The current market value of MBS common stock is $5 per share. Since the risk of forfeiture is substantial, Sarah does not have to report the $5,000 (1,000 shares @ $5) in Gross Income this year.

But let's assume that she does make the election to report it in the current year. She declares $5,000 of compensation income, and MBS gets a deduction this year for $5,000 for compensation paid. Five years later, the stock is selling for $25 per share. Since Sarah reported the stock, she has no further Gross Income, and MBS has no further deductions. Then, in the sixth year, Sarah sells the stock for $30 per share. She must then report a long-term capital gain (05-04) of $25,000 ($30,000 selling price less the basis of $5,000). Yet since capital gains receive favorable tax treatment, she is not unhappy.

On the other hand, if she had not made the election, she would have had to report $25,000 of fully taxable compensation in year 5. She would then have had only $5,000 of long-term capital gain on sale ($30,000 proceeds of sale less the basis of $25,000).

Or if she had quit her job in year 3 and had to forfeit the stock, she would not receive a refund of the taxes paid on the $5,000 of Gross Income reported in year 1.

A *stock option* is the right to purchase a corporation's stock. Corporations grant their employees such options to encourage "identification" with the company. They provide employees a means of participating in the *future* increases in the market value of the stock without having to put up the money to buy the stock and without risking a decline in the stock's value.

Employee Stock Purchase Plan Options 03-06.1

These plans are designed for the publicly held company, since employees with 5% or more of the stock cannot participate. Other important requirements for such a plan are as follows:

1. The exercise price must be at least 85% of the market value at the time the option is issued. *And . . .*
2. The plan must be available to all employees except highly paid executives and officers. And . . .
3. Employees must be employed by the company at the time the option is granted, and they must remain employed until at least three months before the option is exercised. And . . .
4. The term of the option must be for five years or less.

Finally, the plan cannot discriminate in favor of highly paid employees. The amount of stock that can be purchased may be based on salary, but the value of stock cannot exceed $25,000 per year at the time the option is granted.

Under these plans, employees have no Gross Income either at the time the option is granted or upon exercise (that is, the purchase). The employees realize Gross Income only when they sell the stock. At that time, two types of income can be realized: compensation and long-term capital gain (05-04). For any part of the Gross Income to count as long-term capital gain, employees must have held the stock for more than one year, and the sale must have been at least two years after the option was granted. If either of these conditions is not met, the entire gain is considered compensation and fully taxable.

If both conditions are met, then:

1. *compensation* equals the difference between the option price and the fair market value of the stock at the time the option is granted.
2. *gain* equals the difference between the same fair market value and the sale price.

03-06.1A **Example**

John Employee is granted an option under a qualified stock purchase plan. The market value of the stock at the time is $50 per share, and the exercise price of the option is $43 per share. After six months, John exercises his option and purchases 100 shares. Eighteen months later, he sells the stock for $60 per share. Since he held the stock for more than one year, and since he sold it at least two years after the option was granted, he can allocate his gain between compensation and long-term capital gain.

The amount allocated as compensation is $7—that is, the difference between the fair market value at the date the option was granted ($50 per share) and the option exercise price ($43 per share). The remaining profit of $10 ($60 proceeds of sale less the original fair market value of $50) is long-term capital gain.

Sale proceeds		$6,000
Basis for capital gain:		
Cost: $43 per share	$4,300	
Compensation income to be reported in year of sale (100 shares @ $7)	+ 700	−5,000
Long-term capital gain		$1,000

If John had not met the one- and two-year holding period requirements, he would report $700 as compensation income. This circumstance would increase his basis to $5,000, and any gain or loss on sale would be measured from there.

On the other hand, if John did meet the one- and two-year holding period requirements and sold the stock for between $43 and $50, his compensation income would be his profit.

Sale proceeds ($44 per share)		$4,400
Basis for capital gain:		
Cost	$4,300	
Compensation income	+ 100	−4,400
Capital gain		–0–

If he sold it below $43, his cost, he would have no compensation income, but he would have a capital loss for the difference between $43 and his sale price.

Incentive Stock Options

03-06.2

Section 422A of the Code provides for a so-called "Incentive Stock Option plan." Under this plan the employee reports no income in the year the option is granted, and the entire difference between the price paid for the stock and the sale price is long-term capital gain (Chapter 5) or loss.

Among the requirements for an option to qualify under this section of the Code:

1. the option's exercise price must be 100% of the market value of the stock at the time the option is granted;
2. the employee must hold the stock for at least one year after it is transfered into his/her name and for at least two years after the option is granted;
3. the option must be exercised while still in the employ of the grantor or within three months after termination (12 months if the employee is disabled);

4. the term of the option may not exceed ten years;
5. the employee must have no other stock options in effect (see Tax Hint 03-0.2A);
6. the option must be nontransferable;
7. the employee must not own more than 10% (directly or indirectly) of the voting power of all classes of stock.

The employee may use other stock of the company that he/she owns to exercise the option. (See Tax Hint 03-06.2B.)

The maximum amount of options that may be granted in any one year is $100,000. However, one-half of any unused maximum may be carried forward up to three years.

03-06.2A **Tax hint**

For the purpose of determining whether an employee has an open unexercised option, a canceled option is considered to be open until its original expiration date. For this reason, employers may wish to grant options for relatively short periods if there is a reasonable chance the stock may decline in value. An option at $50 per share is worthless with the stock at $40, and no new Incentive Stock Options could be granted until the $50 option's original expiration date.

03-06.2B **Tax hint**

The ability of an employee to use other stock of the employer corporation can be a great help in deferring income tax. Let's say an employee had an option to buy 1,000 shares of stock at $25. At the time the option was granted he/she also purchased 100 shares of that stock at $25. Now the stock is at $100 per share.

Rather then sell the original 100 shares to raise the funds to exercise on 400 shares at $25, the employee uses old stock with a value of $10,000 (100 shares at $100) to buy 400 new shares under the option. This avoids paying the capital gains tax on the old shares.

The basis of the newly acquired shares is the same as the basis of the old shares, in our case $2,500. The basis of the new stock per share would therefore be $6.25 each (400 shares at $2,500).

Tax warning 03-06.2C

If the employee elects to exchange old stock for new stock, the holding period of the old stock is lost. If the new stock were sold or exchanged before the one- and two-year holding periods had passed, the entire gain would be fully taxable ordinary income.

Other Employee Stock Options 03-06.3

Under the current law, any stock option that does not meet the requirements set out in 03-06.1 or 03-06.2 comes under the heading of "other." There are only two possibilities under "other." Either the option (1) has or (2) does not have a readily ascertainable market value.

Options without a readily ascertainable value 03-06.3A

If the option does not have a readily ascertainable value at the date the option is granted, then employees have fully taxable compensation income when they exercise the option. The amount to be included in Gross Income is the difference between the price paid for the option and the fair market value of the stock at the date of exercise.

Options with a readily ascertainable value 03-06.3B

If an option has a readily ascertainable market value, then employees immediately recognize that value as taxable compensation. Any future appreciation of the option (usually because the stock has gone up in value) will be recognized as a capital gain.

Tax *Warning* 03-06.4

The Code discourages the use of "other" employee options. First, if the option does not have a readily ascertainable market value, employees must file written statements with their tax returns, notifying the IRS of the existence of the option. Also, if the option has an ascertainable value, taxpayers must prove it. Here the Regulations are particularly tough. One way to prove the value is if the option is traded on a national stock exchange. This is highly unlikely, since such options are not generally used for employee benefits. In the absence of any trading on a national stock exchange, all of the following become considerations:

1. Employees must be able to freely transfer the option.
2. Employees must be able to exercise the option immediately.
3. The option and the stock must be free of any conditions.
4. The value of the option must be reasonably measurable.

The first three considerations are the last things employers would want if they are using options to help employees identify with their companies. The fourth consideration entails the "time value" of the option: the longer it has to expiration, the more valuable it is—a very difficult component to measure.

Effectively, with options that do not qualify under 03-06.1 or 03-06.2, you are going to run into great difficulty trying to get any portion of the gain classified as capital gain. All the gain on "other" options will probably be ordinary fully taxable compensation.

03-06.5 Minimum Tax Applications

Qualified and restricted options issued prior to May of 1976 can generate income subject to the minimum tax (09-02). The amount subject to the minimum tax is the "bargain" portion of the purchase: It is the difference between the fair market value at the date of exercise and the purchase price. That amount is reported in the year of exercise.

Options granted under the provisions described in 03-06.1 or 03-06.2 do not generate income subject to the minimum tax, nor do the so-called "other" options.

03-07 BARGAIN PURCHASES—EMPLOYEES AND SHAREHOLDERS

Employers may give their employees the right to purchase property from them at a bargain price as part of their compensation. Similarly, independent contractors who provide goods or services may be offered bargain purchases as compensation. In both cases, the receiving parties include in Gross Income the difference between the fair market value and the amount paid, and their basis (04-03) is increased by that amount reported in Gross Income.

Example 03-07.1

MBS Corporation allowed its employee, Sarah, to purchase a widget with a market value of $4,000 for only $1,000. The agreement was considered compensation and not a gift. Sarah must report $3,000 ($4,000 − $1,000) in Gross Income. Her basis for gain or loss in disposition is $4,000.

Bargain Purchases with Stockholders 03-07.2

When a corporation enters into a bargain purchase with stockholders, the difference between the fair market value and the amount paid is considered a stock distribution. To the extent that the corporation has E&P (02-09) the amount is considered a dividend. In that case, the stockholders must include the amount in Gross Income in the same manner as employees; *but* the corporation does not get a deduction since dividends are not deductible for the paying corporation. (See 02-10.1 for distributions in excess of E&P.)

The basis in the hands of individual stockholders is computed the same way it would be if they were employees. Special rules exist for computing the basis in the hands of corporate stockholders receiving a bargain purchase distribution.

TAXABLE INTEREST INCOME 03-08

Interest income is fully taxable ordinary income unless the taxpayer can cite a statute showing it is exempt or partially exempt (02-02).

Interest earned on tax-exempt proceeds is also taxable. As an example, interest paid by an insurance company in addition to the amount payable on account of the death of the insured is taxable. Interest paid by states and their political subdivisions on such items as tax refunds and condemnation awards is fully taxable.

Interest need not be stated as such to be taxable as interest. It may be imputed, as in installment sales (10-12), or it may be part of the discount from face value (03-08.1).

03-08.1 Taxability of Interest from Treasury Bills and Other Discount Instruments

Treasury bills, commercial paper, and bankers' acceptances are typical debt instruments that do not bear interest on their faces. They are normally payable at face, without interest, at maturity. They sell at a discount from face value, and the difference between the purchase price and the face value represents interest income to the holder (03-08.1A). The discount (interest) earned on Treasury bills is included in Gross Income when the bills mature or are sold. Interest on bankers' acceptances and commercial paper accrues ratably.

03-08.1A **Example**

Sarah Investor purchases a $1,000,000 Treasury bill quoted at 12.00% discounted yield, with 91 days to maturity. Her purchase price would be:

Face	$1,000,000
Less: Discount ($1,000,000 × 0.1200 × 91/360	− 30,333
Purchase price	$ 969,667

Twenty days later she sells the bill for a discounted yield of 12.00%. Her ordinary interest income is:

Sale proceeds:	
Face amount	$1,000,000
Less: discount ($1,000,000 × 0.12 00 × 71/360)	− 23,667
Net sale proceeds	$ 976,333
Cost	− 969,667
Interest income	$ 6,666

The interest income on bankers' acceptances and commercial paper is figured in the same way. See 05-11 for the treatment of Treasury Bills sold at a discount higher or lower than the purchase discount.

Original Issue Discount Corporate Debt 03-08.2

Corporate debt that is "original issue discount" can result in interest income. Normally, the difference between the purchase price and the sale or redemption price of corporate debt is a capital gain or loss (05-04). But if the debt is original issue discount, then the prorata increase in value due to the passage of time is interest income. To be considered original issue discount, the discount from face value on the original sale to the first holder must be more than ¼% times the number of full years to maturity.

Example 03-08.2A

Sarah Investor purchases a 10-year MBS Corporation bond for 80 from the underwriters. Since the original issue discount (the difference between par 100 and 80) is more than 2½% (¼% × 10 years), she has an original issue discount bond. She must recognize the accretion of the discount as interest income. Since the discount is $200 ($1,000 face amount − $800 purchase price), she will recognize $1.67 per month ($200 ÷ 120 months) interest income for each month she held the bond. The discount recognized is added to the basis.

After two years, she sells the bond for 85. Her interest income and capital gain would be:

Sale proceeds (85% of $1,000)		$850
Basis:		
Cost	$800	
Plus: Interest income:		
Year 1 ($1.67 × 12 months)	20	
Year 2 ($1.67 × 12 months)	20	840
Capital gain		$ 10

Series EE and Series HH Bonds 03-08.3

Series EE bonds (formally Series E or savings bonds) are sold at a discount from face. The difference between the purchase price and the redemption price is interest income. Since Series EE bonds continue to accrue interest past their maturity, they can be redeemed at greater than face value. The entire difference is still interest income.

Unless taxpayers elect differently, the entire amount

of interest income is reported in Gross Income in the year they redeem bonds. There are two possible elections, which are unique to Series EE bonds:

1. Taxpayers may elect to report the interest income as accrued, rather than in the year of redemption. The election is made at the time of filing the tax return, and it applies to all future years. In the year the election is made, all prior accrued interest must be reported.
2. Taxpayers may elect to "convert" Series EE or Series E bonds into other nonnegotiable U.S. direct obligations, usually Series HH bonds. If they so elect, the accrued interest on the Series EE bonds is not reported until the Series HH bonds mature, normally in ten years. Series HH bonds pay interest semiannually, and taxpayers convert normally for the purpose of creating interest income.

03-08.3A **Tax hint**

Series EE bonds are often used as gifts to children. The parent or guardian need file only a return for the child electing to report Series EE interest as it accrues. This way, when the child matures and cashes in the bonds, there will be no tax to pay. If the child has less than $1,000 per year in income, no further returns are required. But the election is irrevocable, and the child/taxpayer has to continue with it unless the Internal Revenue grants permission to change.

03-08.3B **Tax *warning***

Converting Series EE bonds to Series HH bonds, although tax-free, may be the wrong answer for a few good reasons. First of all, Series HH bonds yield substantially less than other U.S. direct obligations. Second, the interest on Series HH bonds is just as taxable as the interest on other U.S. direct obligations. Third, the yield on Series EE bonds is ½ of 1% higher than on Series HH bonds. Often a programmed redemption of Series EE bonds reinvested in other higher-yielding U.S. direct obligations nets more after-tax dollars. Each taxpayer should work out his or her own situation before jumping into such a conversion.

Sale of Bonds Between Interest Payment Dates 03-08.4

Bonds normally pay interest semiannually. Unless a bond is traded "flat" (03-08.5), the seller is entitled to accrued interest from the last interest payment date up to, but not including, the settlement date of the sale (03-08.4A). That accrued interest is paid by the buyer to the seller on the settlement date, as if it were part of the purchase price. But for federal income tax purposes, the seller realizes interest income just as if it were paid by the bond issuer. If the interest would have been taxable when paid by the issuer, then it is taxable when paid to the seller by the buyer. And if it would have been tax-exempt when paid by the issuer, then it is tax-exempt when paid by the buyer.

Example 03-08.4A

Colin Gordon owns $10,000 face amount of MBS Corporation bonds, 10% coupon, paying interest January 1 and July 1 of each year. For settlement July 15, he sells the bonds to Deborah Ruck for 85. For federal income tax purposes, Colin receives:

Sale of bonds ($10,000 × 0.85)	$8,500
Plus: Interest income ($10,000 × 10% × 14/360)	+ 39
Proceeds of sale	$8,539

He reports $39 of interest income. If these had been municipal bonds, he would have $39 of tax-exempt interest income.

On the other side of the transaction, Deborah pays:

Purchase of bonds (basis)	$8,500
Plus: Prepaid interest	+ 39
Gross payment	$8,539

On January 1st, she collects $500 from MBS Corporation ($10,000 × 10% × ½ year). And reports $461 ($500 − $39) as interest income.

03-08.5 **Bonds Traded "Flat"**

Bonds that are in default on interest and/or principal payments trade without accrued interest payable to the seller. These bonds are said to be trading "flat." When investors collect interest that was in default at the time they bought the bonds, the amount received is *not* interest income, but rather a return of investment. Any interest accruing after the date of purchase and subsequently collected *is* interest income.

03-08.5A **Example**

Brynne Gordon purchases $10,000 face amount of MBS Railroad Company bonds "flat" for a price of 40. At the time of purchase, the bonds have $2,300 of interest past due and in default. Two years later she receives a check from MBS Railroad for $3,400, representing all the interest due and past due. For federal income tax purposes, Brynne reports:

Return of investment	$2,300
Interest income	+1,100
Total received	$3,400

The basis of her bonds, reduced by the $2,300, is now $1,700 ($4,000 purchase price − $2,300). If the interest in default at the time of purchase exceeds the cost of the bonds, then the basis is reduced to zero, and the excess is capital gain (05-04).

Long-Term Savings Accounts 03-08.6

Normally, interest on savings accounts must be included in income when it is constructively received (for a cash basis taxpayer) or when it is earned (for an accrual basis taxpayer). For cash basis taxpayers (in effect, most individual investors), if interest is credited to their accounts on December 31, and if they have the right to withdraw the money (even if they do not), then it is included in income.

Some savings accounts, as well as bank certificates of deposit (CDs), allow the withdrawal of interest only at maturity. In such a case, when the term of the deposit or certificate is more than a year, taxpayers must include the interest in Gross Income when earned.

Example 03-08.6A

Colin Gordon purchases a 36-month, $10,000, 12% bank certificate of deposit. Under the terms, neither the principal nor the interest may be withdrawn until maturity. Withdrawal of either would be penalized by charging the depositor three months' interest. The certificate is dated July 1, 1981.

By December 31, 1981, Colin earns $600. On January 2, 1982, he closes the account and collects $10,300 ($10,000 principal + $600 interest − $300 penalty). So for 1981, he must declare $600 Gross Income from interest. And for 1982, he has a deduction for Adjusted Gross Income of $300.

Amortization of Discount—General Rule 03-08.7

The same general rule that applies to the amortization of original issue discount on corporate and taxable government debt applies also to state and municipal tax-exempt debt (03-08.1). But the rules as to what constitutes original issue discount are stricter when it comes to tax-exempts. The reason is simple: The original issue discount in this case generates tax-exempt interest income. Investors should always read the official statement (similar to a prospectus) of the issuer to insure that the instrument is original issue discount and to determine the monthly accretion of discount.

Bonds purchased in the secondary market (from other investors rather than from the issuing company) present a completely different situation. For taxable issues investors *may* record accretion of discount as interest income. For tax-exempt bonds, investors may *not* record the accretion of discount as tax-exempt interest income. Here is why. The difference between the purchase price and the sale or redemption price is generally tax-favored capital gains (05-04). Since the accretion of discount increases the basis for computing gain or loss, it reduces any gain and increases any loss (03-08.1). So holders of taxable bonds would be foolish to record accretion of discount as currently taxable interest income, when they may, if they elect, report the accretion as tax-favored capital gain on sale. The total tax is not only delayed, but it is also less once it has to be paid.

03-08.8 Amortization of Premium

Amortization of the premium decreases the current interest income (03-08.8A), and it therefore reduces the basis for computing gains and losses. So, by amortizing the premium, holders of tax-exempt bonds simply reduce their nontaxable interest income and increase any subsequent gain or reduce any subsequent loss. Holders of taxable bonds should amortize premium, because they reduce their currently taxable interest income at the small sacrifice of increasing tax-favored capital gains or reducing unwanted capital losses. (Capital losses are only partially deductible—05-05.)

Bonds purchased at a premium (that is, above face value) follow the same rules, regardless of whether they are original issue or purchased in the secondary market. Investors in taxable bonds *may* amortize premium; investors in tax-exempt bonds *must* amortize premium. Premiums must be amortized to maturity date. Investors cannot use the shorter call date to increase the amount of amortization.

Special rules apply to dealers in securities.

No portion of the premium on a convertible bond that relates to the conversion feature may be amortized (03-08.8B).

Example 03-08.8A

Aaron Gordon purchases $10,000 of MBS Corporation bonds at 110, maturing in ten years, coupon 15%. For the first full year he would report:

Interest collected, 15% of $10,000	$1,500
Less: Amortization of premium:	
($1,000 ÷ 10 years)	− 100
Taxable interest income	$1,400

The basis of his bonds is reduced to $10,900 ($11,000 purchase price less amortization of premium $100). Remember, if these were MBS Township (municipal) bonds, he would have to reduce his basis by this amount; doing so is not elective.

Two years later, Aaron sells the bonds for 109. He reports capital *gain* (even though he sold it below 110) of:

Sale proceeds		$10,900
Basis:		
Cost	$11,000	
Two years amortization of premium, 2 × $100	− 200	−10,800
Long-term capital gain		$ 100

Taxpayers may elect to amortize premium on a present value basis, using the bond tables. Doing so creates a slightly lower amortization in the earlier years.

03-08.8B **Example**

Aaron Gordon purchases $10,000 face value of MBS Corporation bonds for 180. The bonds bear interest at 10%, mature in 10 years, and are convertible into 40 shares of MBS common stock. The stock is selling for 42½. The amount of premium that can be amortized is:

Purchase price	$18,000
Less: Price attributed to conversion feature	
(parity) (40 shares × 10 bonds × $42.50)	−17,000
Premium	$ 1,000

03-08.9 **Tax Hint**

There is no problem with a taxpayers' amortizing premium and *not* amortizing discount. No requirement calls for such consistency. But taxpayers must be consistent within each area. If they amortize premium on taxable bonds, they must do so consistently. If they do not amortize discount on taxable bonds, that too must they consistently follow.

03-09 **RENTS AND ROYALTIES**

Payments made for the occupancy of land or building are *rent*. Payments made for the extraction of minerals from land, or for the use of patents, copyrights, trademarks, and the like, are *royalties*. All such payments must be included in Gross Income. (Chapters 6 and 8 discuss the deductions for Adjusted Gross Income that businesspersons or investors may take with regard to rent and royalty income.)

Improvements made by a tenant to property are generally not included in the Gross Income of the renter. If the improvements increase the value of the property, the amount is realized as an increase in the property's selling price. The exception is if the improvements are made in lieu of rent payments. In that case, the improvements would be included in the renter's Gross Income at their fair market value.

Payments received by the *rentee* from the renter to cancel a lease are normally considered to be capital gains (05-04).

FORGIVENESS OF DEBT 03-10

How debt forgiveness is treated for tax purposes depends on all the circumstances surrounding the event. It may be treated in either of four ways:

1. The amount forgiven is a gift and excluded from Gross Income.
2. The amount was forgiven for consideration and is included in Gross Income.
3. The amount forgiven reduces the basis of related property.
4. The amount forgiven was due to bankruptcy or insolvency and is excluded from Gross Income.

The presumption is that debt forgiveness is for consideration, and so it must be included in Gross Income. The responsibility of taxpayers is to prove that a debt forgiveness was in fact a gift.

If the debt forgiven is related to the acquisition of property used in a trade or business, taxpayers may elect to reduce the basis of the property rather than include the amount in Gross Income. Normally, this election would be the wise tax move, since the reduced basis would create a tax liability in the future, rather than currently. If the property is a capital asset, it may result in favorable capital gains treatment.

The settlement of a real estate mortgage, when the mortgage is part of the acquisition transaction, may be included in Gross Income. Or it may reduce the basis of the property, depending on the market value of the property and on the extent of personal liability of the taxpayer. Competent tax counsel should be consulted before entering into such a transaction.

If a taxpayer is adjudicated a bankrupt, then the debts so forgiven are not included in Gross Income. Taxpayers may be insolvent and thus fall into the same category without formal court rulings. But in such cases taxpayers would have to prove that the forgiveness of debt was, in fact, due to their insolvency.

03-11 ALIMONY AND CHILD SUPPORT

When a couple is divorced, three possible financial situations may affect their Gross Income:

1. alimony,
2. child support, and
3. lump sum property settlement.

There is one absolute rule in this area: if it is taxable to the recipient, it is deductible by the payer; if it is not taxable to the recipient, it is not deductible by the payer.

The other basic rule is that alimony is included in Gross Income by the recipient, but child support and lump sum property settlements are not.

For payments to be considered alimony they:

1. must be legally required either under a final or interlocutory decree of divorce, or under a written separation agreement; and
2. must be "periodic"; and
3. must not be labeled as child support.

Payments will be considered periodic if:

1. they are for an indefinite period; *or*
2. they are for a period of more than 10 years; *and* in any one taxable year the payments do not exceed 10% of an agreed-upon principal sum; *or*
3. they are contingent, such as upon the death, remarriage, or income of the payee.

Payments that are labeled "alimony and child support" are considered to be all alimony. The amount of child support must be specifically stated in the agreement.

If an agreement calls for a specific amount of alimony, along with a specific amount of child support, and if the payer pays only part of the total amount, then payments are allocated to child support first (03-11.1).

The source of the payments is not relevant. If a husband was liable for alimony and purchased an annuity to pay it, he would still get the deduction for Adjusted Gross Income for the payments made by the annuity. The amount paid for the annuity would not be a deduction.

Example 03-11.1

As part of the divorce decree, Clark Lane was required to pay his wife, Lois, $5,000 per year in alimony and $5,000 per year in child support for their son. During the year, Clark paid only $8,000. The first $5,000 is allocated to child support, is not taxable to Lois, and is not deductible by Clark. The remaining $3,000 is alimony. Lois must include the $3,000 in Gross Income; Clark gets a deduction for $3,000 for Adjusted Gross Income.

LUMP SUM PROPERTY SETTLEMENT 03-12

When a marriage is dissolved, the parties are entitled to certain marital properties depending on state law. The distribution of that property is normally not a taxable event, due to the simple concept that each party is only taking what is his or hers. Each of the partners retains the same basis in the property that he or she had as a married partner.

03-12.1 Tax *Warning*

If payments to the wife are not considered alimony, they are not automatically lump sum payments. The payments could constitute: *a taxable sale of property*—If one party retains certain assets and makes payments of a lump sum in exchange for the right to retain that property, the result could be a taxable sale. The rights of each party in the divorce, under state law, are the most important factor. This is one area where an attorney is a must.

03-12.2 Tax *Warning*

David agrees to pay Molly $100,000 over a 10-year period. The payments will begin six months after the signing of the agreement, and they will consist of 120 monthly payments of $833.33 each plus interest on the unpaid balance.

Lump sum or alimony? The fact that she will receive the principal amount in ten years or less is fine. *But* the clock starts running when the agreement is signed, not when the first payment is made. So in this case, David is paying alimony, taxable to Molly and deductible by David—even if the agreement states specifically that this is a lump sum payment.

4
RECOGNITION OF GAIN AND LOSS

The phrase "recognition of gain or loss" means that the gain or loss is recognized for tax purposes; it generates either a taxable gain or a loss, which may or may not be deductible. Many gains and losses are not recognized for tax purposes. The classic example is the appreciation in the market value of property. No gain or loss is recognized until the property is disposed of, and even then there may be no gain or loss recognized. This nonrecognition may result from a tax-free trade-in or some other escape hatch.

In many cases, avoiding the taxable event can be the cornerstone of tax avoidance. The careful structuring of the form, as well as of the content, of the realignment of investments can make the difference between a taxable transaction and a tax-free transaction. The more important potentially tax-free exchanges involve insurance policies (04-07.3), exchanges of like-kind property (04-07.4), and the conversion of securities (04-07.1).

Selling short against the box (05-07) is the perfect example of temporarily avoiding the taxable event. The investor has cashed in on the appreciation of the securities, and has delayed paying the taxes at least until the following year.

COMPUTATION OF GAIN OR LOSS 04-02

If the disposition of property results in a taxable event, taxpayers must compute gain or loss. *Gain* exists when the "amount realized" exceeds the "adjusted basis." Although in many instances determining the adjusted basis and the amount realized can be a complicated matter, in the case of the purchase and sale of a security, it is fairly routine:

Amount realized:		
Sell 100 shares of MBS common stock at 53		$5,300
Less: Commission paid		(200)
Less: SEC fee paid		− (2)
Amount realized		$5,098
Adjusted basis:		
MBS common stock purchased at 40	$4,000	
Plus: Commission paid	+ 175	
Less: Return of capital dividend	− (250)	−3,925
Gain		$1,173

If the amount realized is less than the adjusted basis, the taxpayer has a loss.

Note that state transfer tax does not necessarily reduce the amount realized on the sale of securities. The taxpayer may choose either to reduce the amount realized on the sale or to deduct the tax from adjusted gross income. The latter choice may serve to increase long-term gains, which are taxed at a lower rate than ordinary income.

When property is received, the amount realized is the property's fair market value. The amount realized must be reduced by any liabilities assumed by the seller; and it must be increased by any liabilities assumed by the buyer (04-02.1). If the asset disposed of is a capital asset, the seller recognizes a capital gain or loss (Chapter 5).

04-02.1 Example

Dorothy Ghoti owns a piece of land that cost her $50,000. The land has a mortgage against it for $20,000. During the time she holds the land, she spends $5,000 on improvements. She sells the land for $75,000, and the buyer agrees to take over the mortgage and to be responsible for it. Dorothy reports:

Amount realized:		
Sale proceeds		$75,000
Buyer's assumption of mortgage		+20,000
Total realized		$95,000
Adjusted basis:		
Cost	$50,000	
Improvements	+ 5,000	−55,000
Gain		$40,000

04-02.2 Worthless Securities

When a security becomes worthless, it is considered to have been sold on the last day of the year in which it became worthless. The amount realized is zero. But taxpayers must prove the security is *completely* worthless before any loss is allowed.

BASIS OF PROPERTY ACQUIRED BY PURCHASE 04-03

The basis of property acquired through purchase is:

1. the purchase price, plus
2. any liabilities assumed, plus
3. any improvements to the property, less
4. any return of capital.

If property is acquired by the exercise of an option, the cost of the option is added to the basis of the property.

Example 04-03.1

Lillian Ghoti purchases an option to buy a piece of land. The option costs her $4,000, and the exercise price is $23,000. After exercising her option and buying the land, she has a house built on it. She pays the contractor $10,000 in cash, and takes out a mortgage. The bank pays the contractor $50,000 against the mortgage. Several years later, the Water Company pays her $3,000 for an easement across her property. Her basis is:

Cost of options	$ 4,000
Exercise price of option	23,000
Cash paid to contractor	10,000
Mortgage assumed	+50,000
Total	$87,000
Less: Payment for easement	− 3,000
Basis	$84,000

FAIR MARKET VALUE AS A BASIS 04-04

Property can be acquired without the exchange of money.

1. *One property may be exchanged for another in a taxable exchange:* The basis is the fair market value at the

date of receipt. And the taxpayer has either a gain or a loss, depending on the basis of the property given up. Special rules exist for dealers who accept used property in exchange for new property in the normal course of business.

2. *Property may be received for services rendered:* Again, the basis is the fair market value at the date of receipt. But in this case the fair market value is included in the Gross Income of the taxpayer receiving the property.

04-04.1 Example

Saul Colin has a valuable stamp worth $2,000. His basis in the stamp is $100. He trades the stamp for Colin Gordon's bull, which has a similar value. Saul reports $1,900 as gain on the disposition of the stamp ($2,000 realized less $100 basis). His basis in the bull is $2,000, its fair market value.

04-05 BASIS OF PROPERTY ACQUIRED BY GIFT

For property acquired by gift, the general rule is that the basis and the holding period (05-02) are the same in the hands of the donee as they were in the hands of the donor. No gain or loss is recognized by either the donor or the donee. If the property can be depreciated (08-01), the basis in the hands of the donor is used as the basis for depreciation. But if the donee sells the property at a loss, then the amount of loss is figured by using the lower of:

1. the fair market value of the gift at the time of the gift, or
2. the basis in the hands of the donor (04-05.2).

A donee's basis for the gift of the income from a trust for a limited period of time is zero.

Adjustment for Gift Taxes Paid 04-05.1

For gifts made after 1976, the basis of the gift in the hands of the donor—for computing gain or loss but not for depreciation purposes—is increased by the amount of the gift tax (Chapter 13) that is attributable to the increase in market value over basis in the hands of the donor. But the amount added cannot increase the basis above fair market value.

Example 04-05.1A

Mr. Rich gives property with a market value of $500,000 to his son. He pays the gift tax of $240,000. He originally purchased the property for $100,000, and his son sells it for $700,000.

Sale price		$700,000
Basis in the hands of the father	$100,000	
Gift tax added		
($240,000 × $400,000/$500,000)	+192,000	
Basis in the hands of the son		−292,000
Gain		$408,000

In the example, the $192,000 gift tax serves to reduce the capital gain realized by the son.

Example: Gifted Property Sold at a Loss 04-05.2

Mr. Rich gives property with a market value of $500,000 to his son. He pays the gift tax of $240,000. He originally purchased the property for $600,000, and his son sells it for $400,000. There is no adjustment to basis for the gift tax, since that would increase the basis in the hands of the son to more than fair market value. The "prime" basis in the hands of the son is $600,000, the same as in the hands of the donor. Using that basis to compute gain or loss:

Sale proceeds	$400,000
Basis	−600,000
Loss	$200,000

Since that calculation results in a loss, the fair market value at the date of the gift must be used as the basis:

Sale proceeds	$400,000
Basis	−500,000
Loss	$100,000

If the son sold the property for $550,000, there would be neither a gain nor a loss. Using basis in the hands of the donor ($600,000) produces a loss, so that cannot be used. Using the fair market value at the date of the gift ($500,000) produces a gain, so that cannot be used.

04-05.3 Tax *Warning*

The Code effectively prohibits giving away property that has declined in value since acquisition by the donor. Of course, no one can say that you can't give something away, but two rules impose severe tax disadvantages:

1. Only that portion of the gift tax attributable to the appreciation of the property is added to the basis, so no additional basis is obtained by gifting property that has declined in value.
2. No one gets to deduct the loss between the donor's purchase price and the fair market value at the date of the gift. The donor would be better off selling the property, taking the loss and gifting the proceeds of the sale.

The gifting of property that has declined in value is a "nontaxable event" that is to be avoided.

The basis of property acquired from a decedent is the market value shown in the estate tax return—normally, the market value at the date of death. But the executor may choose an alternative valuation date (Chapter 14).

If property is inherited from an estate that is too small to require the filing of an estate tax return, then the basis in the hands of the beneficiary is the fair market value at the date of death.

If the property was held in joint name between the deceased and the beneficiary, and if only part of the asset was included in the estate, then the basis is adjusted only for the part that was included (04-06.1).

The basis of items of income received on account of the death of another is the amount reported in Gross Income by the benefiary (02-13).

Example 04-06.1

When Jack Boerer died, a piece of property was registered jointly with his wife, Ethel. For reasons discussed in Chapter 14, 50% of the property was included in his estate and 50% was not. The property cost $10,000 and was included in the estate with a total market value of $25,000 (one-half of the total). During the period they held the property jointly, they deducted $4,000 in depreciation (08-01 to 08-05). So the adjusted basis at the time of death is:

Cost	$10,000
Less: Depreciation	− 4,000
Adjusted basis	$ 6,000
Ethel's new basis:	
50% of $6,000, her share of original basis	$ 3,000
50% of market value, the amount included in the estate tax return	+25,000
Total new basis	$ 28,000

04-07 PROPERTY ACQUIRED THROUGH NONTAXABLE EXCHANGES

Normally, the exchange of one piece of property for another is a taxable event. Yet the Code specifically exempts certain "exchanges" of property. The key word is "exchange." If property is sold and the proceeds used to invest in another piece of property, that transaction is always a taxable event. For an exchange to be nontaxable, taxpayers must find a specific section of the Code to take that position. In some cases taxpayers do not have a choice, or an election, as to whether they want the transaction to be taxable or tax-free. Many exchanges are automatically nontaxable events.

There is no requirement that cash be left out of the transaction. Taxpayer A can exchange property with Taxpayer B with either one receiving cash in addition. The extra cash, called *boot,* is the portion of the transaction that may be taxable. Actually, "boot" is any nonqualified property included in an otherwise tax-free exchange; most often, that is cash. Even when property is transferred subject to a liability, the person who is relieved of the liability is considered to have received cash.

04-07.1 Exchange of Securities in the Same Corporation

When securities of a corporation are exchanged for different securities of the *same* corporation, the transaction is generally tax-free. If the exchange of stock is nontaxable, then the basis of the new stock is the same as the basis of the old. The most common of these tax-free transactions are:

1. a stock split,
2. a stock spin-off,

3. the conversion of a bond or preferred stock into common stock, and
4. the exchange of voting common stock for nonvoting common.

As the exception, the exchange of common stock for either bonds or preferred stock is normally taxable. The exchange of stock for stock between a family of mutual funds—such as Mutual of Omaha Growth Fund for Mutual of Omaha Bond Income Fund—is also taxable.

Transfer of Property to a Controlled Corporation 04-07.2

When a person, or a group of people, transfer property to a "controlled" corporation, the transfer is tax-free. A corporation is *controlled* if, immediately *after* the transfer, the person or the group has at least 80% of the voting stock of the corporation *and* at least 80% of all other classes of stock.

Gain is recognized to the extent that any "boot" received exceeds the fair market value of the property contributed to the corporation.

1. The basis of the stock in the hands of the stockholder is the basis of the property given up, plus any gain realized.
2. The basis of the property in the hands of the corporation is the basis in the hands of the transferor, plus any gain realized.

Example 1 04-07.2A

Sam and Sarah form a corporation by contributing property to the corporation. Sam contributes land with a basis of $10,000 and a fair market value of $50,000. Sarah contributes AT&T common stock with a basis of $40,000 and a market value of $50,000. Each receives 1,000 shares of New Corporation. The corporation simultaneously issues 50 shares of stock to its lawyer in payment of his fee.

The issuance of stock for services cannot be part of a tax-free contribution to a controlled corporation. So the lawyer must report in his Gross Income the fair market value of the stock he received. The corporation records the issuance of this stock at its fair market values.

Sam and Sarah now own 98% of the stock immediately after the transfer. They are therefore in control, and they must report the contributions as a tax-free transfer. The corporation has a basis of $10,000 for the land; Sam has a basis of $10,000 for his stock. The corporation has a basis of $40,000 in the AT&T stock; and Sarah has a basis of $40,000 in her New Corporation stock.

04-07.2B **Example 2**

Sam contributes property to a corporation and obtains controlling stock. The fair market value of the property is $100,000, but it is transferred subject to a mortgage of $70,000. Sam's basis in the property is $10,000. The assumption of a liability by the corporation in excess of basis is taxable boot. Sam must pay tax on:

Liability assumed by the corporation	$70,000
Less: Sam's basis in the property	−10,000
Reportable gain	$60,000

The corporation's basis in the property is:

Sam's basis	$10,000
Plus: Gain reported by Sam	+60,000
Corporation's basis	$70,000

The basis of Sam's stock is zero:

Original basis	$10,000
Plus: Gain reported	+60,000
	$70,000
Less: Boot (liability assumed)	−70,000
	$ –0–

The corporation has a net "book" value of zero:

Basis of property	$70,000
Less: Mortage liability	−70,000
	$ –0–

The "market value" of the corporation is $30,000 ($100,000 market value of property less $70,000 liability). If Sam were to sell the corporation for $30,000, he would report a gain of $30,000 since his basis in the stock is zero. So the gain reported on contributing the property ($60,000), plus the gain on sale of the stock ($30,000), is the same $90,000 gain Sam would have had if he had sold the property outright ($100,000 market value less $10,000 basis).

Tax *warning* 04-07.2C

This section of the Code is set up to allow for the easy and tax-free creation of a corporation. When a company wants to incorporate its business, this procedure works well. But, getting things back to where they were tax-free may be impossible. Once you are in a corporate form of business, the withdrawal of the assets from the corporation back to the stockholders normally results in a taxable event.

Tax *warning* 04-07.2D

Inasmuch as certain assets may be capital assets (05-01), the gain on the sale of those assets may be subjected to reduced taxation. But transferring those assets to a corporation could change them to ordinary assets, where the gain would be fully taxable.

As an example, Beatrice owns a piece of undeveloped land that is a capital asset in her hands. She transfers the land to the Connie Construction Company for the purpose of building houses. Since the corporation would be classified as a builder, the land would then become an ordinary asset in the hands of the corporation, rather than a capital asset in her hands.

04-07.3 Exchanges of Life Insurance, Endowment, and Annuity Contracts

No gain or loss is recognized on:

1. The exchange of a life insurance contract for:
   a. another life insurance contract,
   b. an endowment contract, or
   c. an annuity contract.
2. The exchange of an endowment contract for:
   a. an annuity contract; or
   b. an endowment contract (provided the payments are not delayed).
3. An annuity contract for another annuity contract.

The key to making an exchange of endowment contracts nontaxable is that the *first* payment under the contract must not be delayed. But the total period over which the contract is to be paid can be extended without creating a taxable exchange.

Notice that the exchange of an annuity for an endowment or life insurance contract is a taxable exchange, and so is the exchange of an endowment for a life insurance policy. If the exchange is taxable, the gain or loss is measured by the fair market value of the contracts and by the cash received over the basis in the contract given up.

Like Kind Property Exchanges 04-07.4

Property held for either business or investment purposes may be exchanged for like kind property used in either a business or an investment. Investment property may be exchanged for business property, and vice versa.

What qualified under this section of the Code as "like kind" can be really tricky. First, several assets are clearly disqualified and are not like kind. They are:

1. inventory held for sale in the normal course of business;
2. securities, including stocks, bonds, and notes; and
3. animals of a different sex.

The last point brings home the basic criterion: Like kind properties must serve the same purpose, and animals of different sexes obviously do not have the same function in life!

Common exchanges that do qualify are:

1. farm for farm,
2. investment real estate for investment real estate,
3. buildings for building lots.

Yet the exchange of buildings for undeveloped property would probably not qualify as a tax-free exchange.

This is another area where competent tax counsel must be sought. Very often, the only way to be sure that a particular exchange will qualify as tax-free is to obtain a private letter ruling.

Boot 04-07.5

As we know, boot is the additional property (usually cash) that is part of a tax-free exchange:

1. Boot *given* increases the basis of the acquired property. When boot is given that is not cash, the taxpayer may realize a gain on the disposition of that property (04-07.5A).
2. Boot *received* may or may not cause part of the transaction to be classified as taxable. When boot is received, whether it is cash or property, the taxpayer may realize a partial gain on the exchange (04-07.5B and 04-07.5C).

04-07.5A **Example: Taxable boot given**

Sam Investor gives the following property in exchange for investment property with a market value of $1,000,000:

1. investment property with a basis of $700,000 and a market value of $800,000, and
2. common stock with a basis of $100,000 and a market value of $200,000.

The common stock is boot, since it does not qualify as part of the like kind exchange. Sam must recognize as taxable gain the *lesser* of the following:

1. *The gain on the nonqualifying property:* That is, $100,000 (market value of $200,000 less his basis of $100,000).
2. *His gain if this had been a taxable exchange:* That is, $200,000 (the market value of the new property of $1,000,000 less the total basis given up $800,000).

Sam's recognized gain of $100,000 is then added to his basis in the new property. The basis is:

Basis in investment land given up	$700,000
Basis in common stock given up	100,000
Reportable gain	+100,000
Total new basis	$900,000

Example: Taxable receipt of boot 04-07.5B

Sam exchanges investment property with a basis of $20,000 and a market value of $30,000 for an investment property with a market value of $25,000. He receives additional cash of $5,000. The cash received is boot, and Sam must recognize income for the lesser of:

1. his gain on a taxable basis, or
2. the amount of boot received.

Since his gain on the property is $10,000 ($30,000 market value less $20,000 basis), he reports the amount of the boot as taxable, $5,000. So his basis in the new property is the basis in the old property ($20,000) plus the amount of gain reported ($5,000) for a total of $25,000.

Example: Receipt of boot on a loss transaction 04-07.5C

Sam exchanges a piece of investment property with a basis of $50,000 and a fair market value of $40,000 for a piece of property with a fair market value of $35,000 plus $5,000 in cash.

Sam realizes no gain on this exchange, because market value of the property given up ($40,000) is less than his basis. Since Sam must recognize the *lesser* of the gain on a taxable basis or the boot received, he has no taxable gain. But the exchange is still not a taxable event, so he recognizes no loss either. The $5,000 boot serves only to reduce the basis in the new property. That basis is $35,000 (the basis given up less the boot received).

ALLOCATING BASIS 04-08

When properties are purchased for a lump sum, or when pieces of a property are sold, taxpayers are required to allocate basis.

04-08.1 **Land and Building**

When land and a building are purchased for a single sum, taxpayers must allocate the portion of the price paid to each of the components. This allocation is required for figuring depreciation expense (08-01). Normally, the allocation is made based on the respective fair market values of the components. For land and building, the allocation used by the local tax assessor is often the basis of the allocation.

04-08.2 **Securities**

04-08.2A **Market Value of Components**

When securities are purchased as a unit, the market value of each of the components is used for the allocation.

04-08.2A-1 ***Example***

Sam Investor purchases a "unit" from MBS Corporation on the initial public offering. He pays $1,000 for the unit, which consists of a $1,000 par value bond and 40 warrants to purchase one share of stock for each warrant. Immediately after the issuance of the unit, the bonds are trading at 98, and the warrants are trading at $2 each. The total market value of the unit is:

$1,000 bond @ 98	$ 980
40 warrants @ $2 each	+ 80
Total	$1,060
Sam's basis:	
Bonds: $1,000 × ($980/$1,060)	$ 925
Warrants: $1,000 × ($80/$1,060)	+ 75
Total	$1,000

Of course, the basis of each warrant would be $1.88 ($75/40 warrants).

Specific Identification Method 04-08.2B

When securities are purchased at different times and for different prices, and when part of the position is sold, taxpayers may use either a first-in/first-out allocation or a specific identification allocation to compute gain or loss.

To use the specific identification method, taxpayers must be able to identify clearly the lot being sold. Identification can be made through reference to certificate numbers, if taxpayers have them. But if the broker or bank is holding the certificates, special rules for identification come into play. Taxpayers must identify the lot being sold *before* the execution of the trade; if they have given trading discretion to their brokers or bankers, then they have until settlement date (normally five business day after execution of the trade) to identify the securities being sold. The broker or banker must confirm in writing the lot identified. Typically, the broker or banker puts on the confirmation of trade: "Sale of stock purchased 10/11/80," or "Sale of stock purchased at 53." The identification must be clear enough to point to a specific lot.

When holders of mutual fund shares leave their shares with the mutual fund custodian, they may use average cost. Special rules apply to security dealers who maintain their securities with a national depository or with the Federal Reserve Bank.

If investors cannot identify the specific lot being sold, they *must* use first-in/first-out (the oldest position is sold first).

Example

Sarah Investor made the following purchases of MBS Corporation common stock: 04-08.2B-1

Date	*Price Per Share*	*Number of Shares*	*Total*
January, 1973	$20	1,000	$20,000
January, 1980	$30	1,000	$30,000
January, 1981	$40	1,000	$40,000

On February 1, 1981, she sells 1,500 shares at $35. Which shares did she sell? If she failed to identify which were sold in a timely manner, she must allocate based on first-in/first-out:

Proceeds of sale		$52,500
First: 1,000 shares @ $20	$20,000	
Then: 500 shares @ $30	+15,000	−35,000
Gain		$17,500

However, if Sarah had been a little "smarter":

Proceeds of sale		$52,500
Lot of 1/81, 1,000 @ $40	$40,000	
Half of lot of 1/80, 500 @ $30	+15,000	−55,000
Loss		$ 2,500

The term "smarter" is in quotes since sometimes taking the gain is a smart tax move (Chapter 5). But by and large, having a tax loss—rather than a taxable gain—is better.

04-08.3 Tax *Warning*

Taxpayers cannot wait until after year-end to decide whether they want a gain or a loss. The specific identification of a lot sold must be made either prior to execution or by the settlement date, depending on the circumstances described.

04-09 BASIS OF INTANGIBLES

The basis of intangibles—patents, copyrights, trademarks, and the like—is cost! What constitutes cost is the only real question. And the rules for purchasers and developers are different:

1. *To purchasers,* the price they pay for the intangible is their basis. Controversy can exist with the purchase of goodwill. Goodwill is the portion of the purchase price of a company that cannot be attributed to specific assets. It includes product identification, employee loyalty, and the fact that "the whole is worth more than the sum of its parts." How much of the purchase price of the acquisition of a company is attributed to goodwill is highly subjective, and it is often the subject of litigation between the IRS and taxpayers.
2. *Developers* have a myriad of elections to make. Should a particular expense of development be considered part of the basis (capitalized)? Or should it be considered an expense of the period (deducted immediately)? When to deduct an expense and when to capitalize it is a highly sophisticated question that entails cash flow and projected future profitability. Normally, once taxpayers elect either to capitalize or to deduct an expense, they must be consistent year to year. Developers get no basis for their own time. The only basis authors would have in their books is the cost of paper, typewriter ribbons, and the like.

INVOLUNTARY CONVERSION 04-10

An *involuntary conversion* occurs when taxpayers lose the use of property due to:

1. casualty, such as fire, windstorm, or other natural phenomena;
2. theft;
3. condemnation for public use; or
4. any other sudden or unexpected destruction.

Taxpayers may elect to defer any gain on an involuntary conversion by reinvesting the proceeds received in similar property. The mechanics work very much like tax-free exchanges (04-07), but taxpayers can first receive the funds and then reinvest them. This part of the mechanics, of course, is prohibited with a tax-free exchange.

If there is a gain on the involuntary conversion, taxpayers may elect to defer that gain and to reduce the basis of the newly acquired property (07-08 for losses).

04-10.1 Example

Colin Gordon owns an apartment house with a basis of $40,000. The apartment burns to the ground, and the insurance company pays Colin $100,000. He reinvests the entire amount in a new apartment house, which costs him $110,000. Colin recognizes no gain, and the basis of the new apartment house would be $50,000, computed as follows:

Purchase of new apartment house		$110,000
Less: Deferred gain:		
Proceeds of insurance	$100,000	
Basis of old apartment house	− 40,000	− 60,000
New basis		$50,000

If Colin invests less than the total received from the insurance company, then the amount of the recognized gain is the excess of the insurance over the amount reinvested. The basis of the new apartment is reduced by the amount of gain *not* recognized. If he reinvests only $90,000, then the deferred gain is computed as follows:

Total gain ($100,000 insurance − basis of $40,000)		$60,000
Amount collected	$100,000	
Amount reinvested	− 90,000	−10,000*
Deferred gain		$50,000

*Gain recognized.

Basis of new apartment house:	
Cost	$90,000
Less: Gain deferred	−50,000
New basis	$40,000

Time Period for the Election 04-10.2

For real property that has been condemned, taxpayers have until three years after the close of the tax year in which the gain is realized. For all other property and occurrences, taxpayers have until two years after the close of the year in which the gain is realized.

Taxpayers may make the election in the year the gain is realized, but then they must complete the election with the return for the year in which the reinvestment is made. On the other hand, taxpayers may pay the tax on the gain and then file an amended return for a refund when the reinvestment is made.

If an election is made to defer the tax and if the reinvestment is not made later, taxpayers must file an amended return declaring the gain.

Tax *Warning* 04-10.3

To qualify for deferring the gain on an involuntary conversion, the reinvestment must be in property with a similar use or function. What qualifies is a matter for competent tax counsel. In some cases the answer may be obvious: farm for farm, cow for cow, and so on. But rental property for rental property may *not* qualify, depending on the use of the property.

SALE OF PRINCIPAL RESIDENCE 04-11

Two tax relief provisions govern the sale of a principal residence: one relates to all taxpayers and the other to taxpayers over 55.

1. Taxes may be deferred when persons sell their principle residences at a gain and reinvest in new principal residences within two years. When the cost of the new principal residence exceeds the sale price of the old principal residence, the entire tax on the gain from the sale of the old principal residence is deferred. When the new principal residence costs less than the old principal residence, the gain must be prorated between currently taxable and deferred.
2. Every taxpayer also has a once-in-a-lifetime election to permanently avoid the tax on $125,000 of gain resulting from the sale of a principal residence. Taxpayers must have reached their 55th birthdays to be eligible for this exclusion.

04-11.1 Sale and Purchase of Principal Residences

The loss on the sale of a residence is a personal one. So it is not deductible; nor may it be added to the basis of a new residence.

But the gain on the sale of a residence is taxable, normally as a capital gain (05-01). However, if the taxpayer qualifies for deferring the gain due to the reinvestment of the proceeds in a new principal residence, then no gain is recognized. The deferring of the gain is not elective; it is mandatory. The gain is totally or partially deferred if the taxpayer buys a new principal residence within two years before or after the sale of the old principal residence.

Special rules apply to members of the armed forces and to taxpayers living abroad. The amount of the gain that is deferred is based on the amount reinvested in the new principal residence. Any deferred gain is used to reduce the basis of the new residence (04-11.1A).

Any amount of "fixing-up" expenses incurred to sell the old principal residence serves to increase the amount of gain that is postponed. It does not reduce the total gain that is eventually reported. Any such fixing-up expenses must be incurred no more than 90 days previous to the sale, and they must be paid within 30 days after the sale.

The nonrecognition of gain applies only to one move every two years, unless the move qualifies for a moving expense deduction (06-11).

Example 04-11.1A

Brynne Gordon sells her principal residence for $100,000. She pays $6,000 in selling commissions, as well as $1,000 in fixing-up expenses. The basis of her old residence was $20,000. Within the time limit, she purchases a new principal residence for $80,000. The computation of the taxable and deferred gain would be:

Selling price of old residence	$100,000
Less: Commissions	− 6,000
Amount realized	$ 94,000
Less: Basis of old residence	− 20,000
Total gain	$ 74,000
Amount realized on sale	$ 94,000
Less: Fixing-up expenses	− 1,000
"Adjusted Sale Price"	$ 93,000
Less: Cost of new residence	− 80,000*
Gain recognized in year of sale	$ 13,000
Basis of new residence:	
Cost	$ 80,000
Less: Gain deferred (total gain $74,000 less $13,000 recognized)	− 61,000
Basis	$ 19,000

*If the cost of the new residence exceeded the adjusted sale price, the entire gain would be deferred.

04-11.2 **Sale of Principal Residence—Over 55**

Taxpayers may elect to exclude the first $125,000 ($67,500 for married persons filing separately) of gain on the sale of their principal residences if:

1. they (or their spouses in joint returns) were 55 years old or older on the date of the sale; *and*
2. they occupied the house as a principal place of residence for at least 3 of the 5 years ending on the date of sale; *and*
3. they or their spouses had not previously made this election.

04-11.2A **Example**

If in example 04-11.1A, Brynne had made this election, then the entire $74,000 of gain would have been tax-free. The basis of the new principal residence would simply be the cost, $80,000. But let's suppose she sells the old principal residence for $225,000, and all other factors remain the same. Then:

Total gain	$199,000
Less: $125,000 exclusion	−125,000
Gain to be allocated between deferred and taxable	$ 74,000

The taxable and deferred gains would then be the same, as would the basis of the new principal residence shown in the first example.

04-11.2B **Tax hint**

As you can see from the example, the two tax advantages can be used together. In fact, they often are.

04-11.2C **Tax *warning***

The $125,000 exclusion is a *once-in-a-lifetime* exclusion. It is not cumulative! In the first case, Brynne used only $74,000 of the total **$125,000** possible. She may never take advantage of this election again! Younger taxpayers should think twice before using this election if the future potential for tax savings on the sale of the new principal residence is evident.

ABANDONMENT AND DESTRUCTION OF PROPERTY 04-12

The tax treatment of the abandonment and/or the destruction of property depends on the intent of the taxpayer. The "loss" could be either a deductible loss or an addition to basis. As an example, let's say a taxpayer purchases land with a building on it but intends to demolish the building to build a new one. The cost of the building, as well as the cost to demolish it, is part of the basis of the land. On the other hand, the loss of the usefulness or the income-producing capability of the property is a deductible loss. The type of loss depends on the kind of property, on its used, and on whether the loss of utility was sudden or gradual.

The sudden and unexpected destruction of property typically falls into the category of a casualty loss (07-08).

If securities become worthless, the loss is a capital loss (Chapter 5 and 04-02.2).

If property held in a business is abandoned, the loss is an ordinary loss. To qualify, the property must be completely and permanently abandoned.

Inventories that become worthless are generally considered an increase in cost of goods sold (10-03). This increase actually decreases any taxable income or increases any deductible loss.

SALES AMONG RELATED TAXPAYERS AND SHAM SALES 04-13

No loss deduction is allowed for a sale to a related party. Related parties include:

1. spouse,
2. siblings,
3. ancestors,
4. lineal descendants,
5. controlled corporations (more than 50%), and
6. any other controlled entity (partnerships, exempt organizations, and so on).

Gains on transactions between related parties are taxable.

When the property subject to a disallowed loss is sold outside the "family," the amount of gain recognized is reduced by the amount of loss previously disallowed. The basis in the hands of the family buyer is not increased.

No loss deduction is allowed for the sale of property in a sham transaction. A *sham transaction* is one made for tax purposes only, with no economic substance. Such sales are obviously a subjective area, and the number of court cases contesting the IRS' classification of a transaction as "sham" is legion.

04-13.1 Example

Colin Gordon purchases a plot of land for $20,000. He sells the land to his sister, Brynne, for $15,000. Colin is not allowed a loss deduction. The basis of the property in Brynne's hands is $15,000. Several years later she sells the land to an outsider for $18,000. She has no gain or loss, since:

Sale proceeds	$18,000
Less: Basis	−15,000
Preliminary gain	$ 3,000
Less: Gain not taxable up to amount of previous loss disallowed ($5,000)	− 3,000
Taxable gain	$ -0-

Tax *Warning* 04-13.2

Sales at a loss among related parties is a "no-win" situation. In Example 04-13.1, Brynne and Colin together lost $2,000 (Colin's purchase at $20,000 and Brynne's sale at $18,000), and no one gets a deduction. Although the Code is written to prevent abuses, even the totally legitimate transaction can get caught in this trap.

5

CAPITAL GAINS AND LOSSES

CAPITAL ASSETS DEFINED 05-01

Capital assets are all assets except:

1. inventories,
2. accounts receivable acquired in the ordinary course of business,
3. real and depreciable property used in a trade or business,
4. certain U.S. government publications, and
5. intangible assets (patents, copyrights, and the like) that are created by or for the taxpayer or that are received as a gift from the creator.

The capital assets that are left fall into two major categories:

1. *Business and investment assets* (stocks, bonds, and so on), which can generate a capital gain or loss when sold or exchanged).

2. *Personal assets* (automobiles, personal residence, jewelry), which can generate a capital gain on sale or exchange, but which do *not* result in deductible losses.

Inventories held for resale in the ordinary course of business, as well as *accounts receivable* resulting from sales of goods or services in the ordinary course of business, are not capital assets. Of all assets, these two have caused the most controversy. As explained later in this chapter and in 07-04 (charitable contributions), the classification of an asset as a capital asset is generally favorable for tax purposes. What constitutes the "ordinary course of business" can be really sticky.

Real and depreciable property—land—is normally considered a capital asset. But if the taxpayer is a real estate dealer or in the business of constructing buildings, then the land is inventory held for sale in the normal course of business.

Special rules apply to dealers in *securities.*

05-02 THE HOLDING PERIOD AND ITS IMPORTANCE

Capital gains and losses are classified as long-term and short-term. They are short-term if the asset is held for less than the prescribed holding period, and they are long-term if held for the holding period or longer. Thus the holding period determines the taxability of any gains (05-04) and the deductibility of any losses (05-05). In general, the holding period begins on the day after acquisition and ends on the day of sale. The prescribed periods are as follows:

Asset	*Holding Period*
Securities	More than one year
Commodity future contracts	(See **05-10**.)
Patents	Always long-term
Livestock	Depends on type of animal and its use
Real and depreciable property	More than one year

Securities 05-02.1

For securities, the holding period begins on the day after the trade date, which is the day the purchase is executed—not the settlement date, which is the day payment is due. When stock is acquired through the exercise of an option, the holding period of the option is *not* added to that of the stock (05-04).

Example 05-02.1A

Robert Colin purchases 100 shares of AT&T common stock for 49. His confirmation shows:

Trade date:	June 24, 1980
Settlement date:	July 1, 1980

The trade date is the date the trade was executed, and the settlement date is the date he has to pay for the stock. So his holding period begins on June 25, 1980, the day after purchase. Robert must hold the stock until the trade date June 25, 1981 to receive long-term treatment. Even if he sells the stock for cash (same-day settlement) and receives his money on June 25, 1981, the transaction would still be long-term.

Robert sells the stock on trade date December 30, 1981 for settlement January 3, 1982. Obviously, the transaction is long-term since he held it for more than one year. But in which year is it taxable? That depends! See Tax Hint 05-02.4.

05-02.2 Short Sales

For securities sold short, the holding period begins on the date of acquisition of the securities. So short sales normally result in short-term holding periods (05-07.4 for exception).

05-02.2A Example

Robert Colin sells 100 shares of AT&T short at 49 on trade date June 24, 1980. On settlement date he arranges to borrow the stock and deliver it to the buyer.

On June 25, 1981, Robert buys back the 100 shares of AT&T for 40. He uses the securities purchased to return the stock borrowed. He has a $900 gain, computed as follows:

Sale proceeds, June 24, 19*80*	$4,900
Purchase price (basis), June 25, 19*81*	−4,000
Gain	$ 900

The gain is *short-term* since the holding period began on June 25, 19*81*, the date of acquisition.

05-02.3 Other Important Points

When *commodities* are acquired through a futures contract, the holding period of the futures contract is added to the holding period of the commodity.

The sale of *patents* comes under special rules in Section 1235. The holding period is not relevant, since the sale by any holder (including the creator) establishes a long-term gain. To qualify, the sale must be for all the rights under the patent.

When *property* is acquired *from a decedent,* the holding period is always long-term.

When property is acquired *by gift,* the holding period in the hands of the donee is the same as in the hands of the donor, except when the property is sold at a loss. In that case, the date of the gift establishes the start of the holding period (04-05).

When property is acquired *through a tax-free exchange,* the holding period of the original property is added to the holding period of the new property.

Tax Hint 05-02.4

The sale of securities at year-end presents a unique situation. The holding period is always based on trade date. But the settlement date determines the year of reporting for gains, while the trade date determines the year of reporting for losses. So in example 05-02.1A, Robert would report any gain in 1982, but any loss in 1981.

Selling stocks or bonds for delayed settlement delays the taxable event *only* if the transaction results in a gain! Such a delay does not allow a short-term transaction to "age" into a long-term transaction. (**See also 10-10.**)

OPTIONS 05-03

Options are contracts. The buyer of such a contract has the right make the seller (or *writer*) perform in either a purchase or sale transaction. For this right, the buyer pays the seller an agreed-upon amount, which is the price of the option. In return, the seller agrees either to sell or to buy a trading round lot of a specified security (the *underlying* security), at a specified price (the *strike price*), and before a specified date (the *expiration date*). All these and other terms are laid out in the contract, which has been standardized since 1973 for options listed on exchanges.

1. A *call option* gives the buyer the right to *buy* the underlying security from the seller (writer). The seller must sell the security if "called" upon to do so.
2. A *put option* gives the buyer the right to sell the underlying security to the seller. The seller must buy it if it is "put" to him or her.

05-03.1 Example

Taxpayer A sells a call contract to Taxpayer B for $300 ($3 per share). The contract gives Taxpayer B the right to buy 100 shares of MBS Corporation common stock (the underlying security) for $50 per share (the strike price) anytime up to June 24 of the following year (the expiration date). If Taxpayer B decides to exercise the call, then Taxpayer A must sell the 100 shares of MBS to B at $50, *regardless of the current market price of the stock.* If B had purchased and exercised a put, then A would have to buy the stock from B at $50, regardless of the current market value.

05-03.2 Alternative Outcomes for Option Holders (Buyers)

Options are not always exercised. In fact, three things can happen to an option contract:

1. The buyer may allow it to expire worthless.
2. The contract may be closed, that is:
   a. the buyer may sell the contract to another buyer, or
   b. The seller may buy it back.
3. The buyer may exercise the contract.

The tax consequences of each of these possible outcomes are quite straightforward.

Expiring worthless 05-03.2A

If, for one reason or another, the buyer chooses not exercise the contract, then it becomes worthless at the expiration date. The money that the buyer laid out for option price is gone; the seller keeps it. And nothing is gained through the option.

Tax consequences 05-03.2A-1

1. *From the buyer's viewpoint,* the option is considered to have been sold for zero on expiration date. This treatment is different from that when stock becomes worthless. When stock becomes worthless, it is considered to have been sold for zero on the *last* day of the year. The distinction is important, since it could mean the difference between a long-term capital loss and a short-term capital loss.
2. *From the writer's viewpoint,* the option is considered to have been repurchased for zero on expiration date. The result is a short-term capital gain, just like the short sale of securities.

Closing the contract 05-03.2B

Since the listing of options on the stock exchanges in 1973, a lively market has developed. But that market would not be so lively had it not been for the liquidity provided by the Options Clearing Corporation (OCC). One of the functions of the OCC is to act as the universal buyer for all sellers and as the universal seller for all buyers. Once a buyer and seller make a transaction on the exchange, they need never come into contact with one another again. Why? Because the OCC then steps in as the contra to both parties.

The benefit is that either the buyer or the seller can

close a contract without regard for the other. Either the buyer sells the contract back to the OCC (in effect, to *some* other buyer), or the seller buys the contract back from the OCC (in effect, from someone else who wants to write the contract).

05-03.2B-1 ***Example***

If Taxpayer B did not want to exercise the option he bought from A, he could simply sell the contract on the stock exchange to anyone who wants to buy it—and the OCC guarantees another "buyer." If Taxpayer A had second thoughts about writing the contract and wanted out, she could simply purchase an identical contract to the one she sold. And, again, the OCC guarantees a contra.

05-03.2B-2 ***Tax consequences***

1. *From the buyer's viewpoint,* if an option is purchased and then sold, it is treated exactly the same as if securities were purchased and sold.
2. *From the writer's viewpoint,* if an option is sold first and later repurchased, the transaction is treated the same as a short sale of stock.

05-03.2C **Exercising the option**

To exercise an option, the buyer merely makes the purchase or sale of the underlying stock, by delivering an exercise notice to the OCC, which then locates an appropriate writer. The day the option holder (buyer) exercises the option is the equivalent of the trade date for establishing the holding period. The holding period for the option is *not* added to that of the stock.

05-03.3C-1 ***Tax consequences***

1. *For the buyer,* the amount paid for the option is added to the price of any purchase or subtracted from the proceeds of any sale.

2. *For the writer,* the amount received for selling an option is added to the proceeds of any sale or subtracted from the price of any purchase.

Example: Exercise of a call option 05-03.2C-2

Brynne Gordon purchases a call option on June 24, 1980. The option allows the purchase of 100 shares of MBS Corporation at $50 per share. The option expires on January 21, 1981. She pays $400 for the option ($4 per share). On September 27, 1980, she exercises her option. Her holding period begins September 28th (the day after trade date), and her basis in the stock is:

Exercise price	$5,000
Cost of option	+ 400
Basis	$5,400

Example: Assignment of a call option 05-03.2C-3

When sellers of options are required to perform under options, they are said to be *assigned.*

In first example, Brynne Gordon sends her notice of exercise to the OCC. It, in turn, assigns a seller to perform under the contract. Let's say that Jim Shields was one of many people who sold MBS options with an exercise price of $50 and an expiration of January 21, 1981. The OCC assigns him to perform—that is, to sell MBS stock at $50 per share. Further, when he sold his option, he received $300 ($3 per share). When he sells the stock, the proceeds of that sale are:

Exercise price	$5,000
Plus: Amount received for the option	+ 300
Total proceeds of sale	$5,300

Now for the big questions: Does he have a gain or a loss? And is it short- or long-term? It depends! Look for the taxable event. Paragraph 04-01 notes that the taxable event is the closing of a position. Jim can do one of three things:

1. He can sell short, and there is no taxable event.
2. He can instruct his broker to deliver stock that has been held long-term, and he has a long-term gain or loss, depending on the basis of the stock delivered.
3. He can instruct his broker to deliver stock held short-term, and he has either a short-term gain or loss depending on the basis of the stock delivered.

See Tax Hint 05-03.3 for the completion of this transaction, assuming Jim delivers long-term stock.

05-03.2C-4 *Example: Exercise of a put option*

The exercise of a put is merely the sale of stock. Brian Greenberg purchases a put of MBS Corporation common stock giving him the right to sell 100 shares at $50 per share. He pays $300 ($3 per share). Three months later he exercises the put. Further, he tells his broker to deliver 100 of MBS, which he purchased four years ago for $30. His tax position is:

Proceeds of sale:	
Exercise of put, sale at $50	$5,000
Less: Cost of put	− 300
Net proceeds of sale	$4,700
Less: Basis of stock delivered	−3,000
Net long-term capital gain	$1,700

The gain is long-term since he delivered stock with a long-term holding period.

05-03.2C-5 *Example: Assignment on a put option*

When Brian exercises his put, the OCC assigns Barney Colin to perform. Barney must buy the stock at $50. He received $250 for the put when he sold it ($2.50 per share). Further, he instructs his broker to use the purchase of MBS on the put option to close a short sale of MBS, which he had made at $60. Barney's tax position is:

Proceeds of short sale		$6,000
Basis of stock purchased with the put:		
Exercise price	$5,000	
Less: Amount received for put sale	− 250	−4,750
Net short-term gain		$1,250

The gain is short-term since the holding period began with the assignment to buy the stock.

Tax Hint 05-03.3

Aaron Gordon got one of those "hot tips." You know the kind: they have oil in Timbuktu or gold in Hoboken. Well, Aaron jumped in ten months ago at $20 per share. Last week the rumor hit Wall Street that they hit oil right in the middle of Newark. The stock has shot up to $50 per share, and Aaron wants out. But it has only been ten months! How can he extend this gain into a long-term gain?

There is no absolute way, but one way will "probably" work. The company has listed options trading. The calls with an exercise price of $20 are selling at $30¼. Why not? The call gives the buyer the right to buy the stock at $20, while it is now selling at $50. So the option has an "intrinsic" value of $30. The extra 25¢ (¼ point) recognizes the fact that the option has another seven months before it expires.

Aaron sells the call option! What does he have to lose? As long as the stock stays over $20 per share, whoever has the option must exercise it. They would be foolish not to call stock at $20 if it is selling above that. Aaron *hopes* it will be more than two months before they call the stock. If they wait that long to exercise their option, the stock Aaron owns will "turn" long-term.

In most cases, option owners wait until the last minute to exercise. Remember, when they exercise, they have to pay Aaron $2,000 to buy the stock. The longer they wait, the more interest they earn on the $2,000.

When Aaron is assigned:

Proceeds of sale:	
Exercise price of option	$2,000
Plus: Proceeds of sale of option	+3,025
	$5,025
Less: Basis of stock	−2,000
Long-term capital gain	$3,025

Not only does Aaron convert the short-term gain into a long-term gain, but he also picks up an extra $25. Actually, the "extra" $25 will be substantially less than he could have earned in interest income had he sold the stock outright, but the tax advantages far outweigh this slight disadvantage.

The *risk*? If the stock drops below $20, Aaron does not get assigned. He then owns the stock. But at least he collected $3,025 for the option he sold. In that event, the money collected for the option is short-term capital gain.

05-03.4 Tax *Warning*

Put options are often considered to be insurance. If a taxpayer purchases 100 shares of MBS Corporation at $50, she might also purchase an MBS put option, exercise $50, say for $3. If the stock goes up, she lets her put option expire worthless. That's like saying, "If the building does not burn, the insurance premium is worthless." But if the stock goes down, she exercises her put and sells the stock at $50. All she loses is the price of the put.

That works fine from an economic viewpoint, but from a tax viewpoint, she must take care:

1. If the stock position being protected is already long-term, no harm is done.

2. If the stock position being protected is short-term, the holding period is *destroyed*! In other words, if the investor held the stock for 11 months and 30 days (but not more than a year), she goes back to day one to start counting the holding period.

There is one exception. If the stock and the put option are purchased as a unit, and if the put option is clearly earmarked to the stock, then the holding period can begin. Since listed options have a maximum life of nine months, there still has to be a three-month period of uninsured exposure.

Conventional (over-the-counter) options can be written for more than a year, but they are normally so expensive as to be economically impractical.

Tax Hint 05-03.5

So if you buy a put to protect a stock position the holding period is destroyed. Is that so bad? Maybe not!

Later in this chapter, we will see that a short-term loss is better than a long-term loss. Suppose the taxpayer has a stock that has gone down in market price, say from $50 to $30. The position is about to become long-term, but the taxpayer wants to hold the stock. Buy a put. That destroys the holding period, and the taxpayer has another year to see if the stock will turn around.

COMPUTATION OF TAXABLE CAPITAL GAINS 05-04

Computing taxable capital gains is a methodical process:

1. First, separate all short-term transactions from all long-term transactions.
2. Then net together all gains and losses from short-term transactions to come up with a *net short-term gain or loss.* If a taxpayer has one or 500 transactions, you end

up with one figure: a net short-term gain or loss. Ignore any net zero.

3. Then net together all gains and losses from long-term transactions to come up with a net long-term gain or loss. Again, the number of transactions does not matter, nor, for that matter, does the number of sources. The taxpayer has one figure: net long-term gain or loss. Ignore any net zero.
4. If both net computations result in zero, ignore both.
5. If the taxpayer has gains in both computations, then
   a. 100% of the net short-term gain is added to Adjusted Gross Income, and
   b. 40% of the net long-term gain is added to Adjusted Gross Income.

   Actually, the Code instructs that 60% of the net long-term gain must be deducted from the total net long-term gain. But thinking of long-term gains as 40% taxable is often easier than thinking of them as a 60% deduction (05-04.1). However, the 60% deduction figure is used in the computation of the alternative minimum tax (09-03).
6. If, after netting all capital gains, you find that one is a gain and the other is a loss, then you have to net down once more; that is, you must offset one net figure against the other. If the result of that netting is a loss, see paragraph 05-05. But if the result is a gain, then the gain is classified as long-term or short-term depending on which one was larger. If the long-term gain was larger than the short-term loss, then the resulting gain is long-term. If the short-term gain was larger than the long-term loss, then the resulting gain is short-term (05-04.2).

05-04.1 Example: Both Long- and Short-Term Gains

Colin Gordon had the following transactions last year:

Short-Term	*Gain (loss)*
Sale of 100 shares MBS Corporation	$ 4,000
Trading MBS options	(2,000)
Purchased gold bar and sold it	$1,000
Net short-term gain	$ 3,000
Long-Term	
Mutual fund capital gain dividend	$ 8,000
Capital gain distribution from partnership (11-02)	2,000
Sale of MBS common stock	(1,000)
Net long-term gain	$ 9,000

In addition, Colin had $50,000 in salary. His Adjusted Gross Income is:

Salary		$50,000
Short-term capital gains		3,000
Long-term capital gains	$9,000	
Less: 60% deduction ($9,000 × 60%)	−5,400	+3,600
Adjusted Gross Income		$56,600

Example: Combination Gain and Loss Netting to a Gain 05-04.2

If in the previous example, Colin also had a short-term loss of $4,500 on another stock trade, his net short-term loss would be $1,500. Since he has both a gain and a loss, he must net once more.

Short-Term	
Original	$ 3,000
New loss	−(4,500)
Net short-term loss	$(1,500)
Long-Term:	
Original	$ 9,000
Net long-term gain	$ 7,500

The gain is long-term, since that is the larger figure of the two. Now his Adjusted Gross Income is:

Salary		$50,000
Net long-term gain	$7,500	
Less: 60% deduction ($7,500 × 60%)	−4,500	+ 3,000
Adjusted Gross Income		$53,000

05-04.3 **Tax Hint**

Notice how the $4,500 loss reduced Colin's Adjusted Gross Income by only $3,600. That's because the net short-term loss of $1,500 reduced net long-term gains. Since that gain was only 40% taxable, Colin only benefits by 40% of the $1,500 short-term loss, or $600. His Adjusted Gross Income is reduced by:

100% of the first $3,000 of loss	$ 3,000
40% of the next $1,500 of loss	+ 600
Total reduction of AGI	$ 3,600

Colin lost forever $900 of tax benefits from the long-term gain. If Colin could have postponed the loss until the following year, it may have been used:

1. to offset short-term gains of that year, or
2. to offset other taxable income (05-05).

05-05 COMPUTATION OF DEDUCTIBLE CAPITAL LOSS

The computation of a deductible capital loss is very similar to the computation of taxable gain. Simply follow steps 1, 2, and 3 in paragraph 05-04.

4. If both figures net down to a loss, then the deductions are as follows (05-05.1):
   a. The short-term loss is 100% deductible to reduce Adjusted Gross Income.
   b. The long-term loss is 50% deductible to reduce Adjusted Gross Income.

(See 05.05.3 for limitations.)

5. If after netting all capital gains and losses, you find that one is a gain and the other is a loss, then you must net down once more. If the result of that netting is a gain, see paragraph 05-04. But if the result is a loss, then it is classified as long-term or short-term depending on which one was larger: If the long-term loss was larger than the short-term gain, then the resulting loss is long-term. If the short-term loss was larger than the long-term gain, then the resulting loss is short-term (05-05.2).

Example: Both Long- and Short-Term Capital Losses 05-05.1

Brynne Gordon had the following transactions last year:

Short-Term	*Gain (Loss)*
Sale of 100 shares MBS Corporation	$(4,000)
Trading MBS options	2,000
Purchased silver bar and sold it	1,000
Net short-term loss	$(1,000)
Long-Term	
Mutual fund capital gain distribution	$ 8,000
Sale of MBS Corporation common stock	(2,000)
Capital loss distribution from partnership (11-02)	(9,000)
Net long-term loss	$(3,000)

In addition, Brynne had $50,000 in salary. Her Adjusted Gross Income is:

Salary		$50,000
Short-term capital loss		(1,000)
Long-term capital loss	$(3,000)	
Less: 50% not deductible		
($3,000 × 50%)	1,500	(1,500)
Adjusted Gross Income		$47,500

05-05.2 **Example: Combination of Gain and Loss Netting to a Loss**

If in the prior example, Brynne also had a short-term gain of $1,500 on another stock trade, her net short-term gain would be $500. Since she has both a gain and a loss, she must net once more.

Short-Term	
Original	$(1,000)
New gain	– 1,500
Net short-term gain	$ 500
Long-Term	
Original	$(3,000)
Net long-term loss	$(2,500)

The loss is long-term, since that was the larger figure of the two. Now her Adjusted Gross Income is:

Salary		$50,000
Net long-term loss	($2,500)	
Less: 50% not deductible		
($2,500 × 50%)	1,250	1,250
Adjusted Gross Income		$48,750

05-05.2A **Tax hint**

Notice how the $1,500 gain increased Adjusted Gross Income by only $1,250. That's because the net short-term gain of $500 reduced the net long-term loss. Since the long-term loss was only 50% deductible, Brynne lost only 50¢ on the dollar. Her Adjusted Gross Income is increased by:

100% of the first $1,000 of gain	$1,000
50% of the next $500 of gain	+ 250
Total increase in AGI	$1,250

The point is that, when short-term gains can be used to offset long-term loss, they should be. If a taxpayer already has substantial short-term gains, that's the time to sell the "old dogs" that have hanging around in the portfolio. Take a loss that is only 50% deductible, and use it to offset 100% taxable income.

Limitations 05-05.3

The amount that Adjusted Gross Income may be reduced in any one year due to capital losses is $3,000 ($1,500 for married taxpayers filing separately). Since long-term capital losses are only 50% deductible, it takes $6,000 of long-term losses to reduce Adjusted Gross Income by $3,000. With both short- and long-term capital losses, a taxpayer must use the short-term losses first. Any unused capital losses are carried forward to the following year.

Losses that are carried forward to the following year actually become the first transaction of the next year. A short-term loss carried forward, becomes the first short-term transaction of the new year. A long-term loss carried forward becomes the first long-term transaction of the new year. For this reason, there is no time limit as to when a carry-forward loss expires; it does not.

Example: Capital loss carry-forward 05-05.3A

Last year, Aaron Gordon had $50,000 in salary. He also had a $2,000 net short-term capital loss, along with a $5,000 net long-term capital loss. His AGI is:

Salary		$50,000
Short-term loss		(2,000)
Long-term loss	$(2,000)	
Less: 50% not deductible		
($2,000 × 50%)	−1,000	(1,000)
AGI		$47,000

Here are the steps in figuring how much capital loss is deductible and how much is carried forward are:

1. Use the short-term loss first.
2. The $2,000 short-term loss is 100% deductible, and the deduction does not exceed the $3,000 annual limitation.
3. Use the long-term loss next
4. Aaron must use $2 of long-term loss to get a $1 deduction.
5. He uses $2,000 to take a $1,000 deduction, which reaches the limitation.
6. He uses $2,000 of his $5,000 net long-term loss, so $3,000 is carried forward.

If Aaron has no other capital transactions next year, the $3,000 long-term carry forward would be used to reduce AGI by $1,500.

05-05.4 Tax Hint

Suppose your client has a $100,000 net long-term loss. First, it is only 50% deductible, and second it will take more than 16 years to use it up if he or she has no further capital gains. Can this loss, somehow, be converted into a currently deductible item—and at the full $100,000 value? It takes work, and a little luck, but it can be done.

When investors sell stock short and the stock pays a dividend while the investor is short, the investor must pay the dividend. (Since the buyer is entitled to a dividend, the short seller must pay it.) As an example, if Investor A is short 100 shares of MBS common stock, which pays a $1 dividend, the investor would be charged for the dividend on "ex-dividend" date. He would have to pay $100. That $100 paid by Investor A is a deduction from Adjusted Gross Income (07-09).

Now suppose you can find a stock selling at $50 that is about to pay a large extra dividend. Normally this news comes out about a month before ex-dividend date. Let's say the dividend is $10. The day before ex-dividend, the stock is selling at $50, and buyers are entitled to the dividend. The next day, on the ex-dividend date, the stock drops in price dramatically (probably about $10 per share), since buyers are no longer entitled to the dividend.

Here is how our client can take advantage of this?

1. On the day before ex-dividend, sell the stock short for $50.
2. On ex-dividend date buy it back for $40.

This transaction results in an economic zero. The gain on the short sale of $10 per share is offset by the dividend charge of $10 for being short on ex-dividend date. *But* the short-term gain offsets the otherwise unusable $100,000 long-term loss, and the dividend charge is fully deductible from Adjusted Gross Income.

This is an area for a knowledgeable broker! Stocks react in strange ways, and your broker must be involved in choosing a stock that reacts properly in a large ex-dividend situation.

See 09-03, for possible alternative minimum tax applications.

CAPITAL GAINS: SPECIAL CONSIDERATIONS 05-06

Certain capital assets get different treatment from normal.

05-06.1 Subdividing Real Estate

At what point does a real estate "investor," who is entitled to capital gains treatment, become a real estate "dealer," who is subject to tax on the sale of inventory? The answer to that question can be sticky.

Yet Section 1237 of the Code provides a safe haven for those who purchase undeveloped real estate and who proceed to have it subdivided and offered for sale on a lot-by-lot basis. A taxpayer can qualify under Section 1237 to receive capital gains treatment on the sale of lots if:

1. the tract of land is held for more than five years or was inherited, and
2. the taxpayer did not make any improvements to the land other than those required for the subdivision.

If the taxpayer meets these criteria, the proceeds of the sale of the first five lots are capital gains. The further sale of the lot calls for an apportionment between capital gain and ordinary income.

05-06.2 Loss on Small Business Corporation Stock

As we've seen, the losses sustained on the investments in common stock are of limited use in reducing Adjusted Gross Income. But Section 1244 of the Code provides relief for investors in small business corporations. To qualify under Section 1244, all three of the following requirements must be met:

1. The taxpayer must be the original buyer of common stock from the corporation.
2. The total original issue of stock was for $1,000,000 or less.
3. The corporation was actively engaged in business, as opposed to holding funds for investment.

If the taxpayer and the stock qualify under Section 1244, the taxpayer is allowed to deduct any loss sustained on the stock as an ordinary loss, up to $50,000 ($100,000 on a joint return without regard to which spouse owned the stock).

Any loss above the limitations would be considered a capital loss subject to those restrictions.

Securities Held by Banks 05-06.3

Special rules exist for the taxation of banks in general. Losses sustained by banks in the trading of securities may be fully deductible and not subject to the limitations on capital losses.

SELLING SHORT AGAINST THE BOX 05-07

Selling stock short is selling stock that the seller does not own. Normally short sellers hope that the market will decline. If so, they buy back the stock at a lower price. The concept of "buy low-sell high" is not violated, just switched to "sell high-buy low." Short sellers must deliver the stock to the buyer. They normally do so by borrowing and delivering similar stock. When they buy back their short positions, they return the borrowed stock.

Deferring Tax Liability 05-07.1

Since the taxable event in the trading of securities is the "closing" of a position (04-01), and since a short sale opens a new position, no taxable event occurs. Hence selling short against the box is normally used to defer the recognition of gain until sometime in the future. Investors typically owns a stock in which they have a large profit. They wish to recognize the profit economically, but without recognizing the profit for tax purposes in the current year. So they sell the same stock short, rather than sell the stock they own. This leaves them in an economically zero position, but no position has been closed, so no taxable event has occurred.

05-07.1A **Example**

Two years ago Aaron Gordon purchased 100 shares of MBS Corporation common stock for $20. On December 15 of this year, Aaron felt that the stock had peaked at $50. But his tax position was such that he wanted to avoid taking the gain for tax purposes. He therefore sold 100 shares of MBS short against the box, which left him with the following position:

Ownership (long) 100 shares, basis	$2,000
Short, proceeds 100 shares	$5,000

At this point Aaron has no economic risk. For every point that the stock goes up, he gains a point on the long and loses a point on the short. For every point the stock goes down, he loses a point on the long and gains a point on the short.

In January of next year, he plans to tell his broker to close the positions by pair-off (05-07.3A), at which time he will realize a long-term gain of $3,000.

How long can an investor hold this "no tax" position? Technically there is no limit. But brokerage industry rules require that margin be maintained in the account. This obligation causes the investor to lose interest income or the "buying power" to acquire more stock. At some point, it becomes uneconomical to continue to hold the short against the box.

05-07.2 Effect on Holding Period

Selling short against the box can affect the *holding period.* If investors are short-term on the stock they are holding, the short against the box destroys the holding period of the stock they own. If they are already long-term on the stock they are holding, there is no effect on the holding period.

See 05-03.5 for a TAX HINT with regard to the positive effects of the destruction of a stock's holding period.

Example 05-07.2A

Barney Colin had the following transactions in MBS common stock:

Date		*Number of Shares*	*Price*
June 2, 1981	Purchased	100	20
January 3, 1981	Sold short	100	50
August 3, 1982	Purchased and closed short position	100	40

The sale on December 3, 1981 is a short against the box, and it does not create a taxable event. But since Barney was short-term on the stock he held, its holding period was destroyed. On August 3, 1982 the holding period for his 100 shares begins anew. He must hold it until August 3, 1983 for it to become long-term.

Barney realizes a short-term gain on the purchase of August 3, 1982 of $1,000: the proceeds of sale $5,000 less basis of $4,000 on the purchase.

Pairing-off 05-07.3

Once investors have sold short against the box, they can unwind the two positions in several ways. The simplest is to wait until the period in which they wish to realize the gain for tax purposes and then instructing the broker to "pair-off" the two positions. To understand a "pair-off," you have to realize that there are really four positions involved. The broker has to maintain these positions for the IRS to accept the fact that the investor has not closed out the position:

1. The stock owned and shown in the investment account as "long."

2. The short stock position shown in the investment account as "short."
3. The stock owned and physically either in the broker's vaults or held by the broker in a depository.
4. A "stock-borrow" position showing that the broker owes the stock to the person from whom it was borrowed.

In a pair-off, the broker returns the customer's stock from the vault to the person from whom the stock was borrowed to cover the short sale. The long and short positions in the investor's account are eliminated by journal entry.

If a short against the box is paired-off, the investor realizes a long- or short-term gain on the date of the pair-off. Whether the gain is long- or short-term has to do with the holding period—or, more specifically, with the date that the investor established the short against the box. Any stock that is held short-term at that time has a holding period of zero.

05-07.4 Tax Hint: A No-Tax Position

Depending on market conditions and the general outlook, investors could take one of two other actions:

1. If *bearish* on the stock, they could sell their "long" position, leaving them with a "real" short position exposed to market risk.
2. If *bullish* on the stock, they could buy back the short position, thus reestablishing their ownership in the stock and again subjecting themselves to market risk.

Except in one case (noted below), the IRS does not link the positions together. The sale of the "long" position results in a long-term or short-term gain depending on the holding period at the time the investor sold short against the box. The buying back of the short position results in a short-term gain if the stock declines in price since the position was established. If the stock rises in price, the investor has a loss when he or she buys back the short position. The loss is:

1. short-term if the "long" position was short-term at the time of the short against the box, or
2. long-term if the "long" position was long-term at the time of the short against the box.

This last item, a long-term loss, is the only time a short sale can result in a long-term transaction; and then it results only in a loss, never in a gain (05-02.2).

Example 05-07.4A

In our first example, Aaron Gordon had the following position:

100 shares MBS Corp. held long-term, basis	$2,000
100 shares MBS Corp. sold short, proceeds	$5,000

At this point, Aaron has a locked-in long-term capital gain of $3,000. In January, when Aaron plans to close out the position, the stock rises to $80 per share.

Then Aaron gets a bright idea. Instead of pairing-off the positions,he closes them in the open market. He figures:

Sale of stock	$8,000
Basis	−2,000
Long-term gain	$6,000
Purchase of short position	$8,000
Sale proceeds of short sale	−5,000
Short-term loss (?)	$3,000

With some other short-term gains, he figures to net this loss against them. In this way he creates a long-term gain taxable at 40%, offset by a short-term loss usable against 100% taxable income. *Wrong*!

This is the exception:

When the closing of a short against the box results in a loss, and when the stock owned at the time of the short sale is already long-term, then the loss is long-term. The rule prevents the creation of long-term gains offset by short-term losses.

Even if Aaron decides just to close the short position and to keep the long position, the loss would be long-term. Of course, long-term losses must first offset long-term gains, and even then they are only 50% usable to offset Adjusted Gross Income (05-05).

05-08 CAPITAL GAINS DIVIDENDS

Regulated Investment Companies (mutual funds) must either distribute or constructively distribute capital gains earned, normally within 45 days after their tax year ends:

1. Capital gains *distributions* are included as long-term capital gains by mutual fund shareholders without regard to the number of days the mutual fund shares are held. The mutual fund pays no federal income taxes.
2. In *constructive distributions,* mutual funds retain the gains and pay the federal income tax on them.

   Shareholders include in income the total capital gain as long-term capital gain; they then take a credit against their taxes for the taxes paid by the mutual fund (09-06.3). The basis of the shareholders' stock is increased by the amount of gain reported and decreased by the tax credit (05-08.1).

Any loss on the sale of mutual fund shares held less than 31 days, when there has been a capital gains distribution or constructive distribution, is a long-term loss. This rule is to prevent investors from creating short-term losses offset by equal long-term gains. (See 05-05.4 regarding the trading of stocks with a large pending dividend.)

The dividend exclusion (02-09.3) does not apply to capital gains dividends.

Example 05-08.1

On May 4, 1981, Aaron Gordon purchased 100 shares of MBS Mutual Fund for $10 per share. On May 15, 1981, the fund constructively distributed a $2-per-share capital gains dividend, and then it constructively passed through a 50¢ per-share federal income tax credit. Even though Aaron has held the stock for less than a month, the dividend is a long-term capital gain. He takes a credit of $50 against his federal income tax (100 shares × 50¢). His basis in the stock is now:

Cost	$1,000
Plus: Dividend constructively received	+ 200
Less: Tax credit received	− (50)
New basis	$1,150

WASH SALES 05-09

The Code prevents taxpayers from taking a capital *loss* in a security if, within 30 days before or after the sale, they:

1. purchase the same security; *or*
2. purchase substantially identical securities; *or*
3. purchase an option to acquire the same or a substantially identical security.

When you are dealing in stocks, a "substantially identical security" could include either a bond or a preferred stock that is convertible into the common stock on which the loss is taken. Rights and warrants to acquire the common stock are clearly substantially identical to the common stock.

The object of this rule is to prevent taxpayers from recognizing a loss on the sale and then reestablishing the position. The 30-days-before rule prevents taxpayers from buying first ("doubling up") and then selling the security with the loss. If the taxpayer enters into a wash sale, the loss is added to the basis of the newly acquired security. In effect, this postpones the deductibility of the loss until the new position is sold. The holding period of the stock on which the loss is disallowed is added to the holding period of the new stock .

The rule does not affect *gains.* If taxpayers wish to recognize a gain and immediately repurchase the same security, no problem.

The wash sale rule also affects *losses on short sales.* In that case taxpayers may not resell the same or a substantially identical security short within 30 days before or after closing the short position.

Dealers in securities are not subject to the wash sale rules.

05-09.1 Example

Colin Gordon had the following transactions in MBS common stock:

Date		*Number of Shares*	*Price*
January 3, 1981	Purchase	100	50 ($5,000)
June 4, 1981	Sell and close position	100	40 ($4,000)
July 1, 1981	Purchase	100	35 ($3,500)
March 9, 1982	Sell and close position	100	80 ($8,000)

On the first purchase, Colin establishes his holding period and a basis of $5,000. The loss on the first sale, $1,000, is disallowed. The $1,000 is added to Colin's basis of the new stock, which is:

New purchase price	$3,500
Disallowed loss on wash sale	+1,000
New basis	$4,500

On July 1, 1981, Colin's holding period is already 5 months, since the holding period of the January 3 purchase is added to the stock acquired on July 1. He held the stock for over an additional 9 months, when he sells it on March 9, 1982. The gain is therefore long-term:

Sale proceeds	$8,000
Basis	$4,500
Long-term capital gain	$3,500

Debt Securities 05-09.2

What constitutes a "similar" security is a well worn path. When dealing in bonds or other debt securities, as long as:

1. either the issuer changes *or*
2. the coupon *and* the due date change,

then the securities are *not* substantially identical. This allows for what is commonly called "tax swaps."

Example 05-09.2A

In January 1982, Barney Colin purchases $10,000 worth of MBS Corporation bonds, 12%, due in 2002 at par. His basis is therefore $10,000.

In December 1982, the bonds are selling for 85. His broker approaches him with the following "swap" idea. He could buy Other Corporation bonds, which are of equal credit rating, yield, and maturity for 85. To raise the needed funds for the purchase, he could sell the MBS Corporation bonds. Since Barney would have no money out-of-pocket, the transaction is called a "swap." He is really swapping one bond for another.

On the sale of MBS Corporation:	
Basis	$10,000
Proceeds of sale	− 8,500
Short-term loss	$ 1,500
Basis of Other Corporation bonds:	
Cost	$ 8,500

Barney has accomplished two things.

1. He has a usable short-term loss to offset other capital gains or Adjusted Gross Income.
2. He prevents the MBS loss from becoming long-term. The holding period for the other Corporation bonds begins with their purchase.

For banks, the loss could be an ordinary loss, usable as a deduction from operating income.

In our example, the issuer changes, so there is no danger of the two bonds being considered substantially identical, causing a wash sale. If the issuer *were* the same, then, to be safe, both the coupon and maturity of the bonds should be different.

In several court cases, holding for the taxpayer, the issuer and the coupon were the same; only the maturity changed. Even though any bond trader will tell that significantly different maturities are not substantially identical, with the vast number of bonds to choose from, this situation should be avoided.

05-09.3 Options

The wash sale rule does not affect the trading of *put* and *call options*. Even if exactly the same option is repurchased, the wash sale rule does not eliminate the deductibility of the loss. But the purchase of an option will invoke the wash sale with regard to the loss on a security trade.

Example 05-09.3A

Last year, Aaron Gordon had the following transactions:

Date		*Quantity*	*Price*
June 4	Purchased Calls, MBS Corp., exercise price 50, exp. Jan. 21	10	4
August 3	Sold above calls	10	2
August 23	Repurchased above calls	10	1
August 23	Purchased common stock Mountainside Corp.	1000	48
October 1	Sold above stock	1000	42
October 10	Purchased Calls Mountainside Corp. Exercise price 40 Exp. Feb. 22	5	3

The sale of 10 call options on August 3 results in a short-term loss of $2,000, as follows:

Basis	
(10 options × 100 shares per option × $4)	$4,000
Sale proceeds	
(10 options × 100 shares per option × $2)	−2,000
Short-term loss	$2,000

Since option trading is not subject to the wash sale rules, the repurchase of the same options on August 23 does not disallow the loss. But the loss on the sale of 1,000 shares of Mountainside Corp. is partially disallowed by the purchase of 5 call options on October 10. Since each option is for 100 shares, only the loss on 500 shares is deductible. The loss on the second 500 shares must be added to the basis of the 5 options purchased on October 10. The deductible loss is:

Basis, 1000 shares	$48,000
Less: Proceeds of sale, 1000 shares	−42,000
Short-term loss	$ 6,000
Less: One-half disallowed by wash sale	− 3,000
Deductible short-term loss	$3,000
Basis of 5 options purchased October 10:	
Cost (5 options × 100 shares × $3)	$ 1,500
Disallowed loss on wash sale	+ 3,000
Basis of 5 options	$ 4,500

Note that the holding period of the stock is added to the holding period of the call options.

05-09.4 Tax Hint

One way of partially avoiding the wash sale rule with common stocks is to purchase the stock of a company in the same industry. Often, stocks within an industry group react in a similar fashion in the market. Your broker may be able to suggest a stock that reacts in a manner similar to the one sold at a loss.

05-09.5 Tax Hint

A wash sale can void a loss that you really do not want. Suppose the taxpayer takes a short-term loss, and then less than a month later takes a large long-term gain. The taxpayer may want to postpone that short-term loss until the following year. In that way the taxpayer will not have to offset the 40% taxable long-term gain with the 100% deductible short-term loss. The investor can retroactively void the short-term loss by intentionally creating a wash sale, by either purchasing the stock back or by buying a call option on the stock.

SPECIAL CONSIDERATIONS—COMMODITY FUTURES 05-10

A commodity future is a contract to deliver or to receive a commodity (corn, silver, and the like) at a fixed price sometime in the future. To be considered a future for tax purposes, it must be traded on an organized exchange and the trades cleared through a clearing corporation. Any other "future" contract is considered a "forward" for tax purposes and is covered in paragraph 05-10.5.

There are three general rules for computing gain or loss on a future contract if that contract is a capital asset:

1. For contracts sold during the year the gain or loss is simply sales proceeds less basis. This is the same as computing gain or loss on a stock, *but* basis may be adjusted as described in number 3 below.
2. If the owner of a long future contract takes delivery of the underlying commodity, the holding period of the future is added to the holding period of the commodity. If delivery is taken, the taxable event is the sale of the commodity. If the holder of a short contract delivers the underlying commodity then that action would be the taxable event. In either case the gain or loss is measured in the same way as in the purchase and sale of any other capital asset.
3. If a future contract is held by the taxpayer at the close of the taxable year, it is treated as sold (or repurchased) at its fair market value. The basis of the contract is adjusted for this mark to the market.

Example—Mark to the Market 05-10.1

Sarah Speculator buys a contract to receive 5,000 troy ounces of silver in October, 1983 for $24.47 per ounce. At the moment she buys the contract, it has no value since that is what October, 1983 silver is selling for. She will have to put up margin to demonstrate financial responsibility to her broker, but that does not enter into the tax computation.

At December 31, 1982, October, 1983 silver is marked to market by the clearing corporation at $35 per ounce. This establishes its fair market value.

Each day the clearing corporation settles gains and losses. Sarah has, or will, receive $52,650 [($35 − $24.47) × 5,000] from the clearing corporation. The clearing corporation receives this money from the loser (someone who sold October, 1983 silver futures short). The clearing corporation is always even—winners collect, losers pay.

Sarah must report the $52,650 as a gain on her future contract. Her basis is now $52,650. Sarah finally closes the contract at $32.00 per ounce. Between the time she declared the $52,650 gain and the time she sold the contract, she had to pay the clearing corporation $15,000 [($35 − $32.00) × 5,000]. This becomes a loss to her, reported as:

Sale of contract ($52,650 − $15,000)	$37,650
Basis	52,650
Loss	$15,000

Of course, if silver continued to rise in price, she would have more gain in the second year rather than a loss.

If Sarah had sold rather than purchased the contract in question, she would have a reportable loss in the first year, and a gain in the second year.

05-10.2 Long-Term or Short-Term?

Both! Gains and losses on futures contracts are reported:

- 40% short-term and
- 60% long-term
- *regardless* of the holding period.

So for the 50% incremental bracket taxpayer, the effective tax rate is 32%. As an example a $1,000 gain would be:

40% short-term (100% reportable)		$400
60% long-term	$600	
less 60% exclusion	360	240
Amount added to AGI		$640
$640 at a 50% tax rate		$320

Hedges 05-10.3

A future that is part of a hedge is *not* marked to the market. It must be closed either under method 1 or 2 of paragaph 05-10, closed in the open market or as part of a transaction in the underlying commodity.

A *hedge* is a form of insurance against loss in the taxpayer's trade or business. As an example, a farmer selling corn futures against his crop, or a potato chip manufacturer buying potato futures to insure her supply at a reasonable price.

For a hedge to be recognized for tax purposes, the taxpayer must identify the contract as such clearly in his other records before the close of the day it is entered into, and it must be part of the trade or business.

However, once a contract is so identified the gain or loss is 100% ordinary gain or loss since the contract is no longer a capital asset.

Tax Warning 05-10.4

Just because the taxpayer says a contract is a hedge or a capital asset does not mean that the IRS or the courts will go along.

The Supreme Court held in Corn Products Refining Co. v Commissioner that the *profitable* futures contracts the company had classified as a capital asset were in fact a hedge. The Court held that the contracts gave them an insured supply of grain and reduced their costs of storing inventory.

But in the Carborundum Co. case, the Tax Court held that "short" futures contracts in British pounds were not a hedge against the company's investments denominated in British pounds. So the losses were only partially deductible capital losses, not fully deductible ordinary losses. In summary, the Court felt the "hedge" was too remote, and the future did not provide a hedge against their investment in the ordinary course of their business.

05-10.5 Tax (Mixed) Straddles

The following rules do *not* apply to straddles where *all* positions are future contracts. Such a straddle is covered under the general rules (05-10).

A tax straddle exists when a taxpayer has two or more positions that work against each other so that little economic exposure is created. As an example, owning silver and selling a silver future. Before Section 1092 was passed, a taxpayer could wait, sell the position with a loss (good deduction) and hold the position with a gain until the following year and/or until it became long-term to be taxed at a favorable rate.

Section 1092 was passed to prevent this, *but* it does not cover only futures! It also covers debt instruments owned, offset by liabilities of a similar maturity, *and* all other personal property not specifically excluded.

As an example of how debt instruments used to be used as a straddle, taxpayers would buy Treasury Bills maturing *next* year, borrowing the money to buy them. Treasury Bill interest is taxable at maturity (unless sold sooner) and the loan interest could be deducted currently. There are two important exclusions:

1. stocks and
2. listed options (but not over-the-counter options)

cannot be part of a tax straddle under Section 1092.

In general what Section 1092 says is that losses cannot be recognized for tax purposes except to the extent that they exceed *unrealized* gains in the position still open (05-10.5A). In addition, any interest or other carry costs related to a straddle are not deductible until the positions are closed.

Example—mixed tax straddle 05-10.5A

Sam Speculator has the following positions:

5,000 ounces of silver at $20	$100,000
Short future contract for 5,000 ounces at 21, value at purchase	–0–
Bank loan, $100,000 at 16%, six months interest paid	8,000

Spot (physical) silver moves to $25 per ounce, and the short future moves to $26.50 per ounce. Sam closes the silver contract and realizes a loss of $27,500. Sam's deduction is only $2,500! Here's why:

Loss on contract [($21 − $26.50) × 5,000]	$27,500
Unrealized gain on spot silver [($25.00 − $20) × 5,000]	25,000
Deductible loss	$ 2,500

The $25,000 loss will be deductible in the year the spot silver is sold. The $8,000 interest expense is not deductible, but rather added to the basis of the spot silver.

Tax warning 05-10.5B

If Sam allows the spot silver to attain a long-term holding period (more than one year), the interest expense will become part of a long-term transaction. This will either reduce favorably taxed long-term capital gain, or increase an only partially usable long-term loss. That is a big difference from being fully deductible interest expense (07-01).

05-10.6 Identified Straddle

Since straddles can be traded for economic gain, and are not just used for tax avoidance, Congress provided for the Identified Straddle. For a straddle to be identified:

1. the taxpayer must clearly identify all of the positions making up the straddle before the close of the day the position is taken, *and*
2. all of the positions must be acquired the same day and all of the positions must either be:

   a. closed the same day *or*

   b. still open on the last day of the tax year.

If a position is identified as a straddle, then the entire position is looked at as a unit. Gain or loss is determined based on the net sale price of the unit versus the net basis of the unit.

Taxpayers who have identified straddles may elect not to have any of the positions marked to the market at the end of the year.

05-10.7 Reporting Requirements

Except for identified straddles, hedges and straddles containing only future contracts, taxpayers must report any position with an unrealized gain if the taxpayer takes a deduction for a loss on a position in a straddle. Although there have not been any regulations issued as to the form of such a report, the format used in Example 05-10.5A should suffice.

05-10.8 Special Carryback Rules for Commodity Losses

The general rule is that if a taxpayer has a net loss from marking future contracts to the market, the taxpayer may elect to carry back the loss three years to apply for a tax refund rather than wait to carry the loss forward as with other capital losses.

The amount **carried back** may be used only to offset net gains from marking future contracts to the market. The amount carried back is carried back as 40% short-term and 60% long-term.

The amounts carried back are the *lower* of:

1. net capital gains (losses) from all sources,
2. net capital gains (losses)from marking futures to the market.

The amount carried back must be used in the oldest year first, and may not be used to increase a net operating loss.

Example—carry back **05-10.8A**

Sam Speculator had the following results:

	1982	1985
Short-term gain (loss):		
Other	–0–	(3,000)
Mark to the Market	20,000	(40,000)
Long-germ gain (loss):		
Other	(30,000)	50,000
Mark to the Market	30,000	(60,000)

Sam must first use $3,000 of his short-term losses to offset 1985 AGI.

His net short-term loss is $43,000, and his net long-term loss is $10,000. His total net capital loss is $53,000. His capital loss from mark to the market only is $50,000. ($40,000 short-term and $10,000 long-term ($60,000–$50,000) The carryback is limited to the amount which would have been carried forward. In this case $50,000 less the amount used in 1985, $3,000.

Of the $50,000 carried back, 40% is short-term and 60% is long-term. That means that $20,000 is short-term and $30,000 is long-term for carryback purposes only. Looking at the short-term first, $20,000 must be used in

1982. None of the $30,000 long-term may be used since net long-term transactions from all sources were zero. The remaining $30,000 not used in 1982 is carried to 1983 as 40% short-term ($12,000) and 60% long-term ($18,000), and the procedure is repeated.

05-10.9 The Last Game in Town

Are straddles dead? *No!* Remember one of the exceptions was listed options. Deep-in-the-money calendar spreads can be used as a tax straddle, escaping the problems of Section 1092.

As an example, suppose Teledyne (or some other volatile stock) was selling at 158 in August. Let's say the January 140 calls were selling at 30 and the April 140 calls were selling at 34. The taxpayer could:

Buy the April call	$34
Sell the January call	30
Maximum potential loss and margin requirement	$ 4

If the stock moves up in price, it is likely that some or all of the 4-point loss will be sustained. But the short January calls will also increase in price. The taxpayer could cover that short, and realize the loss. The April calls, with a built-in profit could be maintained with a different option or the stock sold short to maintain the hedge.

If the stock moved down in price, some economic gain would probably be realized. In that case the option owned could be sold at a loss, and the short option maintained against a new option position or against the stock.

As an alternative, both positions could be liquidated on December 31. Since losses are recognized on a trade date basis and gains on a settlement date basis (next day for listed options) the tax straddle would be fulfilled. Two words of caution:

1. The IRS may contend that the gain on a short sale should be recognized on a trade date basis, rather than on a settlement date basis. The subject has not been ad-

dressed, but the logic would be that the premium already had been received. The logic of postponing the gain until settlement date on a "long" sale is that the money is not received until settlement date.

2. Options are *very* specialized and risky investments. Combining their normal risk with a tax program only adds to the complications of the strategies. An option tax straddle should be entered into only with the advice of a competent investment specialist.

SHORT-TERM GOVERNMENT INSTRUMENTS 05-11

Short-term instruments issued by the federal government (basically Treasury Bills), and taxable short-term instruments issued by other levels of government, are handled in a unique manner. They generally generate fully taxable ordinary income (interest income), but under certain circumstances they can generate short-term capital gains (or capital losses). The reason that the capital gain or loss is always short-term is that the definition of "short-term government instrument" is that its original maturity is one year or less *and* it is issued at a discount and pays no interest.

The rule is that, if these instruments are held to maturity, the entire difference between the purchase price and the redemption price is ordinary interest income. If the instrument is sold at a discounted yield that is higher or lower than the discounted yield at which it was purchased, the difference between the purchase price and the selling price must be allocated between interest income and capital gain or loss. When the instrument is sold at a discount that is different from the discount at which it was purchased, then the amount of ordinary income is the ratable amount of discount earned. The remaining gain or loss on sale is short-term.

Examples 05-11.1

Sarah Investor purchased a $1,000,000 face amount Treasury Bill with 90 days left to maturity at a discount of 14%. Her purchase price is:

Amount of discount:	
$1,000,000 × .14 × 90/360	$ 35,000
Purchase price:	
Face amount	$1,000,000
Less discount	− 35,000
Purchase price	$ 965,000

If she holds the bill to maturity, the government will pay her the face amount, and she will realize $35,000 of interest income. The income will be reported in the year the bill matures.

On the other hand, if she sells the bill 60 days later at a discount of 12%, then:

Face amount	$1,000,000
Discount, $1,000,000 × 0.12 × 30/360	− 10,000
Net proceeds of sale	$ 990,000
Cost of bill	− 965,000
Profit	$ 25,000
Allocation of profit:	
Discount earned at original 14% rate:	
$1,000,000 × 0.14 × 60/360	$ 23,333
Short-term capital gain	+ 1,667
Total profit	$ 25,000

6

BUSINESS-RELATED DEDUCTIONS AND EXPENSES

06-01 DEDUCTIONS FOR ADJUSTED GROSS INCOME

Deductions for the individual taxpayer fall into two categories:

1. deductions *for* (to arrive at) Adjusted Gross Income, and
2. deductions *from* Adjusted Gross Income (AGI) to arrive at Taxable Income (01-05.2).

The distinction is important since Adjusted Gross Income is the basis for computing other deductions, such as medical expense deductions (07-07) or charitable contributions deductions (07-04). In some cases AGI also plays a role in determining whether the Zero Bracket Amount (01-05.2C) benefits the taxpayer in addition to the deduction in question.

Deductions are really expenses. Expenses themselves fall into three categories:

1. *Personal expenses* are generally not deductible. Exceptions are the subject of Chapter 7.
2. "*Nonbusiness expenses*" are the Code's way of indicating expenses related to investments. Is a taxpayer "engaged in the business of—" or simply "investing"? This question helps to determine whether an asset is a capital asset or inventory (Chapter 5). As far as expenses go, it also helps in many cases to determine whether an expense is deductible for, or from, Adjusted Gross Income. In general, and with many exceptions, nonbusiness expenses are deductions from AGI, and business expenses are deductions for AGI.
3. *Business expenses* are generally deductible for AGI, under Section 162. A Section 162 expense is:
   a. "ordinary and necessary" in the conduct of a business,
   b. not against public policy, and
   c. not prohibited by another section of the Code.

These are the general rules for expenses. Due to the many exceptions, taxpayers should examine each expenditure to see not only whether it is deductible, but also whether it is deductible for or from AGI.

EXPENDITURES NOT ALLOWED AS DEDUCTIONS 06-02

As a general rule deductions for expenditures are not allowed unless the taxpayer can cite a specific section of the Code allowing the deduction. Certain expenditures are also specifically *not* allowed as deductions by the Code. Among them are:

1. capital expenditures (06-05.1),
2. expenditures for tax-exempt income (06-05.3),
3. certain accrued, but unpaid, expenditures (10-05.2), and
4. certain payments for insurance (06-08).

06-02.1 Living Expenses

No deduction is allowed for living expenses, such as rent, food, and clothing. Yet we find in the Code a specific allowance for certain types of clothing. The expenses—laundry and cleaning—to purchase and maintain special clothing, uniforms, safety shoes, and the like are deductible from Adjusted Gross Income, if the taxpayer's job requires them. To be deductible, the clothing must not be usable for normal street wear.

Commuting to and from work is a personal expense and not deductible, but the costs of commuting to a second job are a deduction from Adjusted Gross Income. The reasoning is interesting. The IRS' point of view is that your "tax home" is your principal place of work. The deductibility of travel is measured from your tax home to your destination. When you leave your "tax home" to go home, that is a personal expense. When you leave your "tax home" to go to a second job, that is a deductible expense since it is incurred for the production of taxable income, that is, the wages you will earn.

06-03 DEDUCTIONS ALLOWED IN GENERAL

Section 162 of the Code allows the taxpayer to deduct for Adjusted Gross Income any expenses paid or incurred in carrying out a trade or business.

See paragraph 10-05 for a discussion as to when an expense may be deducted for cash and accrual taxpayers.

1. An *ordinary* expense is one that is commonly incurred in the business of the taxpayer. Whether an expense is ordinary depends on the facts of each situation, including the type of business, the industry practice, and the intent of the taxpayer.
2. The term *necessary* should not be taken in the absolute sense. An expense need only be an aid in producing income, not necessarily essential.

Nothing in the Code requires that only the least expensive means be taken. If taxpayers need to visit a customer, they can just as easily take a taxi as a bus. But the amount of the expense must be commensurate with the expected income.

Office in the Home 06-03.1

Normally, if an expense is partially business and partially personal, taxpayers may allocate between the two. As an example, if a doctor uses her car 80% for business and 20% for personal use, then she may deduct 80% of the expenses of running the car for Adjusted Gross Income. Special rules, however, govern the use of part of your personal residence in business. To deduct any part of the expenses for having a place of business in the home:

1. a portion of the home must be set aside for the *exclusive* use in business, *and*
2. the place must be the *principal* business location, *and*
3. the amount of the deduction cannot exceed the "adjusted income" from the business.

These three requirements are strictly enforced, making a deduction for expenses of an office or place of business in the home very difficult to obtain:

1. For any expense to be deductible, a room or a separate building must be set aside for the exclusive use of the business. If the room is also used for personal activities, *no* deduction is allowed.
2. The strict construction of "principal place of business" can be illustrated by the Baie case. In that case the taxpayer owned a hot dog stand. He used part of the kitchen for cooking the food, and he used another room exclusively for bookkeeping. The Tax Court allowed no deduction: The principal place of business was the hot dog stand.

3. The third test, "adjusted income," prevents the taxpayer from taking a loss on the use of an office in the home. "Adjusted income" is the Gross Income from the business, less expenses that would be allowed as a deduction even if the taxpayer were not in business. Normally, if a taxpayer loses money in a business venture, that loss can be used to offset income from other sources (01-05). But the expenses of an office in the home cannot be used to create such a loss.

06-03.1A **Example**

Roland Stone is an itinerant preacher. One of the 20 rooms in his mansion is set aside for the preparation of speeches, answering mail, and other business activities. The room is used exclusively for his business. During the year he earns $1,000 in speaking fees. The interest on his mortgage is $6,000; the real estate taxes are $4,000; depreciation is $2,000; other expenses of running the house are $12,000. Of the above amounts:

1. the interest is deductible as a personal expense (07-01),
2. the real estate taxes are deductible as a personal expense (07-03),
3. the depreciation is deductible only as a business expense (08-01),
4. the other expenses are deductible under Section 162 as ordinary and necessary business expenses.

The amount that Roland can deduct is:

Gross Income	$1,000
Less: Allocated portion of personal expenses deductible:	
5% (1 of 20 rooms) of $6,000 interest	(300)
5% of $4,000 real estate taxes	– (200)
Adjusted Income	$ 500

The Code requires that out-of-pocket expenses be taken before any depreciation is taken as a deduction. Since the total deductible portion of both is only $500, no depreciation is allowed.

Total expenses allocated:	
5% of $12,000	$ 600
5% of depreciation	100
Total	$ 700
Adjusted Income	$ 500
Less: Deductible expenses, limited to $500	− 500
Adjusted Gross Income	$ -0-

"NONBUSINESS" DEDUCTIONS 06-04

Until now we have treated nonbusiness deductions as those in support of investments. Actually, *nonbusiness deductions* are for expenses incurred in:

1. maintaining property held for investment,
2. producing and collecting income, and
3. determining tax liabilities.

Expenses related to these purposes, and not connected with the taxpayer's trade or business, are nonbusiness deductions. Nonbusiness expenses come under Section 212 of the Code, and, like Section 162 deductions:

1. the amounts spent must be commensurate with the expected income;
2. they must not be against public policy; and
3. they must not be prohibited by another section of the Code.

The property in question need not be currently producing income to qualify the expenses under Section 212. As an example, expenses incurred to maintain stock certificates that are not paying dividends, such as a bank safe deposit box, would be deductible.

Expenses incurred to produce rent and royalty income are deductions *for* Adjusted Gross Income. With the exception of such expenses, nonbusiness expenses are otherwise deductions *from* Adjusted Gross Income. Nonbusiness deductions from Adjusted Gross Income include: union dues, the cost of preparing income tax returns, and fees incurred obtaining tax planning advice.

06-04.1 "Vacation" Home Rental

Normally, any losses sustained in the management of rental property can be used to reduce Adjusted Gross Income from other sources.

06-04.1A Example

Ms. Taxpayer has $50,000 of salary, $10,000 of gross rental income, and $12,000 of expenses related to that rental income. Her Adjusted Gross Income would be:

Salary		$50,000
Gross rental income	$10,000	
Less: Rental expenses, deductions for AGI	−12,000	(2,000)
Adjusted Gross Income		$48,000

06-04.1B Limitation of deductions

Special rules apply to so-called "vacation" home rentals. The object of the law is to limit the deductions to no more than the related income, thereby eliminating the reduction of other items of Adjusted Gross Income.

The law is aimed not only at vacation homes, but

also at any home rented to a family member or under a so-called "exchange agreement." In an *exchange agreement,* taxpayers rent homes to each other. Prior to the passage of this section of the Code, taxpayers could convert personal nondeductible living expenses into a deduction, thus:

1. Taxpayer A buys a house and rents to Taxpayer B at a loss.
2. Taxpayer B buys a house and rents to Taxpayer A at a loss.

Now, for a rental to be classified as a "vacation" home, two conditions must be met.

1. The home must *not* be the principal residence of the taxpayer. And . . .
2. It must be used for personal use for the *greater* of 14 days or 10% of the rental period. If a vacation home is rented for less than 14 days during the year, none of the rent income need be reported, nor may any expenses be deducted.

"Personal use" includes:

1. use by the taxpayer or his/her *family, or*
2. use as part of an exchange agreement, *or*
3. rental to anyone at less than fair market value.

As you can see from these definitions, the house need not be used for vacations, although most of the cases fall into this category. Note that the "use by family" prevents taxpayers from buying their parents' homes and renting it back, in order to convert personal nondeductible living expenses into deductions for AGI.

If a rental property qualifies as a vacation home, the deductions are limited to "adjusted income," which in this case is the gross rent collected less personal expenses that would have been deductible as such. First, out-of-pocket expenses are deducted, then any depreciation is deducted.

06-04.1C **Example**

Dorothy Ghoti owns a beach house in Hoboken. She holds it out for rent for eleven months of the year, and uses it herself for one month. Of the months that the house is available for rent, she rents it for three months. The total rent collected is $3,000. Her expenses for the year are:

Real estate taxes (07-03)	$1,000
Mortgage interest (07-01)	1,500
Utilities and maintenance	2,867
Depreciation (08-01)	+1,800
Total	$7,167

Dorothy must allocate the expenses between personal and rental. Since the house is rented for three months (the rental period), and since she uses it for one month, 75% of the utilities and maintenance expenses are allocated to the rental. Expenses that would have been incurred without regard to whether the house was occupied or not are allocated on an annual basis. The unoccupied period is considered personal. In this case 25% of taxes and interest (3 of 12 months) is allocated to the rental. So Dorothy's Adjusted Gross Income from the rental is:

Gross rents received		$3,000
Less: Expenses that would be deductible as personal expenses:		
Real estate taxes ($1,000 × 0.25)	$ 250	
Mortgage interest ($1,500 × 0.25)	+ 375	− 625
Adjusted income		$2,375
Out-of-pocket expenses ($2,867 × 0.75)		−2,150
Income before depreciation		$ 225
Depreciation, limited to $225 $1,800 × 0.25 = $450, limit		− 225
Adjusted Gross Income		$ -0-

If the rental property had not been classified as a vacation home, then Dorothy could deduct the entire depreciation. Her AGI would then be:

Income before depreciation	$ 225
Less: Depreciation	− 450
Adjusted Gross Income (loss)	$(225)

NONDEDUCTIBLE BUSINESS EXPENDITURES 06-05

Under Section 162, most expenditures made by taxpayers in the conduct of a trade or business are deductible. But some expenditures are not deductible by specific provisions of the Code.

Capital Expenditures 06-05.1

Expenditures for the acquisition of assets with a useful life of more than a year are not deductible. Nor are expenditures that increase the useful life of assets beyond the current tax year. Such expenditures, called *capital expenditures,* create assets that must be depreciated over their useful lives (08-01).

If an asset's useful life cannot be determined, then no depreciation is allowed. The expenditure is merely part of the basis of the asset, and it reduces any gain or increases any loss when the asset is sold. Land, franchises, and goodwill fall into this category. *Goodwill* is the amount paid for a going concern above the fair market value of the assets required.

One asset with an undeterminable useful life can be amortized: *Organization expenses* (that is, the costs of starting a business, such as legal fees) have an undeterminable useful life in most cases. Taxpayers may elect to amortize these expenses over a period of 60 months.

06-05.1A **Example**

Aaron and Barney decide to go into business and form a partnership. To draw up the partnership agreement and to register their trade name, they pay $1,000 in legal fees, which are organization expenses. They may elect to carry this asset on their books until they sell the business, and it would be part of their basis in the business. Or they may elect to amortize it over 60 months, and they will show a deductible expense of $16.67 per month ($1,000 divided by 60 months). Any amount taken as a deduction will not be included in their basis.

06-05.2 Political Expenditures

No deduction is allowed for expenses in connection with any candidate for public office or for any support of a political party. This prohibition extends to all such expenses, including dinner tickets, advertisements in political papers, and the like.

Individual taxpayers may claim a credit for one-half of contributions made to political parties or candidates running for public office. The amount of the credit is limited to $50 per taxpayer ($100 on a joint return). (See 09-06 for a discussion of tax credits.)

06-05.3 Expenses for Tax-Exempt Income

No deduction is allowed for any expenses incurred for the production of tax-exempt income. A good illustration of how this prohibition works, as well as how deductions for and from Adjusted Gross Income operate, involves fees paid to attorneys. If an attorney fee is paid:

1. in a business or trade, or for obtaining rental income, the amount is a deduction for AGI;
2. for the procurement of taxable alimony (03-11), the amount is a deduction from AGI, since that is nonbusiness income;

3. for obtaining a tax-free lump sum distribution in divorce (03-11), it is not deductible.

If a *loan* is obtained for the purpose of purchasing tax-exempt municipal bonds, the interest on that loan is not deductible. Municipal bonds used as collateral in a margin account fall into this category. If a loan is obtained to acquire assets, some of which generate taxable income and some of which generate tax-exempt income, the amount of interest disallowed is prorated based on the income received.

Payments Against Public Policy 06-05.4

No deduction is allowed for payments for bribery of public officials or for other payments that violate national or local law. Under this category, payments for traffic tickets and other fines are not deductible (06-05.4A).

Expenses incurred in the production of illegal income, on the other hand, are deductible from such income in figuring the Adjusted Gross Income from such operations.

Example 06-05.4A

The MBS Trucking Company operates between New York and Hoboken. On occasion their trucks are stopped and ticketed for over-weight in violation of local highway laws. After several studies, the company finds that it would be cheaper to continue to pay the over-weight fines than to purchase and operate another truck. So, even though the fines are less expensive than the purchase of a new truck, the payments are not deductible, since that would frustrate the intent of the highway laws.

PENSIONS 06-06

Although this section deals with the income tax aspects of the multitude of pension plans now available, the subject of pension plans under the Internal Revenue Code and under ERISA (Employee Retirement Insurance Security Act) is involved enough to warrant a textbook by itself.

Section 401 deals with the qualification requirements of pension plans. In practice, suffice it to say that most pension plans are submitted to the Internal Revenue Service for a private ruling, or they are part of a prototype that has been previously approved. Following either of these approaches is the only "sure" way to insure that a plan is "qualified." The advantages of qualification are as follows:

1. Employer contributions are deductible.
2. Income earned by the fund is exempt from income tax.
3. Beneficiaries are taxed only on distribution.
4. Under some plans, the distributions are taxed at favorable rates (09-05).
5. Under certain circumstances, the value of the death benefits attributable to the employer's contributions may be excluded for estate tax purposes (14-02).

The thrust of Section 401 is not only to set up a plan that does not discriminate in favor of highly paid employees, but also to insure that the benefits of the average employee are protected.

Although pension plan payments can be made without qualifying under Section 401 (under Section 162, ordinary and necessary), they are impractical. First, the employer must justify the payments as being reasonable as part of an overall compensation program. More importantly, the employer does not get a deduction for the payments until the beneficiary includes them in income. So inclusion occurs only after the employee is vested. Under such a plan, separate accounts must be kept for each employee. Consequently, this section is limited to qualified plans, including those for the self-employed.

Qualification Requirements 06-06.1

To be qualified, a plan's most important points must meet:

1. the minimum vesting requirement,
2. the minimum participation requirements,
3. separate benefits requirement, and
4. nondiscriminatory requirement.

Minimum vesting requirement 06-06.1A

For a plan to qualify, the employees must be immediately vested for all contributions made by the employee, and they must be completely vested for all employer contributions when they attain retirement age. In addition, the employer must choose one of three interim vesting rules:

1. All employes in the plan must be 100% vested after 10 years.
2. Employees become 25% vested after 5 years, with 5% additional vesting accruing each year for the next 5 years, and 10% additional vesting accruing for each of the following 5 years.
3. Employees with at least 5 years of service become 50% vested when the sum of their years of service plus their age equals 45. After that, they become 10% vested for each additional year of service.

Minimum participation requirements 06-06.1B

Employees must be admitted into the plan (although they do not become vested) either when they reach age 25 or when they attain one year of service, whichever comes later. A "year of service" is any 12-month period in which the employee has worked 1,000 hours or more.

A plan still qualifies if it provides vesting after 3

years of service and allows participation to begin after 3 years of service.

A defined benefits plan (06-06.5) is not required to include employees who are hired within 5 years of their normal retirement age.

06-06.1C **Separate Benefits**

Although a qualified plan may include medical and life insurance benefits, no more than 25% of the contribution may be made for these purposes, and special accountability rules must be followed.

06-06.1D **Nondiscriminatory requirement**

The Code sets up several mathematical tests for nondiscrimination. But the real test is that the IRS does not find that the classifications set up by the employer discriminate in favor of highly paid employees or officers. In this area, a private letter ruling or following a prototype is essential.

Special rules allow for separate plans where some employees are covered under a pension plan negotiated as part of collective bargaining.

06-06.2 Defined Contribution Plan

A *defined contribution plan* simply allows the employer to contribute a fixed percentage of employees' salaries into the pension fund. Each employee has his or her own "acount" in which the contributions are accumulated. At retirement, the benefits that the employee receives depend on the amount that has been accumulated in the account.

Contributions for each employee are limited to the *lesser* of 25% of compensation or $41,500 per year (as of January 1, 1981). Compensation may be defined as either including or excluding overtime and bonuses. If bonuses are included, then overtime must also be included. The maximum dollar amount is adjusted periodically to reflect inflation.

Obviously, some discrimination is allowed in favor of highly paid employees since the contributions may be based on compensation. Here, as in all qualified plans, nondiscrimination does not exclude using a percentage of compensation.

Tax hint 06-06.2A

Defined contribution plans are fairly well suited for the large, privately held company, which takes an altruistic approach to its employees. But these plans have no real direction. Other plans (described below) offer far more in terms of rewards to the company and its executives.

Profit-Sharing Trust 06-06.3

A *profit-sharing* trust is a type of defined contribution plan that bases the amount of contribution to the pension trust on income, *if any.* The maximum contribution to the fund for any year is 15% of compensation paid. If in any year, however, the company pays less than the full 15% allowed, that difference may be contributed in any future year. The total contribution for any *one* year cannot exceed 25% of compensation paid in that year.

Tax hint 06-06.3A

Profit-sharing plans are well suited for the company in a cyclical industry where in a bad year the pension plan requirements could be an unwanted burden.

Profit-sharing plans, when sold to the employees properly, can be an excellent tool in promoting "team spirit"—"When the company makes money, we *all* make money!"

06-06.4 Stock Bonus Plan

A qualified *stock bonus plan* is a profit-sharing plan, in which the employer contributes company stock, instead of cash, into the trust. The Code confers special treatment to a qualified stock ownership plan (TRASOP or ESOP). Companies may claim a tax credit for certain payments to the plan.

The effect of the credit is to reduce the cost of the plan, and in some cases the tax credit could pay 100% of the cost.

06-06.4A **Tax *warning***

A TRASOP *must* be approved by the IRS. Written approval of the plan must be obtained within 90 days of claiming the credit.

06-06.5 Defined Benefits Plan

All of the preceding plans ask the question: "How much does the employer wish to contribute?" A defined benefits program asks the question: "How much does the *employee* get out of the plan?" This shift in direction is the key to defined *benefits.* For example, if an employer wants employees to retire at 50% of the pay they are receiving, how much does the employer have to put into the plan to accomplish that goal?

The answer to that question depends on:

1. *The age of the employee:* The total contributed for each employee, in each year, cannot exceed the lesser of 25% of annual compensation *or* $41,500 (as of January 1, 1981, the dollar limit is increased periodically for inflation).
2. *The length of service:* The maximum benefits that can

accrue to any employee vary with the employee's length of service. An employee with at least 10 years of service can receive annual benefits that are the lesser of:

a. $124,500 (as of January 1, 1981), periodically adjusted for inflation, or
b. 100% of the average compensation for his or her highest three consecutive years.

A defined benefits program may be integrated with Social Security. Such coordination provides additional flexibility with regard to how much of the contributions will be for the benefit of each participant.

Example 06-06.5A

Dr. Mark Cummings, D.D.S., P.A. (a professional corporation), set up a defined benefits program for its only two employees. They are:

1. Dr. Mark Cummings, D.D.S., salary $50,000 per year, age 53;
2. Miss Anna Corlin, dental assistant, salary $12,000, age 33.

The benefits are defined as 33.3% of monthly compensation in excess of $900. Benefits are to be integrated with Social Security. The normal retirement age is 65.

Two items enable the dentist to receive a far greater share of each annual contribution. First, he is closer to retirement, and therefore the funds needed to provide his benefits must be accumulated in a shorter period of time. Second, Social Security provides a higher percentage of his assistant's benefits, because Social Security benefits are not directly proportional to salary.

Here is how the annual contribution and the benefits would be computed. (Of course, these figures are for illustration purposes only, and they should not be used in an actual pension plan situation. Each plan should be approved by the IRS, as explained.)

Dr. Cummings:		
Monthly compensation	$4,167	
Monthly payments from pension plan		$1,088
Monthly Social Security		+ 538
Total defined benefit		$1,626
Miss Corlin:		
Monthly compensation	$1,000	
Monthly payments from pension plan		$ 33
Monthly Social Security		+ 438
Total defined benefit		$ 471

Notice that Miss Corlin's total benefits, as a percentage of total salary, actually exceed those of Dr. Cummings. This is quite common due to the Social Security integration. The annual contribution for these benefits would be:

For Dr. Cummings	$11,762
For Miss Corlin	+ 99
Total annual contribution	$11,861

06-06.5B **Tax hint**

What kinds of companies would go for a defined benefits program? Obviously, from our example, those in which the owners wish to "discriminate" in favor of themselves. Although each "employee population" must be studied separately, the defined benefits plan is the one most likely to produce the highest rewards for the older owner of a company.

06-06.6 Self-Employed Retirement Plan (Keogh Plan)

The owner of a sole proprietorship, a partner in a partnership, and a stockholder in a Subchapter S corporation (12-09) are not employees for the purpose of contributions to pension plans. These taxpayers are considered to be self-employed for pension plan purposes. So they are subject to far greater restrictions on contributions for their own benefit.

Yet they may set up Keogh Plans in which the annual deductible contribution limits are the lesser of $15,000 or 15% of earned income. In some cases a minimum contribution is allowed, which is the lesser of $750 or 100% of earned income.

Additional nondeductible contributions may be made up to the lesser of 10% of earned income or $2,500. If such a plan is adopted, all employees must have the same rights to make similar nondeductible contributions. Although no current deduction is allowed, the income earned on that money is not taxed until it is withdrawn from the plan.

These limitations do not apply to a defined benefits plan.

As with any pension plan, employees of the self-employed are protected by nondiscriminatory requirements that apply to Keogh Plans:

1. The self-employed taxpayer may not withdraw funds from the plan before reaching the age of 59½ except due to death or permanent disability. A 10% penalty tax is assessed for any such premature withdrawal.
2. The self-employed taxpayer must begin an organized plan of withdrawal from the plan when reaching age 70½.
3. The maximum amount of earnings from self-employment that may be used in computing whether a defined contribution plan is discriminatory is $200,000.
4. A 6% penalty tax is assessed for any excess contributions not withdrawn by the time the taxpayer's return is filed.

Tax hint 06-06.6A

Keogh Plans are particularly well suited for the part-time consultant. Many professionals are covered by retirement plans with their full-time employers. Often they are called on as expert witnesses, guest speakers, or special consultants of one sort or another. Fees received for such work are generally earnings from self-employment. Since these fees are normally added on to an already high incremental tax bracket, the opportunity to set up a "second" retirement fund in the form of a Keogh Plan should not be overlooked.

06-06.7 Individual Retirement Arrangements (IRAs)

Employees may set up an IRA. The amount they contribute to the IRA is a deduction for Adjusted Gross Income.

Contributions are limited to the lesser of $2,000 or earned income. Married employees, whose spouses do not work, may set up two IRA accounts: one for themselves and a subaccount for their spouses. The amounts contributed to any one account may not exceed $2,000. If such an arrangement is made, the contribution limit is the lesser of earned income or $2,250.

IRA accounts are subject to the same age and tax penalty provisions as a Keogh Plan (06-06.6).

Distributions from an IRA account are *not* subject to lump sum distribution taxation (09-05).

06-06.8 Simplified Pension Plans

Employers may establish IRA accounts for their employees. In such a case, the *employer* may contribute up to a maximum of $7,500 into the account (limited to 15% of compensation) instead of the $2,000 limit imposed on the *employee's* contributions.

No separate account for a nonworking spouse is permitted under a simplified pension plan.

Rollovers 06-06.9

Taxpayers may "transfer" funds from one pension plan to another without tax consequences. A transfer must be directly from one plan to another, and the funds may never be in the hands of the taxpayer.

In a rollover situation, taxpayers do take possession of the pension funds. But, if funds are distributed to taxpayers from their pension plans, they have 60 days to "rollover" the funds into an IRA account and thus to avoid taxation.

Partial rollovers are also permitted. In this way taxpayers may choose to be taxed on some portion of the distribution and defer tax on another portion.

Rollovers and transfers must conform exactly to the Code. It is wise to obtain a written tax opinion prior to any transfer or rollover from either the pension plan manager or outside tax counsel.

EXPENDITURES FOR REAL AND PERSONAL PROPERTY 06-07

Certain expenditures for real and personal property deserve special attention . . .

Repairs Versus Improvements 06-07.1

Repair expenses follow the rules for other expenses, as discussed earlier in this chapter. But the question can arise as to whether an expenditure is a repair or an improvement. An improvement would not be deductible, but rather a capital expenditure (06-05.1). The line between what is a repair and what is an improvement is often a fuzzy one. Yet, as a guide, a *repair* maintains an asset's operating efficiency. An *improvement*, on the other hand, must either:

1. extend the useful life of an asset; *or*
2. add value to the asset; *or*
3. change or increase an asset's productivity.

As an example, a new roof would be a capital expenditure; fixing an existing roof would be a repair.

06-07.2 Lease Cancellation Payments

Lease cancellation payments made by the landlord are generally considered a capital expenditure. The motives for the payment must be examined to determine over what period of time, if any, the payments might be amortized. If, as an example, the payment is made so that a new, and more profitable, lease could be signed, then the lease cancellation payment would be amortized over the life of the new lease (06-07.2A). But if a landlord made such a payment to cancel a lease for the purpose of razing the building, the expenditure might be considered part of the cost of the land. Since land does not have a determinable useful life, no amortization would be allowed.

Lease cancellation payments made by the lessee, however, are generally considered an expense, rather than a capital expenditure. Such a payment would be a deduction if made for business or nonbusiness reasons. See 06-11 for a deduction for personal expenses to cancel a lease as part of a moving expense adjustment.

06-07.2A Example

Sam Landlord pays the tenant of his building $10,000 to cancel the lease he was under and to vacate the property. He does so to sign a more profitable 10-year lease with a new tenant. The expenditure of $10,000 is a capital expenditure, and it must be amortized over the 10-year period. Sam deducts $1,000 per year ($10,000 divided by 10 years) against the rental income on the new lease.

Lease Versus Purchase

06-07.3

In some lease situations the IRS looks through the legality of a contract to its economic reality. The Service can classify what is legally a lease as a sale from the lessor to the lessee. This reclassification can be extremely important. Normally, the "owner" of the property is significantly better off tax-wise than the lessee, because the owner is entitled to:

1. the investment credit (09-07),
2. accelerated cost recovery (08-01), and
3. an interest deduction that is normally higher in the earlier years of a lease or purchase.

Yet a more important consequence hangs on the lease-or-sale question: Are the proceeds capital gains to the seller? Or are they rent or royalty income to the lessor?

The lessee is entitled to deduct "rent" expense. Such a deduction is normally at an even rate over the life of the lease.

No specific event or term of a lease causes the IRS to reclassify the contract as a sale. (See 06-07.3B for a "safe harbor" rule.) Revenue Ruling 55-540 notes that the intent of the parties controls the reclassification, and no test, or combination of tests, is absolutely determinative. However, here are some guidelines as to when this determination might be made:

1. If the lessee can acquire title for a nominal amount.
2. If the terms of the lease cover substantially the full useful life of the asset. Or . . .
3. Part of the rent is called interest, or if the terms of the contract are such that interest payments are apparent.

Regulation 1.48-4 allows the lessor to elect to allow the lessee to claim the investment credit. This election applies only to new property, not to used property. The general rule is that the amount of the credit is based on the fair market value of the asset at the time the lease is entered into. The life of the asset is the lessor's useful life, not the life of the lease.

06-07.3A **Tax *warning***

Not only can the IRS attempt to change a contract from a lease to a sale, or vice versa, but so can one of the parties to the contract. Often, the reason the IRS and the courts get involved is because the two parties to a single contract treat it differently in their tax returns.

In any contract that might be subject to interpretation, it is wise to include how each of the parties should regard it. Keep in mind that intent is important, and that intent should be expressed in the contract. Often, the tax considerations materially affect the amount of "rent" that the lessee is willing to pay and that the lessor is willing to accept.

Take advantage of the ability to "direct" the investment credit. Since this can amount to 10% or more of the fair market value, it is certainly worth putting into the contract.

06-07.3B **Safe harbor for leases**

Section 168(f)(8) provides a safe harbor for leases where the lessor is a corporation and certain conditions are met. If all of the conditions of this section are met, the IRS may not reclassify a lease as a purchase and sale. The more important of these conditions are:

1. the property leased is personal property on which the taxpayer may claim the investment credit; and
2. the lessor at all times during the lease had an investment in the property of at least 10% of his adjusted basis in the property; and
3. the term of the lease is for not more than 90% of the useful life (as defined) of the property.

The safe harbor rule is available only for new property.

The amount of the lessor's investment does not include any financing provided by the lessee or any nonrecourse financing.

INSURANCE PREMIUMS 06-08

Insurance premiums fall into three categories:

1. *Life Insurance Premiums:* As a general rule *life insurance premiums* are nondeductible expenses, even if they are incurred for a business or nonbusiness purpose. The rule makes sense since, by and large, the proceeds payable on death are tax-exempt (02-03).

   Life insurance premiums paid by an employer on behalf of its employees are deductible within limits. As explained in 03-04.1, these premiums may be deductible if they are considered part of the employee's compensation. In such an event, employees may have to include certain amounts in their Gross Income with other compensation earned.
2. *Health Insurance Premiums:* Health insurance is generally a deductible expense. If the premiums are personal in nature, they are deductible, within limits, from Adjusted Gross Income (07-07). Payments by an employer on behalf of its employees are deductible by the employer, but not included in the income of the employee (02-06.3).
3. *All Others:* Other than for life and health, insurance premiums are considered to be an expense, and they follow the general rules for business, nonbusiness, and personal expenses.

TRAVEL AND TRANSPORTATION EXPENSES 06-09

Transportation expenses relate to those expenses incurred in local "travel," normally not requiring an overnight stay. Local transportation expenses (taxis, carfare, automobile expenses, tolls, and the like), incurred in a trade or business, are deductible for Adjusted Gross Income. Transportation expenses incurred for the maintenance of rent and royalty income, or by an "outside salesperson," are also deductible for Adjusted Gross Income. Transportation expenses incurred for other nonbusiness purposes are deductions from Adjusted Gross Income.

Amounts spent by employees (other than outside salespersons) in excess of the amounts reimbursed by their employers are deductible from Adjusted Gross Income.

Travel expenses relate to expenses incurred in distant "travel," normally requiring an overnight stay. Travel expenses include all transportation expenses, plus:

1. food and lodging, and
2. incidental expenses such as laundry.

Travel expenses follow the same general rules as transportation expenses as to deductibility. To be eligible as a travel expense deduction, the trip must be long enough to "normally" require the taxpayer to obtain rest and sleep. There is no need to actually stay overnight.

06-09.1 **Example**

Aaron Gordon's business is in New Jersey. Because he is required to "travel" to Washington, D.C. for a sales meeting, he flies there early in the morning and returns the same night. The trip to Washington is subject only to transportation expense deductions. These include taxis to and from the airports, air fare, and tips to the porter to carry his sample case. He may not deduct the cost of meals in Washington as a travel expense. (See 06-10, as his meals may qualify as entertainment expenses.)

The following week, Aaron has to travel to San Francisco to another sales meeting. He leaves early in the morning and, due to the time zone changes, was there in plenty of time for a 1:00 P.M. meeting. He takes the "red eye" back, which leaves San Francisco at 10:00 P.M., and arrives back in New Jersey the following morning. Although he did not stay overnight, the trip is one that would normally require rest and sleep. The trip qualifies as "travel," and Aaron's cost of meals are deductible travel expenses.

06-09.2 **Automobile Expenses**

Taxpayers may compute actual automobile expenses for the purpose of determining travel and transportation costs. Expenses would include depreciation (08-01) as well as costs of operating the vehicle such as gas, oil, repairs, maintenance, and similar expenses.

If the automobile is used partly for business and partly for personal use, the taxpayer must allocate these expenses between those that are deductible business or nonbusiness expenses and those that are nondeductible personal expenses. The allocation is based on the percentage of mileage used for each purpose.

Alternatively, rather than maintaining the records that would be required to prove the amount of deductible expense, the IRS permits the use of a mileage allowance. This allows taxpayers to keep records only on the mileage used for business and nonbusiness purposes. The mileage allowances for 1980 are equal to the actual parking and tolls, *plus*:

1. 20¢ per mile for the first 15,000 miles of business and nonbusiness use (see below for an exception);
2. 11¢ per mile for all business and nonbusiness mileage over 15,000;
3. 9¢ per mile for transportation for medical (07-07) and charitable (07-04) purposes.

The mileage allowance of 11¢ per mile (rather than 20¢ per mile) must be used for any automobile that has been fully depreciated for tax purposes or that is over five years old.

Tax hint 06-09.2A

Many companies reimburse their employees for mileage expenses based on so many cents per mile. If the amount of such reimbursements is less than the permitted allowances, the difference is deductible. Since many employers use the amount allowed by the IRS as a mileage allowance, and since most of the allowance increases in recent years have been retroactive, many employees have such a deduction.

As an example, the mileage allowance rates for 1980, retroactive to January 1, were not announced until July of 1980. If Mr. Taxpayer had been reimbursed at the old rate of 18½¢ for 10,000 business miles driven between January

1, 1980 and June 30, 1980, he would have a deduction of $150 computed as follows:

10,000 miles at allowable rates, 20¢	$2,000
Less: Amount of reimbursement (18½¢ × 10,000)	1,850
Deductible amount	$ 150

More important, if the employee's *actual* expenses exceed the amount of the reimbursement, the difference is deductible.

06-09.2B **Tax hint**

When an automobile is used partly for business and partly for personal use, the business portion is eligible for the investment credit (09-07). As an example, an automobile cost $10,000, the investment credit on it would be $600. If the automobile were used 40% for business and 60% for personal use, the taxpayer could claim a credit of $240 ($600 × 0.40) in addition to any deductions.

06-09.3 Foreign Travel

For travel within the United States, the entire cost of travel to the destination is deductible if the trip is primarily for business. Of course, any personal expenses, such as side trips while at the destination, would not be deductible. For foreign travel, however, and especially for foreign travel to conventions (other than for conventions in Canada and Mexico), special rules limit the deductibility of travel expenses. For travel abroad, taxpayers must allocate all costs, including transportation to the destination, between business and personal. No allocation (other than that required for domestic travel) is required if:

1. the taxpayer is an employee who has no control over

the destination of the trip and is reimbursed for expenses by the employer;

2. the trip lasts for a week or less; or
3. less than 25% of the time was spent on personal activities.

Taxpayers are allowed to deduct the cost of attending conventions held outside of the United States, Canada, or Mexico only if it is just "as reasonable" for the convention to be held where it is, as it would be for the convention to be held in North America. The purpose, activities, and residence of the members of the sponsoring organization must all be taken into account.

Recordkeeping Requirements 06-09.4

To deduct travel and transportation expenses, the taxpayer must keep accurate records of expenses, including receipts for all expenditures over $25 and for all lodging expenses.

Expenses for a Spouse 06-09.5

The expenses of bringing spouses or other family members along on a business trip are generally not deductible unless the taxpayer can show that their presence was for a business purpose. What constitutes a "business purpose"? Two interesting court cases treat this question. In Wilkins v. U.S., a foreign service officer was allowed to deduct the cost of his wife accompanying him since it relieved him of "incidental" duties and allowed him more time for "substantive" duties. In U.S. v. Disney, the "family type" business required a wife's presence on business trips. Obviously, the type of business and the purpose of the trip must be considered, as well as the spouse's "duties" with regard to business.

Entertainment expenses present a unique tax situation. Over the years, more than any other business or non-business deduction, entertainment has attracted the attention of the Congress and the public. The "three-martini lunch" has been indirectly attacked several times. As a result, the rules for deducting entertainment expenses are a maze of dotting the *i*s and crossing the *t*s. So to be deductible, entertainment expenses must in some case be more than ordinary and necessary; they must be "directly related."

Expenses that may be deducted under the ordinary and necessary test are as follows:

1. *Business meals,* under certain circumstances, are generally considered to be conducive to a business discussion. This same rule applies to beverages served apart from meals. Meals or beverages served in the taxpayer's home would fall into this category if the expenses were commercially, rather than socially, motivated. A night club, or any place where entertainment is a major attraction, is generally not considered a suitable environment for a business discussion. If you establish that the circumstances are conducive to a business discussion, it is not essential that business actually be discussed.
2. The *cost of meals that are part of a business program or banquet* sponsored by a business or professional association are deductible. It is not always necessary that the taxpayer attend the lunch or dinner.
3. *Corporate membership costs* for country club dining facilities, when used by designated officers and executives for entertaining prospective customers, negotiating business, and holiday and similar parties, are deductible business expenses.
4. *Taxpayers' own meals* are deductible while entertaining for business purposes, as long as they are not

claiming deductions for substantial amounts of personal living expenses.

5. The cost of food and beverages furnished for *company cafeterias* or *executive dining rooms* used primarily for employees is deductible.
6. Taxpayers may deduct the ordinary and necessary *cost of providing entertainment* or *recreational facilities* to the general public as a means of advertising or promoting goodwill in the community.
7. Expenses for *business gifts* made directly or indirectly to any individual are deductible. The total of the business gifts made during the tax year to any one individual cannot be more than $25. (See 02-07.3A for an exception for certain gifts made to employees.)

Other than these seven exceptions, entertainment expenses must meet the "directly-related-to-business test" to be deductible. For an entertainment expenditure to meet the directly-related test, taxpayers must show that:

1. they had more than a general expectation of deriving income or some other specific benefit at some future time; and
2. they *did* engage in business during the entertainment period with the person being entertained; and
3. the principal characteristic or aspect of the combined business and entertainment was the transaction of the taxpayer's business.

The taxpayer is not required to show that business income or some other business benefit actually resulted from each and every entertainment expenditure.

Certain other guidelines should be kept in mind:

1. The costs of certain entertainment facilities are not deductible, such as: a yacht, hunting lodge, fishing camp, swimming pool, tennis court, bowling alley, apartment, hotel suite, or a home in a vacation area.

Only the out-of-pocket expenses of a particular event at such a facility are deductible under the general entertainment rules.

2. A country club is considered to be an entertainment facility. Unless the club is used more than 50% for business purposes, no deduction is allowed for dues and fees. If the club is used more than 50% for business, then the dues and fees may be allocated between deductible and nondeductible. The allocation is based on the number of days the club is used for business versus the number of days it is used for personal reasons. Initiation or membership fees that are payable only once to join a country club are not deductible; they are a capital expenditure. Dues to a luncheon club or to any club operated solely to provide business lunches are not considered dues to a country club.
3. Box seats or season tickets to theaters or sporting events are not treated under the country club rules. Taxpayers must allocate the cost of these items to the separate amusement events. The expenses for one event may be deductible regardless of whether or not the box seats or season tickets are used more than 50% for business purposes.

06-10.1 Recordkeeping Rules:

No deduction for entertainment is allowed unless the taxpayer can prove the following:

1. the amount of each separate expenditure;
2. the date the entertainment took place;
3. the name and address of the place of entertainment and the type of entertainment;
4. the reason for the entertainment, including the benefit derived or expected to be derived; and

5. the name, title, and business relationship of the person entertained.

Records should be maintained in a diary or account book, and they should be recorded in a timely manner. If the recorded entries are made later, when there is a lack of accurate recall, they will not comply with the substantiation rules. Receipts for all expenditures of $25 or more must be retained.

Tax *warning* 06-10.2

Keep a current and accurate diary! Entertainment expenses are a "targeted" item in many audits. The expense could be the most legitimate expense of the year; but if it does not meet the recordkeeping requirements, no deduction is allowed. If you pay cash, get a receipt! Tape it into your diary, so it does not get lost.

Tax Hint 06-10.3

The unreimbursed entertainment expenses of an employee are not deductible unless the employer *expects* the employee to make such an expenditure. Most firms expect their professionals and executives to remain current in industry practices and developments. Keeping in touch with the competition may be just as important as keeping in contact with customers. In fact, keeping up-to-date often is essential to "corporate survival."

Before an audit, get a letter from the personnel department of your company to the effect that you are expected to remain current with regard to industry changes. Most taxpayers are very surprised by the amounts of money that is spent in this area. The expense may not be the kind that your employer will reimburse you for, but it may be deductible!

06-10.4 Tax Hint

Bring the spouse along! The cost of the meals and beverages of your spouse while joining you in business entertainment is deductible.

06-11 MOVING EXPENSE ADJUSTMENT

Taxpayers may be entitled to deduct for Adjusted Gross Income the cost of moving to a new location for the purpose of accepting employment. The deductible costs include both the direct and the indirect expenses of moving, including certain costs that would normally be capitalized. To qualify, taxpayers must meet two tests:

1. The *distance test* is that the taxpayer's *new* job must be at least 35 miles farther from the *old* residence than the *old* job. For example, if the old job is 3 miles from the old residence, then the new job must be at least 38 miles from the old residence. (Members of the armed forces need not meet the distance test.)
2. The *time test* is that taxpayers must work full-time at least 39 weeks during the first 12 months after the move. For self-employed taxpayers, the time test requires that they work full-time for:
   a. 39 weeks in the *first* 12 months after the move; *and*
   b. 78 weeks during the first 24 months after the move.

Moving expenses may be deducted in anticipation of meeting the time test. If taxpayers later fail to meet the test, then they must file an amended return. Or they may elect not to claim the deduction until after meeting the time test, and file an amended return for a refund.

Reimbursements from an employer for moving expenses must be included in Gross Income. If employees expect to receive reimbursements from their employers in the following year, they may elect to delay taking the deduction until the year of the reimbursement. This approach prevents having to take the expense in one year and the taxable reimbursement in the next.

The time tests are waived in the case of death, disability, or involuntary termination by the employer, except for misconduct.

More liberal rules exist for foreign moves. Retired persons moving back to the United States may also qualify.

Deductible Expenses 06-11.1

Deductible moving expenses fall into three categories:

1. 100% deductible:
   a. transportation expenses in moving household goods and personal effects.
   b. travel, meals, and lodging expenses in moving from former to new residence;
2. deductible up to a limit of $3,000:
   a. expenses either for the sale of the former residence or for settlement of an unexpired lease if renting,
   b. expenses for buying a new residence, or for getting a new lease if renting,
   c. no more than $1,500 of pre-move and temporary living expenses in the new location during *any* 30 consecutive days *after* getting a job.

Transportation expenses in moving household goods and personal effects include: cost of packing, crating, moving, storing in transit, and insuring the taxpayer's household goods and personal effects.

Travel, meals, and *lodging expenses* in moving from the former to the new residence include the costs on the day of arrival. There is no need for the family to travel together or at the same time, as long as each person is a member of the household before and after the move. Taxpayers who use their own cars may figure the expenses in either of two ways:

1. actual out-of-pocket expenses for gas, oil, repairs, parking and tolls; or
2. 9¢ per mile plus parking and tolls.

Expenses for the *purchase and sale of the two residences,* or for the settlement and acquisition of the leases include:

1. sales commissions,
2. advertising costs,
3. attorney's fees,
4. title and escrow fees,
5. state transfer taxes, and
6. costs to settle an unexpired lease or to buy a new lease.

Expenses that are not deductible include:

1. costs to improve the residence to help it sell,
2. prepayments of interest (but see 07-01), and
3. prepayments or payments for rent.

Pre-moving expenses include the costs of travel before the taxpayer moves, but *after* obtaining the new employment. Travel to seek new employment would be deductible from Adjusted Gross Income (07-09). These expenses are normally for house hunting, and the expenses of the taxpayer's spouse are includible.

Temporary living expenses include the cost of lodging and meals for taxpayers and their families in the area of the new job, but before moving into the new residence.

06-11.2 Example

Aaron Gordon obtains a new job in a city 100 miles away from his present residence and place of employment. His new employer agrees to reimburse him $5,000 for his moving expenses, which he does.

Aaron and his wife make two house-hunting trips prior to the move. He drives the 100 miles and stays at motels that cost him $200. While house hunting, his meals cost him $150.

When he and his family arrive to start his new job, the house they purchased is not ready. The family stays at a local motel for 15 days, for which the bill is $1,125. And the meals for the family cost another $500.

He and his family move to the new location in their car. Meals on the road that day cost them $100. The moving company charges him $3,000 to pack, move, and store his furniture and other effects for the 15 days before moving into the new residence.

When he sold his old house, he had commissions and other expenses of sale of $3,000; and on the purchase of the new house he pays $5,000 in commissions.

His moving expense deduction would be:

Transportation expense in moving household goods and personal effects		$3,000
Travel, meals and lodging expenses in moving from old to new residence (100 miles @ 9¢)		9
Meals on day of move		100
House-hunting trips		
(100 miles × 2 trips @ 9¢)	$ 18	
Motels and meals	350	
Temporary living expenses	1,625	
	$1,993	
Above expenses limited to $1,500	$1,500	
Sale and purchase expenses of old and new residences	8,000*	
	$9,500	
Above expenses limited to $3,000		3,000
Deductible moving expenses		$6,109
Amount of reimbursement		−5,000
Deduction for AGI		$1,109

*Of the $8,000 Aaron paid in commissions for the purchase and sale of his residences, only $1,500 can be used as a deduction for Adjusted Gross Income due to the $3,000 limitation ($3,000 less $1,500 pre-moving and

06-11.3 **Tax Hint**

If the sale of the old residence results in a taxable gain, allocate the tax benefit first to the new residence. This tactic only increases *future* long-term gain on the sale of the new residence, but no current taxable income results.

06-12 EDUCATION EXPENSES

No section of the Code deals with "education" expenses. For an education expense to be deductible, it must qualify under Section 162 as ordinary and necessary. In other words, it must relate to a trade or business or to an income-producing function, in which the taxpayer is *already* engaged. So no deduction is allowed for meeting the minimum requirements of an occupation or for changing occupations. To be deductible, educational expenses must:

1. maintain the skills of a taxpayer's occupation;
2. help the taxpayer to meet new requirements established either by law or by the employer for retaining his or her position; or
3. improve the taxpayer's skills within the current occupation.

The fact that a degree results from a program of education does not automatically make the expenses nondeductible. Yet preparations for the CPA, bar, or similar examinations are clearly not deductible since the examinations represent the minimum requirements of the trade. A CPA taking law courses may not deduct the expenses. The courts have held that being a lawyer is a new occupation, and that the courses are not maintain-

---

temporary expenses). Presuming Aaron took advantage of the tax-free exchange of a new residence for an old residence (04-11), the basis of the new residence must be reduced by the $1,500 tax benefit.

ing CPA skills. On the other hand, a teacher is a teacher regardless of the courses taught or the level. The expenses of an elementary school teacher studying to qualify as a high school teacher *are* deductible.

Obviously, the facts of each situation must be examined to see whether the education expenses are deductible.

Deductible Expenses 06-12.1

Deductible expenses include the cost of books, tuition, laboratory fees, and other contingent outlays. Transportation to the source of education is deductible within limits. If the institution is located in the same general area as the taxpayer's business, then the cost of a one-way trip from the business location to the education is deductible. If the education institution is located outside the general area of the taxpayer's business, then the round trip costs are deductible.

The educational expenses of *employees* (other than travel and transportation) are deductions from their Adjusted Gross Income. The travel and transportation expenses constitute a deduction for Adjusted Gross Income. If the educational expenses are *paid by the employer* (either directly or by reimbursing the employee) and if the expenses meet the critieria of being ordinary and necessary, they are deductible by the employer. They are not included in the Gross Income of the employee.

The educational expenses of the *self-employed*, including outside salespersons and partners in a partnership, are deductions for Adjusted Gross Income.

Tax Hint 06-12.2

When claiming a deduction for educational expenses, taxpayers should complete Form 2106 and file it with their tax returns. This form provides the IRS with the information for determining whether the expense is deductible. Along with the name and address of the institution attended, the taxpayer must answer four questions.

1. *Did you need this education to meet the basic requirements of your job?* A "yes" answer here will probably cause the expense to be disallowed. All is not lost, however, with a "yes" answer. If taxpayers are hired on probation, with the understanding that they would complete a required course of study, the expense will probably be allowed. In one case, Marlor v. Commissioner, the court held that the taxpayer was retaining his present "temporary" position, and the deduction was allowed.
2. *Will this study program qualify you for a new job?* Again, a "yes" answer will probably cause the deduction to be disallowed. Yet intent can be a factor. A doctor taking a course in tax law may become qualified as a tax return preparer, but that possibility would probably not cause the disallowance if the doctor is taking the course to better manage his or her practice.
3. If the answer to the first two questions is "no," the form then asks, *Why are you getting the education and what is the relationship between the courses you took and your job?* Obviously, the answers here are important in establishing that the education meets the ordinary and necessary test.
4. The last question asks for *the names of the courses taken.* The courses must be consistent with the taxpayer's objectives.

06-13 NET OPERATING LOSS (NOL)

Normally taxpayers may offset gains and losses within the tax year to compute Adjusted Gross Income. The Code also allows taxpayers who have a "net economic" loss from all sources for the year to use that loss to offset income in other years. The economic loss for a year is called a *net operating loss,* although the title is somewhat misleading.

To begin the computation of NOL, if any, taxpayers must have a negative figure for Taxable Income for the year. If they have any Taxable Income, no net operating loss can exist. Although rather complicated, the computation of any usable net operating loss is in essence:

1. only the losses from a trade or business (not from a nonbusiness venture) will qualify; and
2. casualty losses (07-08) are considered "business" for the purpose of computing net operating loss.

Gains from nonbusiness ventures may reduce any usable net operating losses, but nonbusiness losses do not serve to increase it (06-13.1).

The taxpayer must make a written election *not* to carry back the net operating loss. The election must be filed before the due date, including extensions, for the year in which the loss is incurred. Once the election is made, it is irrevocable.

There are separate formulas for computing the net operating losses of individuals, partnerships, corporations, Subchapter S corporations, and estates and trusts. The formulas are available in the Regulations, or they may be obtained from any tax service. A copy of the computation of the net operating loss must accompany the claim for the deduction.

The claim for a net operating loss carry-back is made on Form 1040X for individuals and on 1120X for corporations.

Example 06-13.1

Barney Colin loses $12,000 in his business. He also has $500 in interest income, a net long-term capital gain of $10,000 (before the 60% exclusion), and itemized deductions of $5,000 including a casualty loss of $1,000. He files as a single person. His Taxable Income (loss) is therefore:

Loss from business		($12,000)
Interest income		500
Long-term capital gain	$10,000	
Less: 60% exclusion	− 6,000	+$ 4,000
Adjusted Gross Income		$ (7,500)
Itemized deductions: General	$ 4,000	
Itemized deductions: Casualty	+1,000	
loss	$ 5,000	
Zero bracket amount	− 2,300	− 2,700
		$(10,200)
Personal exemption		− 1,000
Taxable Income (loss)		$(11,200)

To find Barney's net operating loss:

Adjusted Gross Income		$ (7,500)
Less: 60% long-term capital gain exclusion		− 6,000
		$ (1,500)
Plus: Nonbusiness income	$ 500	
Casualty loss	+ 1,000	
	$ 1,500	
Itemized deductions	$ 5,000	
Lesser of above figures		(1,500)
Net operating loss		$ 3,000

06-13.2 Carry-Forward and Carry-Back Rules

Taxpayers who have net operating losses may elect:

1. *either* to carry it back three years and forward fifteen,
2. *or* carry it forward fifteen, with no carry back.

06-13.2A Example

Mrs. Taxpayer has a net operating loss in 1980. She could first use it to offset taxable income in 1977, then 1978, and

each year until 1995. Or she could elect to start using it in 1981 and continue to 1995. She may not choose which year to use it in; it must be used consecutively (06-13.3).

Tax Hint 06-13.3

Should Barney elect to carry back the net operating loss, or should he carry it forward? That depends. If the loss is in 1980, he should look at 1977 and see if that year he was in a relatively high incremental tax bracket. If he was, then he should file for a refund and claim the loss against 1977 income. If not, and he expects 1981 to be a year in which he will be in a high incremental tax bracket, he should carry it forward.

7

PERSONAL DEDUCTIONS: INDIVIDUAL TAXPAYERS

INTEREST EXPENSE

07-01

Except as discussed in 07-02, interest expenses are deductible. Interest paid or incurred either in a trade or business, or for the production of rents and royalties, is a deduction for Adjusted Gross Income. Interest expense incurred either for personal reasons or for the nonbusiness production of income is a deduction from Adjusted Gross Income.

To deduct it, a taxpayer must pay or incur the interest expense on debt for which the taxpayer is liable even if the liability is indirect. For example, taxpayers may deduct the interest expense on their portion of a master debt obligation, such as on a cooperative apartment or on a condominium.

- Interest paid on behalf of another individual is a gift to that party, not a deductible interest expense.
- Points paid to obtain a mortgage, to the extent that they represent additional interest, are deductible as interest.

Yet loan origination and placement fees (such as FHA and VA mortgage fees), as well as points paid for services (such as inspection fees), are not deductible interest. Such fees, normally a capital expenditure, are added to the basis of the related property.

- Finance charges, along with other consumer interest charges on purchases, are interest and are deductible as such.
- If an interest charge is not separately stated, but is imputed (such as on an installment note, 10-12), it may still be deducted as interest expense. The burden of proving the amount of interest rests with the taxpayer.

07-02 NONDEDUCTIBLE INTEREST EXPENSE

The Code specifically addresses certain types of interest expense.

1. In some cases the expense is permanently disallowed.
2. In other cases the deduction is postponed to future years.
3. And in still other cases the expense is a capital expenditure and is added to the basis of related property.

07-02.1 Interest to Support Investments

The deduction for interest expenses related to the financing of investments (that are not related to a trade or business) is limited for noncorporate taxpayers, including Subchapter S corporations (12-09). The maximum deduction is $10,000 plus the net income (as defined) on such nonbusiness investments. Though the excess interest is nondeductible because of this limitation, it may be carried forward indefinitely.

The application of this limit is often not as onerous as it sounds. The limitation applies only to property *not* used in a trade or business (07-02.1A). Further, to compute the net income from investments, use only straight-line depreciation (08-04) or cost depletion (08-07). Investment income consists of:

1. interest and dividends; and
2. net short-term capital gains (but not *long*-term capital gains), and
3. net income from rents and royalties, adjusted for straight-line depreciation and cost depletion (07-02.1A); and
4. recapture of depreciation (08-14); and
5. recapture of intangible drilling costs (08-08).

The $10,000 limit is increased by as much as $15,000, for a maximum of $25,000 for interest expense incurred to obtain or carry a 50% or more interest in a corporation. This increase over the $10,000 limit can be no more than the actual interest expense to carry such a holding.

The $10,000 and $15,000 limitations are reduced to $5,000 and $7,500 for married taxpayers filing separate returns. For trusts, the $10,000 limit is reduced to zero.

Example 07-02.1A

Timothy Bryne incurred $100,000 in interest to finance an income-producing piece of property, which yielded the following tax results:

Gross revenue		$1,000,000
Less: Other out-of-pocket expenses	$800,000	
Interest expense	100,000	
Depreciation (200% declining balance)	+150,000	−1,050,000
Net *loss* for income tax purposes		$ (50,000)

To compute the limitation on the deductible interest expense, he must adjust the investment income: (1) to eliminate the interest expense, and (2) to incorporate straight-line depreciation. The income from the investment for limitation purpose is:

Gross revenue		$1,000,000
Less: Other out-of-pocket expenses	$800,000	
Straight-line depreciation	+ 75,000	− 875,000
"Adjusted" net income		$ 125,000
Plus $10,000 allowance		+ 10,000
Maximum deductible interest		$ 135,000

Timothy can therefore deduct the full $100,000 interest expense. If any part of the expense is disallowed due to the limitation, it is added to the following year's interest expense. Its deductibility is thus postponed until a year in which the limitation does not prevent the deduction.

07-02.1B **Tax *warning***

Interest on a margin account is limited by this rule. Note that long-term capital gains are not considered income from investments. If investors have *only* long-term gains in their margin accounts, the deduction for margin interest is limited to $10,000.

The Economic Recovery Tax Act of 1981 did away with accelerated depreciation as such (see 08-04). The Act failed to address any adjustment from lives used under cost recovery (which is a form of acceleration) to the equivalent straight-line rate. It is anticipated that this "oversight" will be corrected by legislation.

07-02.2 Interest to Buy or Purchase Tax-Exempt Securities

Expenses incurred to generate tax-exempt income are not deductible (06-05.3). Under this rule, interest incurred to acquire or to carry tax-exempt securities is not deductible. The key to this disallowance is a "direct" relationship between the investment and the loan. When investors own both taxable and tax-exempt securities, the IRS can allocate interest expense between the two. The portion allocated to the taxable investments is deductible, and the portion allocated to the tax-exempt investments is nondeductible.

The IRS cannot allocate a principal residence as part of taxpayer's investment. So even if taxpayers have large mortgages on their homes, the mortgage interest is still fully deductible even if the taxpayers have extensive investments in tax-exempt securities.

Tax hint 07-02.2A

The best way to avoid having the IRS allocate part or all of the interest on a loan to tax-exempt investments is to never pledge any of those investments as collateral for a loan. Keep tax-exempt securities separate from other securities that are pledged as collateral. Keeping tax-exempt securities in a margin account, where the broker can consider them as part of the overall collateral, invites the assumption that the loan is for the purpose of carrying the tax-exempt securities.

For investors who own tax-exempt securities, careful recordkeeping is essential. When a loan is taken, the use of its proceeds should be clearly traceable to an investment in an asset that generates taxable income. Unfortunately, there is no sure way to avoid an IRS challenge. All the facts in each case must be examined to determine if the loan was used to purchase or to carry tax-exempt securities.

Interest to Purchase or Carry Insurance 07-02.3

In certain cases, the interest incurred to purchase or to carry life insurance, endowment contracts, and annuities is disallowed.

No deduction for interest is allowed for debt incurred for the purchase of a *single premium* life insurance policy, endowment, or annuity. A policy is considered to be "single premium" if a substantial amount of the premium is paid within the first four years.

No deduction is allowed for any debt incurred under a plan to borrow against the cash surrender value of a life insurance, endowment, or annuity unless:

1. four of the first seven annual premiums are paid without borrowing against the policy; or
2. the interest deduction is less than $100; or
3. the proceeds of the loan are invested in a trade or business; or
4. the loan is due to an unforeseen change in circumstances.

The purpose of this disallowance is to prevent taxpayers from generating currently tax-deductible interest that is offset by future income.

07-02.4 Construction Period Interest and Taxes

Under Section 189 of the Code, individual taxpayers, partnerships (Chapter 11), and Subchapter S corporations (12-09) must capitalize interest and taxes incurred in the construction of real property. The interest and taxes so capitalized can be amortized over a period of 10 years (see below for exceptions). The first 10% may be amortized in the year paid or incurred, and the remaining amount may be amortized beginning in the year the property is placed in service or held for resale. Then, if the property is sold or exchanged before the interest and taxes have been completely amortized, the unamortized portion is added to the basis of the property for computing gain or loss on disposition.

The requirement to capitalize interest and taxes is currently being phased in. During the phase-in period, which extends until 1984, real property is divided into three categories: *non-residential, residential,* and *low-income housing.* Interest and taxes incurred in 1981 for:

1. *non-residential* real estate construction may be amortized over 9 years, and after that over the full 10-year period;
2. *residential* real estate construction may be amortized over 7 years, increasing to 10 years in 1984; and
3. *low-income housing* construction period interest and taxes may be amortized 100%, in the year of construction and are not subject to being capitalized.

The capitalization of interest and taxes applies only to property either held in a trade or business or held for income production. Such costs on the construction of personal property are fully deductible, and not subject to these rules.

Section 266 of the Code allows a taxpayer to capitalize construction period interest and taxes 100% if the taxpayer so elects. If the taxpayer makes the election to capitalize these expenses 100%, these rules do not apply.

Tax Hint 07-02.4A

Section 266 election may be made for one year, but not for another. There is no requirement for consistency from one year to the next. If a taxpayer is having a particularly bad year, and if the deductions for interest and taxes incurred in the construction period cannot be fruitfully used, the election to capitalize them should be made. At least this way, they can be used to reduce any gain on disposition or to increase any loss. Further, since they are part of the basis of the asset, they may be depreciated (08-01).

INTEREST TO FINANCE A STRADDLE 07-02.5

Taxpayers may be required to capitalize interest incurred to finance a straddle (05-10.5 for a full discussion).

TAXES 07-03

Taxes fall into three categories. They are either:

1. never deductible,
2. deductible as a business or as a nonbusiness expense, or

3. always deductible, either
   a. for Adjusted Gross Income if incurred in a trade or business or for the production of rents or royalties; or
   b. deductible from Adjusted Gross Income if personal or incurred for the production of income other than rents or royalties.

07-03.1 Never Deductible

Under the heading of "never deductible" are:

1. federal income taxes,
2. federal gift tax, and
3. federal estate tax (except in the case of income received on account of a decedent).

07-03.2 Always Deductible

Under the heading of "always deductible":

1. state and local sales taxes,
2. state and local real estate taxes, unless classified as "special assessment,"
3. state and local income taxes, and
4. state and local personal property taxes if imposed on an annual basis and if imposed on the basis of property values.

In the last category, some states' automobile registration fees are deductible, since the amount of the fee is based on the value of the vehicle. Other states impose a vehicle registration fee based on weight or some other criteria, and they are not deductible.

A "special assessment" tax on real estate is generally not deductible if made for an improvement that increases the value of the property. Such an expenditure would increase the basis of the property. If the special assessment tax is for the maintenance of an existing facility it is generally deductible.

Normally, the tax is deductible by the taxpayer upon whom the tax is imposed. But the Code requires that real estate tax deductions, in most cases, be allocated between the buyer and seller based on the number of days of occupancy, without regard to who must pay the tax under local law.

Business and Nonbusiness Expenses 07-03.3

Some taxes are deductible only as an expense of a business or the nonbusiness production of income. In this category would be such items as cigarette tax, gasoline tax, and the like.

The Social Security tax imposed on an employer is deductible as a business or nonbusiness expense. Social Security tax imposed on the employee is a federal income tax and therefore not deductible.

State unemployment and disability taxes are deductible by an employer if incurred in a business or in the nonbusiness production of income. In some states, employees must contribute to the state unemployment and/or disability fund. These taxes are state and local income taxes, and they are deductible by the employee.

Foreign Taxes 07-03.4

Taxes paid to foreign governments (including those imposed by possessions of the United States, such as Puerto Rico) may be classified as either an "income tax" or as "not an income tax." Foreign income taxes, in many cases, may be taken as a credit against U.S. income taxes (09-08.4). Since a credit generally reduces taxes dollar-for-dollar, it is better than taking the tax as a deduction.

Simply because a tax is labeled an "income" tax by the foreign government, does not necessarily qualify it for the foreign tax credit. The tax must be similar to our income tax. Check the Regulations as to whether any questionable items qualify for the credit. If the tax is not an income tax, it might still be deducted as either a business or nonbusiness expense.

07-04 CHARITABLE CONTRIBUTIONS

Within the limits explained in 07-05, taxpayers are allowed a deduction from Adjusted Gross Income for contributions made to certain charitable organizations. Such organizations include those organized and operated exclusively for religious, charitable, scientific, educational, and literary purposes, as well as certain government units. Treasury Department Publication 78 lists organizations for which contributions are deductible. These include the national charitable organizations with which we are all familiar. Not include on the list are political parties and "exempt organizations" (12-16), whose functions are social rather than charitable.

Charitable organizations are broken down into two basic categories: *public supported* (50% limit) and *private foundations* (20% limit). Although the Code sections and the Regulations defining the two are massive, the truth comes through. Organizations that derive a substantial amount of their support from the public are *public* charities. Those that derive their primary support from a small group of contributors are *private* foundations. Contributions to private foundations are deductible, but the limits are more restrictive (07-05). Contributions to individuals, no matter how "charitable," are not deductible.

Fees paid to charitable organizations for services or products are not deductible as charitable contributions. At the head of this list is tuition. Tuition paid to religious or private schools is not deductible. Some controversy arises with the purchase of tickets, products sold for charity, and other "semicharitable" contributions. The amount paid for such items is generally not deductible.

The taxpayer must prove the amount that is considered a charitable contribution. Just because the ticket says "donation" does not make it a charitable deduction. Yet purchasing tickets to the local church fund raiser, with no intention of attending, would qualify as a deductible contribution.

For the years 1982 to 1986, taxpayers who do not itemize their deductions may take limited deductions for AGI for charitable contributions.

Amount and Timing of the Deduction 07-04.1

The deduction for charitable contributions must be taken in the year "paid," even for accrual basis taxpayers (10-05.2). But a contribution is considered "paid":

1. if charged on a credit card;
2. if paid by check and the check is postmarked before the last day of the year; and
3. if property is delivered to the charitable organization, even if title has not passed.

The contribution is also considered "paid" by an accrual basis corporation if the payment is authorized before the end of its tax year, and if the payment itself is made within 2½ months of the end of its tax year.

If taxpayers deliver property to their *own* agents (rather than to the agents of the charity), then title must be transferred before the contribution is considered "paid."

The amount of the deduction is generally the fair market value of the property donated. But no deduction is allowed for the "donation" of the taxpayer's time or for the temporary use of the taxpayer's property. A deduction can be obtained, however, by the donation of a partial interest in property and for the donation of a future interest in certain properties. Special rules exist for appreciated property (07-04.2).

The taxpayer may deduct out-of-pocket expenses incurred for the benefit of a charitable organization. The IRS allows a deduction for the use of the taxpayer's automobile in the amount of 9¢ per mile.

For a deduction of more than $200 for property donated to a charitable organization, the taxpayer must attach a description of the property, its original cost, the market value (normally the amount of the deduction), and the way the market value was arrived at. Normally, the best way to fix fair market value is to have the property appraised. The appraisal fee is a miscellaneous deduction from Adjusted Gross Income (07-09). For smaller items, such as used clothing, simply keep the charity receipt for the property and give an appraisal of its fair market value.

In considering the fair market value, include all factors, especially whether the quantity is of wholesale or retail amounts. Several taxpayers have tried the "trick" of buying a large product lot, holding it for more than a year (see appreciated property below), and then donating the property at its "retail" value. Revenue Ruling 80-69, among others, makes it clear that the fair market value is the purchase price, not some "artificially" calculated retail market value.

07-04.2 Appreciated Property Donated

When the taxpayer donates property with a fair market value higher than the taxpayer's basis, the amount of the deduction may be determined in a number of ways:

1. If the contributed property results either in ordinary gain or in a short-term capital gain if sold, the deduction is the property's basis (except see entry 2 below).
2. For corporations making donations of appreciated inventory to organizations caring for the ill, needy, or infants, *and* when the inventory is used for that purpose, the deduction is the lesser of one-half of the appreciation or twice the corporation's cost, *plus* the basis.

3. If the sale of Section 1245 property (08-14.1) would result in a profit, part of which would be ordinary income, the amount deductible is its fair market value less the excess depreciation that would be recaptured if sold.
4. If the sale of the property would result in a long-term capital gain when sold, and if it is donated to a private foundation (20% limit), the deduction is its fair market value less 40% of the potential long-term gain.
5. If the property would result in a long-term capital gain when sold, and if it is *tangible* personal property *unrelated* to the donee's qualified function, the deduction is its fair market value less 40% of the potential long-term capital gain.
6. Other than in these cases, when any property, if sold, would result in long-term capital gain, the deduction is the property's fair market value.
7. For corporations making donations of property, constructed by the taxpayer, to a college or university for use in research, the deduction is the lesser of one-half of the appreciation or twice the corporation's cost, *plus* the basis. Counsel must be sought in this area, since specific documentation is required. 07-04.2A

Two points

1. Securities are *in*tangible personal property for these purposes. When donated to a public (50%-limit) charity, their *full* fair market value can be deducted.
2. For corporate taxpayers, other than Subchapter S corporations, the amount of the reduction in list entries 4 and 5 above is 28/46th of the potential long-term capital gain.

07-04.3

Example: Tax Planning Application

Giving appreciated property to charity constitutes one of the cornerstones of tax planning. Tiffany Schuler (single) has taxable income of $200,000. She also has a painting that cost her $10,000 several years ago and that now has a fair

market value of $100,000. If she sells the painting, her tax liability would be:

Taxable income before capital gain		$200,000
Sale of painting:		
Proceeds	$100,000	
Less: Basis	− 10,000	
Long-term capital gain	$ 90,000	
Less: 60% exclusion	− 54,000	36,000
Revised taxable income		$236,000
Tax on $236,000		**$105,935**
Tax on $200,000		**− 87,935**
Increase in taxes		**$ 18,000**

If she donates the painting to a local museum:

Taxable income before donation	$200,000
Less: Charitable donation	−100,000
Revised taxable income	$100,000
Tax on $200,000	**$87,935**
Tax on $100,000	**−37,935**
Decrease in taxes	**$50,000**
Net cash received if sold ($100,000 − taxes of **$18,000**	**$82,000**
Net tax refund if donated	**−50,000**
Net cost of donation	**$32,000**

It only costs her $32,000 to make a $100,000 donation. To many taxpayers, that is very inexpensive satisfaction.

07-04.3A Tax *warning*

Don't donate property that has declined in value! Sell it, take the loss for tax purposes, and donate the cash. *Don't* donate a painting to a medical research charity who is going to sell it! That would be an *unrelated* purpose. Donate it to a museum who will use it, and take the full fair market value as the deduction.

Bargain Sales 07-04.4

Bargain sales made to a charitable organization are considered part sale and part donation. Taxpayers must allocate their bases between the two elements of the transaction.

Example 07-04.4A

Courtney Lee owns a painting worth $100,000 with a basis in her hands of $10,000. She agrees to sell it to the museum for $40,000. Courtney has two transactions: a donation of 60% of the painting and a sale of 40%. On the sale she recognizes capital gain as follows:

Proceeds of sale	$40,000
Less: Basis (40% of $10,000)	−4,000
Long-term capital gain	$36,000

Her charitable contribution deduction is $60,000 (60% of the $100,000 market value of the painting).

Donations Through Trusts 07-04.5

Donations made through trusts must follow strict and complex provisions of the Code for taxpayers to be able to deduct the donation. Even if they follow the "letter" of the law, in many cases taxpayers still do not get the deduction. Unless designed by competent tax counsel to meet specific needs, contributions should not be made through a trust agreement.

07-04.6 Gifts of Future Interest

As a general rule, no deduction is allowed for gifts of future interest in personal property, nor for those in real property with the exception of farms and the taxpayer's residence. The residence need not be the taxpayer's principal residence; a vacation home would quality. The amount of the deduction is the present value of the gift. The present value for donations not given in trust is calculated based on Regulation 1.170A-12.

07-04.6A Example

Aaron Gordon, age 62, donates a remainder interest in his summer cottage to his church, subject to a life estate for himself. At the time of the gift, the land has a value of \$7,000, and the building has a value of \$25,000. The building is expected to have a useful life of 45 years, at which time it will be worth \$5,000. Based on Aaron's expected life span and on the information regarding the land and building, Regulation 1.170A-12 shows the present value of the gift to be \$12,953.

In other words, the current value is \$32,000 (\$25,000 + \$7,000). Yet Aaron will get to live in the house for the rest of his life. That right has some value, which is:

Current value	\$32,000
Present value of the future use	−12,953
Value of Aaron's rights to use the property	\$19,047

Obviously, the longer his life expectancy, the more valuable his right to use the property.

07-04.7 Gifts of Partial Interest

The gift of a partial interest in tangible personal property is deductible.

Example 07-04.7A

Tiffany Schuler has a painting worth $100,000. She "donates" it to the local museum on the terms that they can have it either in 1985 or upon her death. She gets no deduction for the future interest until 1985 when she gives it over to the museum. If she dies first, then she gets no deduction.

But let's say the donation agreement is changed, so that the museum *currently* gets to use the painting three months of the year, and Tiffany gets to use it nine months of the year. She can then deduct 25% of the value of the painting (for the quarter-year it is donated).

Tax *Warning* 07-04.8

Whenever a complex arrangement is entered into, and when the taxpayer expects to receive a deduction for a charitable contribution, seek a private letter ruling before the transaction is completed. The Code, the Regulations, and the court cases in this area are complex and subject to interpretation. So make sure your plan is acceptable to the IRS. It could save court costs and an unpleasant surprise.

LIMITATION ON CONTRIBUTION DEDUCTIONS 07-05

The amount of contribution deductions that taxpayers may take is limited by their Adjusted Gross Income, computed without regard to any net operating loss carryback. The limits are:

1. 50% of Adjusted Gross Income for publicly supported charities and some private foundations,
2. 20% of Adjusted Gross Income for nonoperating private foundations, and

3. 30% of Adjusted Gross Income for donations of appreciated long-term property for which no reduction was taken due to potential long-term capital gains.

If newly formed charitable organizations wish to be classified as 50%-limit organizations, they can request a private letter ruling. If in doubt regarding the status of a particular organization, request a statement from it as to its status.

Taxpayers may elect to reduce all contributions of long-term capital gain property by 40% of the potential long-term gain, and thus to avoid the 30% limit.

Businesses may claim payments made to charitable organizations that are ordinary and necessary under Section 162 without limit. But the limit for a corporation is 10% of its "contribution base," which is:

1. taxable income without regard to charitable contributions,
2. plus the dividend-received exclusion,
3. plus any deductible losses on the reacquisition of the corporation's own convertible debt,
4. plus certain payments made by railroads, and
5. plus any net operating loss carry-back.

07-05.1 Example

The MBS Corporation shows the following annual results:

Taxable income from operations		$100,000
Dividends received from domestic corporations	$50,000	
Less: 85% exclusion	−42,500	+ 7,500
Income before charitable donations		$107,500
Charitable contributions		− 20,000
Net income		$ 87,500

The deduction for charitable contributions is:

Net income	$ 87,500
Plus: Charitable contributions	20,000
85% dividend exclusion	+ 42,500
Contribution base	$150,000
Donation limitation (10% of $150,000)	$ 15,000
Taxable Income:	
Income before charitable donations	$107,500
Allowable contribution deduction	15,000
Taxable Income	$ 92,500

Tax Hint 07-05.2

In most cases, charitable contributions offer a better tax advantage if given by individual stockholders rather than by the closely held corporation. The reason is not only that corporations are subject to a more severe limitation, but also that they are normally in a lower incremental tax bracket.

Further Reduction of 20% Limit 07-05.3

The 20% limit may be reduced further. It is limited to the unused portion of the 50% limit on public charities.

Example 07-05.3A

Last year, Aaron Gordon had Adjusted Gross Income of $30,500. He made the following charitable donations:

1. $10,000 to the ASPCA (a 50%-limit charity);
2. $10,000 to Friends of Lost Poodles (a 20%-limit charity).

To compute the limit on his charitable deductions, first compute the 50% limit donations: 50% of his AGI is $15,250,

50% of AGI	$15,250
Amount used	−10,000
Available for 20% limit donations	$ 5,250
20% of AGI	$ 6,100

Aaron's deduction for the Friends of Lost Poodles is limited to the lesser of $6,100 or $5,250. He therefore loses $4,750 of that donation as a deduction. The deduction in this case is lost forever (07-06).

07-05.3B **Example**

Barney Colin had AGI of $20,000 and made the following contributions:

1. $6,000 in cash to the ASPCA,
2. common stock worth $10,000, which he purchased for $1,000, to Save the Trees (a 50%-limit charity).

The $6,000 cash contribution presents no problem, since it is less than 50% of $20,000 AGI. Barney now has an unused 50% limit available of:

50% of $20,000	$10,000
Amount used	− 6,000
Amount available	$ 4,000

The donation of the $10,000 in stock is limited to the lesser of 30% of AGI ($6,000) or the unused portion of the 50% limit ($4,000). In this case the disallowed deduction may be carried forward (07-06).

If Barney had also made contributions to 20%-limit charities, none of them could be deducted or carried forward.

07-06 CARRY-OVER OF UNUSED CONTRIBUTION DEDUCTIONS

For individual taxpayers, any unused charitable contribution made to 50%-limit charities may be carried forward for 5 years. No carry-forward is allowed for unused contributions made to 20%-limit charities.

Taxpayers must use the current year's deduction first. Then, if any unused 50% limit exists, the amounts carried forward may be deducted (07-06.1). Taxpayers with more than one carry-forward must use the oldest one first. Corporations may also carry forward unused contributions to 50%-limit charities 5 years.

Example 07-06.1

Tiffany Schuler had Adjusted Gross Income of $50,000 and made cash contributions of $10,000 to 50%-limit charities during the year. She also has a carry-forward of $20,000 from last year, along with $10,000 from the year before. Her charitable deduction for this year is:

50% of Adjusted Gross Income	$25,000
First use this year's donations	$10,000
Next use the oldest carry-forward ($10,000 from 2 years ago)	10,000
Then use the next oldest carry-forward ($20,000 from last year to the extent that it can be used)	+ 5,000
Total deduction	$25,000

Tiffany has $15,000 of the $20,000 to carry forward.

Tax Hint 07-06.2

Should the taxpayer elect to make the deduction or reduce the contribution by 40% of the potential capital gain (07-05)? Each situation must be examined both ways.

Example 07-06.2A

Aaron Gordon has Adjusted Gross Income of $50,000. Last year he contributed stock with a market value of $20,000 to his church. The stock cost him $19,000. He also has $4,000 of unused charitable deduction carry-forward. If he makes no election, his deduction for this year is:

Donation of stock, limited to 30% of AGI, or $15,000	$15,000
Carry-forward to the extent it does not increase deduction above the 50% limit	+ 4,000
Total deduction	$19,000

If this route is taken, the new carry-forward is $5,000. The old carry-forward is used.

But if Aaron elects to reduce his contribution for this year by 40% of the potential capital gain:

Stock contributed		$20,000
Potential capital gain $1,000 ($20,000 − basis $19,000)	$1,000	
Reduction of contribution by 40% of capital gain		− (400)
Net		$19,600
Unused carry-forward		4,000
Deduction		$23,600

Obviously, electing to "reduce" the deductible value of a particular gift decreases the total deduction. Without the election, the total is $24,000 ($19,000 this year and $5,000 carried forward), as opposed to $23,600 this year. Aaron must figure how much money he will earn in interest by getting the tax refund now, rather than a year from now.

07-07 MEDICAL EXPENSE

Individual taxpayers are allowed a deduction from Adjusted Gross Income for medical expenses to the extent that they exceed 3% of Adjusted Gross Income.

What constitutes "medical expenses"? The concept

is very broad. Expenses for doctors' fees, hospital fees, nursing, hearing aids, eyeglasses, and the like all are deductible as medical expenses.

Numerous court cases and revenue rulings deal with some borderline situations. The cost of a plastic surgeon's fees were held to be deductible for a face-lift operation even when there was no doctor's recommendation that one was needed. But expenses for the general well being of the taxpayer are not deductible. Items such as trips to a sunny climate, membership in a physical fitness program, and so on are not deductible. In one case, the cost of participating in a stop-smoking program was considered merely helping the "general well being" of the taxpayer and was not deductible.

On the other hand, several expenditures, which are normally considered nondeductible capital expenditures, may be deductible medical expenses under certain circumstances. In the Gerard case, the Tax Court held that a portion of an air conditioning system installed under doctor's advice to provide therapeutic treatment was a deductible medical expense. The portion not deductible was the amount that the value of the house was increased by the air conditioner. In Ferris v. Commissioner, the entire amount of the cost of a swimming pool was a deductible medical expense since it was specially designed for the treatment of polio. Additional costs attributed to creating a sense of esthetic compatibility of the pool with the house were disallowed. The theme that comes through on most capital expenditure situations is this: The portion of the cost that is attributable to medical treatment and that does not add to the value of the premises is a deductible medical expense.

- The cost of *medicines* is considered a medical expense to the extent that they exceed 1% of Adjusted Gross Income (07-07.1). For medicines to qualify for a deduction, they must either be prescribed by a doctor or alleviate a specific health problem. Vitamins and health foods do not generally fall into the category of being deductible.

- Taxpayers may deduct one-half of *medical insurance premiums,* up to $150, without regard to the 3% limitation. Additional medical insurance premiums are added to medical expenses subject to the 3% limitation (07-07.1).
- As a general rule, the *prepayment of medical expenses* is not deductible unless the taxpayer has a legal obligation to make the payment.
- *Transportation* to receive medical care is also deductible as a medical expense. If taxpayers use their personal automobiles for such transportation, the IRS allows 9¢ per mile.
- Taxpayers may deduct the medical expenses of themselves, their spouse and all their dependents (07-07.3).
- Expenses that qualify for the *Child Care Credit* (09-08.3) may not also be deducted as medical expenses.
- The cost of *live-in help,* even if prescribed by a doctor, is not a deductible medical expense unless medical treatment is administered. The person administering the treatment need not be specially qualified or licensed. The important criterion consists of the function performed, not the qualifications of the person performing it.

07-07.1 Example

Lacey Bradshaw had Adjusted Gross Income of $50,000; and the following medical expenses:

Medicines	$ 700
Doctor and dentist fees	1,000
Payment to the hospital	600
Health insurance premiums	800
Eyeglasses	75

Transportation to and from doctors,		
dentists, and hospital (1,000 miles @ 9¢)		90
Tolls and parking		20
Total medical expenses		$3,285

Her deductible medical expenses are:

Medicines		700
Less: 1% of AGI		500
		$ 200
Doctor and dentist fees		1,000
Payments to the hospital		600
Health insurance	$800	
Less: First $150	150	650
Eyeglasses		75
Transportation		90
Tolls and parking		20
Total		$2,635
Less: 3% of AGI		1,500
Net, but not less than zero		$1,135
Insurance premiums not subject to 3% limit		150
Deductible medical expense		$1,285

Reimbursement 07-07.2

A deduction is allowed only for medical expenses that are paid during the year and that are not reimbursed by insurance. If an expense that was deducted in prior years is subsequently reimbursed, the taxpayer may have to report the amount received as income. The amount reportable as income is the amount by which the taxpayer benefited from the deduction.

Example 07-07.2A

If in the Lacey example, she was reimbursed in the following year for the full $1,600 she spent on doctors and the hospital, she would have to include in income only $1,135, since that is the amount of tax benefit she received.

07-07.3 **Tax Hint**

For the $1,000 exemption, obtaining the right to claim a person as the taxpayer's dependent is important (01-08). That right is also important from the standpoint of claiming that person's medical expenses as a deduction. With the elderly or infirmed, this deduction could be even more important than the $1,000 exemption. When a multiple-support agreement is obtained (01-08.1D), the person given the exemption is entitled to claim any medical expenses paid for that dependent.

07-07.4 **Tax Hint**

Beautiful Baby needs orthodontic work. Doctor Pullit, DDS, gives you the bad news: "It'll cost $5,000 over four years. But don't worry! Just pay me $100 a month!" The deal sounds easy, and easy it may be—but tax foolish. Since medical expenses are deductible only to the extent that they exceed 3% of Adjusted Gross Income, each year the first $1,500 is not deductible for a taxpayer with AGI of $50,000. For most high-income taxpayers who are adequately covered by medical insurance, this often precludes any deduction at all, above the $150 for insurance.

Instead of paying Dr. Pullit $1,200 per year, which may or may not be deductible, pay the full $5,000 in one lump sum, even if you have to borrow the money. Make sure to sign a contract with the doctor so that you are legally liable for the payments, and this agreement will not be disallowed as a pre-payment.

07-07.5 **Tax Hint**

Should a high-income taxpayer take out medical or major medical insurance in the first place? For each individual, you must work up the particular figures, which may surprise you in a few cases. For a top-bracket taxpayer, Uncle Sam picks up 50% of all medical expenses in excess of 3% of AGI. For some taxpayers already strapped with recurring medical bills, the 3% of AGI amount may not present the barrier it normally does. The point is that the proceeds of medical and casualty insurance serve only to reduce the tax deduction. For the 50% taxpayer, these proceeds are "worth" only 50¢ on the dollar. Keep this in mind when considering the price of "self-insurance."

CASUALTY LOSSES 07-08

A casualty loss is the *sudden* complete or partial destruction of property due to either damage or theft.

1. The *damage* must be unexpected and sudden. Such items as automobile accidents, fire, and earthquake qualify. Drought damages may qualify if unusual for the area, or if they are more severe than usual for the area. Losses that do not qualify include termite damage, gradual sea erosion, and gradual insect damages.
2. *Theft* does *not* include mysterious disappearance. Just because your gold ring is missing, it is not necessarily stolen. There must be evidence of a theft, and the theft should be reported to the local police authorities and, if applicable, to the insurance company. Property that is simply lost by the taxpayer does not qualify as a casualty loss.

The amount of the loss may be documented by obtaining appraisals of the value of the property before and after the loss. As an alternative, the taxpayer may show the cost of repairs to return the property to its useful state before the loss.

The casualty loss is generally deductible in the year that the loss is determined. If insurance proceeds are expected in a future year, the loss is determined after the insurance proceeds are received. If a deduction is taken for a casualty loss, and if insurance is recovered in a subsequent year, taxpayers must report that recovery to the extent that they receive a tax benefit (07-08.1).

If the casualty loss occurs in an area that is declared a disaster area by the President of the United States, and eligible for federal assistance, the taxpayer may claim the loss either in the year it occurred or in the immediately preceding year. The objective of this election is to allow for a "quick" refund by carrying back the disaster loss. But if taxpayers can wait until filing their returns in the year of the disaster, then compute which year has the higher incremental tax rate and file for the loss deduction in that year; you may increase the amount of the tax refund. The Regulations require that the election be made by the filing date of the year in which the loss occurred, *without* regard to any extensions.

How do the deductions fit into the tax computation?

1. Casualty losses sustained *in a business or trade,* as well as those in the production of *rent or royalty income,* are deductions for Adjusted Gross Income.
2. Casualty losses sustained in a *nonbusiness income producing venture,* or with regard to *personal property,* are deductible from Adjusted Gross Income to the extent they exceed $100 (07-08.1).

07-08.1 **Example**

Courtney Lee owns a home with an adjusted basis of $80,000. Last year the house was struck by lightning, which resulted in a fire causing considerable damage. The fair market value of the house was $120,000 preceding the casualty, and it cost Courtney $9,000 to repair the damage. The insurance company paid only $3,000 of this amount. Her deductible casualty loss is:

Damages	$9,000
Less: Amount reimbursed by insurance	3,000
Net damages	$6,000
Less: First $100	100*
Deductible loss	$5,900

*If this had been business property, the deductible loss would have been $6,000. The $100 reduction in the deductible loss is applied to personal property.

If the next year, Courtney sues the insurance company and recovers the additional $6,000. The amount she would have to include in income would be only $5,900, that is, the amount she deducted. But let's say this is her only itemized deduction from Adjusted Gross Income, and she files as a single person. Since she is entitled to a Zero Bracket Amount of $2,300 in any event, the tax benefit of the loss would be only $3,600:

Deduction taken	$5,900
Zero Bracket Amount	2,300
Tax benefit	$3,600

She would have to include in Gross Income $3,600 of the $6,000 insurance proceeds received.

The Role of Basis 07-08.2

The amount of the allowable deduction is the *lower* of the amount of loss sustained or the basis in the hands of the taxpayer.

Tax *warning* 07-08.2A

In the Courtney example, let's say that the house burns to the ground, that the market value of the lot after the loss is $30,000, and that the insurance proceeds are $40,000. Then:

Fair market value before casualty loss	$120,000
Fair market value after casualty loss	− 30,000
Casualty loss	$ 90,000
Basis	$ 80,000
The lower of basis or loss	$ 80,000
Less: Insurance proceeds	− 40,000
Loss before $100 limit	$ 40,000
Less: First $100 of loss	− 100
Deductible loss	$ 39,900

The point of this computation is that, for appreciated property, the use of the casualty loss deduction to soften the blow of self-insurance is unwise.

An even more dramatic case can be made for the theft of such items of silverware and jewelry. A silverware set that cost, say, $2,000 twenty years ago is probably worth well over $15,000 today. If it were stolen, the casualty loss would be limited to its basis of $2,000.

07-09 MISCELLANEOUS DEDUCTION

In the "miscellaneous deductions" category, all deductions from Adjusted Gross Income are grouped, *except*:

1. medical expenses,
2. taxes
3. interest
4. charitable contributions, and
5. casualty losses.

Miscellaneous expenses are those nonbusiness expenses incurred for the production of income or for the preservation of income-producing assets. Although the list is virtually limitless, some of the items more frequently deducted under this category are:

1. union dues,
2. education expenses,
3. employment agency fees and other costs of seeking employment,
4. expenses for the maintenance of investments,
5. dividend and interest charges on short stock and bond positions,
6. tax return preparation and income tax consultation fees,
7. legal and other professional fees incurred to obtain taxable income,
8. safe deposit box costs,
9. special clothing, uniforms, and safety equipment required by the taxpayer's employment, and
10. vocational supplies.

07-10 DEDUCTION FOR TWO EARNER MARRIED COUPLES

As described in 01-06.1A, married couples may be penalized for filing jointly, as opposed to being single and filing as such. To mitigate this situation, married couples are permitted, as a deduction *for* AGI, the lesser of:

1. 10% (5% for 1982) of $30,000; or
2. 10% (5% for 1982) of the "Qualified Earned Income" of the spouse with the *lower* amount of qualified earned income.

Qualified earned income is:

1. net income from a trade or business; plus
2. salaries and wages;
   less
3. payments to certain pension plans such as IRA and Keogh plans; and
4. employee business expenses.

Example 07-10.1

Sam and Sarah Taxpayer had the following situation for 1983:

Sam's salary		$50,000
Sarah's net income from business		32,000
Sam's IRA contribution		(2,000)
Sarah's Keogh contribution		(3,000)
Sam's employee business expenses		(4,000)
Sam's qualified earned income is:		
Salary		$50,000
Less:		
Contribution to IRA	$2,000	
Employee business expenses	4,000	6,000
Net		$44,000
Sarah's qualified earned income is:		
Net income from business		$32,000
Contribution to Keogh plan		3,000
Net		$29,000
Their deduction for AGI is the lower of:		
10% of $30,000		$ 3,000
10% of $44,000		4,400
10% of $29,000		2,900

8

INVESTMENT-RELATED DEDUCTIONS

DEPRECIABLE PROPERTY

Depreciation is the means of allocating the cost of a long-lived asset over its useful life. Assets that have a useful life extending beyond the tax year, and that are used in the production of income, must be depreciated over their useful lives or as prescribed in the Code. This requirement prevents the full cost of the asset from being deducted in the year of acquisition. Each year during the asset's useful life, some portion of the cost is taken as a tax deduction.

This concept of deducting the expense over the useful life of the asset or as prescribed in the Code remains the same for various types of assets. Only the terminology changes. The term "depreciation" normally applies to tangible assets. The same concept, applied to intangible assets, is called *amortization*. When natural resources are used, the term *depletion* is applied.

Property may be depreciated only if held in a trade or business, or if held for the production of nonbusiness income. For an asset to be depreciable, it must have a determinable useful life. If assets such as land, goodwill, and franchises do not have a termination date, then they do not have a determinable useful life. And no depreciation is allowed on these assets. The full cost is merely part of the basis of the asset, and it serves to increase loss or to decrease gain on sale. Inventory, held for resale, is also not depreciable.

Depreciation expense, as a general rule, begins when the asset is placed into service. It is normally a deduction for Adjusted Gross Income since it is either related to a trade or business or used for the production of rents or royalties.

The mechanics of depreciation involve the simultaneous reduction of the basis of the asset and the increase of tax-deductible expenses.

08-01.1 Example

Colin Gordon purchases a yellow widget stamping machine for his business. He elects to depreciate the machine over 12 years on a straight-line basis, and the cost is $120,000.

Under the straight-line method of depreciation (08-04.1), he can deduct $10,000 per year for 12 years to recover his cost. Each year the basis of the asset will be reduced by the amount of the depreciation. The Code requires (except for real estate) that one-half year's depreciation be taken in the year that the asset is placed in service. So:

First year (half-year)	$ 5,000
Years 2 through 12	10,000 each
Year 13 (half-year)	5,000

At the end of year 2, his basis is:

Cost		$120,000
Less: Depreciation: First year	$ 5,000	
Second year	+10,000	− 15,000
Basis		$105,000

WHO CAN TAKE THE DEPRECIATION DEDUCTION? 08-02

The taxpayer entitled to take the depreciation deduction is the taxpayer with the "economic" exposure to the loss of the value in the asset due to wear and tear. Normally this person is the owner of the property.

Who, then, is the "owner" of the property? In most cases, the answer is fairly straightforward and follows the legal ownership rules. But the IRS can look through the legal veil of a transaction to the economic substance in determining who can claim depreciation.

In a capital, or net, lease transaction (06-07.3B and 10-07), the lessor retains legal title, but the lessee has the economic risks of ownership, as well as the depreciation expense.

A life tenant may deduct the depreciation expense related to an asset. The rate of depreciation expense is based on the useful life of the asset, not on the expected life of the life tenant. The remainderman will deduct the remaining available depreciation upon taking title.

Leasehold Improvements 08-02.1

Lessees may make improvements to property held under lease, and legally they do not have title to the improvements. Most leases convey the improvements to the lessor upon termination of the lease. Yet, from the depreciation standpoint, this situation is a typical example of when legal title is irrelevant. The lessee is entitled to depreciate the leasehold improvements. The period over which the asset should be depreciated is the *shorter* of the life of the improvement as described in the Code *or* the remaining time on the lease.

If a lease is renewable, *and* if the remaining time on the lease is less than 60% of the useful life of the asset, the presumption is that the lease will be renewed. The asset is then depreciated over the shorter of the life as described in the Code or the lease, including the renewal period. The lessee may refute this presumption by presenting facts to the contrary.

When the lessor and lessee are "related," the life prescribed in the Code must be used. The relationship tests are rather complicated, but they include blood relatives, relatives by marriage, corporate interrelationships, and stockholder-corporate relationships.

08-03 BASIS FOR DEPRECIATION

Taxpayers *must* take the depreciation allowable. If they do not, the basis of the asset is still reduced as if they had taken the depreciation. This requirement prevents taxpayers from postponing depreciation to a year when they are in higher tax brackets.

The basis of property for the purposes of computing depreciation is generally the same as the basis for computing *gain.* In several situations involving gifts (04-05), the basis for computing losses is different from the basis for computing gains.

If property starts out being used as personal property, and not subject to depreciation, and if subsequently its use is changed to one of an income-producing nature, then the basis for computing depreciation is the *lower* of:

1. fair market value on the date its use is changed, or
2. the adjusted basis for computing gain.

When several assets are acquired at the same time and for a single price, the cost must be allocated among the different assets for the purpose of computing depreciation.

08-03.1 Example

Brynne Gordon purchases a house for rental purposes for $100,000. She must allocate the cost between land (a non-depreciable asset) and building (a depreciable asset). The allotment may be based on appraisals or on other reliable sources. For tax assessment purposes, the house is appraised at $50,000 and the land at $12,000. After speaking to several realtors, Brynne feels that this is a fair representation of the true fair market values of the land and building. She then allocates the purchase price as:

Land ($100,000 × $12,000/$62,000, the total)	$ 19,355
Building ($100,000 × $50,000/$62,000)	+ 80,645
Total	$100,000

Salvage Value 08-03.2

If an asset is expected to have a salvage value at the end of its useful life, that value is not taken into consideration when computing tax-deductible depreciation. But see 08-14 for recapture of depreciation when an asset is disposed of.

METHODS OF DEPRECIATION 08-04

The Code allows taxpayers to use one of three methods for depreciating tangible property. They are:

1. straight-line over one of the useful lives described in the Code; or
2. the accelerated method prescribed in the Code; or
3. any other reasonable method *not* based on the passage of time.

All tangible assets subject to depreciation are divided into five classes for the purpose of "cost recovery." The taxpayer may elect to use the accelerated method prescribed for that class of assets or depreciate the asset on a straight-line basis over one of the prescribed useful lives.

The only other alternative the taxpayer has is to depreciate the asset under the unit-of-production method or any method of depreciation not expressed in a term of years.

08-04.1 Straight-Line Method

The straight-line method deducts the depreciation expense evenly over the useful life of the asset.

08-04.2 Production Method

The production method ignores the passage of time, and it looks at an asset's productive capability. The method is suitable for assets whose productive capability is a better measure of their useful life than the passage of time. Machinery such as tools, dies, and stamping equipment fall into this category. If a machine is good for, say, 160,000 impressions, it really does not matter over what period of time those impressions are made.

The production method is the basis of cost depletion (08-07.1). If a mine has 160,000 tons of ore and your basis for depletion is $320,000, then the asset is depleted at the rate of $2 per ton (160,000 tons/$320,000). Again, the time involved to remove the ore is irrelevant.

08-04.2A Example

Let's use the figures for Colin Gordon's widget stamper. Assuming that it is capable of stamping 300,000 widgets and that the depreciable cost is $120,000, then the depreciation is calculated as follows:

$$\frac{\text{Depreciable cost}}{\text{Number of impressions}} = \text{Depreciation per widget}$$

$$\$120{,}000/300{,}000 = 40¢$$

Income Forecast Method 08-04.3

The income forecast method of depreciation is a variation of the production method that is often used for movies and video tapes. The cost of the asset is written off based on estimated income production.

Example 08-04.3A

A movie is expected to produce gross revenue of $10,000,000, and it costs $2,000,000 to make. For each dollar of gross revenue earned, 20¢ of the cost is written off as depreciation.

Classes of Tangible Assets 08-04.4

The classes of assets are:

	However, the taxpayer may elect a recovery period of:
3-year property	5 or 12 years
5-year property	12 or 25 years
10-year property	25 or 35 years
15-year real property	35 or 45 years
15-year public utility property	35 or 45 years

All assets of the same cost recovery class (5-year property) acquired during the year must be depreciated over the same period and under the same method (that is, straight-line or accelerated).

Straight-Line Depreciation 08-04.5

The straight-line method deducts the depreciation expense evenly over the useful life of the asset. In the case of Colin Gordon's widget machine, he would have the choice of depeciating it on a straight-line method over either 5 years, 12 years, or 25 years. He cannot choose some figure in between.

If he chose the 5-year period, and if his cost was $120,000, then he would take one-half year's depreciation expense in the year of acquisition ($120,000 divided by 5 years divided by 2) or $12,000. In each of the following years, he would take $24,000 depreciation expense until year 6, when he would take the remaining unrecovered cost of $12,000 as an expense.

08-04.6 Which Assets are in Which Class?

Three-year property includes automobiles, light-duty trucks, machinery and equipment used for research and experimentation, small tools, and any other machinery with a class life under RevPro 77-10 of 4 years or less. Revenue Procedure 77-10 is a listing of assets and their estimated useful lives. This procedure was used under the previous depreciation laws, which covered assets acquired prior to 1981.

Five-year property includes all property not in another class. Basically this includes all machinery, equipment, furniture, and the like. The class includes all Section 1245 property (08-14) with a class life of 18 years or less under RevPro 77-10.

Ten-year property includes all Section 1245 property with a class life of 18½ years or more under RevPro 77-10. It also includes all Section 1250 property (08-14) with a class life of 12½ years or less under RevPro 77-10.

Fifteen-year real property includes almost all real estate.

Fifteen-year public utility property is a special class established for public utilities.

08-04.7 Accelerated Depreciation

Section 168 of the Code contains charts of what accelerated depreciation may be taken in lieu of straight-line depreciation. The amounts are:

"(A) FOR PROPERTY PLACED IN SERVICE AFTER DECEMBER 31, 1980, AND BEFORE JANUARY 1, 1985.—

"If the recovery year is:	The applicable percentage for the class of property is:			
	3-year	5-year	10-year	15-year public utility
1	25	15	8	5
2	38	22	14	10
3	37	21	12	9
4		21	10	8
5		21	10	7
6			10	7
7			9	6
8			9	6
9			9	6
10			9	6
11				6
12				6
13				6
14				6
15				6.

"(B) FOR PROPERTY PLACED IN SERVICE IN 1985.—

"If the recovery year is:	The applicable percentage for the class of property is:			
	3-year	5-year	10-year	15-year public utility
1	29	18	9	6
2	47	33	19	12
3	24	25	16	12
4		16	14	11
5		8	12	10
6			10	9
7			8	8
8			6	7
9			4	6
10			2	5
11				4
12				4
13				3
14				2
15				1.

"(C) FOR PROPERTY PLACED IN SERVICE AFTER DECEMBER 31, 1985.—

"If the recovery year is:	The applicable percentage for the class of property is:			
	3-year	5-year	10-year	15-year public utility
1	33	20	10	7
2	45	32	18	12
3	22	24	16	12
4		16	14	11
5		8	12	10
6			10	9
7			8	8
8			6	7
9			4	6
10			2	5
11				4
12				3
13				3
14				2
15				1.

08-04.7A **Example**

Colin Gordon's widget machine is in the 5-year class. Instead of the straight-line depreciation shown in the previous examples, he could (if the machine were placed in service before January 1, 1985) take the following depreciation:

Year	1	($120,000 × 15%)	$ 18,000
	2	($120,000 × 22%)	26,400
	3	($120,000 × 21%)	25,200
	4	($120,000 × 21%)	25,200
	5	($120,000 × 21%)	25,200
		Total depreciation	$120,000

08-04.7B **Special 15-Year Real Property Considerations**

The Code does not provide a chart for 15-year real property, but it directs the Secretary of the Treasury to devise and publish a chart. To date those regulations have not been forthcoming, *but,* based on the instructions to the Secretary, the taxpayer may construct his/her own chart. For real estate, depreciation begins in the month that the asset is placed into service, and the taxpayer cannot simply take one-half year's depreciation in the year it is placed in service.

The Code directs that 200% declining balance be used for low-income housing, and 175% declining balance be used for all other real property. This formula is not scheduled to change in 1985 and 1986 as do the charts for personal property.

08-04.7C **Declining Balance Method**

To compute annual depreciation under the declining balance method, you must:

1. subtract the depreciation taken in prior years from total cost, and

2. multiply the difference by twice the percentage that you would take under the straight-line method.

Taxpayers must switch to straight-line at the time such a switch would give them a larger deduction.

Example 08-04.7D

Brynne Gordon purchased a piece of real estate for $120,000 (exclusive of the cost of the nondepreciable land). Under the accelerated cost recovery method, her deduction in each of the 15 years would be:

Year	*Cost less total previous depreciation*	× *Rate*	*Depreciation*
1	$120,000	11.67*	$ 14,004
2	105,000	11.67	12,370
3	93,626	11.67	10,926
4	82,700	11.67	9,651
5	73,049	11.67	8,525
6	64,524	11.67	7,530
7	56,994	11.67	6,651
8 to 15	50,743 ($6,343 per year)	**	50,343
			$120,000

* 1/15th is 6.67% per year times 175% is 11.67% per year.
** 50,743 is divided by the remaining 8 years is more than 50,743 times 11.67% ($5,922).

Computation of partial year's depreciation 08-04.7E

When using declining balance depreciation, taxpayers

should compute the depreciation for a full year, and then divide the results by the appropriate number of months.

If Brynne had placed the building in productive use in October of year 1, then in year 1 her depreciation would be:

$14,004 × 3/12	$ 3,501
For Year 2 it would have been:	
$14,004 × 9/12	$10,503
12,370 × 3/12	3,093
Total for Year 2	$13,596

08-04.8 Tax Hint

Which depreciation system should be used? That depends! If the taxpayer anticipates sufficient income to use the deduction, then accelerated depreciation should be used to reduce taxes. If, on the other hand, the taxpayer anticipates little or no taxable income in the near future, then straight-line using a longer useful life should be used to save the deduction for years in which it can be used to offset income taxable in higher tax brackets.

08-04.9 Property Located Outside the United States

Property located outside the United States is subject to different, less liberal, rules.

08-05 ELECTION TO EXPENSE CERTAIN DEPRECIABLE BUSINESS ASSETS

Section 179 allows the taxpayer to elect to expense a limited amount of expenditures for capital assets rather than capitalize them and depreciate them. This is an election, and unlike taking depreciation (which a taxpayer must do), not making this election does not reduce the basis of the property.

Properties eligible for this treatment are those properties for which an investment credit (09-07) could be claimed.

The dollar limits for each year are:

1982	$ 5,000
1983	5,000
1984	7,500
1985	7,500
1986 and thereafter	10,000

Married persons filing separately are entitled only to 50% of the above limits.

If the taxpayer elects to expense a capital asset under this provision, no investment credit is allowed.

DEPLETION 08-06

Depletion is a tax deduction similar to production depreciation (08-04.1). The basic concept is that the taxpayer's investment in the production of natural resources is deductible as those resources are mined or otherwise extracted and sold. The depletion deduction reduces the basis of the investment very much like depreciation (08-01.1), but several aspects of depletion are unique.

First, for most but *not* all natural resources, taxpayers may elect *percentage depletion* rather than *cost depletion* (08-07). For now, the basics of these two methods are as follows:

1. *Cost depletion* amortizes the cost of the investment over the productive life of the asset, in a manner similar to production depreciation.
2. *Percentage depletion* is a direct reduction of taxable income, in lieu of cost depletion, based on a percentage of the selling price (as defined) of the product.

Another unique aspect of depletion is that in many cases the Code is very liberal with regard to which expenses must be capitalized and which may be deducted in the year incurred (08-08). For this reason the depletable basis of the property may be unusually low to begin with. This lower basis, of course, favors the use of percentage depletion based on sales, rather than cost depletion based on the depletable basis.

Finally, depletion is unique with regard to determining who is entitled to the depletion allowance (deduction). Just as the "economic" owner is the taxpayer entitled to the depreciation deduction, the taxpayer with an economic *interest* is the one who may deduct the depletion allowance. This definition allows the total depletion allowance for a given piece of property to be divided among taxpayers.

The most common division of the depletion allowance comes from a lessor-lessee relationship. If the owner of the property leases it to a producer for a royalty of, say, 20% of the ore produced, both are entitled to a depletion allowance. The lessor gets 20% of the depletion allowance, and the lessee 80%. Notice that the total depletion allowance does not increase; it is simply divided among parties.

08-06.1 Economic Interest

What is "economic interest"? The general rule is that taxpayers have an economic interest and are therefore entitled to the depletion allowance, if they look to the production of the natural resource for the recovery of their investment. Specifically, however, the extractive industries have evolved some extremely complex contractual agreements. In many cases it is not obvious who has, and does not have, an economic interest. As a result, the area is one of many private letter rulings. Competent legal counsel is essential since more than one taxpayer may claim depletion on the same property. Too often, these disputes are settled in federal court as part of income tax litigation.

Property Subject to Depletion 08-06.2

The extraction of minerals and other natural deposits are subject to depletion. The cutting of timber is subject only to cost depletion. Oil and gas is generally also limited to cost depletion, except for small producers and royalty owners (08-07.2, percentage depletion).

Treatment of Contract Bonuses 08-06.3

Since the depletion allowance relates to the extraction of natural resources, logic has it that the allowance may be taken only when there has been such an extraction. Yet an exception is made when a lessor receives a bonus plus royalties based on extraction.

1. In figuring the amount of the *cost depletion* allowed, you add the bonus to the expected royalties to compute the total amount expected to be received under the contract. (See 08-07 for an example of how cost depletion is computed.)
2. *Percentage depletion* for bonuses received on oil and gas property may not be used. Only cost depletion may be used. Percentage depletion, however, may be used for bonuses received on properties other than gas and oil.

METHODS OF DEPLETION 08-07

There are two methods of computing the depletion allowance: *cost* and *percentage.* Cost depletion may be taken for the extraction of all natural resources. Percentage depletion is restricted both by the type of product extracted and, in the cases of oil and gas, by the size and type of the taxpayer's business.

08-07.1 Cost Depletion

Cost depletion is based on the taxpayer's basis—in most cases, the capitalized cost—in the property for computing gain. Depletion is taken only on the cost of the mine or well. The costs of buildings, equipment, and other collateral items are subject to depreciation expense.

To compute the amount of depletion per unit of production, divide the basis of the property by the total anticipated production. When more than one taxpayer is entitled to the depletion allowance, the amount is prorated among them based on their proportionate share of the economic interest.

If the anticipated production is corrected due to new knowledge in subsequent years, the depletion allowance is recomputed for the year of the correction and for subsequent years. No adjustment for previous depletion is made.

08-07.1A Example

Aaron Gordon leases uranium land to MBS Hot Rock Company in 1979. The terms of the lease run as long as uranium can be produced from the property. Aaron is to receive a royalty of 20% of the uranium produced, and he receives a bonus of $250,000 upon signing the lease. The recoverable ore is estimated to be 4 million tons, and Aaron's share of the sales, his royalties, are expected to be $1,800,000.

During 1979, no uranium is extracted. Aaron's basis in the property is $800,000. Aaron's cost depletion per dollar of royalties to be received as computed as:

Total to be received under the contract ($250,000 bonus + $1,800,000 royalties)	$2,050,000
Aaron's basis in the property	$ 800,000
Cost depletion per dollar of revenue ($800,000/$2,050,000)	39.02¢
For 1979, he reports:	
Royalty received (bonus)	$250,000
Less: Depletion allowance [$250,000 (amount received) × ($800,000/$2,050,000)]	− 97,561
Adjusted Gross Income	$152,439

The depletion allowance could just as well be calculated as $250,000 × 0.3902, or $97,550 (the difference is in rounding).

Other than for oil and gas, Aaron could use percentage depletion. But in this case doing so would not be to his advantage (08-07.2A). Aaron's basis in the mine is now:

Original basis	$800,000
Depletion allowed	− 97,561
Adjusted basis	$702,439

Percentage Depletion 08-07.2

The Code requires taxpayers to choose the *higher* of cost depletion or percentage depletion. The computation is made each year, and the percentage is figured on the selling price at the site of extraction. The selling price may include some transportation and processing required to sell the "raw" product, but it does not include processing to a finished product.

For each product, consult the Code, the Regulations, and the court cases to determine exactly how much processing is allowed for that particular natural resource. The percentages allowed for each type of ore vary from 5% to 22%. As an example, uranium is 22%, gold is 15%, sand and gravel 5%. In this complex area, however, the use of the material must be considered in some cases, as well as the mixture of various ores in one mine.

As a general rule, oil and gas wells are not allowed a percentage depletion, with two exceptions. The first is for natural gas produced from geopressured wells, and the second is for oil and gas produced by "small" producers. Again, the rules are complex, but the general limit is either 1,000 barrels per day average for the year, or 6,000,000 cubic feet per day average for the year. For those who qualify, the rate is being reduced gradually from 22% in 1980 to 15% for 1984 and later. A further limitation is that the percentage depletion cannot exceed 65% of the taxpayer's taxable income (as defined) from all sources, without regard to the depletion allowance.

Percentage depletion for all natural resources is limited to 50% of taxable income from the mine, or well, without regard to the depletion allowance (08-07.2B).

08-07.2A **Example**

From example 08-07.1A, we can see that Aaron is better off using cost depletion. The percentage depletion is 22% of $250,000 or only $55,000. Let's carry through the same problem.

In 1980 MBS mines 200,000 tons of ore and received gross income (subject to depletion) of $2,000,000. After taking all deductions, except depletion, MBS's taxable income from the property is $1,500,000. If Aaron's royalty is $400,000 (20% of production), then his depletion allowance is the *greater* of:

22% of $400,000	$ 88,000
or	
$400,000 × ($800,000/$2,050,000)	$156,098

Obviously, he would choose the cost depletion again.

But let's say his basis in the property is $80,000 instead of $800,000. Then on the bonus payment of $250,000 his depletion would be the greater of:

22% of $250,000	$ 55,000
or	
$250,000 × ($80,000/$2,050,000)	$ 9,756

He would use the $55,000, and his basis would be:

Original basis	$ 80,000
Depletion allowed	55,000
Adjusted basis	$ 25,000

On the payment of 1980 royalties in the amount of $400,000, his depletion allowance would be:

22% of $400,000	$ 88,000
or	
$400,000 × ($25,000*/$1,800,000**)	$ 5,556

*His adjusted basis
**Anticipated future collection

Note that the total depletion allowance taken exceeds his basis. $55,000 in 1979 and $88,000 in 1980 equals $143,000 which is greater than his basis of $80,000. His basis in the property is now zero.

This highlights one of the major tax advantages of percentage depletion. The total depletion can exceed total cost.

Example 08-07.2B

MBS's percentage depletion would be computed as:

Gross income (mine selling price)	$2,000,000
Less: Current royalties paid	400,000*
	$1,600,000

Less: Allocation of royalty bonus	
[200,000 (extracted)/4,000,000 total) × $250,000]	12,500*
	$1,587,500
22% of $1,587,500	$ 349,250

*These items must be subtracted from the gross selling price that MBS can use to compute depletion, to avoid both parties claiming the same depletion allowance. This is, in effect, the allocation of economic interest.

MBS's taxable income from the property, before depletion, is $1,500,000. The limit on percentage depletion is 50% of that, or $750,000. MBS is well within that limit.

08-08 EXPLORATION AND DEVELOPMENT EXPENDITURES

One of the major tax advantages to investing in the extraction of natural resources arises from the rules distinguishing what is a deductible expense and what has to be capitalized. Normally, when an asset is constructed, all the expenses involved in the construction are capitalized, and they can be deducted only over the useful life of the asset. In the area of natural resources, many of these expenses can be deducted immediately. The rules fall into three categories:

1. exploration for other than oil and gas,
2. development for other than oil and gas, and
3. intangible oil and gas expenses, including those for geothermal wells.

08-08.1 Exploration Expenditures

Exploration expenditures include all the expenses of finding any mineral deposit other than oil and gas, as well as all the expenses of testing for quality and quantity.

Taxpayers may elect to deduct these expenses currently rather than capitalize them. The election is made in the first year that such expenses are incurred, and it is binding for future years.

For foreign exploration, the deduction is limited to $400,000 for the lifetime of the taxpayer.

When the mine reaches the development stage (08-08.2), taxpayers must make an election regarding the recapture of the previously deducted exploration expenses. They can either include them in gross income immediately or defer them until the mine comes into production. The election is made annually.

If taxpayers make the election to defer the recapture until the mine has become productive, the depletion allowance may not be deducted until the total depletion allowance equals the previously deducted exploration costs. The effect is to use the first depletion deductions to offset the gross income from the recapture of the exploration costs.

Development Expenditures 08-08.2

Taxpayers may elect annually either to capitalize or to deduct mine development expenses. Once a mine has shown that it has commercially producible ore, expenses must normally be incurred to develop the production. These expenses may be deducted immediately, as they are paid or incurred, rather than capitalized.

Intangible Drilling Costs 08-08.3

The line between tangible and intangible rests with salvage value. If the expenditure results in an asset with a salvage value (drilling rigs, tools, and so on), it must be capitalized. Expenditures that result in an asset without salvage value—such as wages, fuel, supplies, and the like—are intangible, and they can be deducted, rather than capitalized, as they are incurred or paid.

08-09 SPECIAL FARM CONSIDERATIONS

The Code gives special tax treatment to farmers and ranchers. To understand the nature of this treatment, you must understand the objectives of the Code. The Code attempts to ease the bookkeeping burdens of the "real" farmer, while excluding the "investor" from taking undue advantage of the liberal rules. There are two sides of the liberal tax rules: the income side and the expense side.

On the *income* side, farmers may, in certain cases, postpone the recognition of income to a future year. This option, of course, delays paying the tax on that income. And it is normally allowed for the collection of funds due to the destruction of a crop that would have been sold in a future year.

What about *expenses*? Although most businesses are required to show inventories at the end of their tax year, thereby reducing their deductible expenses (10-03), farmers may elect a "pure" cash basis and not show inventories, thereby increasing their deductions.

Again, to simplify their accounting, farmers may deduct many expenditures that would normally be capitalized. Items such as feed, seed, and fertilizer may be deducted when purchased, even if they have not yet been used. This election gives farmers deductions for expenses in year 1, but they do not have to show the income until year 2, when the crop or animals are sold. For example, ground improvements, such as soil and water conservation programs, which obviously improve the value and productivity of the land, would normally be capitalized. Yet these expenditures may be deducted in the year of the expenditure (within limits).

Having established ease for the "real" farmer, how does the Code prevent the "investor" from reaping the harvest? There are several attacks. The primary attack is the requirement that farming be undertaken for *profit*. If farming is a hobby (08-11), or if it is run in a manner indicating that it is not for profit, the IRS will attempt to disallow all the losses.

Another attack is the limitation of the deductions that may be taken by a *farm syndicate*, which is basically a farm tax shelter. As an example, if 35% or more of the losses are allocated to limited partners (11-02.5), then the limitations apply. As an example of the limitations, the deduction for feed is limited to the amount *used*.

Finally, in the area of soil and water conservation expenses, if the farm is sold within 10 years, some or all of the profit may be recaptured as ordinary income rather than as long-term capital gains.

Tax *Warning* 08-09.1

If your investment in a farm or ranch is tax motivated, *beware*! Taking a current deduction for the creation of an asset and then selling the asset at a long-term capital gain is a fine idea. Go ahead and buy that breeding goat, feed it for 12 months (24 months for horses and cattle), take a deduction for what it eats, and then sell it for a long-term capital gain. That's a fine idea—if the goat does not die, *and* if the market for breeding goats is still as strong as you thought it would be.

Farming and ranching are for professionals! One of the reasons Congress has allowed favorable tax treatment is due to the high degree of risk. If you are a farmer, enjoy them. If you are an investor, there are probably easier rows to hoe.

WINDFALL PROFITS TAX 08-10

The windfall profits tax is not an income tax, but rather an excise tax on the production of crude oil. Although the tax is limited to 90% of the taxable net income of the producer, it is withheld by the first purchaser of the crude who remits the tax. The tax rate depends on which of four groups the oil fits into:

1. *Tier I:* Most oil discovered before 1979	70%
2. *Tier II:* Oil from the National Petroleum Reserves and stripper wells	60%
3. *Tier III:* Most newly discovered oil	30%*
4. *Exempt:* Some Alaskan oil, Indian oil, and some oil produced by states and localities	0%

* For year:		1984	22 %
1982	27½%	1985	20 %
1983	25 %	1986 and thereafter	15 %

For 1983 and subsequent years, certain stripper wells owned by independent producers will be exempt.

The tax is imposed on the difference between a base price, which is adjusted periodically for inflation, and the selling price. Lower rates are applied if the producers are independent contractors and if their average daily production is 1,000 barrels or less. Those rates are:

- *Tier I:* 50%
- *Tier II* and *Tier III:* 30%

Royalty owners are entitled to a credit of $2,500 in 1981, **for the first two** barrels per day for 1982 to 1984. This increases to three barrels per day in 1985.

The taxable portion of the selling price is reduced by the state severance tax that applies to the difference between the base price and the selling price.

08-10.1 Example

The MBS Oil Company sells 1,000,000 barrels of Tier I oil, which it produced, at $35 per barrel. The base price at the time is $15 per barrel, and the state severance tax is 10% of selling price.

Selling price (1,000,000 × $35)	$35,000,000
Base price (1,000,000 × $15)	−15,000,000
Taxable portion	$20,000,000
State severance tax on $20,000,000	− 2,000,000
Taxable selling price	$18,000,000

The tax is computed to be \$12,600,000 (\$18,000,000 × 0.70). And the tax is limited to 90% of the taxable profit from production. Therefore, as long as MBS makes at least \$14,000,000 net on the gross selling price of \$35,000,000, the limit would not come into effect.

HOBBY LOSSES 08-11

Section 183, hobby losses, is a two-edged sword. The section itself is simple(!?). For losses to be deductible, taxpayers must be engaged in profit-making ventures. That requirement does not mean they have to succeed. Somewhere between a legitimate attempt at a business venture and my becoming a professional bowler is the potential for a lot of court cases. So, to avoid as much litigation as possible, Section 183 places the burden of proof on the taxpayer, *unless* that taxpayer shows a profit in 2 of 5 consecutive years (2 of 7 years for horse "players" such as breeders). In that case, the burden of proof shifts to the IRS.

If the IRS challenges a deduction on the grounds that it is a hobby loss, not that of a legitimate business, the taxpayer may force the IRS to "wait and see" by making a binding election: The taxpayer who makes money must say, "Leave me alone"; whoever loses money must say, "I will pay."

Tax *Warning* 08-11.1

Watch for the two-edged sword. Let's say that you are raising goats for breeding and deducting like mad. The IRS jumps in to say that raising breeding goats on Montgomery Street in San Francisco is a hobby—no deductions. You can make the IRS "go away" by saying, in effect, "Wait till next year!" You can rest assured that the IRS *will* be back next year, but for the time being you have put them off.

Here comes the second edge! To put off the IRS, you sign the agreement that *you* will make money in 2 of the 5 consecutive years. For years 1, 2, and 3, you take big deductions. In year 4, you are up to your ears in goats, and the goat market takes off. The Dow Jones goat index smashes 1,000, and you are about to cash in. But before you sell your goats, you die. The executor sells your goats in years 4 and 5 at enormous profits. So you are "square" with the IRS, right? No! *You* signed the agreement to make money in five years, not your estate. You and your estate are two different taxpayers. *You* failed the 2-of-5 test, and the IRS will prevail.

08-12 BAD DEBT DEDUCTIONS

Bad debts are normally deductible in one form or another. The deduction is the basis in the hands of the taxpayer. Any amount not included in gross income would not be included in the basis. (See also 08-12.4.)

08-12.1 Example: Individual

Dr. Barney Colin, MD, reports income from patients when he collects his fees. During the year he bills $1,000 for his services, but fails to collect the money. He gets no deduction, since the bad debts were never included in his Gross Income. His basis in the receivable is zero, and therefore his deduction is zero.

08-12.2 Direct Write-Off System

If a corporation is on the *direct write-off* system, they take a deduction for Adjusted Gross Income of the bad debts as they are realized.

Example 08-12.2A

The MBS Service Company recognizes income when services are performed. During the year they include $200,000 in income. Of the amount so included, $1,200 is considered uncollectible. In addition, they are forced to abandon collection efforts on $500 included in income for the previous year. With the direct write-off system, the deduction is $1,700 ($1,200 identified from this year's sales and $500 identified from previous year's sales).

The Black Motor's Formula 08-12.3

In lieu of taking a deduction for specific bad debts as they are identified, taxpayers may elect to provide a reserve for bad debts based on past history. The deduction is then taken based on an estimate, and bad debts are charged against the reserve as they are identified. The reserve method does not increase the bad debt deduction; merely accelerates the deduction since taxpayers do not have to wait to identify the specific bad debt.

Taxpayers make such an election with the first return showing a bad debt expense. If they wish to switch from a direct write-off method to a reserve method, the taxpayer must receive the permission of the Commissioner of the Internal Revenue. This is obtained by filing Form 3115 during the *first* 180 days of the tax year in which the change is desired.

How does the taxpayer estimate bad debts? Taxpayers may use their own formulas if they more clearly reflect income. But the question has been answered by the Black Motors' formula. The formula was tested to the Supreme Court level in the Black Motors case, and the IRS approves of its use. The Black Motors formula uses a "six-year" average. Taxpayers total the outstanding accounts receivable at the end of the previous five years and at the end of the current year. Then they compare that total to the *net* bad debt losses for the six years, which the bad debts *after* reduction for recoveries of bad debts previously written off.

08-12.3A **Example**

Year	Ending Accounts Receivable	Actual Bad Debts
1	$20,000	$ 500
2	30,000	700
3	40,000	1,000
4	35,000	400
5	38,000	500
Current year	42,000	800
Total	$205,000	$3,900

The taxpayer's average percentage of bad debts to ending accounts receivable is 1.9% ($3,900 ÷ $205,000). The reserve at the end of the current year should be $798 (1.9% of $42,000).

Let's say the reserve at the *beginning* of the current year is $900. During the year the taxpayer identifies $800 of bad debts (see the chart) and charges them against the reserve. There is no tax deduction for that charge. It simply reduces the reserve from $900 to $100. Since the reserve has $100 and it should have $798, the taxpayer increases the reserve by $698 and takes a deduction for that amount.

08-12.4 Corporate Bonds

Corporate bonds are, of course, debt instruments. When they become worthless, taxpayers have a capital loss. The date that the bonds are considered to have become worthless is the last day of the taxpayer's year, normally December 31. So any bond purchased in a previous year results in a long-term loss. Banks receive a more favorable treatment, and they can normally take an ordinary loss for worthless bonds. Except for banks, there is no deduction for partial worthlessness or for a decline in value.

Example 08-12.4A

Barney Colin purchases $10,000 MBS Corporation bonds for 97 ($9,700) on March 1, 1980. On January 3, 1981, the Company is declared bankrupt, and the bonds are worthless. Barney has a *long*-term loss since the bonds are considered to have become worthless on December 31, 1981, and his holding period is more than a year.

Personal Debt 08-12.5

Nonbusiness bad debts are considered to be short-term capital losses, regardless of the time the debt is held. No deduction is allowed for purely personal bad debts.

Example 08-12.5A

Aaron Gordon loans his friend Tiffany Schuler $5,000. To evidence that loan, she gives him a note, bearing interest at 10% annually, and agrees to pay it back when she sells her house, which she expected to do shortly. Two years later, Tiffany declares bankruptcy and has no assets. The debt is declared worthless by the bankruptcy court as part of the overall debt cancellation.

Aaron has a short-term loss in the amount of $5,000. He gets no deduction for the lost interest on the note since he never included that amount in his Gross Income.

The key is that he obtained written documentation of the loan and handled the transaction in a businesslike manner. If he simply gave her the money in a personal relationship situation, the IRS would contend that there was no debt and therefore no deduction.

Tax Hint 08-12.6

What happens if you lend someone money who never intended to pay you back? Fraud? If so, then the amount you lose is deductible as a casualty loss (07-08)! You get to deduct the full amount, less the first $100. The deduction is not limited as to amount, nor does it offset long-term capital gains as do short-term losses.

08-13 RESEARCH AND DEVELOPMENT EXPENDITURES

Research and development expenditures are truly one of the tax-favored investments. The Code is designed to encourage the development of new ideas and products. Hence the objectives are rather straightforward. Congress wants taxpayers to develop new ideas that help the economy. Taxpayers may even choose the method of accounting for those expenditures that is most advantageous under the current circumstances. The only restriction is that, if the expenditure is capitalized, it must be amortized over a period of 60 months or more.

What is *not* classified as research and development? Exploration for minerals, gas, or oil is not covered by these rules (08-08). Nor are expenditures to improve land or to create depreciable property.

What is research and development? *Research and development* relates to "soft" expenses—such as salaries, legal fees, laboratory costs, and the like—that are expended to create a new product. Taxpayers have two choices:

1. Expense all such expenditures *immediately* and take a tax deduction. Or . . .
2. Capitalize the expenditure and depreciate it over a period of 60 months or more.

The election to capitalize or to deduct expenses must be made as they relate to *each* project—an unusual degree of flexibility. See 09-08.12 for a credit for research and development expenditures.

DEPRECIATION RECAPTURE 08-14

The depreciation recapture rules attempt to find an equitable tax treatment for depreciable property used either in a trade or business or for the production of income. If the property is sold at a loss, then the loss is really an adjustment of depreciation. In other words, the taxpayer (using hindsight) should have taken more depreciation. So rather than classify the loss as a capital loss, which would be only partially deductible, the loss is classified as an ordinary loss, which is fully deductible. (See Chapter 5 for the favorable tax treatment of gains on the sale of long-term capital assets, as well as the deductibility of capital losses.)

Although the intent of the law is fairly straightforward, the application is rather complex. It is important to understand the application, since it affects tax planning, especially timing for the disposition of an asset. Since the recapture rules were phased in over a period extending from 1961 to 1981, property acquired prior to 1981 may receive a more favorable treatment than the ones described in the following sections.

Gains are handled under two rules:

1. *Section 1245 property* (substantially depreciable personal property); and
2. *Section 1250 property* (substantially depreciable real property.

Section 1245 Recapture 08-14.1

If Section 1245 property is sold at a gain, then to the extent that the gain is merely recapture of depreciation, it is fully taxable. To the extent that the gain is a true economic gain, it is afforded capital gains treatment.

08-14.1A **Example**

Five years ago, Aaron Gordon purchased a widget stamping machine for $10,000. He depreciated it over 12 years on the straight-line method. This year he sells the machine for $11,000. His gain is computed as:

Cost	$10,000
Depreciation taken	– 4,167
Adjusted basis	$ 5,833
Sale proceeds	$11,000
Adjusted basis	– 5,833
Gain*	$ 5,167

*Gain is attributed to:

Recapture of depreciation (Section 1245 gain, fully taxable)	$4,167
True economic gain (Section 1231 gain, taxable as long-term capital gain)	+1,000
Total	$5,167

08-14.2 Section 1250 Recapture

If the Section 1250 property is *nonresidential* and the taxpayer used the accelerated method of depreciation, the recapture rules are the same as for Section 1245 property. On the other hand, if the taxpayer used the straight-line method of depreciation, then the entire gain is Section 1231 gain, long-term capital gain.

For residential Section 1250 property, the amount of ordinary gain is only the difference between straight-line depreciation and accelerated depreciation. So, any straight-line depreciation that was used to offset fully taxable ordinary income is recaptured as long-term capital gain.

08-14.2A **Example**

Three years ago, Aaron purchased a new in use apartment house for $50,000 (exclusive of the cost of land). He depreciated it based on the 15-year 175% declining balance method (DDB). He sold it for $70,000. His gain is:

DEPRECIATION RECAPTURE

Cost	$50,000
Less: Depreciation taken	−15,538
Adjusted basis	$34,462
Sale proceeds	$70,000
Less: Adjusted basis	−34,462
Gain*	$35,538
Depreciation taken	$15,538
Straight-line depreciation (50,000 ÷ 15 × 3)	−10,000
Excess depreciation over straight-line rate	$ 5,538

*Gain is attributed to:

Recapture of *excess* depreciation (Section 1250 gain, fully taxable)	$ 5,538
Section 1231 gain ($20,000 of true economic gain plus $10,000 recapture of straight-line depreciation)	+30,000
Total	$35,538

Section 1231 08-14.3

Step one towards understanding depreciation recapture is the understanding of Section 1231. Section 1231 affords long-term capital gains treatment to certain noncapital assets. Depreciable real and personal property used either in a trade or business or for the production of income are not capital assets (05-01).

But they *may* be Section 1231 assets. Section 1231 assets are *depreciable* real and personal property held in a trade or business, or for the production of income, for *more* than a year. They include certain depreciable livestock (horses and cattle must be held for more than 24 months), certain unharvested crops, and certain coal and iron ores. So keep in mind that, if the property is not held for more than a year, it is *not* Section 1231 property. Any gain or loss is ordinary gain or loss.

Section 1231 computation of gain or loss requires several steps.

1. The Sections 1245 and 1250 recapture of depreciation is *added* to ordinary income and *subtracted* from the proceeds of sale in computing Section 1231 gain or loss.

2. The taxpayer then nets down all Section 1231 gains and losses to come up with a *net* Section 1231 gain *or* loss.
3. a. If the result in Step 2 is a gain, it is added to other long-term capital gains.
   b. If the result is a loss, it is a fully deductible loss.

08-14.3A **Example: Netting section 1231 gains**

Aaron Gordon has the following sales of assets held in his trade:

1. Widget stamping machine (08-14.1A):	
Section 1245 gain	$ 4,167
Section 1231 gain	$ 1,000
2. Building (08-04.2)	
Section 1250 gain	$ 5,538
Section 1231 gain	$30,000
3. Truck held 3 years, cost	$ 8,000
Depreciation taken	− 4,800
Adjusted basis	3,200
Sale proceeds	− 1,000
Section 1231 loss	$ 2,200

Aaron's gains and loss are as follows:

Fully taxable ordinary income:	
Section 1245 gain	$ 4,167
Section 1250 gain	+ 5,538
Total	$ 9,705
Amount added to long-term capital gains:	
Section 1231 gain, machine	$ 1,000
Section 1231 gain, building	+30,000
	$31,000
Less: Section 1231 loss, truck	− 2,200
Net Section 1231 gain	$28,800

Tax hint 08-14.3B

That $2,200 loss offsets only 40% taxable income. Two lessons should be learned:

1. If the sale of the truck could have been postponed or accelerated into a year without any Section 1231 gains, it would have been 100% deductible, instead of offsetting 40% taxable income.
2. Don't *under*depreciate assets. First, doing so reduces current deductions and therefore increases current taxes. Second, the loss may or may *not* be fully deductible depending on the results of the sale of other assets.

Involuntary Conversion 08-14.4

If a Section 1231 asset is involuntarily converted due to a casualty loss (but not due to condemnation), an additional favorable tax break is afforded. Such a loss need not be netted against other Section 1231 gains. If the casualty results in a gain (presuming the insurance payout exceeds basis), then the gain is netted with other Section 1231 transactions.

Example 08-14.4A

If, in the previous example, the loss on the truck is due to an uninsured accident, it is not used to reduce other Section 1231 gains. In that case, the $2,200 is fully deductible, and the full $31,000 is added to other long-term capital gains. But if there is a gain on the accident because the insurance proceeds exceed the basis of the truck, it is added to other Section 1231 transactions.

Tax hint 08-14.4B

If a casualty "loss" results in a gain, it is time to think before acting. Taxpayers can avoid reporting the gain by obtaining a new truck and reporting the transaction as an involuntary conversion (04-10). Here is the decision:

1. If the gain adds to Section 1231 gains, it is probably better to report the gain since it is only 40% taxable. The replacement property will have a basis of the full new cost, and that increased depreciation will offset 100% taxable income in the future. But . . .
2. If the gain serves only to reduce Section 1231 losses, which are 100% deductible, go the involuntary conversion route. Any reduction in future depreciation expense due to lower basis is immediately offset by a current deduction.

08-15 SECTION 1231: TIMBER, COAL, AND IRON ORE

To encourage the production of timber, coal, and iron ore, Congress has granted special treatment with regard to gains and losses. If the property is held for more than one year, some or all of the gains and losses can come under Section 1231. So gains are effectively long-term capital gains, and losses will be fully deductible.

08-15.1 Timber

The outright sale of standing timber does *not* qualify under these special rules. The sale of standing timber could:

1. be a capital gain or loss if held for investment; or
2. be ordinary income if held in a trade or business; or
3. qualify under Section 1231 if held in a trade or business, *but* only if the business was not the sale of timber.

To qualify for the special Section 1231 treatment, the timber must be cut by the taxpayer, and he or she must retain an economic interest in the timber at the time of cutting. The taxpayer must have owned either the land or the right to cut the timber for at least one year. This means that the lessee can get the Section 1231 treatment, rather than the owner.

To qualify, the taxpayer must elect Section 1231 treatment in the year the timber is cut, without regard to when it is sold. Doing so may require the reporting of taxable income before any proceeds of sale are received. The election increases the basis of the timber to current fair market value. Any subsequent sale results in an ordinary gain or loss.

Example 08-15.2

Barney Colin owns 5,000,000 feet of standing timber with a basis for depletion of $40,000 and a fair market value of $100,000. In 1981, he cuts the timber, retained an economic interest in the timber, and elected Section 1231 treatment. In 1982, he sold the timber for $120,000. The cost of the cutting was $5,000, the costs relating to the sale were $2,000. Barney's taxable income for 1981 and 1982 is:

1981:	
Fair market value of timber	$100,000
Basis	− 40,000
Section 1231 gain	$ 60,000

At the end of 1981, Barney has timber with a basis of:

Fair market	$100,000
Cutting costs	+ 5,000
Basis	$105,000

1982:	
Sale proceeds	$120,000
Less: Selling expenses	− 2,000
	$118,000
Basis	−105,000
Ordinary income	$ 13,000

08-15.3 Tax Hint

If Barney had not made the election, and if the timber was *not* a capital asset in his hands (i.e., inventory), then he would have reported no income in 1981 and $73,000 fully taxable ordinary income in 1982, computed as:

Sale proceeds		$120,000
Less: Basis	$40,000	
Cutting costs	5,000	
Selling costs	+ 2,000	−47,000
Profit		$73,000

But if the timber were a capital asset in Barney's hands, there would be no advantage to electing Section 1231 treatment since the entire gain would be long-term capital gain in 1982. The danger is having the IRS classify Barney as a dealer in timber, which would make the timber inventory if he had not made the election.

In the event that the sale of timber that is held for an investment has a market value below basis, then the election under Section 1231 permits a 100% loss deduction, rather than the limited long-term capital loss deduction.

08-15.4 Coal and Iron Ore

The owner, but not the miner or the lessee, of a coal or iron ore mine receives Section 1231 treatment for royalties received if the property is held more than one year. The taxpayer must also:

1. use cost depletion only, and
2. treat expenditures for the maintenance of the property as a reduction of the Section 1231 gain.

Expenses—such as taxes and other expenses of maintaining income-producing property—are normally deductions from Adjusted Gross Income. Yet these expenses must be deducted from the favorably taxed Section 1231 gain.

In a year when no royalties are received, the deductions may still be taken from Adjusted Gross Income.

Example 08-15.5

Aaron Gordon owns a coal mine that he leases under a royalty agreement. His basis for cost depletion is $8 per ton, and he receives royalties of $14 per ton. If during the year he receives royalties on 100,000 tons mined, and if he has expenses of $5,000 for maintaining the mine, his tax computation would be:

Royalties received		$1,400,000
Less: Cost depletion	$800,000	
Cost of maintaining the mine	+ 5,000	− 805,000
Section 1231 gain		$ 595,000

9

SPECIAL TAX COMPUTATIONS: AND CREDITS

INCOME AVERAGING (5-YEAR METHOD) 09-01

The income tax is, of course, a progressive tax: the more the taxpayer earns, the higher the tax rate. But these varying rates can place an unfair burden on taxpayers with inconsistent income from one year to another. As an example, if Artie Dahl, a single taxpayer, has taxable income of $5,000 in one year and $100,000 in another, he pays tax at the 11% incremental rate in the first year and at the 50% incremental rate in the second year. If he earned $52,500 in each year ($105,000 ÷ 2), then the *maximum* incremental tax rate would have been only 42%, rather than 50%.

To ease this burden, Congress enacted the *5-year averaging method.* Income from all sources, other than from the premature withdrawal of an owner-employees' pension plan, qualifies. If income is excluded because it was earned outside the U.S. or within a U.S. possession, an adjustment is required. This adjustment, along with a rather complex description of eligibility for 5-year income averaging, intends to prevent taxpayers either who are newly in the work force or who excluded foreign source income from averaging.

Taxpayers who provide more than 50% of their own support and who were either citizens or residents of the U.S. during the previous four years are eligible. Failure to provide more than 50% of their own support does not automatically make taxpayers ineligible, as there are many exceptions.

Taxpayers who elect the 5-year averaging method may not also exclude foreign source income.

The amount of income that is subject to income averaging is the amount by which the current year's taxable income exceeds 120% of the average of the previous four years' income—provided it is at least $3,000 (09-01.1). The computation effectively reduces the maximum incremental rate of taxation to a level *nearly* as low as if the income had been earned evenly over the period.

09-01.1 Example

Courtney Lee had the following taxable income:

Year	*Taxable Income*
1	$20,000
2	10,000
3	21,000
4	18,000
Total	$69,000
Current year	$80,000

Taxable income, current year	$80,000
120% of average of last four years ($69,000 ÷ 4) × 120%	−20,700*
Averagable income (must be at least $3,000)	$59,300
120% of average of last four years' income	$20,700

20% of averagable income		+11,860
Income level on which highest incremental tax rate is charged		$32,560
Tax on $32,560 (incremental rate, 34%)		$ 6,983
Above tax	$6,983	
Less tax on $20,700	−3,387	
Net	$3,596	
$3,596 × 4		+14,384
Total tax		$21,367
Compared to tax on $80,000, incremental bracket 48%		$27,971

*The form, Schedule G of Form 1040, computes this figure somewhat differently, but the answer is the same.

Married Couples 09-01.2

Married couples who filed jointly during the 5-year period need make no adjustment. But if a taxpayer who is married and who files separately in a community property state may have to make an adjustment to reflect community property income.

A person who was married during the base period and who is now either single or married to another must make an allocation to reflect income earned by each of the taxpayers.

Taxpayers who were previously single and who are now filing jointly simply add their taxable incomes together.

MINIMUM TAX ON PREFERENCE ITEMS 09-02

Previous chapters have shown that taxpayers get "a break" on many items in areas that Congress wants to help through tax incentives. But Congress also says, in effect, "Don't drink too much from the fountain!" If you have too many tax preference items, then you face the possibility of a minimum tax. There are actually two minimum taxes: the one discussed in this paragraph, and the Alternative Minimum Tax discussed in 09-03.

The minimum tax is actually a tax that is *added* to other income taxes. In general, the tax is 15% of tax preference items. However, the tax preference items are "reduced" by the greater of either $10,000 ($5,000 for a married taxpayer filing separately) or one-half of the taxpayer's tax liability (as defined) prior to computing the tax. In other words, taxpayers with less than $10,000 of tax preference items will face no minimum tax. Additionally, taxpayers with a high income tax liability will have either no—or a relatively small—minimum tax.

Taxpayers with a net operating loss (06-13) may be able to defer paying the minimum tax.

09-02.1 Tax Preference Items

09-02.1A Accelerated depreciation on real property

We know that accelerated depreciation allows you to take greater deductions on real property than you would be allowed to take on a straight-line basis (08-04). The amount of depreciation you take in excess of straight-line depreciation is a tax preference item.

09-02.1A-1 *Example*

A building with a 15-year recovery period and a basis for depreciation of $100,000 would show in the first year:

Accelerated depreciation, 175% declining balance method	$11,667
Straight-line method	− 6,667
Tax preference item	$ 5,000

Accelerated depreciation on personal property subject to lease 09-02.1B

Accelerated depreciation on personal property is generally not subject to the minimum tax. But if that personal property is subject to a lease, then the difference between the amount deducted and the amount that would have been deducted using the straight-line method is a tax preference item.

This is not a tax preference item for corporations, except for Subchapter S corporations (12-09) and personal holding companies (12-12).

Reserves for losses on bad debts of financial institutions 09-02.1C

Taxpayers may use the reserve method for computing bad debt expenses rather than specifically identifying worthless accounts (08-12). As a general rule, the estimates that are added to the reserve account and taken as a tax deduction must be based on actual experience. But certain financial institutions (mainly banks and other thrift institutions) are permitted to add amounts to their bad debt reserve account above that which their experience warrants. This additional amount is a tax preference item.

09-02.1D Depletion

Taxpayers may take a depletion allowance (deduction) in excess of their basis, normally cost (08-06). The amount of that depletion is a tax preference item.

09-02.1D-1 *Example*

Mine subject to percentage depletion (cost)	$100,000
Depletion taken in prior years	− 90,000
Basis, January 1	$ 10,000
Depletion allowance current year	−(50,000)
Tax preference item	$ 40,000

Obviously, *all* future depletion will be a tax preference item.

09-02.1E Intangible Drilling Costs

Taxpayers may take a current deduction for intangible drilling costs, even though such costs would normally be capitalized (08-08.3). For productive wells only—since the costs for a nonproductive well would normally be deductible in any event—intangible drilling cost deductions *may* be a tax preference item. The tax preference item consists of the amount by which intangible drilling costs exceed net income from oil, gas, and geothermal properties. The amount of tax preference must be determined based on each oil and gas property separately, and all geothermal properties combined.

This is not a preference item for corporations.

You should figure "excess" intangible drilling costs two ways and use whichever is more favorable for the taxpayer. Subtract from the total allowable intangible drilling costs the amount that would have been allowed if the costs had been capitalized.

1. and then amortized over a 120-month period beginning with the month that production begins, or
2. amortized as cost depletion.

Example 09-02.1E-1

The intangible drilling expenses allowable are $100,000, and the well goes into production on October 23. Assuming that the 120-month amortization is more favorable for the taxpayer, then:

Total intangible drilling expenses	$100,000
$100,000 × 3/120	− 2,500
Excess intangible drilling expenses	$ 97,500

Net income is gross income less all expenses except intangible drilling expenses. If the well produces $200,000 of gross income, $44,000 of depletion expense, and $70,000 of other allocable expenses, then:

Gross income		$200,000
Less: Other expenses	$70,000	
Percentage depletion	+44,000	−114,000
Net income for tax preference purposes		$ 86,000

In this case, $11,500 is a tax preference item ($97,500 less $86,000).

Capital gains 09-02.1F

Capital gains are a tax preference item for corporations only. Corporations have a choice: they may either include capital gains in ordinary income or elect an alternative tax (12-02). The tax preference applies only if the corporation elects the alternative tax. The minimum tax would also apply to any alternative tax election with regard to Section 1231 gain on the sale of timber. Individuals are subject only to the Alternative Minimum Tax (09-03).

The tax preference amount is the difference between the two taxes figured under the "regular" method and under the alternative method divided by 0.46.

09-02.1F-1 ***Example***

Regular tax	$48,000
Alternative tax due to long-term capital gains or Section 1231 gains on timber	−45,000
Net savings	$ 3,000
Tax preference amount ($3,000 ÷ 0.46)	$ 6,522

09-02.1G **Municipal bond interest**

Tax-exempt interest on municipal bonds is *not* a tax preference item.

09-02.2 Computation of "Net Income Taxes"

Part of the minimum tax computation requires the computation of the taxpayer's other "net income taxes." So to compute the minimum tax on individuals, here's what you have to do:

1. Find the tax on Taxable Income before (that is, not including):
   a. the tax on Accumulation Distribution of Trusts (09-11),
   b. the 10-year lump-sum tax (09-05), and
   c. the tax on premature withdrawals of pension plans.

2. Then add the tax from recomputing prior-year investment credits (09-07).
3. Also *add* the tax on the premature redemption of individual retirement bonds.
4. Now *subtract* the following credits (09-07 and 09-08):
   a. credit for contributions to candidates,
   b. credit for the elderly,
   c. credit for child and dependent care,
   d. investment credit,
   e. foreign tax credit,
   f. WIN credit,
   g. jobs credit, and
   h. residential energy credit.

Translated into English, this calculation means that, in most cases, the "tax" will be the taxpayer's net tax, before any payments and not including Social Security or self-employment tax.

Similar definitions of "net income taxes" exist for corporations, as well as for estates and trusts.

Example: Computation without a net operating loss or unused credits 09-02.2A

Aaron Gordon's tax return showed the following data:

Tax preference items (09-02.1)	$85,000
Net income tax liability (09-02.2)	$22,500

The computation of his minimum tax would be:

Tax preference items	$85,000
Less: The *greater* of $10,000 or one-half of his income tax liability ($22,500 × 50%)	−11,250
Amount subject to minimum tax	$73,750
Amount of tax ($73,750 × 0.15)	$11,063

The $11,063 would be added to his other income tax liabilities.

09-02.3 Effect of Net Operating Loss and Unused Credits

If a taxpayer has unused net operating loss carry-forward (06-13), the Code allows for deferring the minimum tax. It does not forgive the tax; it merely postpones the payment. Certain credits may be used to offset the minimum tax. They are:

- Credit for the elderly
- Credit for political contributions
- Credit for child and dependent care
- Residential energy credit.

09-02.3A **Example**

Aaron Gordon's return shows the following calculation for his minimum tax:

Tax preference items	$85,000
Net income tax liability	–0–
Net operating loss carry-over	$10,000
Unused child care credit	$ 100

Tax preference items	$85,000
Less: $10,000 minimum allowance	10,000
Amount subject to minimum tax	$75,000
Minimum tax, $75,000 × 0.15	$11,250
Less: 15% of net operating loss carry-forward $10,000 × 15%	1,500*
Net	$9,750
Less unused child and dependent care credit	100**
Net minimum tax payable	$ 9,650

*This amount is added to Aaron's minimum tax next year.
**Most credits cannot be used to offset the minimum tax. If this were, say, the investment credit, it could not be used against the minimum tax.

Allocation of $10,000 Allowance 09-02.4

For estates and trusts, for Subchapter S corporations, and for personal holding companies, the $10,000 allowance is based on the number of taxpayers involved. Each taxpayer is entitled to the $10,000 allowance. Controlled corporations must allocate the $10,000 allowance among the controlled members.

Tax Hint 09-02.5

How much does the minimum tax hurt? Does it prevent the taxpayer from entering into more tax-preferred investments? In some cases, the answer is that, although it reduces the effectiveness of tax-advantaged investments, it does not eliminate the advantages. So you must examine each case in relation to all the relevant facts.

Example 09-02.5A

In 1982 Barney Colin is about to enter into a lease transaction involving personal property. He has other preference items, so all the accelerated depreciation is subject to the minimum tax.

The asset's cost is $100,000 with a recovery life of 5 years, Barney's incremental tax rate is 50%, and the return on his investments is 12% compounded annually. If he elects accelerated depreciation, it produces these results:

Year	*Accelerated*	*Straight-Line*	*Difference*
1	$ 15,000	$ 10,000	$ 5,000
2	22,000	20,000	2,000
3	21,000	20,000	1,000
4	21,000	20,000	1,000
5	21,000	20,000	1,000
6	–0–	10,000	(10,000)
Totals	$100,000	$100,000	–0–

The total minimum tax over the life of the investment will be $10,000 × 15% or $1,500.

The comparison between straight-line (thus avoiding the minimum tax) and accelerated depreciation (and paying the minimum tax) is:

		Net Investable Funds	Interest Earned on Investable Funds
1	50% of 5,000	$ 2,500	
	minimum tax		
	(15% of $5,000)	(750)	
		$ 1,750	
	6% (net of tax) of $1,750	105	$ 105
2	50% of $2,000	1,000	
	minimum tax		
	($2,000 × 15%)	(300)	
		$ 2,555	
	6% of $2,555	153	153
3	50% of $1,000	500	
	minimum tax		
	($1,000 × 15%)	(150)	
		$ 3,058	
	6% of $3,058	183	183
4	50% of $1,000	500	
	minimum tax	(150)	
		$ 3,591	
	6% of $3,591	215	215
5	50% of $1,000	500	
	minimum tax	(150)	
		$ 4,156	
	6% of $4,156	249	249
6	50% of $10,000	(5,000)	
	Net	$ (595)	$ 905
	Minimum tax paid		(1500)
	Net *loss*		$ (595)

In this case the minimum tax *kills* the accelerated depreciation. With an internal taxable rate of return of 12%, the amount that the taxpayer earns on the deferred taxes is less than the minimum tax. Of course, if the internal rate of return is higher, you might come up with a different answer.

ALTERNATIVE MINIMUM TAX 09-03

Individuals, estates, and trusts are subject to an Alternative Minimum Tax (AMT). The tax is truly an "alternative," since it comes into play only if it exceeds the net "regular" tax liability. The AMT is a two-pronged attack:

1. there are two tax-preference items to consider, and
2. taxpayers with large credits (09-06) may lose some of the benefits of those credits.

The tax is a graduated tax. For income that is *subject* to the tax, the rates are:

0 to $20,000	0%
$20,001 to $60,000	10%
$60,001 and higher	20%

Long-Term Capital Gains 09-03.1

The 60% long-term capital gain deduction, other than as it applies to the sale of the taxpayer's principal residence, is a preference item for AMT purposes. Some exceptions exist for estates and trusts.

"Excess" Itemized Deductions 09-03.2

If deductions *from* Adjusted Gross Income (itemized deductions) are more than 60% of Adjusted Gross Income, they *may* be a preference item. The following deductions, however, are not subject to the minimum tax:

1. medical and dental expenses,
2. state, local, and foreign taxes,
3. casualty and theft losses,
4. certain deductions for estate taxes (Chapter 14).

Example 09-03.2A

Aaron Gordon's return shows the following information:

Adjusted Gross Income		$60,000
Medical deductions (net after the 3% limit)	$ 4,000	
State and local taxes	5,000	
Interest expense	10,000	
Charitable contributions	15,000	
Casualty loss	6,000	
Dividends on short positions	+ 8,000	
Total itemized deductions	$48,000	
Zero Bracket Amount	− 3,400	−44,600
Taxable Income before personal exemptions		$15,400

The computation of his excess itemized deductions would be:

Total itemized deduction		$48,000*
Less: Medical and dental expenses	$ 4,000	
State and local taxes	5,000	
Casualty loss	+ 6,000	−15,000
Net itemized deductions		$33,000
Adjusted Gross Income		$60,000
Less itemized deductions not subject to AMT		−15,000
Net Adjusted Gross Income		$45,000
Net itemized deductions		$33,000
60% of net Adjusted Gross Income ($45,000 × 0.60)		−27,000
Excess Itemized Deductions		$ 6,000

*See tax hint 09-03.2B.

09-03.2B **Tax hint**

The taxpayer's itemized deductions should not exceed the Adjusted Gross Income, since there will be no tax benefit. If the itemized deductions do exceed Adjusted Gross Income, the taxpayer should reduce a deduction *subject* to the AMT.

09-03.3 Computation of the Alternative Minimum Tax

First you must compute the amount of income subject to the AMT:

1. From Adjusted Gross Income,
2. *subtract*
   a. the full amount of itemized deductions, before reduction for the Zero Bracket Amount, and
   b. personal exemptions.
3. Then *add* tax preference items,
   a. excess itemized deductions, and
   b. the 60% capital gain deduction.

Once you compute the AMT based on this income, then subtract the following from that tax.

1. net income tax as defined in 09-02.2, not including the tax on the premature redemption of individual retirement bonds, and
2. the minimum tax.

If the result is zero, then there is no AMT. If the result is a positive figure, then that is the AMT.

The only credit that may be used to offset the AMT is the foreign tax credit (09-08.4), and this is of limited use. For this reason, taxpayers with *no* items of preference but with large credits (09-06) may still be subject to the AMT.

Example 09-03.4

Aaron Gordon's tax return shows the following information:

Salary		$30,000
Long-term capital gain (none of which relates to the sale of his personal residence)	$75,000	
Less: 60% deduction	−45,000	+30,000
Adjusted Gross Income		$60,000
Itemized deductions (09-03.2A)		−44,600
Taxable Income before personal exemptions		$15,400

Tax on $15,400, married, two exemptions	$ 1,325
Less: Investment credit	100
Net tax	$ 1,225

The computation of the AMT would be:

Adjusted Gross Income		$60,000
Less: Itemized deductions	$44,600	
Zero Bracket Amount	3,400	
Personal exemptions	+ 2,000	−50,000
		$10,000
Plus: Excess itemized deductions (09-03.2A)	$ 6,000	
60% long-term capital gains deduction	+45,000	+51,000
Income subject to AMT		$61,000
Tax on first $20,000		$ 0
Tax on next $40,000 @ 10%		4,000
Tax on last $1,000 @ 20%		+ 200
Total		$ 4,200
Less: Regular tax		− 1,225
Additional tax to be paid due to AMT		$ 2,975

Aaron's total tax is $4,200, which is actually the higher of the two taxes. Yet the way the forms are structured, the AMT is added to the regular tax.

09-04 10-YEAR LUMP-SUM INCOME AVERAGING

Employees may receive a lump-sum distribution from a pension plan due to leaving the employ of the company that sponsors the plan. In many cases the employees may reinvest the proceeds in a new retirement plan and thereby avoid paying the income tax on the distribution (06-06). In other cases, employees may wish to retain the funds and pay the tax on the distribution. If so, the distribution may be relatively large compared to the taxpayer's other income, and simply adding the amount to other taxable income would substantially increase the taxpayer's incremental tax rate.

To alleviate the burden of paying tax at a higher-than-normal tax rate, Congress enacted the special 10-year averaging rules. These rules allow the taxpayer to pay a relatively low tax on a lump-sum distribution. The tax rate is actually lower than it would be had the employee taken the funds prorata over any 10-year period.

Distributions That Qualify 09-04.1

For a lump-sum distribution to qualify for the 10-year averaging method, it must meet *all* of the following conditions:

1. The distribution must come from a qualified pension, profit-sharing, or stock bonus plan.
2. If the employer had more than one plan of the same kind (pension, profit-sharing, or stock bonus), then the distribution must be from all the plans of the same kind.
3. The distribution must be for the entire amount to the employee's credit.
4. The distribution must be made in a single tax year.
5. The distribution must be made for one of the following reasons:
   a. the employee died,
   b. the employee is aged 59½ or over,
   c. the employee quit, retired, was laid off, or was fired,
   d. a self-employed owner/beneficiary became totally and permanently disabled.

Among the distributions that do *not* qualify are:

1. U.S. retirement bonds distributed with the lump-sum,
2. any distribution made before the employee has participated in the plan for 5 years, unless it was paid because the employee died,
3. the capital gains portion of the distribution (09-05.1), or
4. the current actuarial value of any annuity included in the lump-sum.

The method can be used any number of times as long as the employee is under 59½ years old. Afterwards, it can be used for only one distribution to the employee.

Capital Gains Distributions 09-04.1A

Certain pension plans in force before 1974 may generate a distribution of capital gains. To elect the 10-year averaging method for the capital gains portion, the employee must make an irrevocable statement to forgo capital gains treatments on the particular distribution in question, *as well as* all future distributions from any plan. In most cases, this election benefits the taxpayer since the 10-year averaging method produces a lower tax than you would get by including the capital gains in with other income. But work out each situation both ways to be sure.

09-04.2 Death Benefits

Taxpayers may be entitled to a death benefit exclusion of up to $5,000 (03-03.2). The 10-year lump-sum method takes this benefit into account, and it is not lost if the 10-year averaging method is elected.

09-04.3 Method of Computation

The first step in the computation is to figure the amount of the distribution that is taxable. For distributions under $20,000, only one-half of the distribution is considered taxable. The excluded amount (a maximum of $10,000, one-half of $20,000), is reduced by 20¢ for each additional $1 of distribution over $20,000. Once the distribution equals $70,000, there is no exclusion (09-05.5).

Then you must compute the tax:

1. Divide the taxable amount by 10.
2. Figure the tax that a single taxpayer would pay on the one-tenth.
3. Multiply the tax you find by 10 to get the tax on the distribution (09-05.5).

09-04.4 Estate Tax

Amounts received on account of the death of another must be included in the recipient's income to the extent that the amount would have been income to the deceased. The recipient need not include this amount, however, if it has already been included in the income of the estate of the deceased (02-13).

In most cases, distributions from pension plans fall into this category, when they are made on account of death. Beneficiaries include the distributions on their tax returns. To avoid some of the double taxation, however, the amount of estate tax (Chapter 14) that is attributable to the inclusion of the pension plan in the estate tax return is deducted from the taxable portion of the distribution (09-05.5).

Example 09-04.5

Aaron Gordon is the sole beneficiary of the pension plan of Jennifer Hagney. When she dies, he receives the distribution for her plan. The amount of the distribution is $50,000, and he elects to report the amount on the 10-year averaging basis. The amount of estate tax attributable to the pension plan is $4,000. The computation of Aaron's tax liability is:

Amount of the distribution		$50,000
Death benefit exclusion		− 5,000
Net		$45,000
Less: 50% of $45,000 but not more than $10,000	$10,000	
$45,000 − $20,000 is $25,000		
20% of $25,000	− 5,000	− 5,000
Net		$40,000
Federal estate tax attributable to lump-sum distribution		− 4,000
Taxable amount		$36,000
10% of taxable amount		$ 3,600
Plus: $2,300 to adjust for Zero Bracket Amounts included in Tax Tables		+ 2,300
Amount used for tax computation		$ 5,900

Tax on $5,900, using tax table for singles	$ 451*
10 × $451	$4,510

* Note that the maximum incremental rate is 14%, and that the overall effective tax rate is only 10%.
Note: Tax Table for singles must be used for this computation regardless of the filing status of the taxpayer.

Aaron then excludes the entire $50,000 from his Gross Income, and adds $4,510 to his tax liability.

09-05 TAX CREDITS AND HOW THEY WORK

A *tax credit* is a direct reduction of the taxpayer's liability. It comes into play after all deductions from gross income have been taken to arrive at Taxable Income, which forms the basis for computing the tax liability (01-05). Once the liability is computed, the credits are used to figure the actual amount to be paid.

09-05.1 Example

From Figure 1-2 a married taxpayer files jointly Taxable Income of $36,375. In this case, the tax liability is $6,662. If the taxpayer also has a credit of $1,000, he or she would pay only $5,662 ($6,662 less the credit of $1,000).

09-05.2 Credits Compared with Deductions and Exemptions

In terms of "cash in hand," credits are worth 100¢ on the dollar, while deductions and exemptions are always worth less. Credits directly reduce the amount of taxes payable. Yet deductions and exemptions reduce only taxable income, and so they generate cash equal only to the deduction or exemption times the taxpayer's marginal income tax rate.

Example 09-05.2A

Herbie Russell, a single taxpayer, has taxable income of $50,000 before item X of $5,000. If item X is a deduction, you can compute his taxes payable by referring to Schedule X in Figure 1-1:

Tax on $50,000	$13,889
Less: Incremental Tax rate (42% of $5,000)	− 2,100
Tax payable	$11,789
or	
Tax on $45,000 taxable income	$11,789

On the other hand, if the $5,000 is a credit:

Tax on $50,000	$13,889
Less credit	− 5,000
Tax payable	$ 8,889

The difference of $2,900 ($11,789 − $8,889) is equal to 5,000 × 58% (100% − his 42% incremental tax rate).

Refundable Credits 09-05.3

A *refundable credit* is one that generates a tax refund. The most common of such credits consists of income taxes paid in advance, such as by withholding (10-01) or by payment of estimated taxes (10-02). In such a case, if the credit is greater than the tax liability, the difference is refunded to the taxpayer. Refundable credits include:

1. federal income tax withheld,
2. credit from previous year's overpayment,
3. earned income credit,

4. payments made with request for extension to file,
5. excess FICA and RRTA tax withheld (two or more employers),
6. credit for federal tax on special fuels and oils, and
7. regulated investment company credit (05-08).

09-05.3A **Example**

If in the previous example the credit had been $20,000, then:

Tax on $50,000	$13,889
Less: Credit	−20,000
Amount to be refunded to taxpayer	$ 6,111

09-05.4 Nonrefundable Credits

A *nonrefundable credit* is one that can only reduce the tax liability to zero and that does not enable the taxpayer to receive any money back. If in the previous example, the $20,000 credit was nonrefundable, then the $6,111 would *not* be refunded. The taxpayer would simply not have to pay any tax. Some credits are lost forever if they cannot be used in the year that they are generated. Others can be either carried back or carried forward to offset the tax liabilities of other years. Nonrefundable credits include:

1. credit for contributions to candidates for public office,
2. credit for the elderly,
3. credit for child and dependent care expenses,
4. investment credit (with some exceptions),
5. foreign tax credit,
6. work incentive (WIN) credit,
7. job credit, and
8. residential energy credits, and

9. Research and development.

Example 09-05.4A

A taxpayer has the following situation in 1980 with regard to a nonrefundable credit that could be carried back three years and forward five years:

Tax liability before credits	$18,067
Less credit	20,000
Net liability (not less than zero)	–0–
Unused credit, 1980 ($20,000 – $18,067)	$ 1,933
Original return, 1977, tax liability	$15,000
Carry-back of unused credit	1,933
Refund of 1977 taxes	1,933

In most cases, unused credits must be carried back first before they can be carried forward. In this case all the 1977, 1978, and 1979 taxes would have to be recovered before any remaining unused credit could be used to offset 1981 taxes. The carry-back of unused credits may be claimed by filing either Form 1040X (individuals) or Form 1120X (corporations).

INVESTMENT CREDIT 09-06

Sections 38, 46, 47, and 48 of the Code allow a credit against income taxes for investment in certain qualified property. The base amount of the credit is 10% of cost, but the credit could be as high as 25%, and as low as 6%.

The amount of the credit is dependent upon:

1. the cost of the property,
2. use of the property, and
3. recovery life of the property for computing depreciation (08-04).

Qualified property (or "Section 38 property" as it is often referred to) is, simplistically, tangible personal property used in a trade or business. Although realty and intangible property do not qualify, the categories are not that clearly defined in practice (as discussed later). To be "fully" qualified, the property must have a recovery life of at least 5 years, although exceptions are discussed later. The percentages of cost that qualifies, based on useful life, are:

Recovery Life	*Percentage of Cost*
Less than 3 years	0
3 or 4 years	60%
5 or more	100%

Only $125,000 ($150,000 in 1985 and later) cost of used equipment may be used in figuring the credit.

09-06.1 Example

During 1980, Sharon Goldfinger purchases or constructs the following tangible personal property:

Item	*Recovery Life*	*Cost*	*Qualified Cost*
Automobile	3 years	$ 10,000	$ 6,000
Machine B	5 years	100,000	100,000
Machine C	5 years	150,000	150,000
Machine D	5 years	200,000	200,000
Machine E (used)	5 years	300,000	125,000*
		Total qualified	$581,000

* Maximum amount of used equipment.

The investment credit is $58,100 (10% of $581,000).

09-06.2 Rehabilitation Credit

To encourage businesses to remain in the inner city, rather than build new facilities in the suburbs, the rehabilitation credit was passed. The amount of the credit is:

15% for buildings at least 30-years old;
20% for buildings at least 40-years old; and
25% for certified historic structures.

With some exceptions, the minimum amount of the expenditure is the greater of the taxpayer's basis in the property or $5,000 and at least 75% of the outer walls must remain standing.

A certified historic structure is any building listed in the National Register or certified by the Secretary of the Interior as being of historic significance to a registered historic district.

Expenditures by lessees may qualify for the credit if the term of the lease is at least 15 years after the completion of the work.

Rehabilitation expenses include such items as new electric wiring, plumbing, and the like. It does not include the cost of the land or the building itself. If the taxpayer claims the rehabilitation credit:

1. the basis must be reduced by the amount of the credit; and
2. only straight-line depreciation may be taken on the building, normally over the 15-year cost recovery period.

The credit may be taken only on nonresidential buildings except for historic structures, which may be put to any income-producing use.

Eligible Property 09-06.3

Eligible property includes:

1. tangible personal property (except portable heaters and air conditioners),
2. some research and storage facilities,
3. certain expenditures for rehabilitating business buildings, and,
4. investments in certain energy property such as those that are solar or wind powered.

Always check to see if a particular asset is eligible. As an example, elevators *do* qualify while catwalks to get to the elevators *do not.*

09-06.4 Limitations

Except for solar and wind energy property, the credit is a nonrefundable credit. But unused credits may be carried back three years and forward fifteen.

A further limitation is that, for 1980, only the first $25,000 of tax liability plus 70% of the excess can be offset by the investment credit. The percentage of the liability over $25,000 that may be offset increases to 80% in 1981 and to 90% in 1982.

09-06.4A **Example**

Total tax liability, 1980		$1,000,000
Investment credit	$1,500,000	
Use of investment credit		– 25,000
Net		$ 975,000
70% of remaining liability ($975,000)		– 682,500
Net payable, 1980		$ 292,500
Unused investment credit:		
Total generated		$1,500,000
Amount used ($25,000 + $682,500)		707,500
Amount available for carry-back and/or -forward		$ 792,500

09-06.4B **Tax *warning***

In some cases the amount of the investment credit may be limited to the fair market value of the asset rather than its cost (10-11.3B) or the amount the taxpayer has at risk.

The at-risk rules are similar to, but slightly more liberal than, the at-risk rules for deducting losses.

Further, in some situations, the amount of "cost" is the lower of:

1. cost to the taxpayer or
2. the cost to actually manufacture the property.

These limitations are directed at certain tax shelters. When the investment credit is a significant portion of the advantages of a tax shelter, it is wise to have your *own* tax advisor consulted.

Special Consideration 09-06.5

More liberal, and sometimes more restrictive, rules apply to certain industries such as public utilities and railroads. Often the use of the property must be considered. As an example, a Commuter Highway Vehicle used to transport workers to their place of employment qualifies 100% for the investment credit even though its recovery life is three years.

Keep in mind that Congress has used the investment credit to encourage certain endeavors and to discourage others. Before relying on an investment credit when making an investment decision, seek competent tax advice.

Credit for Qualified Research Expenditures 09-07

To encourage research and development, Section 44F of the Code provides for a 25% tax credit for certain increases in research and development made during the period June 30, 1981 to December 31, 1985. The research must be conducted in the United States. To encourage multinational companies to do their research in the U.S., special provisions are made to allow them to take the credit without regard to income earned within the U.S.

The credit is available for the amount that the current year's research and development expenditures exceed the base period's research and development expenditures.

Research and development expenditures that qualify for the credit include:

1. 100% of the salaries and wages paid to those doing research and development, as well as of the salaries and wages of those supervising;

2. 100% of the cost of materials and supplies consumed in research and development;
3. 65% of the amounts paid to outside contractors for research and development;
4. 65% of the amounts paid to qualified educational institutions for basic research and development for the advancement of scientific knowledge not having a specific commercial objective.

The base period is the average expenses for the three immediately preceding years. However,

1. for the first year ending after June 30, 1981, it is the amount spent in the previous year;
2. for the second year ending after June 30, 1981, it is the average of the two preceding years; and
3. in no event may the base amount be less than 50% of the current amount.

The credit is nonrefundable, but any unused credit may be carried back three years and forward fifteen years.

09-07.1 **Example**

The MBS Corporation had the following research and development expenditures:

	1980	*1981*	*1982*	*1983*
Wages	$10,000	$12,000	$15,000	$ 20,000
Supplies	5,000	2,000	3,000	10,000
Paid to contractors				
& universities	3,000	5,000	6,000	100,000
Total	$18,000	$19,000	$24,000	$130,000

Their preliminary base period amount is:

Wages (10,000 + 12,000 + 15,000)	$37,000
Supplies (5,000 + 2,000 + 3,000)	10,000
Outsiders (3,000 + 5,000 + 6,000) × 65%	9,100
	$56,100
$56,100 divided by 3 years (average)	$18,700

Current year:	
Wages and supplies	$30,000
Outsiders (100,000 × 65%)	65,000
	$95,000
Base, the *higher* of $18,700 or	
50% of $95,000	47,500
Amount subject to the credit	$47,500
Credit, 25% of $47,500	$11,875

Tax Hint 09-07.2

Research and development can be deducted as well as a credit taken. What is the most a 46% incremental taxpayer has to spend out of pocket if it more than doubles its research and development expenditures? 41½¢ per dollar!

As an example, if current research and development were $100,000 and the base period research and development were $50,000 or less:

Expenditure		$100,000
Deduction at 46%	$46,000	
Credit (25% of $50,000)	12,500	58,500
Net cost after taxes		$ 41,500

Not bad, expecially if the research and development will increase future sales and competitive edge.

Tax warning 09.07.3

This credit will not work in a tax-sheltered investment.

09-08 OTHER CREDITS

09-08.1 Credit for Contributions to Candidates for Public Office

Taxpayers may take a credit for one-half of contributions to candidates for public office, to political newsletter funds, to political committees of candidates, and to elected public officials. The credit is limited to $50 ($100 for taxpayers filing jointly). The credit is nonrefundable.

09-08.2 Credit for the Elderly

Taxpayers who are 65 or older, as well as those who are on public retirement, may be entitled to a nonrefundable credit of $375 ($562.50 if both spouses qualify and file jointly). The amount of credit is reduced for:

1. amounts received under Social Security, Railroad Retirement Act, and certain other tax-free government pensions, and
2. amounts of Adjusted Gross Income in excess of $7,500 ($10,000 on a joint return).

The credit is zero for persons receiving $2,500 or more ($3,750 if both spouses are 65 or over) in Social Security or other government tax-free pensions.

09-08.2A **Example**

Aaron Gordon is over 65, has Adjusted Gross Income of $10,000, and receives $1,000 in Social Security. His credit for the elderly is:

Maximum base (single, 65 or over)		$2,500
Less: Social Security received	$1,000	
One-half the amount that his Adjusted Gross Income exceeds $7,500 ($10,000 − $7,500) × 0.50	1,250	2,250
Base for credit		$ 250
Credit ($250 × 0.15)		$ 38

Credit for Child and Dependent Care Expenses 09-08.3

If a taxpayer has to pay someone to care for a "qualifying person" so that the taxpayer can either work or look for work, then up to 30% of such expenses may be taken as a nonrefundable credit. The amount of the credit is reduced 1% for each $2,000 of AGI above $10,000. The minimum credit is 20% for those with an AGI of $30,000 or more. *Qualifying expenses* include housekeeping, cooking, babysitting, and other general household services. A *qualifying person* must meet one of the following tests:

1. The person must be under the age of 15 and the taxpayer's dependent.
2. The person must be the taxpayer's spouse and physically or mentally incapable of self care or a full-time student.
3. The person may be any person who is not capable of self-care and who could have qualified as the taxpayer's dependent except that he/she had income of $1,000 or more.

Married taxpayers must file jointly to be eligible for the credit, *and* the amount of the eligible expenses is the *lower* of:

1. the actual amount spent,
2. $2,400 ($4,800 for more than one qualifying person),
3. the earned income of the taxpayer, or
4. on a joint return, the earned income of the spouse with the smaller income.

If a spouse is unable to care for him- or herself, or is a full-time student, then the minimum earned income is $200 ($400 for two or more qualified reasons) per month.

09-08.3A **Example**

Aaron and Tiffany Gordon have two children. He works full-time and earns $50,000. She spends most of the year looking for work. In October, she finally gets a job, and her earnings for the year are $3,500. During the year, the Gordons spend $4,500 on babysitters, first to allow Tiffany to look for work and then to allow her to take the employment at the end of the year. The credit they are entitled to on a joint return is 20% (since their AGI exceeds $30,000) of the lower of:

1. the amount they spend, $4,500,
2. $4,800 (they had two children), or
3. the amount she earned, $3,500.

In this case, the credit is $700, 20% of $3,500.

If an employer pays dependent care expenses for an employee under a qualified plan, the employee may exclude such payments from Gross Income up to the $2,400 and $4,800 limits discussed. In that case, the employee gets no credit.

09-08.4 Foreign Tax Credit

To avoid international double taxation, taxpayers may take a nonrefundable credit for foreign *income* taxes paid on foreign-source income that is also subject to U.S. taxation. Although the foreign tax credit is nonrefundable, any unused credits may be carried back two years and then forward five years. So taxpayers who pay foreign income taxes should complete Form 1116 to determine how much of those payments may be used to offset U.S. income taxes. The amount of this credit is limited in many respects, including:

1. by the relationship the foreign-source income bears to the taxpayer's total income; and
2. by the country imposing the tax; and
3. by the type of industry or business generating the income.

Taxpayers may elect to deduct foreign taxes, rather than claim the credit. But, in most cases, taking the credit rather than the deduction results in lower taxes.

Work Incentive (WIN) Credit 09-08.5

The WIN credit is part of an incentive program for employers to hire the economically disadvantaged. Employers receive the credit, in lieu of a deduction, for certain qualified wages. The credit is *not* in addition to the deduction for wages paid, but rather in place of it. There are two WIN programs:

- One deals with employees who have been certified either by the Department of Labor or by the appropriate state or local agency as having been eligible to receive Aid to Families with Dependent Children throughout the 90 days just before they were hired.
- The other program deals with substantially the same type of employee hired under Section 432(b)(1) of the Social Security Act. This program requires that no current employees be displaced, and it does not apply to migrant workers.

This nonrefundable credit ranges from 25% to 50% of the first $6,000 of wages paid or owed to qualifying employees. Any unused credit may be carried back three years and then forward seven years.

09-08.6 Jobs Credit

The jobs credit is so similar to the WIN credit that an employer may not take both a job credit and a WIN credit for the same employee. The job credit gives a credit of up to 50% of the first $6,000 of wages paid to an employee who is certified to be in one of seven targeted groups of the economically disadvantaged. The certification that an employee is in one of the targeted groups is normally given by a local agency, which is an office of the State Employment Security Agency. Certification is obtained on Form 6199. The credit is nonrefundable, but it may be carried back three years and then forward seven years.

09-08.7 Residential Energy Credits

There are two *once*-in-a-lifetime credits for reducing the need for energy in your residence:

- The first is a 15% credit of the first $2,000 (for a maximum credit of $300) spent for such items as insulation, storm windows, caulking, weatherstripping, and the like.
- The second is a 40% credit of the first $10,000 (maximum $4,000) spent on renewable energy sources. Items in this category include solar, geothermal, and wind energy sources if used in the taxpayer's residence.

Unfortunately, wood-burning stoves do not fit into either category.

09-08.8 Regulated Investment Company Credit

Mutual funds may elect to "pay the tax in lieu of the taxpayer's paying the tax" (05-08). As the taxpayer, you are eligible for a *refundable* credit, since the mutual fund has, in effect, prepaid *your* taxes on capital gains.

09-08.9 Credit for Federal Tax on Special Fuels and Oils

This refundable credit *may* be used against the taxpayer's income tax liability. Taxpayers may file for a quarterly refund if the quarterly amount exceeds $1,000. The credit is a refund of the federal highway gasoline and motor fuels tax. The refund ranges from 2¢ to 7¢ per gallon for fuel used:

1. in nonhighway vehicle use, such as farming, aviation, and the like (motor boats do *not* qualify),
2. in certain approved public transportation, and
3. in the production of gasahol.

Prepaid Taxes 09-08.10

Taxpayers are required to prepay their federal income tax liability (10-01 and 10-02). To the extent that these prepayments represent an overpayment of taxes, they are a refundable credit. Payments that fall into this category are:

1. federal income tax withheld from wages,
2. estimated tax payments,
3. refunds due from prior years and applied to the current year,
4. payments with requests for extensions, and
5. excess FICA (Social Security) and RRTA (Railroad Retirement Act) taxes withheld from wages.

This last category includes employees who have two or more employers and whose total earnings exceed the base for withholding. The base in 1981 was $29,700, and the maximum tax was $1,975.05—but these amounts change frequently.

Earned Income Credit 09-08.11

The earned income credit is a "negative" income tax. This is the one time a taxpayer can receive a refund for taxes that were never paid. To be eligible for the earned income credit, the taxpayer must:

1. have Adjusted Gross Income of $10,000 or less,
2. have earned income such as wages and earnings from self-employment, *and*
3. have a child who lived with the taxpayer during the *entire* year.

The credit, based on earned income, reaches a maximum of $500 when the taxpayer's earned income (or Adjusted Gross Income in some cases) reaches $6,000. The credit is gradually phased out and reaches zero at an Adjusted Gross Income of $10,000.

First, the research and development must be incurred in carrying on a trade or business. Second, the credit may be used only to offset the tax on the income from that trade or business for the individual taxpayer.

09-09 INCOME TAX LIABILITIES OF ESTATES AND TRUSTS

When a taxpayer dies, the estate becomes a new taxpayer. Accordingly, the administrator of the estate must file a tax return for income earned by the estate. The tax rates are similar, but slightly lower, than the tax rates for a single taxpayer.

Trusts are also separate taxpayers, provided they meet the requirements of the Code. (See 09-10 for instances where the income is taxed to the grantor, rather than to the trust.)

Trust income is taxed at the same rates as estate income. The taxable income of a trust deviates in one major respect from other taxable entities: The trust receives a deduction for amounts distributed to the beneficiaries, and those amounts are then taxable to the beneficiaries (09-11).

Income retained by the trust is taxable to the trust. This liability does not constitute double taxation, since the beneficiary receives a credit for taxes paid by the trust when the income is distributed and becomes taxable to the beneficiary.

Income distributed by the trust retains its characteristics, and the trust is merely a conduit. As an example, tax-exempt municipal bond interest would retain its tax-exempt character when distributed. Similarly, interest and dividend income distributed would be subject to the dividend and interest exclusion.

Beneficiaries receive a Form K-1 from the trust. This

form outlines the income received and its character. As an example, dividends "passing through" the trust are shown as "dividends" on the Form K-1, and the beneficiaries add that to other dividends on their tax returns.

Since the expenses of the trust administration must be allocated to each source of income, as well as to administering the corpus (principal), the pass-through is not "pure."

TRUST INCOME TAXABLE TO THE GRANTOR 09-10

Obviously, the ability to create a "new" taxpayer in the form of a trust has enormous potential for abuse. For one thing, the progressive income tax rates begin again, so income can be diverted to the trust for the purpose of obtaining lower rates. Additionally, the beneficiaries may be in lower tax brackets than the grantor. In this manner, the beneficiaries' lower tax rates similarly "shelter" the income.

For these reasons, the Code requires that the grantor give up control of the principal of the trust for more than 10 years. This gives rise to the so-called Clifford trust. In a Clifford trust, the income goes to a beneficiary, and the principal reverts to the grantor in no less than 10 years and one day. Even in this case, capital gains may be taxable to the grantor or taxed at the rate the grantor would have paid.

What is the key to creating a trust that is upheld? The grantor must not have control, directly or *indirectly*, over the income or principal. Also, the income must not be used for the benefit of the grantor. The establishment of a trust that is recognized for income tax purposes, and that is legal under state law, must be handled by an attorney who is fully competent in such matters.

THE "THROWBACK" RULE ON EXCESS TRUST DISTRIBUTIONS 09-11

What happens when a trust distributes more, for the *year*, than it had in distributable income? One of two tax consequences comes into play. First, the distribution could be considered a tax-free distribution of corpus (principal). That is exactly what happens in the following situations:

1. If the distributed income was earned in 1968 or prior, the distribution is tax-free to the beneficiary.
2. If the distributed income was earned while the beneficiary was a minor, the distribution is tax-free. For these purposes, being a minor means under the age of 21, including the years before the beneficiary was born.
3. If the distribution is of capital gains, then it is tax-free.

Any other distribution comes under the "throwback" rules. These rules are designed to reduce the benefits of a trust's paying taxes on retained income at a low tax rate, and then distributing that income in later years to a beneficiary in a higher incremental tax bracket. Hence the rules are designed to tax beneficiaries at approximately the same rates as they would have paid had the distribution been made in the year earned.

1. The computation of the throwback tax is a two-step problem. The distributed income is considered to come from the first year after 1968 that has distributable income. The distribution is considered to be both the undistributed income and the income taxes paid by the trust. Beneficiaries receive credit for the taxes paid.
2. Beneficiaries then go through a 5-year averaging technique to determine the amount of taxes due. They look at the income they had last year and for the four preceding years. Then they disregard the highest and lowest years, and add the distribution (divided by the number of years to which it relates) to the middle three years' income. The taxpayers then refigure the tax for those three years, and compute the increase in taxes for each year. They take the average increase in taxes for those three years, and multiply by the number of years to which the distribution relates.

Example

09-11.1

Colin Gordon is the beneficiary of a trust that accumulated income for five years. The trust distributes those five years' income to him this year, along with this year's distributable income.

Five years' distributable net income	$100,000
Income tax paid on $100,000	− 29,000
Undistributed net income	$ 71,000
Current year's income distributed	$ 22,000

Colin had other taxable income of:

- this year $50,000;
- last year, $45,000;
- year 3, $40,000;
- year 4, $35,000;
- year 5, $30,000;
- year 6, $25,000

Colin's regular tax for this year, before the throwback, is based on $72,000 taxable income ($50,000 from other sources and $22,000 current distribution). If Colin were a single taxpayer, this tax would be $24,131. (This year's tax does not enter into the throwback computation.)

Colin must then add to this tax his throwback tax. He first selects three of the base years, dropping the highest and the lowest. This leaves $40,000, $35,000, and $30,000 taxable income for his base years.

The $100,000 distribution (including the taxes paid) must be divided by 5, the number of years to which the income relates. That amount is added to his taxable income in the base years.

	Year 3	Year 4	Year 5
Original taxable income	$40,000	$35,000	$30,000
Additional income due to throwback ($100,000 divided by 5 years)	+20,000	+20,000	+20,000
Taxable income	$60,000	$55,000	$50,000
Tax on taxable income	$18,371	$15,989	$13,889
Tax on original taxable income	− 9,299	− 7,399	− 6,113
Increase in taxes	$ 9,072	$ 8,590	$ 7,776
The average of the increases is ($9,072 + $8,590 + $7,776) ÷ 3			$ 8,479
$8,479 × 5 (the number of years)			$42,395
Less: Taxes paid by the trust			−29,000
Net throwback taxes due			$13,395

Note that, if this computation shows that the trust paid more taxes on the income than the beneficiary's throwback liability, there is *no* refund.

09-12 OTHER TYPES OF TRUSTS

09-12.1 Employee Trusts

Employee trusts are designed to hold and manage the assets of employee pension, profit-sharing, and stock bonus plans. They are governed by the Internal Revenue Code and the Employee Retirement Income Security Act (ERISA, 06-06). Income earned by an employee trust is exempt from federal income taxes. The income is eventually taxed to the beneficiaries when it is distributed.

09-12.2 Common Trust Funds

A common trust fund is a pool of assets managed by a bank for a number of participants. Such funds are treated as partnerships (Chapter 11), and they are not subject to federal income tax. Each participant pays tax on his or her share of the income, whether distributed or not.

Business Trust 09-12.3

A so-called business trust is one set up to run a business, rather than to manage investments. The Code does not recognize such a trust, but it may consider them to be a corporations (Chapter 12).

Whether the IRS classifies such a trust as a corporation doing business—and therefore subject to corporate income taxes—depends on all the facts and circumstances. Some of the factors to be considered are:

1. Does the trust afford limited liability (a characteristic of a corporation)?
2. Can interest in the trust be transferred (another characteristic of a corporation)?
3. Does the trust have a business purpose? In other words, does it hold itself out as doing business in the community, rather than merely investing in, and maintaining, property?

10
TAXES AND ACCOUNTING

WITHHOLDING 10-01

Since taxpayers are expected to pay their taxes *during* the year, filing returns at the end of the year is merely a determination of the taxes due. Most individual taxpayers pay their taxes during the year by two methods: withholding and estimates (10-02). Generally, employees are subject to withholding. Whether taxpayers are employees is a more critical question than merely which way they will pay taxes. The reasons are:

1. The system of withholding by the *employer* is a means of enforcement. Employees are generally more "fluid" in their movements, and harder for the IRS to catch up with. If an employer fails to withhold taxes *and* if the employee fails to pay them, the employer can be held liable for those taxes.
2. The FICA tax falls into two categories: Social Security and self-employment tax. Employees, subject to withholding, pay Social Security; others pay self-employment

tax. The Social Security rates are higher than the self-employment rates. In 1981, the combined rate for Social Security was 13.30% of the first $29,700 in wages. Of this amount, the employer is supposed to pay half and the employee half. At the same time, the self-employment tax was only 9.3% of the first $29,700 of earnings. This is paid entirely by the self-employed person. Employees who fail to withhold FICA tax can be held liable for their portion (6.65%) if employees properly report the income. If employees fail to pay taxes on their wages, the employer can be held liable for the full 13.30%.

3. Federal (FUI) and state (SUI) unemployment insurance is based on wages subject to withholding. Except for a few states, the employer is entirely responsible for these taxes.

4. Since pension plans must not discriminate against certain employees (06-06), failure to classify a "worker" as an employee, subject to withholding, could violate these requirements.

10-01.1 Employer-Employee Relationship

When is withholding required? The answer depends on the relationship between the person offering work and the person accepting it. If the employer offers a place of work, supervises that work, and is in control of the worker, then an employer-employee relationship exists. Independent contractors, partners in a partnership and sole proprietors are not employees. Whether a person is an independent contractor depends on all the circumstances of the relationship. The key element is control and supervision. Wages paid to farm workers and to domestic servants working in a household are not subject to withholding, but they may be subject to FICA tax.

Wages Subject to Withholding 10-01.2

The general rule is that all wages, salaries, bonuses, commissions, and other compensation are subject to withholding. The employer is responsible for finding any specific exceptions that exist in the Code. Some of the more common exceptions are:

1. moving expense reimbursements (06-11),
2. payments made on account of a deceased employee,
3. expense reimbursements when the employee adequately documents the expenses and when they are deductible by the employer or excludable by the employee, and
4. payments from an employee trust.

Amount of Withholding 10-01.3

The amount the employer is required to withhold is based on information supplied by the employee on Form W-4 or W-5. This information includes the marital status of the employees, their exemptions, and additional exemptions from withholding based on their anticipation of deductions from or for Adjusted Gross Income.

The employer then consults tables designed to "estimate" the employee's tax liability. Although these tables are based on the progressive income tax, they do not go up to the highest incremental tax bracket of 50%. Employees who expect to have higher tax liabilities may request additional withholding or may file estimated payments.

The responsibility for filing an "honest" W-4 or W-5 rests with the employee. Employers are responsible only for maintaining a reasonable level of prudence. Any W-4 form with more than 9 exemptions and no withholding must be filed with the IRS.

Most states have a withholding tax, and some states also have a SUI withholding. These amounts are also deducted from employees' wages.

10-01.4 Example

Brynne Gordon receives her semi-monthly pay of $1,010. She files a W-4 claiming to be married and having 4 exemptions, including herself. Her federal withholding, and net pay would be:

Gross wages paid		$1,010.00
Less: Federal income tax withheld	$148.50	
FICA withheld	+ 67.17	− 215.67
Net pay		$ 794.33

10-01.5 Payments

Employers are required to deposit with a local bank amounts withheld from employees. They do so by filing Form 501 with the payments. The period between the time that the amounts are withheld and the time that the deposit must be made varies between 3 days and 3 months depending on the amount withheld.

Employers are required to obtain a taxpayer identification number from the federal government prior to having employees and withholding taxes. This number is obtained by filing Form SS-4 with the employer's local IRS computer center.

10-01.6 Tax *Warning*

Of all the areas in the Code requiring a warning, this is the most severe! Failure to turn over to the IRS amounts withheld from employees' wages carries extremely high penalties. Not paying your own taxes is one thing, but not paying over your employees' withholding is a position that you should never allow yourself to get into.

When in doubt, withhold! Treating workers as independent contractors is obviously less expensive than treating them as employees. Payroll taxes and bookkeeping expenses are lowered. But if you undergo an audit and the IRS disagrees, the employer is held liable for the taxes. When this happens, the state unemployment authorities are normally right behind the IRS auditor.

PAYMENT OF ESTIMATED TAXES 10-02

All taxpayers are required to pay their taxes during the year. Even corporations are taxable entities, and they too must estimate and prepay their taxes (Chapter 12). But how do you estimate the taxes that are going to be due and payable? And what happens if the taxpayer underpays on the estimate?

Individual Taxpayers 10-02.1

Individuals must estimate their federal income tax liability and pay those taxes during the year. The total tax liability includes *all* taxes, including self-employment taxes and the recapture of investment credit. If the withholding on wages (10-01) is sufficient to cover the tax liability, no further action is required. But if withholdings are not enough to cover the liability, the taxpayer may have to file Form 1040ES. This form is filed quarterly (April 15, June 15, September 15, and January 15 of the following year). The taxpayer may compute the estimated tax liability, and pay the estimates based on the *lowest* figure derived from five computations. In the five computations, taxpayers may consider withholding taxes as being "paid" evenly over the year (10-01).

10-02.1A **Method 1**

If, upon filing a return (normally on or before April 15 of the following year), the taxpayer has *in fact* paid 80% of the *total tax* liability evenly over the year, the taxpayer has complied with the prepayment rules.

If taxpayers pass the 80% test, there can never be a penalty for the underpayment of income taxes. But if they file for an extension of time to file (normally granted to June 15 of the following year), they must pay 100% of the taxes due with the request for an extension.

10-02.1B **Method 2**

Taxpayers may take last year's actual total tax liability and pay one-fourth of that amount with each quarterly return. In that case, there is no penalty for the underpayment of taxes. The key to this position is that each of the four Forms 1040ES must be filed on time!

10-02.1C **Method 3**

The taxpayer may take last year's taxable income and compute the tax liability using *this* year's rates and exemptions. Normally this method will produce the lowest payments, since there is always a reduction in tax rates from one year to the next.

10-02.1D **Method 4**

Taxpayers may choose to annualize their current year's actual income. They figure actual income and deductions through the end of the month preceding the date the payment is due. Then they annualize these figures by presuming the same monthly average for the rest of the year. They must pay 80% of the tax liability computed in this manner.

Method 5 10-02.1E

Taxpayers may compute income and deductions through March 31, June 30, and September 30. They then presume that they will have no further income or deductions for the year. They must pay 90% of the tax computed in this manner.

Corporations 10-02.2

Corporations are required to pay estimated taxes based on the actual amount of taxes expected to be due. But they pay no penalties for underpayment of taxes if:

1. the payments of estimated taxes equaled 80% of the actual amount due,
2. the estimates were equal to the previous year's tax,
3. the estimates were equal to the tax on the previous year's income using the current rates, or
4. 80% of the tax due based on annualizing income was paid on each required quarterly installment.

Large corporations, with more than $1 million of taxable income in any of the previous three years, have a greater estimated tax payment requirement.

Tax Hint 10-02.3

Taxes deferred mean interest earned. With this tenet in mind, highly paid executives can have their employers withhold enough to meet their liabilities in December. Since withholdings may be considered to have been taken out evenly during the year, there would be no penalty.

Penalties 10-02.4

There is a nondeductible penalty of 12% annual "interest" on the amount of each underpayment. The penalty is figured very much like interest is, but the amount is not deductible.

10-02.4A **Example**

Ms. Taxpayer underpays the June 15 installment by $400 and files her return on April 4 of the following year. The penalty for *that* installment would be:

$400 × 292/365* × 12% is	$38.40

*The fraction accounts for the number of days the payment was late.

A separate computation must be made for each installment.

10-02.5 Tax Hint

Whenever the amount of estimated taxes paid is less than 80% of the final tax due, taxpayers should file Form 2210 (individuals) or Form 2220 (corporations). This form is not required, but if the taxpayer does not compute the penalty, the IRS computer will. The IRS computer will not allow for any of the exceptions and different methods explained. It just assumes there is an underpayment.

10-03 INVENTORIES, A NONDEDUCTIBLE EXPENSE

Inventories are goods held for sale in the normal course of business. They may be purchased or manufactured by the taxpayer.

If inventories are a material item in computing income, then all taxpayers, regardless of their accounting systems, must carry inventories as an asset—rather than take them as a deduction—until they are sold. Once sold, inventories become part of the cost of goods sold, which is a deduction.

Example 10-03.1

Brynne Gordon started her furniture business two years ago. During each of the two years she purchased $200,000 and $250,000 of furniture for sale. At the end of the first year, she had $50,000 of furniture unsold in inventory, and at the end of the second year she had $60,000 of inventory. Her tax-deductible cost of goods sold is computed as follows:

First year:	
Beginning inventory	$ –
Purchases	200,000
	$200,000
Ending inventory	– 50,000
Cost of goods sold	$150,000
Second year:	
Beginning inventory	$ 50,000
Purchases	+250,000
	$300,000
Ending inventory	– 60,000
Cost of goods sold	$240,000

METHODS OF VALUING INVENTORIES 10-04

Determining the value of inventories at the end of the tax year can be one of the most significant factors in determining taxable income: the lower the ending inventory, the higher the cost of goods sold (see 10-03.1); and the higher the cost of goods sold, the lower the taxable income.

Inventory can be valued in a multitude of ways, but three are by far the most popular:

1. average cost
2. first-in/first-out (FIFO), and
3. last-in/first-out (LIFO).

These three methods are a means of determining the *cost* of the inventory on hand. Taxpayers using the average cost or FIFO methods may reduce the value of inventory to "market value" in certain cases; this practice is often referred to as carrying inventories at the lower of cost or market. Users of LIFO may use only cost and cannot reduce inventory for a decline in market.

10-04.1 Average Cost

Average cost presumes that the units remaining in inventory were acquired at the average price during the year.

10-04.1A Example

A company's records show the following, with 7,000 units remaining in inventory:

	Quantity	*Unit Price*	*Total*
Beginning inventory	10,000	$1.00	$10,000
Purchase, March 31	5,000	1.10	5,500
Purchase, June 30	5,000	1.20	6,000
Purchase, September 30	5,000	1.30	6,500
Purchase, December 31	5,000	1.40	7,000
	30,000		$35,000

The average price per unit is $1.17 ($35,000/30,000 units). So the ending inventory is:

7,000 units × $1.17	$ 8,190

10-04.2 FIFO Method

FIFO presumes that the oldest inventory is *sold* first. So what is left in inventory must be the most recently acquired items.

Example 10-04.2A

Under FIFO, the inventory in the prior example would be:

Purchase, December 31, 5,000 units	$ 7,000
Purchase, September 30, 2,000 of the 5,000 units remain unsold, 2,000 @ $1.30	+ 2,600
Ending inventory	$ 9,600

LIFO Method 10-04.3

LIFO presumes that the *newest* inventory is sold first. So what is left in inventory must be the *oldest* items. You might picture this type of "flow" like a coal bin: The coal used is off the top of the pile; the oldest delivery is left underneath. True, almost no situations actually use LIFO, but the presumption is acceptable for tax purposes. Although they are beyond the scope of this book, there are some excellent accounting theory arguments for LIFO costing of inventory, even if the true flow of goods is FIFO.

Example 10-04.3A

In the previous example, all 7,000 units of the ending inventory under LIFO are presumed to be from the opening inventory of 10,000 units. So:

7,000 units @ $1.00	$ 7,000

Comparison of Methods 10-04.4

Obviously, in periods of inflation, LIFO gives a lower inventory value than any other method. One way of remembering which is which: *LIFO* means *Lower* taxes. There are only two problems with adopting the LIFO method to save taxes.

- First, under LIFO, taxpayers must use cost. So if the market value of inventory declines, they may end up with a higher valuation than the lower of cost or market.
- Second, the Code requires that taxpayers use the same method for tax and book purposes. In other words, taxpayers' financial statements must also show the lower income and the lower asset valuation. This requirement, however, should not be an overwhelming problem, since most readers of financial statements understand the effects of LIFO, and taxpayers are allowed to disclose some of the effects of being on LIFO as supplemental information.

10-04.5 Market Value

Taxpayers, other than those using LIFO, may reduce the carrying value of their inventories to market value. It is incumbent on taxpayers to prove that the market is lower than cost. Normally they may do so by offering the goods for sale below cost.

Taxpayers may not write down their inventories to market simply because they have too much on hand. In the Thor Power Tool case, the Supreme Court made this point: If there is too much on hand and if the taxpayer wants to take a tax deduction, then the taxpayer must sell or destroy the inventory.

10-04.6 Tax Hint

Using LIFO gives taxpayers a much larger degree of flexibility than you might think. In the prior example, with LIFO we had a cost of goods sold of $28,000:

Total available for sale	$35,000
Ending inventory	− 7,000
Cost of goods sold	$28,000

But let's suppose that last purchase on December 31 had been for 23,000 units, instead of 5,000 units, at $1.40. The ending inventory would then be 25,000 units, since we acquired 18,000 more, and the chart would read:

	Quantity	*Unit Price*	*Total*
Opening inventory	10,000	$1.00	$10,000
Purchase, March 31	5,000	1.10	5,500
Purchase, June 30	5,000	1.20	6,000
Purchase, September 30	5,000	1.30	6,500
Purchase, December 31	23,000	1.40	32,200
	48,000		$60,200

The ending inventory of 25,000 units with LIFO basis is:

10,000 units @ $1.00	$10,000
5,000 units @ $1.10	5,500
5,000 units @ $1.20	6,000
5,000 units @ $1.30	6,500
25,000	$28,000

Now the ending cost of goods sold is:

Total available	$60,200
Ending inventory	−28,000
Cost of goods sold	$32,200
Original cost of goods sold	−28,000
Increase in cost of goods sold	$ 4,200

Interesting! The cost of goods goes up and so deductions go up, and nothing was sold. The mechanics of LIFO cause this effect for a large, late purchase. What happens is that the difference between the $1.40 (the inventory presumed to have been sold) and the oldest price in inventory becomes an immediate deduction. Although the increase in inventory is received on the last day of the year and even though we "know" it is not sold, the LIFO procedure presumes it is. The reconciliation of the $4,200 increase is as follows:

3,000 units (part of the original 10,000) are added to inventory	$ 3,000
15,000 units are added to inventory at a total cost of $18,000 ($5,500 + $6,000 + $6,500)	+18,000
	$21,000
Deducted from inventory and presumed sold are 18,000 units @ 1.40	−(25,200)
Net decrease in inventory *and* increase in cost of goods sold	$ 4,200

10-04.7 Simplified LIFO

The Code makes it easy for small businesses to switch to LIFO and then to compute their inventories on LIFO without having to keep historical records on each item in inventory or the need to construct their own indexes for what is called "dollar value LIFO."

10-04.7A The switch

When a taxpayer switchs to LIFO, the inventory must be priced at cost. For all other methods, the inventory is priced at the lower of cost or market. This means that the taxpayer must first recognize an item of income, either the increase in value from lower of cost or market to cost. Section 472(d) allows the income to be reported ratably over three years rather than be taken in all in the year of the switch. This, of course, delays payment of the tax, but it can also serve to have the income taxed at a lower incremental rate.

10-04.7B LIFO Computation for the small business

A business whose averge annual gross receipts for the preceding three years were $2,000,000 or less may elect under Section 474:

1. to include all inventory for a given trade or business in one pool, and
2. Section 472(f) allows the use of government-published indexes for computing LIFO.

Example 10-04.7C

At this writing the Secretary of the Treasury has not yet published any indexes. But let's assume that the Consumer Price Index (CPI) is allowed for a particular taxpayer:

Inventory, cost:	
1981	$2,000,000
1982	3,000,000
1983	4,000,000
CPI	
1981	100
1982	105
1983	110
LIFO would be	
1981 layer, $2,000,000 × 100/110	$1,818,200
1982 layer, $1,000,000 × 105/110	954,555
1983 layer, $1,000,000 × 110/110	1,000,000
Inventory at LIFO	$3,762,755

That is fairly simple math to obtain a $237,245 deduction ($4,000,000 − $3,762,755), and each year it will get bigger even with the slightest amount of inflation if inventory increases.

CASH, ACCRUAL, AND HYBRID ACCOUNTING METHODS 10-05

The Code requires taxpayers to adopt a consistent method of accounting that clearly reflects income. But because these rules affect such a diversity of taxpayers, they are flexible. Hence the Code allows for cash methods, accrual methods, or certain methods that are combinations of the first two.

10-05.1 Cash Method

Most individual taxpayers are on a *cash basis* of accounting—by far the simplest method. Income is recognized for tax purposes when it *can* be collected (see below for constructive receipt), and expenses are recognized when paid. Most taxpayers establish their method of accounting when they file their first tax return.

In most cases, however, "pure" cash accounting is not permitted. Inventory (10-03) is one area where a cash system falls short; *constructive receipt* is another. Cash basis taxpayers must report as income receipts that they could have obtained, even if they failed to do so. In other words, taxpayers cannot defer the tax on income by simply failing to collect it. For example, taxpayers have right to withdraw interest credited to a savings account on December 31, and it is taxable in the year credited, even if it is not withdrawn.

10-05.2 Accrual Method

The *accrual basis* of accounting is more sophisticated. Income is recognized when *earned* (regardless of when it is collected), and expenses are recognized when incurred (regardless of when paid). Again, there are exceptions, such as:

1. rent income *received* by an accrual basis taxpayer must be declared in the year received, even if it is prepaid rent; and
2. expenses accrued to a related party must be paid within two and a half months after the year end, or the deduction is lost.

Certain large corporations, those whose gross receipts are over $1 million and not closely held, are required to be on the accrual method.

10-05.3 Hybrid Method

Somewhere between pure cash and pure accrual accounting are myriad *hybrid methods*—part cash, part accrual. The IRS accepts hybrid accounting, as long as it is consistently applied and as long as it clearly reflects income. The key to acceptance is that each item of expense or income is handled consistently from year to year.

Taxpayers who wish to switch from one method of accounting to another must request permission from the Commissioner of the IRS.

ASSIGNMENT OF INCOME 10-06

One of the most used and abused techniques for tax planning is the assignment of income to a third party. The concept is quite simple: Assign the income to a taxpayer in a lower tax bracket—normally someone, such as a child, to whom the taxpayer would be giving the money anyway. When examining the assignment of income, look at the two basic sources of income for the tax answers:

- *Income from services* rendered, or from services to be rendered in the future, can*not* be assigned to a third party. Compensation is taxable to the person performing the services. Creating a trust or some other device does not change the facts of the situation.
- Assigning the *income from property* is another matter. The only way to transfer income from property to a third person is to transfer title in the property. The simple assignment of income from the property is not recognized. If taxpayers retain title or *control* over income-producing property, the income is taxed to them. But title to and control of income-producing property can be transferred, and the income assigned in that manner. The transfer can be either direct or indirect through a trust, and the trust assignment may be temporary. To be recognized for tax purposes as a transfer of the income from the property, a transfer through a trust must meet certain requirements (09-09, 09-10).

LEASE VERSUS SALE 10-07

Transferring the "use" of property for "consideration" is one of the most complex—and court-involved—business transactions. Did the taxpayer "sell" the property? Or was it merely "rented"? The first hurdle to get over is the legality of the transaction: The Code looks at the "reality" rather than at the "legality."

With an outright sale of property, there is normally no problem. But when a piece of property is leased under terms that approximate the transfer of the *risks* of ownership to the lessee, the questions begin to arise. Sometimes, the answers can be found in absolute mathematical terms; sometimes they involve "all the facts and circumstances."

Establishing the "owner" of the property for tax purposes is important from three standpoints:

1. Who is entitled to depreciation (08-02)?
2. Who is entitled to the investment credit (09-07)?
3. Is the "owner's" interest expense subject to the investment interest limitation (07-02)?

One of the key terms to understand is "net lease" (10-07.3). If a piece of property is under *net lease,* it may be considered to be a sale.

10-07.1 Depreciation

"Who is entitled to depreciation?" is the question without a pat answer. The courts have said that you must go by the intent of the parties, as outlined in the contract and after due consideration of all the relevant facts. There are, however, certain guideposts. If the lessee has an option to purchase the property at a bargain price, either during or prior to the expiration of the lease, the transaction is considered a sale. If the lease extends beyond the useful life of the asset, then another indication of the intent of the parties is available. (See 06-07.3B for a safe harbor for leases.)

10-07.1A Tax hint

What's the difference between being the owner or not? The taxpayer gets either depreciation or rent expense as a deduction. True! But, with accelerated depreciation, the difference can be enormous in the earlier years of the contract.

Investment Credit 10-07.2

The denial of the investment credit because property has been leased is purely mechanical. But when the investment credit is denied to the lessor, the lessor can pass that credit to the lessee.

For property that is manufactured or produced by the lessor, the lessor is entitled to the investment credit, even if the property is leased, *unless* all the facts and circumstances indicate that the lease is really a sale. In other words, you use the same basic rule as for depreciation. But if the property is purchased by the lessor, the investment credit is *denied* the lessor, unless:

1. the property was first used in the lessor's trade or business for a period of 24 months before the lease; *or*
2. the period of the lease (including all renewals) is less than 50% of the useful life of the asset; *and,* during the first 12 months of the lease, the lessor's Section 162 expenses were at least 15% of gross rents received.

But see 06-07.3B for an exception.

Remember, Section 162 expenses are those ordinary and necessary expenses required in a trade or business, but they do not include depreciation.

The credit is not totally lost. On any lease of new property (but not used property), the lessor can pass through the credit to the lessee. The amount of the credit is based on the fair market value and on the useful life of the asset in the hands of the lessor.

These rules do not apply to corporations, except Subchapter S types (12-09).

Investment Interest 10-07.3

The limitation on the deduction for investment interest expense (07-02) applies to interest expense to support property under net lease. The rationale is that the asset has been sold and that the lessor has an account receivable bearing interest income—or just an investment in interest-producing property.

Property is *net lease property* if:

1. the lessor is guaranteed either a specific return or against loss; *or*
2. Section 162 expenses are less than 15% of gross rental.

The 15% test must be made for each property, and the test must be made *annually.* Taxpayers may make two elections in making the 15% test. They may either combine or separate multiple leases on the same or adjacent property. They may also include or exclude property that has been in use for more than 5 years.

These rules do not apply to corporations, except Subchapter S types.

10-07.4 Tax Warning

Obviously, the purpose of these rules is to treat a rental as a rental and a sale as a sale, without regard to the legal form of the transaction. Yet these very same rules can trap a complacent owner of property. Watch out anytime a lessor:

- enters into a long-term lease,
- expects to be entitled to depreciation and the investment credit, and
- expects to deduct interest expense without limit.

If these features may somehow be lost to the lessor (and gained by the lessee), seek competent tax counsel. The entire economic structure of the lease is changed.

Taxpayers are required to compute their tax liability on an annual basis, which is, for most taxpayers, a calendar year. Actually, however, taxpayers elect their own tax years.

Corporations (Chapter 12) elect their tax year when filing their first returns. Many corporations elect a *fiscal year,* which is any 12-month period ending on the last day of any month. Corporations may also elect a 52-53-week fiscal year. Rather than ending on the last day of the month, the year ends on the last Friday, Monday, Tuesday, or any day of the month.

Individuals also make that election with the first tax returns they file. Technically, individuals may have a fiscal year like corporations, but very rarely.

Partnerships (Chapter 11) must elect a fiscal year that coincides with the fiscal year of the majority of the partners. When the partners are individuals, their filing requirements normally lock the partnership into a calendar year for taxes.

Any taxpayer, however, may file an application with the IRS to change to any fiscal year. Normally, the IRS grants such a change if there is a substantial business reason for it. But the IRS may also require adjustments to income so that the change does not distort the taxpayer's tax liability.

Normally, taxpayers have to file short-year returns in the first and last years of their existence. These returns are filed as if they were annual returns, with no special adjustments required. Returns for a period of more than a year are not permitted.

Importance of Choosing a Fiscal Year 10-08.1

The tax consequences of choosing a fiscal year are discussed in more detail later in the book. For now, suffice it to say that, for *partnerships* (11-02) and *Subchapter S corporations* (12-09), the choice of a fiscal year determines when undistributed income is taxed to the owners. For new *Subchapter C* (regular corporations, 12-02), the choice can affect the tax rates that are paid in the first year of operations.

10-09 PERIOD IN WHICH GROSS INCOME MUST BE REPORTED

Although cash basis taxpayers report income when received and accrual basis taxpayers report income when earned (10-05), certain special situations and exceptions should be noted.

10-09.1 Rent Received in Advance

Rent received in advance is reported in gross income when received, regardless of the taxpayer's method of accounting.

10-09.2 Compensation Received in Advance

The general rule is that compensation received in advance by a cash basis taxpayer is reportable in Gross Income when received. But if the amount received is treated as a loan by the employer and employee, the amount is not included in Gross Income until the debt is forgiven or offset by compensation earned. The most common situation involves advances to salespersons. If they have a debt obligation to repay the advances, then there is no income to the salespersons at the time of receipt.

10-09.3 Checks in the Mail

Cash basis taxpayers are considered to have received payment when they receive the check. Even if the check is not cashed, taxpayers have constructive receipt, and they must include the amount in income. But, even if the check is dated in year 1 but not received by the taxpayer until year 2 (normally because it is in the mail), the taxpayer has Gross Income in year 2.

A similar situation arises if a check is received and is not cashed at the request of the maker. Payment is considered to be received when the taxpayer *can* cash the check. If the maker requests the check not be cashed, no income has been received.

Savings Certificates 10-09.4

When taxpayers receive interest on bank or similar savings certificates that have maturities of more than one year, they must include the interest in their income, prorated over the life of the certificate. They must do so even if the interest would be forfeited if withdrawn. If interest has been reported and then forfeited, taxpayers take a deduction for Adjusted Gross Income for the amount forfeited.

The bank or savings institution must notify taxpayers of the amount of interest to be included in gross income on Form 1099, which must be sent to taxpayers before the last day of February for the preceding year.

SPECIAL CONSIDERATIONS FOR SECURITIES SALES 10-10

What is the "taxable event" (04-01)? When is a transaction recognized for tax purposes?

Although accrual basis taxpayers recognize gains and losses when earned or incurred, a special rule is invoked for *cash* basis taxpayers for the sale of securities *through a broker*. Cash basis taxpayers recognize losses on trade date and gains on settlement date. The trade date is the day the trade is actually done, and, in all economic senses, it establishes the gain or loss. The settlement date is the day the buyer actually pays for the purchase and receive the securities; the seller receives his or her money and delivers the securities. The brokerage community has established a pattern of settlement dates, but, as a general rule, the settlement date is five business days after trade date.

The settlement date, however, can be changed! A trade for "cash" means that trade date *is* the settlement date. In most cases, the settlement date can be changed if the taxpayer wishes to do so.

These rules present an interesting (and useful) dichotomy. Taxpayers have almost no flexibility in recognizing a loss (the trade date fixes true economic loss), but they enjoy great flexibility in establishing a gain (by adjusting the settlement date).

10-10.1 Gaining Flexibility on a Loss

Sell short against the box to "avoid" a loss! The technique of selling short against the box to avoid recognizing a gain (05-07) can also be used to avoid recognizing a loss.

10-10.2 Tax Hint

In consideration of the settlement and trade date rules, as well as of the short against the box technique, the cash-basis taxpayers who understand "how to play the game" are the ones who enjoy the greatest degree of flexibility.

10-11 PERIOD IN WHICH EXPENSE MUST BE REPORTED

While the general rule is that cash basis taxpayers deduct expenses when paid and accrual basis taxpayers deduct expenses when incurred (10-05), there are many exceptions and interpretations as to when something is actually paid or incurred.

For some expenses, taxpayers, whether cash or accrual, can elect when the deduction is to be taken. Among these are:

1. research and development expenses (08-13),
2. exploration and development expenditures (08-08),
3. certain farm development and soil and water conservation expenditures (08-09), and
4. certain corporate and partnership organization expenses (12-05.2).

Timing a deduction is extremely important in view of the statute of limitations. In most cases, taxpayers may not amend or correct tax returns after three years. They could lose a perfectly good deduction because they took it in the wrong year.

Example 10-11.1

> In late 1981, the IRS disallows a deduction for 1978 as a result of an audit, because the deduction should have been taken in 1977. If Marvin Taxpayer filed his 1977 return on April 15, 1978, then 1977 would be closed to amending the return. So the deduction is not allowed *at all* because it was taken in 1978 and because 1977 is closed. This sort of slip-up happens quite often with taxpayers who try to "push" a deduction forward into a year with a higher incremental tax rate.

Cash Basis Taxpayers and Borrowed Money 10-11.2

In this area, form takes priority over substance. If the taxpayer borrows funds from one party and uses those funds to pay expenses to another party, the expenses are "paid" and a deduction is allowed. But if a cash basis taxpayer pays for an item by giving a note to the supplier, *no* deduction is allowed. Giving a note is not considered payment.

What about the use of a credit card? That seems to be OK. The courts have held that the use of a credit card to make a charitable contribution establishes a liability on the part of the taxpayer, which is therefore a deduction. As of 1981, that theory has not been tested for Section 162 expenses, but it should follow through.

10-11.3 Nonrecourse Debt

Nonrecourse debt exists when the creditor may look only to the income of the property being financed for payment of principal and interest. *Recourse debt* exists when the borrower is liable for the payment of principal and interest without regard to the value or income-producing capacity of the property being financed.

Except for loans secured by real estate and certain other exceptions (which will be noted), taxpayers' deductible expenses are limited to the amount they have "at risk." If taxpayers are not at risk for the payment of a debt, that debt cannot be used to establish a deductible expense. The amount they have at risk is:

1. the amount invested in the property,
2. plus any recourse debt,
3. plus any profits left in the business, and
4. less any amount of profit or investment withdrawn from the business.

If recourse debt is converted into nonrecourse debt, the amount of deductions taken that relate to the debt is recaptured and becomes taxable income.

Any deductions lost due to the at-risk rule may be deducted in the year that thc taxpayer has sufficient amounts at risk to take the deduction.

The at-risk limitations do not apply to most corporations. They do apply to any corporation where 5 or fewer people own 50% or more of the stock (except as noted below), as well as to Subchapter S corporations. The rules do not apply to any corporation regularly engaged in the leasing of Section 1245 assets, except Subchapter S corporations.

Example 10-11.3A

Colin Gordon acquires a piece of medical diagnostic equipment for $100,000, with the intention of charging a fee for its use in the local hospital. He pays $10,000 in cash, and the seller takes a nonrecourse loan for the remaining $90,000 at 12% interest. Colin is not personally liable for the note. The proceeds of the rental activity and the equipment itself are the only collateral for the loan. Colin uses 5-year accelerated cost recovery for depreciation. All operating expenses are to be paid by the users.

During the first year he collects $12,000 in rental. Out of that income, he pays $9,600 interest expense and $400 in principal on the loan, and he takes the remaining $2,000 for personal use. His loss for the year is:

Rental income		$12,000
Less: Interest expense	$ 9,600	
Depreciation		
($100,000 × 0.15)	+15,000	−24,600
Net loss		$12,600
Tax deduction limited by at risk amount:		
Original investment		$10,000
Profits retained in business		+ 400
Tax deduction		$10,400

The remaining $2,200 ($12,600 − $10,400) is deductible when Colin's at-risk amount is increased.

Tax *warning* 10-11.3B

What about the investment credit? Does Colin get a $10,000 investment credit ($100,000 cost × 0.10)? If Colin were a 50% taxpayer, that credit would be the equivalent of another $20,000 deduction ($10,000/0.50). This is what "shelter sellers" call a *3-for-1 write off.* For every $1 of investment, the taxpayer gets the equivalent of $3 of deductions; $10,000 of investment credit (worth the same as a $20,000 deduction), and the $10,000 deduction (actually $10,400 in our case). Will it work? Not in this case!

The Code does limit the investment credit because of nonrecourse financing. The rules for computing the "at-risk" amount for purposes of allowing the investment credit are the same as above, except:

1. The amount at risk is measured by the original purchase. Profit kept in the business does not increase the amount at risk. And,
2. If the taxpayer was at risk for at least 20% of the cost at all times, and if the nonrecourse loan was obtained from a qualified lender (basically banks, insurance companies, and similar financial institutions), then the entire cost is considered to be at risk.

Further, the IRS has taken the position that the fair market value of the machine must be less than $100,000, or why the need for a nonrecourse loan? If the property could be sold for $100,000, the seller would do so. Another approach the IRS has taken is that the terms of the loan are such that Colin and the seller are really partners; so there is no increase in basis above the basis that the seller had. In either case the investment credit would be lost or at least reduced.

Investor beware! The investment credit is not as secure as just reading the Code would lead you to believe. If the sale is above fair market value or if the debt has little chance of being paid, the IRS will attack the investment credit!

10-11.4 Prepaid Interest

For cash basis taxpayers, an expense is deductible when paid. But, even for cash basis taxpayers, prepaid interest must be allocated over the life of the loan.

The installment sale method simply allows taxpayers to report the gain on the sale of property as they receive the money from the sale. But installment sales must be broken down into two categories:

1. *Those by dealers*: Installment sales afford dealers a type of tax relief similar to other installment sales, but they are beyond the scope of this book.
2. For *those by persons other than dealers,* the sale of property on which a *gain* is realized is automatically reported under the installment method. These taxpayers must elect not to report under the installment method, and they must report the entire gain in the year of sale.

Example 10-12.1

Aaron Gordon has a piece of property with a basis of $20,000. He sells it for $100,000. The means of payment is a note of 5 installments, with each installment due annually and with interest at 12% (10-12.2). His profit of $80,000 ($100,000 sales proceeds less $20,000 basis) is reported as he collects the payments. If the sale were on January 20 of year 1, and if the first payment is January 20 of year 2, then in year 2, he reports:

Long-term capital gain ($80,000/5 payments	$16,000
Interest income ($100,000 × 0.12)	+12,000
Total income, Year 2	$28,000

He continues to report the capital gain as collected, along with the appropriate amount of interest income.

Imputed Interest 10-12.2

Obviously, Aaron could have written the installment contract to read: "Sale price $136,000, no interest." He would then collect $136,000 over the life of the contract. So why not make the whole sale price capital gains (favorably taxed), instead of part interest income? To prevent taxpayers from doing just that, the IRS insists that interest at the rate of 6%, simple, be charged on an installment or deferred payment (10-13) contract. If it is not, then the IRS imputes 7% interest on the discounted present value method. A chart on how to compute imputed interest can be found in Regulation 1.483-1(g)(2). The rates are frequently changed. So the taxpayers should check the current rates before entering into an installment contract.

10-12.3 Sales Between Related Parties

There used to be an old trick. John has stock with a very low basis. He sells it under an installment plan to his wife. He has no tax to report until she pays him. Now his wife sells the stock. She has no tax because her basis was increased to fair market value when she purchased the stock.

To prevent this abuse, the Code was amended. When an installment sale has been made between related parties (10-12.4), and when the buyer sells the property within two years of the purchase, the profit to the first seller is triggered and becomes taxable. The Code goes further for the sale of securities, since even the 2-year waiting period is not enough to stop the triggering of profits to the first seller. For the purpose of these rules, "related" means: spouse, linear relatives, corporations, partnerships, and trusts over which the taxpayer has control.

10-12.4 Example

Aaron Gordon, in the prior example, sells the property to his son. So far, so good—no problem. Within two years, the son sells the land. *Now* here's the problem: The entire profit that Aaron realized on the sale and that he had not yet reported is taxable to him. If the property is securities, then whenever his son sells the securities, the remaining unreported profit becomes immediately taxable.

10-12.5 Tax Hint

Losses cannot be deferred by the installment method.

But, if you have to sell securities at a great gain, you might want to sell them to the brokerage house in an installment sale for more flexibility on the tax return.

Example 10-12.5A

Tiffany Schuler has 100,000 shares of MBS stock that she got years ago. Her basis is only $1 per share, and the stock has just been tendered at $30. She has no choice; she must tender. Some tax problem!

Proceeds of sale	$3,000,000
Basis	− 100,000
Long-term capital gain	$2,900,000

Tiffany will never have a year like this again. How can we spread out the gain over several years, to reduce both her regular tax and her Alternative Minimum Tax?

Have her sell the stock on an installment plan to the brokerage firm! The broker gets paid when it tenders the stock, so it is not out any money. In fact, if the broker pays Tiffany an interest rate lower than its borrowing rate, it actually makes more money on the deal.

SALE OF PROPERTY VERSUS CONTINGENT PAYMENTS 10-13

If taxpayers sell property for an undeterminable amount, due to contingencies in the contract, they are entitled to a full return of basis before reporting any profit.

Example 10-13.1

Barney Colin sells his cleaning establishment, in which he has a basis of $50,000, under the following conditions:

1. $20,000 cash at the signing of the contract; and
2. 30% of the net profits for the next five years.

At the time he signs the contract, Barney has no income. The $20,000 received reduces his basis from $50,000 to $30,000. In the next five years, he receives: $20,000, $22,000, $23,000, $34,000, and $27,000. He reports:

Year 1, basis	$30,000
Recovery of basis	−20,000
Basis, beginning of year 2	$10,000
First $10,000 collected in year 2 is recovery of basis	−10,000
Remaining basis	$ –0–
Year 2 collection	$22,000
Recovery of basis	−10,000
Reportable gain	$12,000

All the remaining payments are reported as gains in the year collected. Presuming the asset sold is a capital asset in the hands of the seller, the gains are reported as capital gains.

11

PARTNERSHIPS

11-01 WHAT IS A PARTNERSHIP?

Under the Code, a *partnership* is an untaxed *reporting* unit. When two or more taxpayers combine their efforts or funds in a business venture, they constitute a partnership. There is no requirement that a formal partnership agreement be in effect.

All joint ventures, however, are not necessarily partnerships. As an example, if two taxpayers own investment property as tenants in common, they are not a partnership. They report their share of the income and expenses on their own tax returns.

When a partnership does exist, it must file an information return on Form 1065. The return, in effect, notifies the IRS how each of the taxable items in the partnership will be treated by the partners on their own separate returns.

11-01.1 Tax *Warning*

If you have any doubt as to whether a partnership exists, the wise move is to file Form 1065, since it is merely an information return, and no tax payments are required. On the other hand, failure to file this form when one is due carries severe penalties. The penalty is $50 per partner, per month that the return is late. For example, if two years after the form is due, the IRS determines that a partnership existed between two taxpayers, the penalty would be $2,400 ($50 × 2 taxpayers × 24 months).

THE CONDUIT THEORY 11-02

A partnership is the closest thing to a pure conduit that exists in taxation. In a "simple" partnership, each "piece" of income or expense passes through to the partners in the exact same form as if they had earned it separately, in proportion to their respective interests in the partnership. If a partnership, in its simplest form, receives dividend income, then each partner is considered to have received a share of the dividend income.

But many partnerships are not "simple." As a result, the Code sets certain limitations on the pure pass-through approach. The two major exceptions to the pure conduit approach are as follows:

1. No partner may take a *loss* in excess of his or her basis.
2. Partners may divide income and expenses in any way they choose, *except* that the division must have economic substance.

Example: Loss in Excess of Basis 11-02.1

Aaron Gordon and Barney Colin form a partnership. Aaron contributes $50,000 in cash. Barney contributes property worth $50,000, in which he has a basis of $10,000. Each partner has a 50% interest in profits and losses. In their first year of operations, the partnership loses $40,000. On the books of the partnership, each of them takes a $20,000 loss. Aaron reports that loss on his personal tax return, and his remaining basis in the partnership is $30,000

($50,000 cash contributed less $20,000 loss). Barney, on the other hand, has a problem. The loss ($20,000) exceeds his basis ($10,000). He can deduct the loss on his personal tax return up to his basis. His basis is then zero. The remaining $10,000 loss is in a state of "suspension." He can deduct it only when his basis is sufficient to cover it.

Aaron and Barney's agreement specifies that any profits on the sale of Barney's property must be credited to his account. In the second year of operation, the land is sold for $55,000, and Barney is credited with the $45,000 in profit. The profit is $45,000, because the partnership has the same basis for the property, as Barney had ($10,000). Barney reports a long-term gain of $45,000 on his personal return, which increases his basis from zero to $45,000. Now he may deduct the $10,000 that he could not deduct last year.

11-02.2 Division of Profits

Partners may make changes to their agreed division of profits even after year-end, until the partnership return is due. The IRS recognizes any division of profits that is agreed to by the partners, with two exceptions:

1. in the case of family partnerships (11-04), and
2. when the division of profits has no substance other than the avoidance of income taxes.

11-02.3 Example

Aaron and Barney form the A$B Partnership. Barney agrees to contribute $100,000, and Aaron agrees to do all the work. They agree also to divide the partnership income or loss as follows:

1. Each partner gets 10% interest on the average balance in his capital account.

2. Aaron gets a salary of $20,000.
3. Any remaining income or loss is divided evenly.

In its first year the partnership earns $1,000, before consideration of the agreement. The partnership's ordinary loss (11-03) is:

Net income		$ 1,000
Less partners' guaranteed payments:		
Interest paid Barney	$10,000	
Salary paid Aaron	+20,000	−30,000
Ordinary loss		$29,000

Barney would report on his personal return:

One-half of ordinary loss	$14,500
Less: Guaranteed payment, interest	−10,000
Net *loss* from partnership	$ 4,500

Aaron would report on his personal return:

Guaranteed payment, salary	$20,000
Less: One-half of ordinary loss	−14,500
Net *income* from partnership	$ 5,500

An important point to note is that, although Barney and Aaron call these guaranteed payments "interest" and "salary," they are *not*. They are merely a means of computing the division of gain or loss in the partnership. On Form K-1 (11-03.4), they show up as income or loss from a partership, not as interest or salary.

On the other hand, let's say Aaron and Barney arbitrarily divide the $1,000, so that Barney gets a $10,000 loss and Aaron gets an $11,000 gain, because Barney is in a higher incremental tax bracket and needs the deduction. The IRS would disallow such an arrangement.

11-02.4 Other Allocations

Other items of income and expense can be specifically allocated to one partner or another, if the allocation has economic substance. In the first example, we saw the gain on the sale of property allocated to the partner contributing the property. Similarly, such items as Section 1245 recapture could be allocated to the partner contributing the asset.

Allocations can also be made based on state income tax considerations. In the A$B example, if Barney were a New York resident, A$B might allocate any interest on New York State tax-exempt bonds to him. Under New York law, Barney does not have to pay any state income tax on that interest. But if that interest were allocated to Aaron (a New Jersey resident), he would have to pay New Jersey state income tax on it.

11-02.5 Limited Partners

All states allow what is called a *limited partnership,* which consists of at least one general partner and one or more limited partners. In most cases the general partner has unlimited personal liability for the debts of the partnership. The liability of the limited partners is limited to the amount they invest in the partnership. Hence limited partners are normally investors in a business, rather than part of the management. Most states require that limited partners not be active in the business.

The Code recognizes a limited partner in the same way as a general partner. But keep in mind that the two limitations on deducting losses apply to both limited and general partners:

1. The amount deducted cannot exceed the partner's basis in the partnership.
2. The amount deducted cannot exceed the amount that the partner has at risk (10-11).

RECONCILIATION OF BOOK PROFIT TO FORM 1065

Since a partnership is a conduit, Form 1065 breaks down the various elements of income and loss for reporting. To insure the reporting of all items of income and loss, the form requires a reconciliation of the partners' capital accounts.

The first figure to be derived is "ordinary" income or loss. This figure is a compilation of all the income and expense accounts that would simply be added to, or deducted from, the Adjusted Gross Income of the partners, if each one were reporting individually. Ordinary income therefore includes two elements: (1) all items of income that do not require special consideration before being added to Adjusted Gross Income, and (2) all expenses that are deductions *for* Adjusted Gross Income. The items of income are:

1. gross profit (sales less cost of goods sold),
2. ordinary income from other partnerships and fiduciaries,
3. nonqualifying dividends (those that do not qualify for the corporate 85% exclusion or the $100 individual exclusion),
4. net income from rents and royalties (after deductions for Adjusted Gross Income),
5. net farm profits (after deductions for AGI), and
6. Sections 1245 and 1250 recapture of depreciation, along with Section 1231 losses.
7. Interest income until 1985, when the interest exclusion comes into effect.

The items of expense are:

1. guaranteed payments to partners and
2. Section 162 expenses.

Guaranteed payments to partners are deducted in figuring ordinary income, but they are added back as ordinary income to each partner later in the reconciliation.

11-03.1 Example

The A$B partnership books showed the following for the year:

Sales		$500,000
Cost of goods sold		−300,000
Gross profit		$200,000
Other income:		
Rent income	$14,000	
Interest on City of Hoboken, N.J. bonds	5,000	
Gain on the sale of MBS Corporation common stock	+10,000	+29,000
Gross income		$229,000
Less expenses:		
Salaries paid to employees	$16,000	
Partners' guaranteed payments:		
Salaries	60,000	
Interest on capital	12,000	
Contributions to partners' qualified retirement plans (Keogh Plans)	5,000	
Contributions to the ASPCA (a qualified charity)	4,000	
Other business expenses	+16,000	−113,000
Net income		$116,000

The ordinary income would be:

Net income		$116,000
Plus: Contribution to the ASPCA (a deduction from Adjusted Gross Income)	$ 4,000	

Keogh Plan contributions (amount must be reported separately since the deductibility is limited by each partner's income)	+ 5,000	+ 9,000
		$125,000
Less: Interest on City of Hoboken bond since that is tax-exempt interest	$5,000	
Gain of sale of MBS stock since each partner must compute the amount of capital gain or deductible loss including all other capital gains or losses	+10,000	− 15,000
Ordinary income		$110,000

Schedule K 11-03.2

The reconciliation then moves to Schedule K of Form 1065, where the items of income and expense are summarized. As we will see later, Schedule K forms the basis of Schedule K-1, which is the report sent to the partners to enable them to file their personal tax returns.

Example 11-03.2A

In the A&B example, the Schedule K would read:

Ordinary income	$110,000
Guaranteed payments to partners (combining the $60,000 salary and the $12,000 interest)	72,000
Net long-term capital gain (presuming MBS is held long-term; if not, then net short-term capital gain)	10,000
Charitable contributions (50% qualifying)	4,000

Payments to partners' Keogh Plans	5,000
Net earnings from self employment	168,000*

*This is for the computation of self-employment taxes (FICA), which is:

Ordinary income	$110,000
Plus: Partners' guaranteed payments (remember that is just a way of dividing the profits)	+ 72,000
	$182,000
Less: Rental income (not subject to FICA—only earned income is)	14,000
Earnings from self-employment	$168,000

11-03.3 Schedule M

The last reconciliation before the completion of Schedule K-1 is the reconciliation of beginning and ending partners' capital. This comparison insures that all items are reported somewhere. In our case, let's presume that the partners withdrew only the salaries and interest from the business and that their beginning capital accounts at the start of the year equal $100,000.

Capital account at the beginning of the year		$100,000
Capital contributed during the year	$ –0–	
Ordinary income	110,000	
Plus other income:		
Partners' guaranteed payments	72,000	
Tax-exempt interest	5,000	
Long-term capital gain	+10,000	+197,000
		$297,000
Less other expenses and losses:		
Contributions	$ 4,000	
Keogh Plan contributions	5,000	
Partner drawings	+ 72,000	− 81,000
Capital accounts, end of year		$216,000

Schedule K-1 11-03.4

The last step in the partnership return is the completion of Schedule K-1. This schedule tells each partner how to report each of the items. The total of all K-1s must equal the totals on Schedule K, since this is merely a breakdown of those figures and of the figures on Schedule M.

Example 11-03.5

Barney is entitled to the interest, and Aaron is entitled to the salary. All other items of income and expense are divided equally.

The two page 1s of their Forms K-1 are shown in Figures 11-1a and b. The questions on page 1 are directed to the tax shelter partnerships. We presume that there is no nonrecourse financing and that each of them is one-half liable for $80,000 of partnership debts.

Neither Aaron nor Barney needed to complete any of the items on page 2 of Form K-1 (Figure 11-1c). But the items here are important, since they further emphasize the conduit approach.

Items of tax preference, interest on investment indebtedness, investment credits, and the other items that require special treatment on the individual's tax return are shown separately.

Note the extreme right-hand column of the form. The form even tells the taxpayer the Form 1040 line on which to enter the item. As an example, the $2,000 charitable contribution is entered on Schedule A, line 21 or 22 of Form 1040, and it is added to all the other contributions the taxpayer makes. The $60,000 income from self-employment goes on Schedule SE of Form 1040, which is the schedule used to compute the self-employment tax. This amount is added to all other self-employment income.

FAMILY PARTNERSHIPS 11-04

Family partnerships come under special rules that allow the IRS broad discretion in allocating income. For these

FIGURE 11-1a. Barney's Schedule K-1

SCHEDULE K–1 (Form 1065)
Department of the Treasury
Internal Revenue Service

Partner's Share of Income, Credits, Deductions, etc.—1980

For calendar year 1980 or fiscal year
beginning ...., 1980, and ending ...., 19......
(Instructions for partners attached. Complete for each partner—See instructions on back of Copy B)

Copy A (File with Form 1065)

Partner's identifying number ▶ 123-45-6789

Partner's name, address, and ZIP code
Barney Colin
123 East 69th Street
New York, N. Y. 10011

Partnership's identifying number ▶ 22-1990019

Partnership's name, address, and ZIP code
A$B Partnership
70 Pine Street
New York, N. Y. 10005

	Yes	No
A (i) Date(s) partner acquired any partnership interest during the year ▶ n/a		
(ii) Did partner have any partnership interest before 1/1/77?		X
B Is partner a nonresident alien?		X
C (i) Is partner a limited partner (see page 2 of Instructions)?		X
(ii) If "Yes," is partner also a general partner?		
D (i) Did partner ever contribute property other than money to the partnership?		X
If "Yes," enter: a Basis to partnership of contributed property (other than money) at time(s) of contribution to the partnership . . $		
b Value of contributed property in "a" above as reflected in the partner's capital account $		
(ii) Did partner ever receive a distribution other than money from the partnership?		X
If "Yes," enter: a Basis to partnership of distributed property (other than money) at time(s) of distribution to the partner . . . $		
b Value of distributed property in "a" above as reflected in the partner's capital account $		
E Was any part of the partner's interest ever acquired from another partner?		X

	Yes	No
F (i) Did partnership interest terminate during the year?		X
(ii) Did partnership interest decrease during the year?		X

G Enter partner's percentage of:

	(i) Before decrease or termination	(ii) End of year
Profit sharing	%	50 %
Loss sharing	%	50 %
Ownership of capital		73 %
Time devoted to business		none %

H IRS Center where partnership filed return ▶ Holtsville

I What type of entity is this partner? ▶ Individual

J Partner's share of liabilities (see page 7 of Instructions):

	(i) Incurred before 1/1/77	(ii) Incurred after 12/31/76
Nonrecourse	$	$
Other	$	$ 40,000

K Enter total amount of liabilities other than nonrecourse for which the partner is protected against loss through guarantees, stop loss agreements, or similar arrangements of which the partnership has knowledge:

Incurred before 1/1/77 . . . . . . $ none
Incurred after 12/31/76 . . . . . . $ none

L Partner's share of any pre-1976 loss(es) from a section 465(c)(1) activity (i.e., film or video tape, section 1245 property leasing, farm, or oil and gas property) for which there existed a corresponding amount of nonrecourse liability at the end of the year in which loss(es) occurred . . . . . . $ none

M Reconciliation of partner's capital account:

a. Capital account at beginning of year	b. Capital contributed during year	c. Ordinary income (loss) from line 1b	d. Income not included in column c, plus nontaxable income	e. Losses not included in column c, plus unallowable deductions	f. Withdrawals and distributions	g. Capital account at end of year
100,000		55,000	19,500	4,500	12,000	158,000

a. Distributive share item	b. Amount	c. 1040 filers enter the amount in column b on:
1 a Guaranteed payments to partner: (1) Deductible by the partnership	12,000	Sch. E, Part III
(2) Capitalized by the partnership		Sch. E, Part III
b Ordinary income (loss)	55,000	Sch. E, Part III
2 Additional first-year depreciation (Basis ....)		Sch. E, Part III
3 Gross farming or fishing income		Sch. E, Part IV
4 Dividends qualifying for exclusion		Sch. B, Part II, line 3
5 Net short-term capital gain (loss)		Sch. D, line 3, col. f or g
6 Net long-term capital gain (loss)	5,000	Sch. D, line 10, col. f or g
7 Net gain (loss) from involuntary conversions due to casualty or theft		Form 4684
8 Other net gain (loss) under section 1231		Form 4797, line 1
9 Net earnings (loss) from self-employment	60,000	Sch. SE, Part I or Part II
10 a Charitable contributions: 50% 2,000, 30% ...., 20%	2,000	Sch. A, line 21 or 22
b Other itemized deductions (attach list)		See Sch. A
11 Expense account allowance		
12 Jobs credit		Form 5884
13 Taxes paid by regulated investment company		Form 1040, line 61, add words "from 1065"
14 a Payments for partner to a Keogh Plan (Type of plan ▶ H.R. 10)	2,500	Form 1040, line 26
b Payments for partner to an IRA		Form 1040, line 25
c Payments for partner to Simplified Employee Pension (SEP)		Form 1040, line 26

FIGURE 11-1b. Aaron's Schedule K-1

SCHEDULE K–1 (Form 1065)
Department of the Treasury
Internal Revenue Service

Partner's Share of Income, Credits, Deductions, etc.—1980

For calendar year 1980 or fiscal year
beginning ...., 1980, and ending ...., 19......
(Instructions for partners attached. Complete for each partner—See instructions on back of Copy B)

Copy A (File with Form 1065)

Partner's identifying number ▶ 234-56-7890

Partner's name, address, and ZIP code
Aaron Gordon
324 Partridge Run
Mountainside, N. J. 07092

Partnership's identifying number ▶ 22-1990019

Partnership's name, address, and ZIP code
A$B Partnership
70 Pine Street
New York, N. Y. 10005

	Yes	No
A (i) Date(s) partner acquired any partnership interest during the year ▶ n/a		
(ii) Did partner have any partnership interest before 1/1/77?		X
B Is partner a nonresident alien?		X
C (i) Is partner a limited partner (see page 2 of Instructions)?		X
(ii) If "Yes," is partner also a general partner?		
D (i) Did partner ever contribute property other than money to the partnership?		X
If "Yes," enter: a Basis to partnership of contributed property (other than money) at time(s) of contribution to the partnership . . $..........		
b Value of contributed property in "a" above as reflected in the partner's capital account $..........		
(ii) Did partner ever receive a distribution other than money from the partnership?		X
If "Yes," enter: a Basis to partnership of distributed property (other than money) at time(s) of distribution to the partner . . . $..........		
b Value of distributed property in "a" above as reflected in the partner's capital account $..........		
E Was any part of the partner's interest ever acquired from another partner?		X

	Yes	No
F (i) Did partnership interest terminate during the year?		X
(ii) Did partnership interest decrease during the year?		X

G Enter partner's percentage of:	(i) Before decrease or termination	(ii) End of year
Profit sharing	%	50 %
Loss sharing	%	50 %
Ownership of capital		27 %
Time devoted to business		100 %

H IRS Center where partnership filed return ▶ Holtsville

I What type of entity is this partner? ▶ Individual

J Partner's share of liabilities (see page 7 of Instructions):

	(i) Incurred before 1/1/77	(ii) Incurred after 12/31/76
Nonrecourse	$	$
Other	$	$ 40,000

K Enter total amount of liabilities other than nonrecourse for which the partner is protected against loss through guarantees, stop loss agreements, or similar arrangements of which the partnership has knowledge:

Incurred before 1/1/77 . . . . . . $ none
Incurred after 12/31/76 . . . . . . $ none

L Partner's share of any pre-1976 loss(es) from a section 465(c)(1) activity (i.e., film or video tape, section 1245 property leasing, farm, or oil and gas property) for which there existed a corresponding amount of nonrecourse liability at the end of the year in which loss(es) occurred . . . . . $ none

M Reconciliation of partner's capital account:

a. Capital account at beginning of year	b. Capital contributed during year	c. Ordinary income (loss) from line 1b	d. Income not included in column c, plus non-taxable income	e. Losses not included in column c, plus unallowable deductions	f. Withdrawals and distributions	g. Capital account at end of year
		55,000	67,500	4,500	60,000	58,000

a. Distributive share item	b. Amount	c. 1040 filers enter the amount in column b on:
1 a Guaranteed payments to partner: (1) Deductible by the partnership	60,000	Sch. E, Part III
(2) Capitalized by the partnership		Sch. E, Part III
b Ordinary income (loss)	55,000	Sch. E, Part III
2 Additional first-year depreciation (Basis ....)		Sch. E, Part III
3 Gross farming or fishing income		Sch. E, Part IV
4 Dividends qualifying for exclusion		Sch. B, Part II, line 3
5 Net short-term capital gain (loss)		Sch. D, line 3, col. f or g
6 Net long-term capital gain (loss)	5,000	Sch. D, line 10, col. f or g
7 Net gain (loss) from involuntary conversions due to casualty or theft		Form 4684
8 Other net gain (loss) under section 1231		Form 4797, line 1
9 Net earnings (loss) from self-employment	108,000	Sch. SE, Part I or Part II
10 a Charitable contributions: 50% 2,000, 30% ...., 20%	2,000	Sch. A, line 21 or 22
b Other itemized deductions (attach list)		See Sch. A
11 Expense account allowance		
12 Jobs credit		Form 5884
13 Taxes paid by regulated investment company		Form 1040, line 61, add words "from 1065"
14 a Payments for partner to a Keogh Plan (Type of plan ▶ H.R. 10)	2,500	Form 1040, line 26
b Payments for partner to an IRA		Form 1040, line 25
c Payments for partner to Simplified Employee Pension (SEP)		Form 1040, line 26

FIGURE 11-1c. Reverse Side of Schedule K-1

15 a Foreign taxes paid (attach schedule)		Form 1116
b Other income, deductions, etc. (attach schedule)		(Enter on applicable lines of your return)
16 Oil and gas depletion. (Enter amount—not for partner's use ▶ ....)		For IRS use only.
17 Specially allocated items (attach schedule): a Short-term capital gain (loss)		Sch. D, line 3, col. f or g
b Long-term capital gain (loss)		Sch. D, line 10, col. f or g
c Ordinary gain (loss)		Form 4797, line 9
d Other		Sch. E, Part III
18 Items of tax preference: a Accelerated depreciation on real property—		
(1) Certified historic structure rehabilitation (167(o) or amortization under 191)		Form 4625, line 1(a)(1)
(2) Low-income rental housing (167(k))		Form 4625, line 1(a)(2)
(3) Other government-assisted low-income housing		Form 4625, line 1(a)(2)
(4) Other real property		Form 4625, line 1(a)(3)
b Accelerated depreciation on personal property subject to a lease		Form 4625, line 1(b)
Amortization: c ...., d ...., e ...., f		Form 4625, line 1(c) thru (f)
g Reserves for losses on bad debts of financial institutions		Form 4625, line 1(g)
h Depletion (other than oil and gas)		Form 4625, line 1(i)
i (1) Excess intangible drilling costs from oil, gas, or geothermal wells		See Form 4625 instr.
(2) Net income from oil, gas, or geothermal wells		
19 Interest on investment indebtedness: a Investment interest expense—		
(1) Indebtedness incurred before 12/17/69		Form 4952, line 1
(2) Indebtedness incurred before 9/11/75, but after 12/16/69		Form 4952, line 15
(3) Indebtedness incurred after 9/10/75		Form 4952, line 5
b Net investment income (loss)		Form 4952, line 2 or line 10(a)
c Excess expenses from "net lease property"		Form 4952, lines 11 and 19
d Excess of net long-term capital gain over net short-term capital loss from investment property		Form 4952, line 20
20 Property qualified for investment credit:		
New property — a 3 or more but less than 5 years		Form 3468, line 1(a)
b 5 or more but less than 7 years		Form 3468, line 1(b)
c 7 or more years		Form 3468, line 1(c)
New commuter highway vehicle — d 3 or more years		Form 3468, line 1(d)
Qualified progress expenditures — e 7 or more years		Form 3468, line 1(e)
Used property — f 3 or more but less than 5 years		Form 3468, line 1(f)
g 5 or more but less than 7 years		Form 3468, line 1(g)
h 7 or more years		Form 3468, line 1(h)
Used commuter highway vehicle — i 3 or more years		Form 3468, line 1(i)
21 a Credit for alcohol used as fuel		Form 6478, line 15
b Nonconventional source fuel credit		
c Unused credits from cooperatives		

22 Property used in recomputing a prior year investment credit (enter on corresponding line of Form 4255):

	Description of property (also state whether new or used)	(1) Rate	(2) Date placed in service	(3) Cost or basis	(4) Estimated useful life	(5) Applicable percentage	(6) Original qualified investment (column 3 × column 5)	(8) Date item ceased to be investment credit property	(9) Period actually used	(10) Applicable percentage	(11) Qualified investment (column 3 × column 10)
A											
B											

Instructions for the Partnership

Complete Schedule K-1 (Form 1065) for each partner. File Copy A with Form 1065 and send Copy C to the appropriate partner. Schedule K-1 and Schedule K have the same line numbers to make it easier for the partnership to prepare Schedule K-1. (In addition, Schedule K-1 has questions A through L, item M, and line 22.) Refer to the Schedule K instructions before preparing Schedule K and Schedule K-1, especially the instructions for line 15b. Also, refer to the instructions for the lettered items at the top of Schedule K-1. Additional copies of Schedule K-1 are available from your District Director. The total amount of the distributive share items (column b) reported on each line on all of the partners' Schedules K-1 should equal the amount reported on the same line of Schedule K (Form 1065). Similarly, the total of the amounts reported in each column of item M of all the partners' Schedules K-1 should equal the amounts reported in the same column in Schedule M of Form 1065.

Substitute forms.—Prior IRS approval is not required for (a) a substitute Schedule K-1 that shows only the line items required for use by a taxpayer if those line items have the same numbers and titles and are in the same order as on the comparable IRS Schedule K-1; and (b) a substitute Schedule K-1 that is an exact facsimile of an IRS Schedule K-1. Other substitute Schedules K-1 require prior approval. You may apply for approval of a substitute form by writing to: Internal Revenue Service, Attention TX:R, 1111 Constitution Avenue, NW., Washington, DC 20224.

purposes "family" includes: spouse, parents, grandparents, children, and grandchildren.

The IRS recognizes a family partnership, along with the agreed-upon distribution of income, if the distribution fairly takes into account compensation to those providing services and to those providing capital. Since taxpayers cannot simply assign income to others to avoid income tax (10-06), a family partnership cannot be used for that purpose.

But when capital is an important income-producing item, there is an opportunity for income splitting. To split income, the "producer" in the family gives a portion of the partnership to members of the family (normally the children). The transfer may take place over a period that enables the giver to avoid gift taxation (Chapter 13). The gifts may avoid estate taxation (Chapter 14) when the family breadwinner dies, since the business is no longer his or hers. The gifts must be made in such a way that the breadwinner gives up control of the asset. This can be done through a trust, and it should be done with the help of competent legal counsel. The partnership then divides the income in such a manner as to give proper compensation to the providers of capital—now the children who are in a lower incremental tax bracket than the parent.

This concept is extremely useful in tax planning when capital is a significant income-producing item. It is less effective in a business where services provided by the breadwinner are the most significant income-producing item.

Subchapter S corporations (12-09) provide a similar, and often more flexible, vehicle for family income splitting.

TAX YEARS OF PARTNERS AND THEIR PARTNERSHIPS 11-05

When do partners include their distributive shares of the partnership's income expense items in their returns? The answer is "with or within" the tax year that the partnership's tax year ends. For example, if the partnership's tax year ended on, say, November 30, 1981, then calendar year partners would include the income from the 12 months ended November 30 in their 1981 income. The partnership's income from December of 1981 would not be reported by the partners until 1982. If the partnership's year ends December 31, 1981, then taxpayers would report a full 12 months of income in 1981.

If profitable partnerships were free to choose their fiscal year, they would all choose one that ends on January 31. In that way 11 months of income would be permanently delayed from being reported by the partners on their own tax returns. Unfortunately, partnerships are not free to choose whatever fiscal years they wish. Unless they get the permission of the Commissioner of the IRS, partnerships must use a fiscal year that is the same as those of all their principal partners. A *principal partner* is one with a 5% or more interest. This definition effectively forces all partnerships with individuals as principal partners to use a December 31 fiscal year. Only rarely does the Commissioner grant permission for a partnership to be on a fiscal year different from the partners. Even then, adjustments must usually be made to partially offset the tax advantages.

A partnership year can end prematurely, which triggers the reporting of income. This "trigger" applies to particular partners (but not to the partnership) if they sell or transfer their *entire* interest in the partnership. Transfer by gift or inheritance (and therefore by death) does not prematurely end the partnership year.

The partnership year could close prematurely, causing income and expenses to be reportable, if the partnership ceases to do business. It might also close sooner than planned if more than 50% of the ownership changes hands by sale or exchange (but not by gift or inheritance) within 12 months.

TRANSACTIONS AMONG PARTNERS AND THEIR PARTNERSHIP 11-06

In most respects, transactions between partners and the company in which they are partners are handled for tax purposes as if the parties were not related. But special rules, affecting some transactions, are designed to prevent tax abuse.

For a transaction between a partner and a partnership in which he or she owns more than a 50% interest, no deduction for a loss is allowed. The recognition of a gain, however, is normally allowed. For these purposes there are family attribution rules. As an example, an interest held by a taxpayer's child, spouse, or sibling would be attributed to the taxpayer for the purpose of determining whether a 50% interest exists.

Gains and Double Taxation 11-06.1

When the partnership sells property on which a loss has been disallowed, the gain is taxable only to the extent that it exceeds the disallowed loss. Thus double taxation on the same gain is prevented.

Example 11-06.1A

Colin Gordon sells a piece of property, in which he has a basis of $10,000, to his partnership for $5,000. Colin owns 51% of the partnership. On the sale to the partnership, Colin recognizes no loss.

Two years later, the partnership sells the property for $12,000, but it recognizes only $2,000 of the gain:

Proceeds of sale	$12,000
Basis (cost)	− 5,000
Preliminary gain	$ 7,000
Loss previously disallowed	− 5,000
Taxable gain	$ 2,000

11-06.1B **Tax warning**

Avoid this type of transaction for two reasons:

1. The basis of the property to the partnership is reduced to $5,000 (from $10,000), and any depreciation is similarly reduced.
2. If the property had been sold for between $5,000 and $10,000, no one would get to deduct the loss between Colin's basis of $10,000 and the sale price.

11-06.2 Ordinary Versus Capital Gains

If a partner owns more than 80% of a partnership (including family attribution) and sells a capital asset to a partnership in whose hands the asset is not a capital asset, the gain is an ordinary gain rather than a capital gain.

11-06.2A **Example**

Brynne Gordon owns a painting that was a capital asset in her hands and that had a basis of $5,000. Brynne also owns directly 10% of Art Dealer Partnership. Through family attribution (her brother owns 45% and her father owns 30% of the partnership), however, she is considered to own more than 80% of the partnership. She sells the painting to Art Dealer Partnership, in whose hands the painting is not a capital asset, for $24,000. The $19,000 gain ($24,000 proceeds less $5,000 basis) is an ordinary gain, not a capital gain.

11-06.2B **Tax *warning***

This rule is designed to prevent a partner from realizing a capital gain on the sale of an asset and then having the partnership realize an ordinary loss. The family attribution rules can inadvertently convert a capital gain into an ordinary gain for the unwary taxpayer dealing in the "family" business.

Expenses Accrued to Partners 11-06.3

The Code denies a deduction to an accrual basis partnership for expenses that are accrued to a "person" related to one of the partners but not paid by that person within 2½ months of the end of the partnership's year. The deduction is denied only to the partner involved, and the other partners get their share of the deduction. The deduction is lost permanently, and does not become deductible when paid!

Example 11-06.3A

Colin Gordon is a 40% owner of the Bowling Partnership, an accrual basis taxpayer. He also owns 100% of the MBS Corporation, a cash basis taxpayer. Bowling Partnership borrowed money from MBS Corporation. Both companies are calendar year taxpayers.

On December 31, Bowling accrues interest payable to MBS Corporation in the amount of $10,000. They do not pay that interest to MBS until April 2 of the following year (more than 2½ months after this year end). Bowling's other partners may deduct their portion of the accrued interest ($6,000), but Colin may not deduct his portion of the expense to the partnership, and that deduction is permanently lost. Even if the payment had been made on March 16 of the following year—too late, no deduction!

PARTNERS' BASIS FOR INTEREST IN THE PARTNERSHIP 11-07

Each partner must compute his or her own basis for partnership interest in order to determine:

1. gain or loss on disposition, and
2. the amount of deductible losses and expenses (11-02).

The computation of a partner's basis is a three-step operation:

1. computing the interest at *the time of investment,*
2. computing *increases* in the basis during ownership, and
3. computing *decreases* in basis during ownership.

11-07.1 Computing Interest at the Time of Investment

In establishing an original basis, a partner normally contributes either services, cash, or property.

1. *Cash* contributions simply add a similar amount to the partner's basis.
2. The partnership may either deduct or capitalize the value of one of the partners' *services,* and that amount becomes taxable income to the partner (and is added to his or her basis).
3. In most cases, a partner's contributions of *property* to a partnership, in exchange for an interest in the partnership, is a nontaxable event. The partnership assumes the same basis in the property as in the hands of the contributing partner. The partner's basis in the partnership is his or her basis in the contributed property. Any potential Section 1245 or Section 1250 recapture of depreciation stays with the asset. The partnership has to account for any recapture when the asset is sold.

   Farm property subject to recapture is an exception to the rule. If farm property that is subject to recapture is contributed to a partnership, the difference between the fair market value of the partnership interest and the taxpayer's basis in the property is recognized as ordinary gain, but not as a loss. The partnership then assumes a basis of fair market value in the property.

   Another important exception is the exchange of *securities* for an interest in an "investment" partnership. An *investment partnership* is one whose assets are more than 80% in readily marketable securities. In such a case, the partner recognizes capital gain, but not a loss, on the transfer that is equal to the difference between the fair market value of the securities contributed and the taxpayer's basis. This rule prevents taxpayers from diversifying their portfolios through a partnership device, while avoiding capital gains taxes.

Increase in Basis 11-07.2

A partner's basis is increased by all *income* allocated to him or her, whether it is taxable or not. This requirement avoids double taxation on such items. If the items are left in the business and if the business is sold, the value of that business includes income on which the partner had already paid tax. Any income left in the business obviously also increases the amount that the taxpayer has at risk, and so it increases the amount of deductible losses and expenses in the future.

The partner's basis is also increased by any *depletion allowance* allocated to him or her in excess of the basis in the asset. This adjustment is required since the partner's income has been "artificially" reduced by this amount.

Decreases in Basis 11-07.3

A partner's basis is reduced by all *losses* and *expenses,* whether deductible or not. But not reduced by capital expenditures since a reduction would duplicate the depreciation expense.

The basis is further reduced by any *oil or gas depletion allowance.* This rule is effectively a "penalty" imposed in 1976 to reduce the tax advantages of oil and gas investments.

The basis is also reduced for any *withdrawals* by the partner.

The basis cannot be decreased below zero for any of these items. (See 11-08 for distributions in excess of basis.)

11-07.3A **Example**

Brynne Gordon invests $10,000 in an oil well partnership. In the first year of operations, her share of the taxable income is:

Sales		$100,000
Out-of-pocket expenses	$10,000	
Percentage depletion	+22,000	− 32,000
Taxable income		$ 68,000

At the end of the year, the well is dry, and Brynne's cash position is:

Original investment		$ 10,000
Gross receipts		+100,000
		$110,000
Less: Amount spent on oil well	$10,000	
Out-of-pocket expenses	+10,000	− 20,000
Net cash		$ 90,000

Her basis in the partnership was:

Original investment	$ 10,000
Net income	68,000
Excess of percentage depletion over basis in oil well ($22,000 − $10,000)	+ 12,000
Basis before oil and gas adjustment	$ 90,000
Less: Oil and gas depletion	− 22,000
Basis	$ 68,000

Note that, before the oil and gas depletion subtraction, Brynne's basis is the same as the cash to be distributed. If the cash is distributed, then her basis is zero. But after the oil and gas depletion adjustment, her basis is only $68,000. In other words, if she withdraws the full $90,000, she has a gain of $22,000 ($90,000 − $68,000). (See 11-08.1 for treatment of that gain.)

There is an easy way to understand the tax effects—or normally the *non*tax effects—of a distribution to a partner. Consider a partnership something like tenants in common. Although from a legal point of view this analogy is not true, the Code looks at each partner as owning a piece of the pie. So when partners receive money or property from the partnership, the general rule is that they are merely taking what is already theirs. The distribution therefore simply reduces the partner's basis, but not below zero.

Distribution of Cash 11-08.1

Partners who receive distributions of cash in excess of their basis have a capital gain. If partners receive cash distributions in *complete* liquidation of their interests in the partnership, and if those distributions are less than their basis in the partnership, then they have a capital loss.

Example 11-08.1A

Aaron, Barney, and Tiffany are equal partners in the MBS Partnership. On April 30, MBS's balance sheet shows the following:

Cash		$100,000
Asset A		25,000
Asset B		30,000
Asset C		35,000
Total assets		$190,000
Liabilities		$115,000
Capital accounts: Aaron	$25,000	
Barney	25,000	
Tiffany	+25,000	+ 75,000
Total liabilities and capital		$190,000

The partners agree to buy out Tiffany's interest for $40,000. The reason for the additional $15,000 ($40,000 less her capital account of $25,000) is that Asset A has a fair market value of $70,000. Of the total unrealized appreciation in value ($45,000), Tiffany is entitled to one-third. So Tiffany now reports a capital gain of $15,000, which is the excess cash she receives over her basis in the partnership.

Aaron and Barney may now elect to adjust the basis of the partnership assets to reflect the sale. Actually, they *must* elect to do so, or they will end up paying tax on the same profit twice. Since the entire gain that Tiffany reports is attributable to Asset A, Asset A's basis in the hands of the partnership is increased by the $15,000 of profit Tiffany reports. If more than one asset is involved in the valuation of the partnership's worth, then the $15,000 is allocated among them. The balance sheet of MBS now shows:

Cash ($100,000 − $40,000 paid)		$ 60,000
Asset A ($25,000 + $15,000 adjustment)		40,000
Assets B & C		+ 65,000
Total assets		$165,000
Liabilities		$115,000
Capital accounts: Aaron	$25,000	
Barney	+25,000	+ 50,000
Total liabilities and capital		$165,000

If MBS were to sell Asset A for its market value of $70,000, each partner would report $15,000 of capital gain (one-half of the difference between $70,000 and the $40,000 basis). The effect of the transaction is that Barney and Aaron bought Tiffany's share of Asset A. She realized the profit, and they increased their basis by their cost (the $15,000 over the $25,000 in her capital account).

Of course, the partners could withdraw up to $25,000 each in cash with no tax consequences. The drawing would simply reduce their capital accounts and their basis.

Distributions of Property 11-08.2

If a partner receives property in a distribution from a partnership, the property retains the same basis in the hands of the partner as it had in the hands of the partnership. The partner's capital account is reduced by that same amount. Again, observe the conduit approach. The partner is merely taking what is his or hers, and there should be no change in basis—and no taxable event.

When partners receive property in complete liquidation of their interests, there is again a strong bias towards not having a taxable event. Partners must first reduce their basis by any cash received; the remaining basis is allocated among the assets received. The one major exception to this rule, however, is Section 751 property (11-10). Obviously, certain property generates ordinary income, and other property generates capital gains. When there is a disproportionate distribution of such assets to one partner, special adjustments must be made, and a taxable event can occur. The effect of these adjustments is to correct the inequity of the distribution and effectively to put everyone back to the state of tenants in common.

Example 11-08.2A

If in the prior example, Tiffany elects to take Asset B (with a basis and fair market value of $30,000) and $10,000 in cash, the tax answer changes slightly. Presuming none of the assets are Section 751 assets (11-10), Tiffany has no taxable gain until she sells Asset B. First, she reduces her basis by the cash received. Her basis is then $15,000 ($25,000 less $10,000 cash). Her remaining basis is then allocated to Asset B, and in her hands the asset's basis is $15,000. She realizes a gain when she sells the Asset.

The remaining partners should again elect to allocate the $15,000 adjustment in the basis of Asset B to the remaining assets. In this case, since the entire difference is due to the value of Asset A, the $15,000 is allocated to it. The assets of MBS would then be:

Cash ($100,000 − $10,000 paid)	$ 90,000
Asset A ($25,000 + $15,000 adjustment)	40,000
Asset C	+ 35,000
Total assets	$165,000

Again, Aaron and Barney realize their portions of the $45,000 gain ($15,000 each) when they sell Asset A. Tiffany realizes her portion of the $15,000 gain when she sells Asset B.

11-08.3 Distribution of Property to Transferee Partners

The last complication involves the distribution of property to a transferee partner. Again the complications arise from the need to treat each partner as owning his or her share of a particular asset in the partnership. Transferees can elect either to apply or to allocate the amount they pay for an interest in the partnership to particular assets, rather than consider their investments as "buying a piece" of an entire enterprise. This election normally benefits transferee partners. The adjustments to basis of the individual assets benefit only the new partner, not the remaining partners. Again, the conduit approach is preserved, since the assets are not involved in the transfer of the partnership interest.

11-08.3A Example

If in the prior example, Tiffany sells her interest in the partnership to Courtney Lee for $40,000 in cash. In this event, the tax consequences again change slightly, but still only to retain the conduit concept or tenants-in-common approach. Tiffany realizes a $15,000 capital gain on the sale of her partnership interest in the same manner as if she were selling stock in a corporation.

But Courtney is now at a tax disadvantage. She has a basis for her interest in the partnership of $40,000 (cost), but the assets allocated to her are on the books for only $25,000 net after liabilities. To correct this inequity the partnership may (and should) elect to adjust the basis of the assets, as they relate to Courtney *only*. The other partners are unaffected. Since the entire $15,000 relates to Asset A, the new balance sheet of MBS shows:

Cash		$100,000
Asset A (partnership basis)		25,000
Asset A (additional basis—Courtney)		15,000
Assets B & C		+ 65,000
Total assets		$205,000
Liabilities		$115,000
Capital accounts: Aaron	$25,000	
Barney	25,000	
Courtney (regular)	25,000	
Courtney (Asset A)	+15,000	+ 90,000
Total liabilities and capital		$205,000

Now if asset A is sold, the partnership reports:

Proceeds of sale	$ 70,000
Basis	− 25,000
Gain	$ 45,000

Aaron and Barney each show one-third of that gain, which is added to their capital accounts and to their bases in the partnership. But Courtney reports:

Gain on sale of Asset A	$ 15,000
Less: Special basis allocated to Asset A as transferee partner	− 15,000
Reportable gain, and net addition to capital account	$ –0–

Now each of the partners has a $40,000 basis in the partnership. Aaron's and Barney's are $25,000 plus the reported gain of $15,000. Courtney's account shows $40,000, her cost. And remember, Tiffany reports her $15,000 gain earlier.

11-08.3B **Tax *warning***

What happens if you do not elect the special allocation adjustment to the basis of specific assets retained in the partnership? In that case, you allocate the gain to goodwill. The costs allocated to goodwill cannot be recovered until the partner's interest in the partnership is terminated.

The allocation procedures (especially as they relate to assets with potential ordinary income, 11-10) are complex. Competent tax counsel should be obtained whenever a partnership interest is transferred or whenever property is distributed to a partner.

11-09 DEATH OR RETIREMENT OF A PARTNER

Major tax confrontations occur when partners either die or retire. Are payments to the partners ordinary fully taxable income? Or are they capital gains? In two situations, you have no choice: (1) the payments received that are distributions of partnership income are fully taxable ordinary income; and (2) payments received for Section 751 assets (11-10) are also fully taxable ordinary income. But some of the payments received by retired partners are nontaxable return of basis—or, in other words, the distribution of their assets held in the partnership.

After these distributions, if partners still have basis in the partnership, and if they are not entitled to any further distribution, they have a capital loss.

If, however, partners receive distributions in addition to and above their bases, what is the character of that income? Is it ordinary income? Or is it capital gains? Here the confrontation occurs. The outgoing partner wants those payments to be capital gains. If they are, then to the remaining partners the payments represent goodwill—for which the remaining partners do not get a deduction.

The goodwill is just added to their basis and used to determine their capital gain or loss when they retire. On the other hand, if the payments to the outgoing partner are in the form of compensation for past or future services, then the amounts are deductible by the remaining partners and fully taxable ordinary income to the retiring partner.

So are these payments for goodwill, or are they "other" payments? The rule is that, unless the partners have a written agreement that specifies otherwise, the payments are "other": that is, they are deductible by the partnership and taxable to the outgoing partner. If an agreement is made to pay a retired partner in a fixed number of installments, the partner may allocate portions of each installment to the reasons for the payments—the return of investment, compensation, and so on.

Payments made to the beneficiary of a deceased partner are taxable to the beneficiary in the same manner as if they had been received by the deceased. (See 14-10 for possible credits for estate tax paid on the distributions.)

Example 11-09.1

Colin Gordon is a 20% partner in the MBS Partnership. The partnership's balance sheet on the date of his retirement is:

Cash		$100,000
Asset A		20,000
Other assets		+ 80,000
Total assets		$200,000
Liabilities		$ 50,000
Capital accounts: Colin Gordon	$ 30,000	
others	+120,000	+150,000
Total liabilities and capital		$200,000

In complete liquidation of Colin's interest, the other partners agree to give him:

Asset A		$ 20,000
Less: Mortgage loan against Asset A, which Colin assumes		− 5,000
Net		$ 15,000
Cash representing:		
Colin's distributive share of this year's income	$15,000	
Goodwill	7,000	
Payment of 20% of the estimated income for next year	+18,000	+40,000
Total		$ 55,000

None of the partnership assets are Section 751 assets. Colin reports:

Nontaxable return of investment up to the amount in his capital account:	
Net value of Asset A	$15,000
Distribution of this year's income (he will pay tax on this as ordinary income as part of his Form K-1, without regard to the fact that it has been distributed to him)	+15,000
Balance in his capital account	$30,000
Goodwill reported as long-term capital gain	7,000
Distribution of future income reported as fully taxable ordinary income	+18,000
Total received	$55,000

11-10 SECTION 751 ASSETS

Section 751 assets are essentially inventory and accounts receivable, which generate ordinary income. The definition is much broader than simply inventories and receivables.

Almost any asset that generates ordinary income is included in the definition of receivables for this purpose. Among them are:

1. property subject to depreciation recapture,
2. stock in a DISC corporation (12-17), and
3. certain mining and oil and gas properties.

Again, the liquidation of a partner's interest brings about a tax confrontation. Most cash basis partnerships have a significant amount of unrealized receivables, since they are not reported for tax purposes until they are collected. All the partners, realizing that they have this unrecorded asset, could give recognition to this by paying goodwill to the retiring partner, but they also realize that they would get no deduction for the goodwill (11-09). Moreover, when the receivables are collected, the remaining partners would have to pay tax on them as ordinary income.

If, however, the partners take into account the value of those receivables then we have a taxable event. Someone (either the remaining or outgoing partners) will retain the receivables. Whoever does receive them is considered to have purchased the receivables from the partner(s), who do not keep them. The selling partners realize fully taxable ordinary income on the sale, and the buying partners get a stepped-up basis for the cost of the purchase.

Example 11-10.1

The MBS Widget Partnership is engaged in the business of selling widgets. Brynne Gordon is a 30% partner in MBS. The partnership balance sheet is as follows:

	Basis	*Market Value*
Cash	$ 54,000	$ 54,000
Accounts receivable	4,500	7,200

Widget inventory	4,500	36,000
Land and building	+ 45,000	+ 46,800
Total assets	$108,000	$144,000
Capital accounts: Brynne	$ 32,400	$ 43,200
Others	+ 75,600	+100,800
Total capital	$108,000	$144,000

Straight-line depreciation (no recapture problem) is used for the building that Brynne contributed to the partnership 13 months before she liquidated her partnership interest. On the date of this balance sheet, the partnership distributes the widget inventory and the accounts receivable to Brynne, in complete liquidation of her partnership interest.

In this case the Section 751 assets consist of the accounts receivable and the inventory whose book value is below market value. When these assets are finally realized into cash, they result in ordinary income. The other assets, including cash, are not Section 751 assets, since they do not have ordinary income potential.

Before the remaining partners can use the Section 751 assets to buy Brynne out, they must pay the tax on them as if they had been realized into cash. But remember the conduit theory. Brynne already owns 30% of the Section 751 property, so she cannot sell them to herself. She takes her 30% at their basis, and the remaining partners must pay the tax on the 70% that is theirs. They report as ordinary income:

70% of accounts receivable market value		$ 5,040
70% of inventory market value		+ 25,200
		$ 30,240
Less basis: 70% of receivables	$3,150	
70% of inventory	+3,150	− 6,300
Taxable income		$ 23,940

Brynne's basis for these assets will be:

30% of receivables ($4,500) and inventory ($4,500), which was "hers"	$ 2,700
Plus: Amount "purchased" from the other partners (fair market value)	+30,240
Basis	$32,940

When she sells them, she realizes her share of the ordinary income:

Total market value ($7,200 + $36,000)	$43,200
Her basis	−32,940
Ordinary income	$10,260

But we're not finished yet! Brynne not only purchased Section 751 property, but she also sold the other property! She received property with a market value of $30,240 (remember, we do not count her share of her own property), for giving up 30% of the other property. Her basis in the other property was:

Cash	$54,000
Land and building	+45,000
Total partnership basis	$99,000
30% of $99,000	$29,700
Amount received	$30,240
Basis	−29,700
Long-term capital gain	$ 540

Tax *Warning* 11-10.2

When a partnership is liquidated, you have probably no clearer example of the tax complications that can arise. In our example, the partners could have structured the entire event as one with no tax consequences by simply paying Brynne off in cash. The excess over her basis in the partnership would have been a capital gain to her, and no one would have ordinary income. But the remaining partners would have been "stuck" with Brynne's share of the ordinary income on the receivables and inventory ($10,260).

Obviously, there are real dollars and cents considerations in the wording and structure of a partnership liquidation, and competent legal counsel is a must.

12
CORPORATIONS

12-01 WHAT IS A CORPORATION UNDER THE CODE?

Corporations are separate taxable entities under the Code. Sometimes that separateness can be an advantage, and sometimes it can be a disadvantage.

Business entities that are incorporated under state law are obviously corporations, and they are taxable as such. But the Code imposes the corporation income tax on some nonincorporated entities. The corporation income tax is imposed on any entity that more closely resembles a corporation than it does a partnership or nonincorporated association. Some of the factors that lead to such a determination are as follows:

1. Is the purpose of the entity to conduct business and to distribute its profits?
2. Is there a continuity of the entity's life, even after the death of one or more owners?
3. Is there limited liability conferred on the active owners of the business?

4. Can the interests in the entity be freely transferred?
5. Is there central management?

If the answer to these questions is yes, then the IRS may determine that a corporation exists, even if under state law there is no corporation.

Tax *Warning* 12-01.1

Unlike a limited partnership, which is a nontaxable conduit for income and the attendant tax liability, a corporation is the taxable entity. For this reason, corporations can (and do) create a double taxation on the same income. The income is first taxed at the corporate level, and then, when the income is distributed to the owners (in the form of a dividend), the owners pay another tax. If the taxpayer's form of business turned out to be a corporation for tax purposes, the effects on the taxpayer's after-tax dollar could be disastrous.

Example 12-01.1A

Colin Gordon is the sole stockholder of the MBS Corporation, and the corporation has income before income taxes of $100,000:

Income before income taxes	$100,000
Income tax (12-02)	− 25,750
Net income	$ 74,250

If Colin is in the 50% incremental tax bracket, and the entire $74,250 is distributed to him, then:

Dividend received	$74,250
Income tax, 50% rate	−37,125
Net after *double* taxation	$37,125

Since the corporate rates go as high as 46% and since the personal rates go as high as 50%, the net after double tax benefits of corporate income could be as low as 27%—for an effective tax rate of 73%.

Limited partners would obviously be shocked to find themselves classified as stockholders of a corporation! The answer is competent counsel to make sure that this is one tax trap that is clearly avoided.

12-02 THE CORPORATE INCOME TAX STRUCTURE

Three basis income taxes are imposed on corporations:

1. the minimum tax (09-02),
2. the regular income tax, and
3. the tax on capital gains.

Additional "penalty-type" taxes may also be imposed on corporations (discussed later in the chapter).

12-02.1 The Regular Income Tax

The basic income tax is imposed on "net income" 12-03, which for a corporation is similar to Adjusted Gross Income for individuals. The tax rates on net income are gradually being reduced each year. So that for 1983 and subsequent years, they will be:

Taxable income up to $25,000	15%
Taxable income between $25,001 and $50,000	18%
Taxable income between $50,001 and $75,000	30%
Taxable income between $75,001 and $100,000	40%
Taxable income over $100,000	46%

We will use these rates for illustrations.

Although the tax rates are graduated, the "effective" rate for *major* United States corporations is 46% on most of their income. Since most states also impose an income tax on corporations, it is often convenient to think of major corporations as being in the 50% incremental tax bracket.

The Tax on Capital Gains 12-02.2

Net short-term capital gains are simply added to other ordinary taxable income for corporations. For long-term capital gains, the corporation may either pay a flat 28% tax or add the net long-term gains to other taxable income. Obviously, the choice depends on the corporation's incremental tax bracket.

Example 12-02.2A

The MBS Corporation has $64,500 in taxable ordinary income, along with $4,000 in net long-term capital gains (after netting against all long-term and net short-term losses). MBS' income tax liability is the *lower* of:

Regular Method	
Ordinary taxable income	$64,500
Long-term capital gains	+ 4,000
Total	$68,500
Tax on first $25,000 @ 15%	$ 3,750
Tax on second $25,000 @ 18%	4,500
Tax on remaining $18,500 @ 30%	+ 5,550
Total tax, regular method	$13,800

Alternate Method	
Ordinary taxable income	$64,500
Tax on first $25,000 @ 15%	$ 3,750
Tax on second $25,000 @ 18%	4,500
Tax on remaining $14,500 @ 30%	4,350
Tax on long-term capital gain @ 28%	+ 1,120
Total tax, alternate method	$13,720

Obviously, the difference of $80 ($13,800 − $13,720) is

$4,000 @ 2% (30% highest incremental rate and 28% capital gains rate). The corporation pays the lower of the two taxes.

12-02.3 Capital Losses

Net capital losses, whether long- or short-term, are not deductible against any other type of income. Capital losses may be used only to offset capital gains. But corporations may carry back capital losses three years and then forward five years to offset *capital* gains in those years. This is substantially different from the case of individuals, who can carry forward unused capital losses indefinitely.

12-02.3A Example

If, in the prior example, MBS had either a net long-term or a net short-term loss (after netting against all capital gains for the year), they would still have to pay the $12,600 income tax due on $64,500 of ordinary taxable income for the year. Suppose, however, that two years ago, MBS had a taxable long-term gain of $2,000 and a taxable short-term gain of $10,000, which was taxed at the 46% rate.

Capital loss carry-backs and carry-forwards *must* be used to offset short-term gains first, and they cannot create or increase a net operating loss. In this case, the $4,000 loss is used to offset the short-term gain by $4,000, even if this year's loss is long-term in nature. This produces a refund of $1,840 ($4,000 × 0.46). Any unused capital losses are carried forward in the same manner—that is, offsetting short-term gains first and not creating or increasing a net operating loss.

12-02.4 Tax Hint

The timing of capital gains and losses is even more critical for corporations than it is for individuals. For one thing, you might need an accelerated recognition of a capital gain due to an expiring capital loss carry-forward. But the conversion of a long-term loss into a short-term loss, when it is carried backwards or forwards, is a powerful tax tool with great potential flexibility!

Example 12-02.4A

The MBS Corporation is a 46% incremental tax bracket corporation. In 1980, the corporation already realized a long-term capital gain of $100,000. In 1978, the corporation had a short-term capital gain of $100,000. MBS has a potential $100,000 long-term loss, which they could realize in either 1980 or 1981. They expect no further capital transactions in 1981.

If MBS realizes the loss in 1980, then it will offset this year's long-term gain and save $28,000 in taxes. But if they postpone the loss to 1981, when they must carry it back, they are *required* to carry it back to the first available year, which is 1978. At that point they get a refund for 1978 taxes in the amount of $46,000. Worth waiting for?

Tax hint 12-02.4B

Don't forget, the wash sale rule affects only losses! If you have to accelerate a gain to utilize an expiring capital loss carry-forward, consider selling to recognize the gain and then immediately rebuying the stock.

Fiscal Year Considerations 12-02.5

Each corporation may choose a fiscal year ended sometime in the first 12 months of its existence. For the moderately successful corporation, the choice of a fiscal year could create a small permanent tax savings.

Example 12-02.5A

A corporation expects to earn $100,000 per year for the next few years. In any full fiscal year, the tax liability would be $25,750. But due to the graduated income tax, the tax on the last $50,000 is $17,500, averaging 35%. The corporation could elect a fiscal year ending six months after its start-up. This way the second $50,000 would fall in the second fiscal year, and the tax on it would be only $8,250, averaging only 16½%. Of course, this is only a one-time savings of $9,250 ($17,500 − $8,250), but it is a worthwhile thought.

12-03 COMPOSITION OF CORPORATE INCOME

A corporation's Gross Income is composed of basically the same things as you find in the Gross Income of individual taxpayers. From Gross Income, the corporation deducts certain items to arrive at Taxable Income. Although the deductions allowed to a corporation are generally the same as those allowed to individuals as deductions for Adjusted Gross Income, all the deductions are for Taxable Income, since a corporation does not have Adjusted Gross Income. Corporations are also allowed certain deductions that individuals are not—primarily the deduction for 85%, subject to limitations, of dividends received from certain domestic corporations (02-16). The deductibility of some corporate expenses is limited (12-05).

In theory the computation of corporate Taxable Income is quite simple: Gross Income less expenses that are ordinary and necessary to generate that Gross Income. Closely held corporations often present problems. At times the IRS attempts to consider income received directly by stockholders as attributable to the corporation. As an example, rent for the use of corporate property is taxable to the corporation even if it is received directly by stockholders. This situation has the potential for double taxation, since the IRS "reconstructs" the flow of funds first to the corporation and then as a dividend to the stockholder.

The IRS has successfully imputed income to a corporation for providing services or property to a stockholder.

As an example, if a stockholder were allowed to live rent-free in corporate-owned property, the IRS might impute rent income to the corporation for the fair market value of the rental. Since rent is generally not deductible by individuals, the corporation would have taxable income, and the stockholder would have no deduction.

The IRS has not been successful in imputing interest income to a corporation for interest-free loans to stockholders. Although the IRS apparently continues to challenge these arrangements, making interest-free loans to stockholders can form the basis of tax planning. (See 12-08 for the potential of an additional tax, the accumulated earnings tax.)

RECONCILIATION BETWEEN BOOK PROFIT AND TAXABLE INCOME 12-04

Corporations file Form 1120, which includes two schedules:

1. Schedule M-1—Reconciliation of Income per Books with Taxable Income, and
2. Schedule M-2—Analysis of Retained Earnings.

For an understanding of federal income taxation in general, and for corporations specifically, these schedules provide an excellent tool. It holds no surprises, since this kind of schedule exists, at least in the tax preparer's head, for all taxpayers.

Example 12-04.1

The MBS Corporate books show the following:

Sales	$100,000
Cost of goods sold	40,000
Gross profit	$ 60,000

FIGURE 12-1. Schedules M-1 and M-2

Schedule M-1 Reconciliation of Income Per Books With Income Per Return

1 Net income per books	$31,608	7 Income recorded on books this year not included in this return (itemize)	
2 Federal income tax	$5,892	(a) Tax-exempt interest $ 1,300	
3 Excess of capital losses over capital gains	1,500		1,300
4 Income subject to tax not recorded on books this year (itemize)		8 Deductions in this tax return not charged against book income this year (itemize)	
5 Expenses recorded on books this year not deducted in this return (itemize)		(a) Depreciation $ 800	
(a) Depreciation $		(b) Contributions carryover $	
(b) Contributions carryover $			800
		9 Total of lines 7 and 8	2,100
6 Total of lines 1 through 5	39,000	10 Income (line 28, page 1)—line 6 less 9	36,900

Schedule M-2 Analysis of Unappropriated Retained Earnings Per Books (line 24 above)

1 Balance at beginning of year	45,000	5 Distributions: (a) Cash	15,000
2 Net income per books	31,608	(b) Stock	
3 Other increases (itemize)		(c) Property	
		6 Other decreases (itemize)	
		7 Total of lines 5 and 6	15,000
4 Total of lines 1, 2, and 3	76,608	8 Balance at end of year (line 4 less 7)	61,608

☆ U.S. GOVERNMENT PRINTING OFFICE: 1980—O-313-457 58-0401110

Other expenses:		
Officers' salaries	$15,000	
Office expenses	4,000	
Depreciation (straight-line)	2,000	
Other Section 162 expenses	+ 3,000	− 24,000
Operating income		$ 36,000
Long-term capital loss	$ (1,500)	
Interest income (U.S. Bonds)	1,700	
Interest income (N.J. State Bonds)	+ 1,300	+ 1,500
Income before income taxes		$ 37,500
Federal income taxes		− 5,892
Net income		$ 31,608
Retained earnings—beginning of year		+ 45,000
		$ 76,608
Dividends		15,000
Retained earnings—end of year		$ 61,608

Taxable income is:	
Income from operations	$ 36,000
Plus: Interest on U.S. bonds	1,700

Less: Accelerated depreciation taken for tax purposes	$ 2,800	
Straight-line depreciation on books	− 2,000	− (800)
Taxable income		$ 36,900

The income tax on $36,900 is $5,892. Figure 12-1 shows the resulting Schedules M-1 and M-2.

Tax Hint 12-04.2

If the officer is the same person as the stockholder, is there a better way? *Yes*! Instead of paying a dividend (which the corporation cannot deduct in determining Taxable Income), pay the money as salary, which is deductible. The resulting Taxable Income would be $21,900, and the tax $3,285—a savings of $2,607.

An officer/stockholder cannot simply pay excessive salaries to avoid paying a dividend. The IRS looks at all salaries of officer/stockholders to insure that the amounts paid as salary are reasonable in relation to the services performed. But this area is rife with court cases: Taxpayers pull for salaries, and the IRS pulls for dividends. Unfortunately, neither the Code nor the Regulations give any reliable guidelines for what is "reasonable" compensation.

LIMITATIONS ON THE DEDUCTIBILITY OF CERTAIN EXPENSES 12-05

Charitable Contributions 12-05.1

Corporations may not deduct contributions made for use outside the United States or its possessions. In addition, the amount that may be deducted in any one year is limited to no more than 10% of taxable income figured *without* regard to:

1. the charitable donations,
2. the dividends received deduction,
3. any net operating loss carry-*back*, and
4. any net capital loss carry-*back*.

Unused contribution deductions may be carried forward five years. (See also 07-04.)

12-05.1A **Tax hint**

Charitable contributions are generally more favorably treated on the individual return. First, the limitations are higher. Second, the individual taxpayer is usually in a higher tax bracket than the corporation, so more after tax dollars are realized.

Stockholders of closely held corporations often face the question as to who should do the giving. In most cases, the individual doing the giving gains a bigger tax advantage.

12-05.1B **Tax hint**

Amounts paid to charitable organizations that are, in fact, ordinary and necessary business expenses are deductible without limit. But what precisely *must* a corporation pay under certain circumstances? And what is truly given out of charitable considerations? The answers are best left to the facts of each situation.

12-05.2 Organization Expenses

Both partnerships and corporations are faced with what to do with organization expenses—that is, legal and accounting fees that are incurred or paid to form the company. Since the life of the asset is the life of the enterprise, over what period of time may the expenses be amortized?

Fortunately, the Code gives a clear answer. Taxpayers may choose *not* to amortize the expenses at all (rarely the correct choice), or to amortize them over a period of not less than 60 months. Generally, corporations and partnerships choose the 60-month period, since this is the fastest available.

One group of expenses that are *not* organization expenses and that cannot be amortized are the costs of selling stock in the company. The same rule applies to the costs of selling partnership interests. The expenses that fall into this category include printing, SEC registration costs, legal and accounting services, and advertising. Since such expenses constitute a permanent asset, they can be used only as part of basis when the enterprise is liquidated and when the final capital gain or loss is computed.

CORPORATIONS DEALING IN THEIR OWN SECURITIES 12-06

The Code's treatment of corporations dealing in their own securities is logical, yet complex. A true profit (or a reduction of expense) comes through the maze as taxable. Receipts of funds that are truly investments in the enterprise come through as excludable. (See 02-01—investments in an enterprise are not included in Gross Income.) To understand the tax consequences of corporations dealing in their own securities, we must divide those securities into three categories:

1. "pure" equity, such as common and preferred stock,
2. "pure" debt, such as bonds, and
3. convertible bonds.

Stock (Equity) 12-06.1

A corporation, dealing for cash, cannot recognize a gain or loss when trading its own stock.

12-06.1A **Example**

MBS stock is selling for $10 per share. The company feels that this is too low a price and buys some. Some time later, the stock is selling for $15, and MBS sells. Do they realize a profit? No!

Here's why. If MBS issues *new* stock instead of selling the stock they bought, there would be no gain. Although they buy their own stock, called "treasury stock," and resell the *very* same shares, they are still only issuing their own stock to a *new* investor. Any gain or loss is excludable from Gross Income as an investment in an enterprise (02-01).

12-06.1B **Noncash transactions**

On the other hand, a noncash transaction can cause a gain or loss. The gain or loss does not involve the stock, but rather the asset used in the exchange.

12-06.1B-1 ***Example***

The MBS Corporation issues 100,000 shares of its own stock for $10 cash each. Cash is increased by $1,000,000, and corporate capital is increased by $1,000,000. But there is no taxable event.

Some time later, MBS purchases back 1,000 shares of stock for $15 per share. Again, no taxable event. Cash is reduced by $15,000, and corporate capital is reduced by $15,000.

Some time still later, MBS sells the 1,000 shares they purchased for $15 at a price of $18,000. Still no taxable event. Cash is increased by $18,000, and corporate capital is increased by $18,000.

12-06.1B-2 ***Example***

The MBS Corporation owns land with a basis of $2,000. They exchange that land for 1,000 shares of their own stock while the stock has a fair market value of $15 per share. MBS recognizes a gain on the exchange of the land in the amount of:

"Sale" proceeds, 1,000 shares × $15	$15,000
Basis	− 2,000
Gain	$13,000

Bonds (Debt) 12-06.2

When a corporation either purchases its own bonds or prematurely retires similar debt, it may recognize gain or loss. Gain or loss on the early retirement of debt is ordinary gain or loss, and so it is reported in a manner similar to interest income (gains) or interest expense (losses). When a corporation retires its debts for *more* than its book carrying value, there is a deductible loss (12-06.2A). When a corporation retires its debts for *less* than book carrying value, the corporation may elect to:

1. recognize the gain, or
2. adjust the basis of the related property or other property.

The reduction of property basis is appealing because it postpones the recognition of gain. But, if the property is depreciable property, then future depreciation is reduced since there is a reduced basis.

Taxpayers may not arbitrarily reduce the basis of any property. The Code has a priority list of which assets must be reduced. The first item on the list is the asset against which the debt was issued. If this asset is an asset subject to receiving the investment credit, the investment credit may be recaptured upon the adjustment of basis. If it is a capital asset, then the reduction of basis, rather than the recognition of income, may create a capital gain, rather than an ordinary gain.

Example 12-06.2A

Ten years ago, MBS Corporation issued $1,000,000 face

amount of 20-year bonds for a price of 98. The book carrying value of those bonds is currently:

Face amount	$1,000,000
Less: One-half of original discount	− 10,000
Net carrying value	$ 990,000

MBS recently acquired $10,000 face amount of those bonds for $10,000, their face value. MBS has an ordinary loss of:

Price paid for bonds	$ 10,000
Book carrying value	− 9,900
Ordinary loss	$ 100

On the other hand, if they had purchased the bonds for $8,000, then:

Book carrying value	$ 9,900
Price paid for bonds	− 8,000
Potential gain	$ 1,900

MBS could report that gain, or it could elect to reduce the basis of related property.

12-06.3 Convertible Debt Issues

When convertible debt is repurchased at a loss, the deductible loss is limited to the portion of the purchase price that relates to the debt obligation. The portion of the purchase price that relates to the convertibility feature is not deductible. The logic is that part of the purchase price really relates to the purchase of the corporation's own stock, and that is not a deduction, but merely a reduction of corporate capital.

The computation of the deductible amount is quite complicated, and it involves an estimation of the "normal" price of the bond without the convertible feature.

Example 12-06.3A

Ten years ago, MBS Corporation issued $1,000,000 face value of convertible bonds at a price of 98. Each bond was convertible into 50 shares of MBS common stock. The bonds bear interest of 10%, and they are callable this year at a price of 102. The common stock is now selling for $30 per share, and the bonds are selling at 160. MBS purchases $10,000 face amount of these bonds for 160. Their deductible loss is:

Current carrying value of bonds:	
Original issue price (10 bonds @ 98)	$ 9,800
50% of original discount that has since been recognized as interest expense	+ 100
Carrying value	$ 9,900
Allocation of purchase price:	
Original issue price	$ 9,800
Plus: Any discount recognized as interest expense	100
Call premium (subject to certain limitations)	+ 200
Amount allocated to debt feature	$10,100
Amount allocated to conversion feature (the difference)	+ 5,900
Total purchase price	$16,000
Amount of purchase price allocated to debt feature	$10,100
Carrying value	− 9,900
Deductible loss	$ 200

This problem assumes that the call provision fairly represented the call provision of a similar nonconvertible debt.

LIQUIDATING AND CHANGING THE CORPORATE STRUCTURE 12-07

The creation of a corporation is normally a relatively simple, and often tax-free, matter. Further, the transfer of property to a controlled corporation is a tax-free transfer (04-07.2). Each corporation, however, is a separate legal person. Transactions among corporations, as well as those between corporations and their stockholders, must be considered a taxable event unless taxpayers can cite specific sections of the Code that allow for a tax-free transaction.

In the area of reorganizations and liquidations, the Code is replete with tax-free mechanisms. Each case requires highly technical conformity to the Code, to the Regulations, and to Revenue Procedures. The available alternatives are discussed here simply to give you a working familiarity. A corporate reorganization, however, should never be undertaken without both competent legal and tax counsel.

12-07.1 One-Month Liquidation

The one-month liquidation is designed to allow the closely held corporation to liquidate completely by distributing its assets to its stockholders. The stockholders receive the property distributed, and they have the same basis for the property as the corporation had.

The transfer of assets to the stockholders is not completely tax-free. First, there may be a recapture of investment credit and depreciation, depending on the use the property by the receiving stockholders. Stockholders may also recognize a gain up to the *greater* of the amount of cash and marketable securities received from the corporation or the E&P (12-07.6). Under different circumstances, that gain may be realized as either dividend income or a capital gain.

12-07.2 Twelve-Month Liquidation

The twelve-month liquidation is designed to avoid the double taxation of a corporation being liquidated. The corporation may elect not to report any gain on the disposition of most of its assets during the liquidation period. So there is little or no tax at the corporate level. The corporation distributes the proceeds to the stockholders, who realize a capital gain or loss depending on their basis in the stock.

Reorganizations 12-07.3

Corporations may change their form without changing their business purpose or continuity of ownership. Although the Code provides for certain types of reorganizations to be made tax-free, the taxpayer's responsibility is to prove that the reorganization had a business purpose and that it was not entered into solely to save taxes.

Six types of reorganization are specifically recognized as tax-free in the Code.

Type A reorganization 12-07.3A

The merger, or consolidation, of two or more corporations into one new corporation is a type A reorganization. Although stockholders of one or more of the corporations may participate to a small degree in the mergers (such as buying out a small minority interest), too much participation by the stockholders disqualifies a merger from being tax-free under type A.

Type B reorganization 12-07.3B

A tax-free type B reorganization occurs when one corporation uses its voting stock to acquire the voting stock of another corporation. The section allows for the tax-free takeover of a corporation purely on a stock-for-stock basis. To qualify, at least 80% of the stock of the acquired corporation must be obtained by the new parent corporation.

12-07.3C **Type C reorganization**

A type C reorganization is similar to a type B. But, instead of the new parent receiving the stock of the acquired corporation, the parent acquires substantially all of the assets. The phrase "substantially all of the assets" is not defined in either the Code or the Regulations, but it is generally considered to mean 80% of the gross assets or 90% of net assets. The IRS, however, has been somewhat flexible. So, instead of being purely for the voting stock of the new parent, a type C reorganization allows some flexibility in the use of cash or other property.

12-07.3D **Type D reorganization**

A type D reorganization is essentially a form of liquidation. A transferor corporation transfers its assets to a transferee corporation, in exchange for the voting stock of the transferee corporation. The transferor corporation then distributes the stock it acquires to its stockholders. To qualify as a type D, the transferor corporation must acquire control of the transferee corporation. For these purposes "control" means 80% of the voting stock and of all other classes of stock.

A type D reorganization is similar to the contribution of property to a controlled corporation (04-07.2). The main difference is that, in a type D, a corporation intervenes between the individual investor and the corporation which it ends up controlling.

12-07.3E **Type E reorganization**

A type E reorganization is essentially a recapitalization. A recapitalization may occur as a result of a compromise settlement with creditors or with preferred stockholders; or it might result simply from an exchange of one type of security for another by the investors. A type E reorganization substantially involves the kind of exchanges described in 04-07.1.

Type F reorganization 12-07.3F

A type F reorganization allows for the tax-free change by a corporation of its name or place of incorporation.

Spin-Off Reorganizations 12-07.4

Corporations may, for good business reasons, wish to divide into two or more corporations. Such an act may be referred to as either a "split-up," "split-off," or "spin-off." Although each is technically different from the other in the Code, they all accomplish the same thing: The stockholders of the old corporation end up owning stock in two or more corporations. The total assets the stockholders control is not increased, just spread over more corporations. And the Code's purpose is effectively the same: It prohibits the use of a spin-off to avoid paying dividends.

Collapsible Corporations 12-07.5

In a normal liquidation proceeding, if a corporation sells off its inventory, it must pay income tax at the ordinary rate (Chapter 12). Then, when it distributes the remaining cash to the stockholders, they have to pay an additional tax on the capital gain realized through such a liquidation dividend (02-09).

A *collapsible corporation* is one that is formed to convert ordinary income into capital gains. It is designed to construct or to purchase inventory—such as buildings, movies, and the like—and then liquidate (or "collapse") before realizing a profit on that inventory. The inventory is then distributed to the stockholders at its fair market value as a liquidation dividend. The difference between their basis in the stock and the fair market value of the inventory represents a capital gain, on which they are liable for tax. But they can then sell the inventory at no additional gain—or tax.

If, however, the IRS finds a corporation to be collapsible, the distribution in liquidation is ordinary fully taxable income, not capital gain. In the case the gain on the distribution will be recognized as ordinary income of a collapsible corporation, only if all three of the following conditions exist:

1. The shareholder in question owns directly or indirectly more than 5% of the corporation's stock.
2. 70% or more of the stockholder's gain on disposition of the stock is related to inventory manufactured or purchased by the corporation.
3. The stockholder realizes a gain within three years of the purchase or completion of construction of the inventory.

There are many ways to avoid having a corporation classified as collapsible that go beyond the scope of this book. Since the IRS will not issue a private letter ruling as to whether a specific corporation is collapsible or not, this is an area that requires competent tax counsel. If there is any danger that a corporation will be classified as collapsible, get written tax opinions from tax counsel.

12-07.6 Preferred Stock Bailout

To understand a preferred stock bailout, you must first understand *earnings and profits* (E&P), which is essentially the earnings of a corporation from which dividends must be paid. Although not defined anywhere in the Code, simplistically it is equal to net income less any dividends paid. In some respects it is similar to retained earnings, but there are some technical differences.

A preferred stock bailout used to be a way of converting fully taxable dividend income for the stockholder into long-term capital gains. The corporation would declare a nontaxable stock dividend (02-13), payable in preferred stock. The stockholder would then sell it to a third party, realizing a capital gain, and the third party would redeem the stock. Since the third party's basis was the value of the stock at redemption (the purchase price), he or she realized no tax liability.

To seal off this escape hatch, Section 306 essentially says that any stock dividend payable in other than common stock, issued when a corporation has E&P, is "Section 306" stock. The gain on such a sale is ordinary income.

The Section actually imposes a penalty on the stockholder and on the corporation. If a cash dividend were declared, E&P would be reduced, but the redemption of the preferred stock by a third party does not reduce E&P. So future distributions may also be considered dividends since the corporation has a higher E&P than it would otherwise have. Distributions in excess of E&P are not taxable dividends to the stockholders, but rather a liquidating dividend or a return of investment.

ACCUMULATED EARNINGS TAX 12-08

Stockholders of closely held corporations would prefer to leave any accumulated earnings in the corporation. They could then either sell the corporation or liquidate it, and thereby realize the gain as a long-term capital gain, rather than as dividend income.

The Accumulated Earnings Tax (AET) is a penalty tax that the IRS may seek to impose upon a corporation for the *unreasonable* accumulation of earnings for the *purpose* of avoiding the double taxation of paying a dividend to its stockholders. Both conditions must exist for the IRS to prevail in this assessment.

The tax is imposed on the annual earnings retained in the business in excess of what is reasonably needed for the expansion and growth of the corporation. Obviously, this determination is subjective. Yet certain criteria have been developed to ascertain whether excess accumulation exists and, if it does, how much is subject to the tax (12-08.1). The first $250,000* of earnings and

* $150,000 for corporations whose principle function is the performance of services in the field of health, law, engineering, architecture, accounting, actuarial science, performing arts, or consulting.

profits (the amount available for dividends) is exempt from the tax (12-08.2). The *additional* tax, over the regular corporate income tax, is:

First $100,000 of excess earnings	27½%
Amount over $100,000 of excess earnings	38½%

The maximum incremental tax that may be imposed on a corporation is 84½% (46% maximum income tax and 38½% accumulated earnings tax).

12-08.1 Existence of Excess Accumulated Earnings

Whether excess earnings have been accumulated, as well as whether such earnings may be subject to the penalty tax, depends on all the facts and circumstances. In any given case, the burden of proof of "excess" accumulated earnings is initially on the IRS. They normally file a statement of a proposed deficiency, which the taxpayer must respond to. If the taxpayer fails to respond, the IRS proceeds to Tax Court, where the burden of proof shifts to the taxpayer.

Indications that the condition exists include:

1. loans to shareholders,
2. loans made to outsiders that do not relate to the corporation's normal business, or
3. investments in unrelated properties or securities.

Indicators that earnings are being accumulated for a "reasonable" purpose include documentation that the funds are being accumulated for:

1. expansion of the business or the replacement of assets,
2. the acquisition of another company,
3. the payment of debt obligations, and

4. needed working capital, such as the acquisition of inventories or the financing of receivables.

The key word is "documentation." Vague planning or accumulation of funds to provide for unspecified purposes is not sufficient.

Computation of Income Subject to the Tax 12-08.2

The computation begins with Taxable Income for the year. Taxable Income is then adjusted to reflect the amount available for dividends. Subtractions from Taxable Income would include expenditures that reduce the amount available for dividends, but that are not deductions, such as:

1. federal income tax liability (but not the accumulated earnings tax),
2. charitable contributions made in excess of the amount deductible, and
3. dividends paid, including those paid in the first 2½ months of the following year.

Some items that are not normally taxable are added to Taxable Income to arrive at the amount available for dividends. These included:

1. long-term capital gains not included in Taxable Income, less the alternative income tax payable on those gains,
2. the 85% dividends received exclusion, and
3. prior year items, such as net operating loss carry-back and carry-forward, along with capital loss carry-back and carry-forward.

Many other adjustments are required in the Code, but they all get to the heart of computing how much of this year's income is available for dividends.

The last step of the computation is the "accumulated earnings credit." The first $250,000 of a corporation's earnings and profits are not subject to the AET (see exception for certain service industries in 12-08). The credit is the *greater* of:

1. earnings and profits retained for the *reasonable* needs of the business, less *this* year's net capital gain, *or*
2. $250,000 less the accumulated earnings and profits at the beginning of the year, less any dividends paid during the first 2½ months of *this* year, since credit was given for that in the prior year.

12-08.3 Tax Hint

Here is the key to avoiding the accumulated earnings tax: The first credit against earnings that might be subject to the tax is the amount reasonably accumulated for business purposes. Keep in mind that the IRS must also prove the second part of the reason for the accumulation—that is, it must prove that the accumulation's purpose is to avoid paying a dividend.

Do not overlook a possible escape hatch—increasing salaries to officer/stockholders. The corporation receives a deduction for the payments, and the salary is subject to the maximum tax of 50%. This escape hatch, however, is not foolproof. The IRS may attack the salaries, calling them dividends, if they are excessive. It would then disallow the deduction to the corporation and make the amounts subject to the 46% normal income tax.

What constitutes excessive salaries is often a point requiring interpretation by the courts. Traditionally, however, the courts have been more lenient in this area than the IRS has been. The courts have accepted relatively high salaries as being reasonable where taxpayers have shown that, in a nonclosely held corporation, they could have earned a similar amount. Keep in mind that most major publicly held corporations pay salaries in six figures.

Example 12-08.4

MBS Corporation's tax return includes the following information:

Taxable income	$1,000,000
Federal income tax	$ 413,000
Gross amount of dividends received subject to the 85% exclusion	$ 50,000
Long-term capital gain	$ 100,000
Tax on long-term capital gain	$ 28,000
Dividend paid in the first month of the year	$ 20,000

Accumulated earnings and profits at the beginning of the year are $225,000. MBS could not justify accumulating any of the amounts not paid as dividends. The accumulated earnings tax is:

Taxable income		$1,000,000
Plus: Dividend exclusion ($50,000 × 0.85)		42,500
Long-term capital gain		+ 100,000
		$1,142,500
Less: Federal income tax		(413,000)
Tax on long-term capital gain		− (28,000)
Adjusted taxable income		$ 701,500
Credit:		
$250,000 exclusion	$250,000	
Beginning earnings and profits of $225,000 reduced by the dividend paid of $20,000	−205,000	− 45,000
Income subject to AET		$ 656,500
Tax on first $100,000 @ 27½%		$ 27,500
Tax on next $556,500 @ 38½%		+ 214,253
Total Accumulated Earnings Tax		$ 241,753

SUBCHAPTER S CORPORATIONS 12-09

A Subchapter S corporation is one that elects *not* to be taxed at the corporate level. Net income or loss, as well as net long-term capital gains, pass through to the stockholders in a manner similar to a partnership. Yet it is significantly different from a partnership, in two main ways:

1. The income or loss does not retain its characteristic by source, except for *net* long-term capital *gains.* Since only net long-term capital gains are passed through, the net long-term capital gain must be reduced by the amount of any operating loss.
2. Distributions to the stockholders may result in taxable income to the stockholders at the time of distribution, rather than having the taxability of the distribution depend on the company's full year results.

Only three credits may be passed through to the stockholder: the investment credit, the research and development credit, and the Job Credit. Stockholders are required to report their shares of the interest on investment indebtedness and the items of tax preference that the corporation has. These amounts are added to other amounts of a similar nature to see whether the taxpayer has either a loss of interest deductions due to the investment limits or a minimum tax due to the tax preference items.

12-09.1 Example

The MBS Corporation (a Subchapter S corporation) had the following results last year:

Loss from operations	$35,000
Net long-term capital gain (after netting against capital loss)	50,000

Stockholders report on their personal returns a net long-term capital gain of $15,000 ($50,000 − $35,000). In a partnership, the partners would report a net loss from operations of $35,000 (deductible for AGI), along with a long-term capital gain of $50,000 (only 40% added to AGI).

Three Year Taxable Potential 12-09.2

Long-term capital gains *may* be taxable at the corporate level for a Subchapter S corporation. Any long-term gain is taxable only if it occurs during the first three years of a corporation's election. Corporations that have been Subchapter S corporations since their inception are not subject to the three-year waiting period. Further, the long-term capital gain is not taxed at the corporate level unless it exceeds *both* $25,000 and 50% of the corporation's taxable income. This rule was enacted to prevent a corporation from electing Subchapter S status for the express purpose of passing through an unusual long-term gain.

Example 12-09.2A

A corporation has a long-term capital gain of $100,000 and other income of $50,000. The long-term capital gain would be taxable at the corporate level, but if the other income were more than $100,000, then there would be no capital gains tax at the corporate level.

Tax and Distribution 12-09.3

Payments made to stockholder/employees for *services rendered* are deductible by the corporation as salaries and wages. Unlike a partnership, such payments are subject to withholding taxes and FICA tax. Individuals treat such payments exactly as if they had been received from any employer.

Stockholders are also taxed on any *undistributed income.* Undistributed taxable income is taxed to stockholders who own the stock on the last day of the corporation's fiscal year, and they must report the income in the year that the corporation's fiscal year ends. For a corporation with a December 31 year end, an entire year's undistributed income is taxed to a calendar year stockholder. But for a corporation with a January 31 fiscal year, eleven months of undistributed income is rolled into the following year. If a corporation has $100,000 of undistributed taxable income for fiscal year ended January 31, 1982, then the entire amount is reported in 1982 by a calendar year stockholder.

If a Subchapter S corporation has an *operating loss* (capital losses do not pass through but can be carried forward five years), the stockholders may deduct that loss on their personal tax returns. But at the end of the fiscal year current stockholders are not the ones who receive the deduction. Instead, losses must be prorated to all the stockholders who held stock during the year, based on the number of days they held the stock.

This system gives rise to four layers of income retained in the corporation:

1. *Undistributed taxable income* (UTI) is the *current* year's earnings retained by the corporation.
2. *Previously taxed income* (PTI) is the income reported by the stockholders in prior years and retained by the corporation.
3. Some earnings and profits (E&P) are retained from years before the election was made to become a Subchapter S corporation.
4. Other earnings and profits of years are accumulated after the Subchapter S election.

These tiers are important in distinguishing a tax-free distribution of UTI or PTI from a taxable distribution of E&P. Distributions in the first 2½ months of the current fiscal year are considered to be from the previous year's income. Distributions in the last 9½ months are considered to be from the current year's income.

12-09.4 Tax *Warning*

Determining whether a distribution is from UTI, PTI, or E&P can be rather complex, especially if loss years are involved. The point is that a Subchapter S election *can* cause a double taxation: first when the UTI is reported by individual stockholders, and again when the stockholders liquidate their interest. At that point it would be a capital gain.

Previously taxed income can get locked into a Subchapter S corporation. Suppose:

Income Year 1	\$10,000
Income Year 2	\$15,000
Income Year 3	\$20,000

There have been no distributions. In years 1 and 2, the corporation was a Subchapter S corporation, and the stockholders reported the income on their returns. In year 3 the corporation was a "regular" (Subchapter C corporation).

If a dividend is paid in the last 9½ months of year 3, it is considered to be from current E&P, and it is a taxable dividend. The \$25,000 from years 1 and 2 could not be distributed tax-free until all the current E&P is paid out.

Tax *Warning* 12-09.5

PTI is *personal* to the stockholders who report the income. If stockholders sell their stock, the PTI does *not* go with it. New stockholders cannot withdraw someone else's PTI as a tax-free distribution. Another possible taxation trap!

Eligible Corporations 12-09.6

To be eligible to elect Subchapter S status, a corporation must meet all the following conditions:

1. There must be no more than 25 shareholders. A husband and wife are considered one shareholder;

2. The corporation must not own 80% or more of another active corporation.
3. The corporation must be a domestic corporation, and all the stockholders must be U.S. citizens or residents.
4. All the stockholders must be individuals, estates of individuals, or certain trusts under limited circumstances. (Partnership and corporate stockholders are not allowed.)
5. There must be only one class of stock outstanding.
6. The corporation must not derive more than 80% of its gross receipts from foreign sources.
7. The corporation must not derive more than 20% of its gross receipts from passive sources, such as rents, interest, dividends, and the like. An exception is made for interest of $3,000 or less earned in the formation year of a potentially active corporation.

The election is made by filing Form 2553. All the stockholders must consent to the election. The election may be filed either in the previous year or in the first 75 days of the current year.

The election is terminated by:

1. the corporation's failure to meet the requirements of a Subchapter S corporation,
2. the refusal of any new stockholder to accept the Subchapter election, or
3. a voluntary revocation statement sent to the IRS prior to the beginning of a fiscal year.

Once a Subchapter S status has been terminated, it may not be reinstated for a period of 5 years.

12-09.7 Example

Barney Colin and Aaron Gordon are 50% stockholders of the MBS Corporation (a Subchapter S corporation). During

FIGURE 12-2. Schedule K

Schedule K Computation of Undistributed Taxable Income and Summary of Distributions and Other Items

Computation of Corporation's Undistributed Taxable Income		
1 Taxable income (line 28, page 1)		23,000
2 Less: a Money distributed as dividends out of earnings and profits for the tax year	4,000	
b Tax imposed on certain capital gains (line 31, page 1)		4,000
3 Corporation's undistributed taxable income (subtract line 2 from line 1)		19,000
4 Actual dividend distributions taxable as ordinary income. (Do not include amounts shown on line 6.)		3,478
5 Actual dividend distributions taxable as long-term capital gains (after tax)		522
6 Actual dividend distributions taxable as ordinary income and qualifying for dividend exclusion		
7 Nondividend distributions		2,000
8 Undistributed taxable income—taxable as ordinary income or (loss) (see instructions)		16,522
9 Undistributed taxable income—taxable as long-term capital gain (after tax) (see instructions)		2,478
10 Investment credit property		Cost or basis

Property Qualified for Investment Credit		Cost or basis
Basis of new investment property	a 3 or more but less than 5 years	
	b 5 or more but less than 7 years	
	c 7 or more years	5,000
New commuter highway vehicle	d 3 or more years	
Qualified progress expenditures	e 7 or more years	
Cost of used investment property	f 3 or more but less than 5 years	
	g 5 or more but less than 7 years	
	h 7 or more years	
Used commuter highway vehicle	i 3 or more years	

11 Interest on investment indebtedness:	
a 1 Interest on investment indebtedness incurred before 12–17–69	
2 Interest on investment indebtedness incurred before 9–11–75, but after 12–16–69	
3 Interest on investment indebtedness incurred after 9–10–75	
b Net investment income or (loss)	
c Excess expenses from "net lease property"	
d Net capital gain attributable to investment property	
12 Items of tax preference (see instructions): a Accelerated depreciation on:	
1 Certified historic structure rehabilitation (167(o) or amortization under 191)	
2 Low-income rental housing (167(k))	
3 Other real property	
4 Personal property subject to a lease	
b Amortization: 1 ...., 2 ...., 3 ...., 4	
c Reserve for losses on bad debts of financial institutions	
d Depletion	
e Intangible drilling costs	
f Net capital gain (after tax)	
13 Jobs credit	

1979 (their first year) the corporation earns $14,000, each of the stockholders reporting $7,000 as ordinary income on their returns. During 1980, the corporation's books show the following:

Income from operations	$20,000
Long-term capital gain	$ 3,000
Purchase of equipment eligible for the investment credit (10-year life)	$ 5,000
Dividend paid, March 1, 1980	$ 2,000
Dividend paid, September 30, 1980	$ 4,000

FIGURE 12-3. Schedule K-1 for Aaron Gordon

SCHEDULE K-1 (Form 1120S)
Department of the Treasury Internal Revenue Service

Shareholder's Share of Undistributed Taxable Income, etc.—1980

For calendar year 1980 or other tax year beginning ...., 1980, ending .... 19......

(Complete a separate Schedule K-1 for each shareholder—See instructions on back of Copy C)

Copy A File with Form 1120S

Part I Income

	(a) Amount	(b) Form 1040 references; for Form 1041, see Instruction A.
1 Undistributed taxable income—ordinary income or (loss) (If line 1 is a loss, see instruction C for deductible amount.)	8,261	Schedule E, Part III
2 Undistributed taxable income—net long-term capital gain (after tax)	1,239	Schedule D, Part II
3 Shareholder's distributive share of losses from section 465 activities (see instruction D)		
4 Amount of loan repayments for "Loans from Shareholders." (See instruction E.)		

Part II Interest on Investment Indebtedness

		Form 4952 references
1 (a) Interest on investment indebtedness incurred before 12–17–69		line 1
(b) Interest on investment indebtedness incurred before 9–11–75 but after 12–16–69		line 15
(c) Interest on investment indebtedness incurred after 9–10–75		line 5
2 Net investment income or (loss)		line 2 or 10
3 Excess expenses from "net lease property"		lines 11 and 19
4 Net capital gain attributable to investment property		line 20

Part III Items of Tax Preference (See Instructions)

		Form 4625 references
1 Accelerated depreciation on:		
(a) Certified historic structure rehabilitation (167(o) or amortization under 191)		line 1(a)(1)
(b) Low-income rental housing (167(k))		line 1(a)(2)
(c) Other real property		line 1(a)(3)
(d) Personal property subject to a lease		line 1(b)
2 Amortization: (a) ...., (b) ...., (c) ...., (d)		lines 1(c), (d), (e) and (f)
3 Reserves for losses on bad debts of financial institutions		line 1(g)
4 Depletion		line 1(i)
5 Intangible drilling costs		line 1(j)
6 Net capital gain (after tax) (see General Instruction A)	1,239	

Part IV Property Eligible for Investment Credit

			Form 3468 references
Basis of new investment property	(a) 3 or more but less than 5 years		line 1(a)
	(b) 5 or more but less than 7 years		line 1(b)
	(c) 7 or more years	2,500	line 1(c)
New commuter highway vehicle	(d) 3 or more years		line 1(d)
Qualified progress expenditures	(e) 7 or more years		line 1(e)
Cost of used investment property	(f) 3 or more but less than 5 years		line 1(f)
	(g) 5 or more but less than 7 years		line 1(g)
	(h) 7 or more years		line 1(h)
Used commuter highway vehicle	(i) 3 or more years		line 1(i)

Part V Property Used in Refiguring an Earlier Year Investment Credit (Enter on corresponding lines of Form 4255).

Description of property (also state whether new or used)	(1) Rate	(2) Date placed in service	(3) Cost or basis	(4) Estimated useful life	(5) Applicable percentage	(6) Original qualified investment (column 3 × column 5)	(8) Date item ceased to be investment credit property	(9) Period actually used	(10) Applicable percentage	(11) Qualified investment (column 3 × column 10)
A										
B										

Part VI Jobs Credit

	(a) Amount	
1 Jobs credit		Form 5884

Part VII Other Shareholder Information

1. Name and address of shareholder	2. Social security number	3. Stock ownership: Number of shares	Period held: Date acquired	Period held: Date of disposition
Aaron Gordon Mountainside, N. J. 07092	123-45-7890	50	1/1/79	--

4. Compensation	5. Percentage of time devoted to business	6. Corporation's name, identifying number, and address (including ZIP code)
$30,000	100%	MBS Corporation 22-1990019 14 River Street Hoboken, N. J. 07102

FIGURE 12-4. Schedule K-1 for Barney Colin

SCHEDULE K-1 (Form 1120S) Department of the Treasury Internal Revenue Service	**Shareholder's Share of Undistributed Taxable Income, etc.—1979** For calendar year 1979 or other taxable year beginning ...., 1979, ending ...., 19....	Copy B For Shareholder

Part I Income	(a) Amount	(b) Form 1040 filers enter col. (a) amount as indicated below. Form 1041 filers enter col. (a) amount in corresponding line of that form.
1 Undistributed taxable income—ordinary income or (loss)	8,261	Schedule E, Part III
2 (a) Undistributed taxable income—net long-term capital gain from transactions entered into after 10/31/78 (after tax)	1,239	Schedule D, Part II
(b) Undistributed taxable income—net long-term capital gain from transactions entered into before 11/1/78 (after tax)		Schedule D, Part II
Part II Losses from Section 465 Activities		
1 Shareholder's distributive share of losses from section 465 activities (see instructions)		
Part III Interest on Investment Indebtedness		Form 4952 line reference
1 (a) Interest on investment indebtedness incurred before 12–17–69		line 1
(b) Interest on investment indebtedness incurred before 9–11–75 but after 12–16–69		line 15
(c) Interest on investment indebtedness incurred after 9–10–75		line 5
2 Net investment income or (loss)		line 2 or 10
3 Excess expenses from "net lease property"		line 11 and 19
4 Net capital gain attributable to investment property		line 20
Part IV Items of Tax Preference (See Instructions)		Form 4625 line reference
1 Accelerated depreciation on: (a) Low income rental housing		line 1(a)(1)
(b) Other real property		line 1(a)(2)
(c) Personal property subject to a lease		line 1(b)
2 Amortization: (a) ...., (b) ...., (c) ...., (d)		line 1(c), (d), (e) and (f)
3 Reserves for losses on bad debts of financial institutions		line 1(g)
4 Depletion		line 1(i)
5 Intangible drilling costs		line 1(j)
6 Net capital gain (after tax) (see General Instruction A)	1,239	

Part V Property Eligible for Investment Credit			Form 3468 line reference
Basis of new investment property	(a) 3 or more but less than 5 years		line 1(a)
	(b) 5 or more but less than 7 years		line 1(b)
	(c) 7 or more years	2,500	line 1(c)
New commuter highway vehicle	(d) 3 or more years		line 1(d)
Qualified progress expenditures	(e) 7 or more years — 1974 through 1978		line 1(e)
	(f) 7 or more years — 1979		line 1(f)
Cost of used investment property	(g) 3 or more but less than 5 years		line 1(g)
	(h) 5 or more but less than 7 years		line 1(h)
	(i) 7 or more years		line 1(i)
Used commuter highway vehicle	(j) 3 or more years		line 1(j)

Part VI Property Used in Recomputing a Prior Year Investment Credit (Enter in corresponding column of Form 4255.)

	(1) Description of property (also state whether new or used)	(2) Date placed in service	(3) Cost or basis	(4) Estimated useful life	(5) Applicable percentage	(6) Original qualified investment (column 3 × column 5)	(8) Date item ceased to be investment credit property	(9) Period actually used	(10) Applicable percentage	(11) Qualified investment (column 3 × column 10)
A										
B										

Part VII Jobs Credit	(a) Amount	Form 5884 line reference
1 Jobs credit		line 9

Part VIII Other Information

1. Name and address of shareholder	2. Social security number	3. Stock ownership: Number of shares	Period held: Date acquired	Date of disposition
Barney Colin Mountainside, N. J. 07092	345-67-8901	50	1/1/79	--

4. Compensation	5. Percentage of time devoted to business	6. Corporation's name, identifying number, and address (including ZIP code)
$30,000	100%	MBS Corporation 22-1990019 14 River Street Hoboken, N. J. 07102

The resulting Schedule K (Form 1120S) for the corporation and the Schedules K-1 for each of the stockholders are shown in Figures 12-2, 12-3, and 12-4. The distribution of the $2,000 dividend on March 1, 1980 reduces the prior year's PTI. That amount, now $12,000 ($14,000 − $2,000), is shown on line 7 of Schedule K, as a nontaxable distribution.

The dividend of September 30, 1980 must be allocated between the ordinary income and the long-term capital gain. This is done on a simple ratio basis:

Ordinary income portion [$4,000 × $20,000/$23,000 (total income)]	$3,478
Capital gain portion ($4,000 × $3,000/$23,000)	+ 522
Total	$4,000

These amounts appear on Schedule K, lines 4 and 5, but they do not appear on the Schedules K-1 for the stockholders. The amounts of dividend distribution are shown on Form 1099-DIV, as are all corporate dividends. They are taxable in the year distributed, and they are *not* subject to the dividend exclusion (02.09.3).

The dividend of $4,000 leaves undistributed taxable income of $16,522 ordinary ($20,000 − $3,478), along with $2,478 long-term capital gain ($3,000 − $522). These items appear on Schedule K, lines 8 and 9, and on Schedule K-1, lines 1 and 2.

The amount of equipment eligible for the investment credit is shown in Part IV of Schedules K-1 and on line 10 of Schedule K. The stockholders simply add these amounts to any other investment credits to which they are entitled. The credit reduces their personal income tax liability.

12-09.8 Tax Hint: When Are Subchapter S Corporations Useful?

Subchapter S elections are generally not well suited for profitable corporations. First the income is taxed to the individual, who is probably in a higher tax bracket than the corporation would be. (Keep in mind that, with progressive income tax, the corporation forms an additional taxpayer that starts at the bottom of the scale.) Second many of the pension and insurance benefits available to stockholder/employees of Subchapter C corporations are lost in a Subchapter S corporation.

Yet Subchapter S elections are excellent for the start-up years of a corporation when losses are anticipated. The losses may be deducted by the stockholders directly, whereas the corporation has no previous taxable income with which to use a net operating loss (06-13).

Tax Hint: Family Income Splitting 12-09.9

Subchapter S corporations present an excellent opportunity for family income splitting. Since undistributed taxable income is attributed to the person holding the stock on the last day of the year, some last-minute tax planning is available.

Take care, however, to insure that the active stockholder/employees are adequately compensated for their labor. The IRS can allocate some of the income attributed to stock ownership back to the income producer in a "family" corporation. But when a bonafide gift of stock is made to children and capital is an income-producing factor, the income is taxed to the children in the lower tax bracket.

TO INCORPORATE OR NOT TO INCORPORATE? 12-10

Whether or not to incorporate depends on the objectives of the enterprise and the projections of capital needs. The corporate form of business has only two major tax drawbacks:

1. Income distributed to shareholders is doubly taxed, and

2. losses cannot be deducted by the stockholders directly.

Both drawbacks can be avoided by the election of Subchapter S status, but doing so is really electing not to be a corporation for tax purposes.

On the other hand, the corporate form provides a number of advantages. If a firm plans to retain significant earnings for expansion, then the corporation provides the best vehicle. Corporation taxes are lower than the individual tax rates, and another taxpayer has been created that starts at the bottom of the progressive income tax ladder. Also, the corporate form allows for easier transfer of a partial interest in the business, and the transfer of shares of ownership to those who would be beneficiaries under a will forms the heart of much estate planning (Chapter 14). Finally, with a corporation, stockholder/employees have more flexibility in installing pension plans, deferred compensation plans, medical and life insurance plans, and other employee benefits. It is often most helpful to have a "benevolent" employer, and the owner of a corporation can easily create one.

The corporate form of business is usually inappropriate in two major cases:

1. When the income of the business is expected to be withdrawn, instead of reinvested. In this area, the threat of double taxation is the highest.
2. When the character of the income is best suited for direct pass-through to the individual owner's tax return. This is the reason most tax shelters are in the form of a partnership.

Keep in mind that a Subchapter S election is not going to help most tax-sheltered investments. The character of the deductions is lost, but, more importantly, Subchapter S corporate income from passive sources is limited to 20% of gross receipts. This restriction kills the possibility of casting a real estate shelter (and most other passive investments) a Subchapter S format.

Corporations may be related in one of two ways: brother-sister or parent-subsidiary. A *parent-subsidiary* is a relationship where a corporation owns, directly or indirectly, 80% of the voting and nonvoting stock of another. Indirect ownership comes about when one corporation owns a subsidiary, and when the parent and the subsidiary combined satisfy the 80% test. A *brother-sister* relationship exists when 5 or fewer stockholders own 80% of two or more corporations.

When corporations have a common parent, they may, if they elect, file a consolidated tax return, in which all their incomes and losses are simply added together. Consolidation can provide the group with considerable tax benefits. The major benefit is that the operating gains of one company can be offset by the operating losses of another. Likewise, the capital gains of one company may offset the losses of another. This trading off provides an immediate tax benefit from a loss, rather than a carried forward benefit. It also makes a capital loss carry-forward or an NOL carry-forward less likely to expire. Limitations, such as on the use of the investment credit, may be avoided by the use of the credit against the income of an affiliated company.

Consolidating brings no loss of the graduated income tax provisions since affiliated companies *must* allocate what is called the "surtax exemption," that is, the first $100,000 taxed at a rate below 46% (12-11.1). Both parent-subsidiary and brother-sister corporations must allocate the surtax exemption.

This rule exists to prevent one taxpayer from creating many corporations to obtain a series of surtax exemptions.

Example 12-11.1

Barney and Colin each own 50% of both the MBS Corporation of Newark and the MBS Corporation of Hoboken.

During the year MBS-Newark has taxable income of $200,000, and MBS-Hoboken has taxable income of $300,000.

The corporations may choose to allocate the surtax exemption in any way they see fit. If they fail to make an election, the surtax exemption is divided equally. Assuming they elect to divide it equally, each corporation pays the following tax on the first $100,000 of taxable income:

First $12,500 @ 15%	$ 1,875
Next $12,500 @ 18%	2,250
Next $12,500 @ 30%	3,750
Next $12,500 @ 40%	5,000
Next $50,000 @ 46%	23,000
Total	$35,875

They would, of course, pay 46% on all income over $100,000.

12-11.2 Other Effects of a Corporate Relationship

When corporations are related, they must also share the $250,000 accumulated earnings credit and the $10,000 minimum tax exemption.

12-11.3 Exceptions

Certain corporations are never considered to be part of a controlled relationship. They are:

1. regulated investment companies (12-13),
2. certain insurance companies (12-15),
3. exempt corporations (12-16),
4. DISC corporations (12-17), and
5. foreign corporations.

A corporation that is a personal holding company (PHC) is subject to a "penalty" tax of 50% of the *undistributed* PHC income. This penalty tax is unlike the accumulated earnings tax (12-08) in that the taxpayer may elect to assess this tax themselves by filing Form 1120PH. The tax is designed to prevent the misuse of the low corporate tax rates to shelter passive personal income. As an example, a 50% bracket taxpayer could form a corporation to hold assets bearing interest. The corporation would pay a maximum tax rate of only 46%—and even less than that on the first $100,000 of income. And, if the individual taxpayer dies before disposing of the corporation, the income from disposing of the corporation would escape any additional income tax (Chapter 14). Or the taxpayer could dispose of the corporation and realize the income at the capital gains rate in years when he or she is in a lower tax bracket. To prevent this abuse, the PHC tax is imposed.

For a corporation to be PHC, it must meet *both* a stockholder test and an income test.

Stockholder Test 12-12.1

To be a PHC, 50% of the *value* of the outstanding stock of the corporation must be owned by 5 or fewer persons during the *second* half of the corporation's fiscal year.

Constructive ownership of the stock is part of the test. One individual is attributed with the stock, convertible securities, and options owned by the family or the controlled corporation.

Income Test 12-12.2

PHC income consists of:

1. Dividends and interest.

2. Taxable income received from estates and trusts.
3. Payments received under a personal service contract, *if*:
   a. the person is named in the contract or can be designated by someone other than the corporation, *and*
   b. the person performing the services owned directly or indirectly 25% or more of the value of the corporation anytime during the year;
4. Rent payments received from shareholders who own directly or indirectly 25% or more of the corporation's stock *may* be PHC income depending on several complex tests.
5. Royalties other than for copyrights, minerals, oil and gas (see below for the exclusions).
6. Copyright royalties *may* be included as PHC income if they constitute less than 50% of ordinary gross income (before capital gains and Section 1231 gains).
7. Rents *may* be PHC income if they do not constitute at least 50% of "adjusted" ordinary gross income.
8. Minerals, oil and gas royalties *may* be PHC income if they do not exceed 50% of "adjusted" ordinary gross income.

Reviewing these eight items makes the point of this tax clear. Rents and royalties that are part of a corporation's normal business are excluded. Items that are included are those that an individual would typically transfer to a corporation to take advantage of the reduced tax rates.

For PHC purposes, both ordinary income and PHC income are reduced by certain expenses related to rents and royalties from minerals, oil, and gas. They are also reduced for certain interest and lease income not related to investments. The reduced ordinary income is called *adjusted ordinary income.*

If PHC income is 60% or more of "adjusted" ordinary income, then the corporation is a PHC corporation. When both the numerator (PHC income) and the denominator adjusted ordinary income) are reduced before the computation to see if the 60% test has been met, the chance of a corporation's being classified as a PHC is increased.

Distribution Dividends 12-12.3

Since the point of the PHC tax is to prevent taxpayers from taking advantage of the lower corporate tax rates, dividends paid to stockholders reduce PHC income. They obviously do not reduce taxable income for the computation of the regular income tax.

Dividends paid in the first two months of the following year can be used to reduce PHC income of the previous year. This allowance permits taxpayers to compute how much in dividends must be paid to avoid the PHC tax.

The Code even permits a dividend to be paid in subsequent years if the IRS determines that a deficiency in PHC tax existed in a prior year. Taxpayers normally have 90 days after receiving a deficiency notice to pay such a dividend and thus to reduce or eliminate the PHC tax. But, in such a case, taxpayers still have to pay the interest on the PHC tax. This remedy is available only in the case of an error on the part of the taxpayer in computing the PHC tax, not for cases of fraud or willful failure to pay the tax.

Example 12-12.4

The tax return of the MBS Corporation shows the following:

Interest income		$100,000
Dividends received from domestic corporations	$100,000	
Dividend received exclusion	− 85,000	+ 15,000
Total income		$115,000

Charitable contributions	$ 50,000	
Amount not allowed due to 10% limitation	− 21,000	− 29,000
Taxable ordinary income		$ 86,000
Long-term capital gain		$ 90,000
Income tax on $86,000		$ 20,150
Tax on capital gain		+ 25,200
Total income tax		$ 45,350
Dividends paid during the year		$ 10,000
Dividend paid March 1st of following year		+ 5,000
Total dividends		$ 15,000

The PHC tax would be computed as:

Taxable income		$ 86,000
Plus: 85% dividends received exclusion		+ 85,000
		$171,000
Less: Federal income taxes	$ 45,350	
Contributions not allowed	21,000	
Taxable dividends paid	15,000	− 81,350
Undistributed PHC income		$ 89,650
PHC Tax: 50% of $89,650		$ 44,825

12-12.5 Tax *Warning*

This example is a highly simplified situation. If there is any possibility that a corporation *might* have a PHC tax liability, it should seek competent counsel.

12-13 REGULATED INVESTMENT COMPANIES AND REAL ESTATE INVESTMENT TRUSTS (REITS)

Both Regulated Investment Companies and Real Estate Investment Trusts are restricted as to the types of investments that they may make and as to the types of income that they may earn. These restrictions are set out in the Code, in the Investment Companies Act of 1940, and in the rules and regulations of the Securites and Exchange Commission.

Regulated Investment Companies 12-13.1

Regulated investment companies are often referred to as mutual funds or investment trusts. They are corporations registered under the Investment Companies Act of 1940 and subject to the jurisdiction of the Securities and Exchange Commission. They are formed for the express purpose of acting as investment conduits. Small investors buy shares of the regulated investment company, which reinvests the money in stocks, in bonds, and in other public investment vehicles.

Regulated investment companies may elect to pay no income taxes and instead pass the income earned directly to the shareholders in a manner similar to Subchapter S corporations. Individual stockholders then report the income on their individual returns and pay the income tax based on their incremental tax brackets.

Regulated investment companies may also elect to pay tax as a regular corporation. In that event, they pass the tax back to the shareholders, who receive a credit against their individual taxes (09-08.8).

These companies can pass through to the shareholders only four types of income: dividend income, tax-exempt interest income, taxable interest income, and long-term capital gains. Included in dividend income are dividends and short-term capital gains earned by the corporation. To the extent that the dividend paid to shareholders relates to dividends received by the investment company, the dividends from the investment company qualify for the dividends exclusion. To the extent that the dividends relate to short-term capital gains, they do not.

12-13.2 Real Estate Investment Trusts (REITs)

Real estate investment trusts are similar to investment companies, but they are designed as investment vehicles for real estate and real estate secured indebtedness.

12-14 BANKS

Banks come under the same rules for income taxation as other corporations, but with three major exceptions:

1. the handling of net operating losses,
2. the computation of bad debt reserves, and
3. the reporting of gains and losses on securities transactions.

12-14.1 Net Operating Losses

Corporations are allowed to carry back net operating losses for three years and forward for fifteen years (06-13). But banks may carry back their net operating losses ten years, as well as forward fifteen.

12-14.2 Bad Debt Reserves

Until 1988, all banks will be allowed to compute their bad debt reserve based on a percentage of outstanding loans without regard to their actual experience. Other corporations must use their actual experience (08-12). Thus banks are allowed an "extra" deduction above that to which they would normally be entitled—one that would be justified by their experience. The difference between the bad debt deduction taken and the amount that can be justified by experience is a tax preference item (09-02.1C).

Savings and loans associations, as well as other savings institutions, also use a percentage factor to compute their reserve for bad debts. Under current legislation they are able to continue this practice after 1988, when the banks must begin using the experience method only.

Gains and Losses on Securities Transactions 12-14.3

When banks realize gains and losses from trading securities, they are ordinary gains and losses, not capital gains and losses. Interestingly enough, this rule allows banks to deduct their trading losses against other income, where regular corporations cannot. Inasmuch as the banking industry lobbied for this treatment, and since a bank's gains are fully taxable, it would appear that banks anticipate more losses then gains. Or so it would appear.

INSURANCE COMPANIES 12-15

Insurance companies are *not* taxed in the same manner as other corporations. They are covered by separate sections of the Code, which relate to them only. The reasons for this special treatment are the uncertainties of the insurance business. For the most part, their tax burdens are significantly lighter than regular corporations, and the timing of the payments is often delayed offering them additional liquidity.

Insurance companies, however, are not treated uniformly. The Code recognizes that different companies incur different degrees of risk and uncertainty. The Code recognizes four basic categories of insurance companies, with subcategories based on the type of insurance written. The four basic categories are:

1. life insurance companies;
2. Section 831 companies, which include all companies that are not life or mutual insurance companies, as

well as some mutual companies that write marine and fire insurance;

3. Section 821 companies, which include most mutual companies; and
4. foreign insurance companies.

While insurance company taxation is a textbook in itself, here are some general concepts of the differences from regular corporate taxation:

- Life insurance companies pay income tax on only a portion of their investment income. For this reason, they are not as big a buyer of tax-exempt securities as other insurance companies. Further, they pay tax on only 50% of their underwriting income when earned. The tax on the remaining 50% of underwriting income is normally paid when it is distributed to the stockholders.
- Section 831 companies pay tax in the same manner as other corporations. But the taxable income is computed in a manner designed to reduce the current tax liability of the company and thereby to provide additional liquidity.
- Section 821 companies pay tax on a specially defined income, also designed to provide the company with additional liquidity.
- Foreign insurance companies are taxed on their U.S. insurance business as if they were domestic companies. But special treatment may be given to them by treaties, or if their reserves for U.S. losses are below certain minimums.

12-16 EXEMPT CORPORATIONS

Section 501 of the Code lists many corporations that are exempt from federal income tax. The common threads that run through all the exemptions are that the corporation is not designed for making a profit *and* that, if any profits are made, none of the benefits of those profits may inure to any stockholder.

Some of the corporations that you might expect to find exempt from federal income tax include charitable organizations (those to which contributions may be deducted), as well as pension and retirement plans. But the list is far more encompassing. Most corporations organized on a "not-for-profit" basis are exempt from federal income tax on receipts related to their primary function. Fund-raising activities, for example, are generally considered related to an exempt organization's functions. Included on the list of corporations that may apply for a tax-exempt status are:

1. civic leagues organized to promote social welfare,
2. business leagues such as real estate boards if they are not organized for profit.
3. social clubs, including country clubs, if they are not organized for profit,
4. political organizations designed to assist public office seekers, and
5. mutual insurance companies (other than life or mrine) may be tax-exempt.

Exempt organizations, however, must pay income tax on any unrelated income, to prevent unfair competition with taxable entities. As an example, a country club could have significant revenues from its bar and restaurant. As long as they are serving members, this income would be related and therefore tax-exempt. But if the club advertises to encourage nonmembers to use their facilities, such revenues could be classified as nonrelated, and be taxable.

More than twenty subsections under Section 501(c) list the various organizations that qualify for tax-exempt status—and that is a subsection under Section 501. For each of these sections there are related Regulations. Competent legal counsel must be obtained to insure compliance if an organization wishes to be exempt under any of these Sections.

Exemption from paying federal income taxes does not necessarily confer an exemption from state franchise (income) taxes. Many states do impose their franchise tax on organizations that are exempt from federal taxes.

12-17 DISC CORPORATIONS

The domestic international sales corporation (DISC), generally the selling arm of one or more manufacturing corporations, was designed by Congress to increase exports. To qualify as a DISC, a company must pass sales and asset tests, which are designed to insure that the primary business of the DISC is export. To meet these requirements, it is essential for a manufacturer, or a group of manufacturers, to set up a separate corporation.

A DISC pays no income tax. But the stockholders are deemed to have received a taxable dividend of a portion of the DISC's taxable income. This portion can be as low as 50% of the taxable income. Taxable income actually distributed to the stockholders is taxable at the time of distribution if it has not been previously deemed distributed and taxed. Yet DISCs may "lend" money to their stockholders and continue to defer the income tax. Due to the way that the deemed taxable dividend to the stockholders is computed, the DISC must continually increase its profitability for the stockholders to reap the maximum tax benefits. While the computation is rather complex, it fits the objective Congress had when it authorized DISCs.

13
GIFT TAXES

CONCEPTS

The federal gift and estate taxes (Chapter 14) are excise taxes imposed upon taxpayers' right to transfer property. The fact that these taxes are excise taxes is important since:

1. the tax is not deductible from or for federal income tax (except with regard to income received on account of a decedent), and
2. all property is subject to the tax, even property exempted from federal income tax.

The gift tax is a tentative tax since it is based on the total lifetime giving of taxable gifts. Every time taxpayers make a taxable gift, they must refigure their total gift tax liability. They then take credit for previous gift taxes paid. This process is important since the gift tax is a progressive tax: the more you give, the higher the tax rate.

The final determination of the tax liability is made upon a taxpayer's last transfer—from the estate to the

ABLE 13-1. Unified Gift and Estate Tax Table for 1985 and hereafter

Column A	Column B	Column C	Column D
Taxable Amount Over—	Taxable Amount Not Over—	Tax on Amount in Column A	Rate of Tax on Excess Over Amount in Column A
	$10,000		18%
$10,000	20,000	$1,800	20%
20,000	40,000	3,800	22%
40,000	60,000	8,200	24%
60,000	80,000	13,000	26%
80,000	100,000	18,200	28%
100,000	150,000	23,800	30%
150,000	250,000	38,800	32%
250,000	500,000	70,800	34%
500,000	750,000	155,800	37%
750,000	1,000,000	248,300	39%
1,000,000	1,250,000	345,800	41%
1,250,000	1,500,000	448,300	43%
1,500,000	2,000,000	555,800	45%
2,000,000	2,500,000	780,800	49%
2,500,000		1,025,800	50%

beneficiaries. Total lifetime taxable gifts are added back to the taxable estate, and the estate tax is then computed (Chapter 14). The gift taxes paid during one's lifetime are then taken as a credit against the estate tax payable. Table 13-1 shows the *unified* gift and estate tax rates, which run as high as 50% for 1985 and thereafter.

The tax rates are gradually being reduced. The top rates for 1982, 1983, and 1984 are:

Year	*Top Rate*	*Taxable Amount Over*
1982	65%	$4,000,000
1983	60%	$3,500,000
1984	55%	$3,000,000

The tax rates for taxable amounts of $2,500,000 and less are not scheduled to change under current law.

The unified credit is gradually being increased. The scheduled increases are:

Year	*Credit*	*Exemption Equivalent*
1982	$ 62,800	$225,000
1983	$ 79,300	$275,000
1984	$ 96,300	$325,000
1985	$121,800	$400,000
1986	$155,800	$500,000
1987 and thereafter	$192,800	$600,000

For illustrative purposes we will use the rates and credits in effect for 1987.

Each person has a lifetime credit of $192,800 (lesser amounts in 1986 and prior years), which must be used to reduce any gift tax liability. Any credit not used to reduce gift tax liability is available to reduce estate tax liability.

13-01.1 Example

Alan Larkin, who previously made taxable gifts of $2,000,000, makes an additional taxable gift of $1,000,000. The gift tax on the $1,000,000 is:

Total prior gifts		$2,000,000
New gift		+1,000,000
Total lifetime gifts		$3,000,000
Tax on $3,000,000 (Table 13-1)		$1,275,800
Credit for prior gift taxes:		
Taxes paid	$ 588,000	
Lifetime credit	+192,800	− 780,800
Net payable		$ 495,000

13-02 WHAT ARE TAXABLE GIFTS?

The term "gift" in the Code means much the same as it does in English. It is the gratuitous transfer of property without full and adequate consideration in money or in money's worth. To be a gift, the intent need *not* be there.

While this distinction is rarely a problem in business (a bad business deal is not a gift), it has been a major problem for transactions among family members.

Certain gifts are *excluded* from being subject to gift taxes at all times. They are:

1. gifts to charitable and some political organizations,
2. gifts to the U.S. or to its political subdivisions,
3. gifts of $10,000 per year/per donee,
4. gifts between husbands and wives, and
5. gifts for the education or medical treatment of the donee.

The third item deserves amplification. Each donor may give up to $10,000 per year to each donee, every year. In other words, a father could give $10,000 to *each* of his children, or a husband and wife may consider gifts to be given half by each. If the nongiving spouse consents to the gift-splitting, the donor could give $20,000 each year to each donee.

If the gift is less than $10,000, no forms need be filed. But if the gift-splitting technique is used, both spouses must file a gift tax return, even if no tax is due and even if no lifetime credit is used. This election is made by filing Form 709 or Form 709A (13-12).

Love and the promise of love, or marriage and the promise to marry, do not have "money's worth." Giving a gift to acquire such an "asset" is a taxable gift.

POWERS OF APPOINTMENT 13-03

A *power of appointment* gives the possessor the right to determine who is to receive property. The donor of the power has title to the property and gives the possessor of the power the right to dispose of it. This right is conferred through the operation of the donor's will. A *general* power of appointment allows possessors to name themselves as the beneficiaries. A *limited* power does not give possessors such a right, except within clearly defined areas of support, health, education, or the maintenance of the power.

The creation of a general power of appointment does not invoke the gift tax. But its exercise does cause a gift tax liability on the part of the possessor of the power. The exercise of a limited power generally does not cause a gift tax liability to be imposed on the possessor of the power.

If a power is allowed to lapse, the possessor may still be liable for a gift tax. The one way the possessor can avoid a gift tax liability is to disclaim the power within 9 months of the creation of the power. And even then the disclaimer must conform to requirements set out in the Code.

13-04 COMMUNITY PROPERTY CONSIDERATION

When a husband and wife make a gift of community property, the gift is considered to be made one-half by each. No gift splitting election need be made.

13-05 GIFTS MADE WITHIN THREE YEARS OF DEATH

One of the purposes of making gifts is to reduce the amount of estate tax payable upon the death of the donor (Chapter 14). Although the amount of all gifts made after December 31, 1976 are added back to the estate before figuring the estate tax, when the gift was made is important in figuring how much will be added back.

- The general rule is that only the fair market value of the gift at the date of the gift is added back to the estate. This valuation eliminates two elements from the estate: appreciation of the asset subsequent to the gift, and the gift taxes paid by the donor.

- But if the gift is made within three years of the date of the donor's death, *and* if the gift consisted of an insurance policy (and certain other assets in limited situations), the fair market value of the property at the date of death is added back to the estate. The gift taxes paid are also added back to the estate. This inclusion does not create a double taxation, since the estate still receives credit for the gift taxes paid (14-03).

TAX BASED ON FAIR MARKET VALUE 13-06

The gift tax is based on the fair market value of the property on the date of the gift. Fair market value is the price that a willing buyer would pay and that a willing seller would accept, neither of whom is compelled to complete the transaction.

For *listed stocks and bonds,* the fair market value is the mean between the high and low prices for the day. For *over-the-counter securities,* it is the mean between the bid and the ask.

The fair market value of an *insurance policy* is the amount an insurance company would charge for a similar policy based on the age of the insured, the cash value of the policy, and the loans against the policy.

If the donor has a *reversionary interest* in the property, the gift tax is based on actuarial tables in the Regulations.

THE ANNUAL AND MARITAL EXCLUSIONS 13-07

The annual exclusion of $10,000 per donee/per donor/per year (13-02) is not automatic. For the exclusion to apply, the gift must be of a *present* interest in property; that is, the donee must have the absolute right to enjoy the property at the time of the gift. If the donee is required to wait to enjoy the gift, the gift is taxable, and no $10,000 exclusion is allowed. For instance, if the donor gives a stamp collection with the proviso that the donee must wait until some future time to take possession, then the market value of the gift is fully taxable.

13-08 GIFTS TO CHARITIES

Gifts to charities for which a deduction is allowed and to some political organizations are not subject to the gift tax (07-04).

Gifts to political corporations qualified under Section 527 are exempt from gift tax. These corporations are organized for the purpose of supporting the campaign of persons running for political office. The funds may not be used to influence legislation.

Gifts to private charitable tax-exempt foundations are generally not subject to the gift tax. But private foundations are subject to strict regulations that could cause their loss of tax-exempt status or the imposition of a penalty tax. If either of these conditions exists, any "donations" to them would be taxed as a gift. Further, the Code requires that private foundations include certain wording in their governing instruments. If this wording is not included, the donation could be taxable. Since determining whether a private foundation qualifies is normally beyond the ability of an outsider, ask for a copy of the exemption letter that each private foundation must obtain from the IRS, before making any donations. Further, the foundation should provide the taxpayer with a letter noting that the donation is *both* deductible for income tax purposes and exempt from gift tax.

13-09 HOW THE TAX IS FIGURED

The taxpayer figures the gift tax on all taxable gifts made *subsequent to June 6, 1932* using the table shown in Table 13-1. That tax is reduced by previous gift taxes paid and the lifetime credit.

Gifts made *prior to January 1, 1985* may require special adjustments to reflect changes in the gift tax laws and rates. The tax credit given for "taxes paid on gifts prior to January

1, 1985" is based on the current rates with some adjustments to reflect changes in the law.

Gift tax returns are due annually on April 15 of the following year.

Example

13-09.1

Aaron Gordon gives his daughter $250,000 in 1979. At the time he files a gift tax return showing:

Total current gift	$250,000
Exclusion (amount in 1979)	− 3,000
Taxable gift	$247,000
Tax on $247,000	$ 69,840
Less: The unified credit (amount in 1979)	− 38,000
Gift tax paid	$ 31,840

In 1982, he sells his ranch to his son for $20,000. Aaron recently received a firm offer of $280,000 for the ranch. If Aaron and his wife do *not* elect gift splitting, then his gift tax liability would be:

Current gift ($280,000 − $20,000)		$260,000
Less: Annual exclusion		− 10,000
Taxable current gift		$250,000
Total prior taxable gifts		+247,000
Basis for computation		$497,000
Gift tax on $497,000		$154,780
Less: Unified credit (for 1982)	$ 62,800	
Previous gift taxes paid	+ 31,840	94,640
Gift tax payable		$ 60,140

For illustrative purposes we are showing the form that was in use for 1981 and prior, when gift tax returns were due quarterly. The new form was not available at this printing. No major changes are expected in the form other than changing the title to Annual Gift Tax Return.

FIGURE 13-1. Aaron Gordon's Form 709 (Page 1)

Form **709** (Rev. December 1980) Department of the Treasury Internal Revenue Service

United States Quarterly Gift Tax Return

(Section 6019 of the Internal Revenue Code) (For gifts made after December 31, 1976)
Calendar quarter(s) ending ☐ March, ☐ June, ☐ September, ☑ December, 19 82

For "Privacy Act" notification, see the Instructions for Form 1040.

Donor's first name and middle initial	Donor's last name	Social security number
AARON	GORDON	137-30-5585
Address (number and street)		Residence (domicile)
324 PARTRIDGE RUN		USA
City, State, and ZIP code		Citizenship
MOUNTAINSIDE N. J. 07092		USA

	Yes	No
If you (the donor) filed a previous Form 709, has your address changed since the last Form 709 was filed?		✓
A Gifts by husband or wife to third parties.—Do you consent to have the gifts by you and by your spouse to third parties during the calendar quarter(s) considered as made one-half by each of you? (See instructions.)	✓	
(If the answer is "Yes," the following information must be furnished and your spouse is to sign the consent shown below. If the answer is "No," skip lines 1–6 and go to Schedule A.)		
1(a) Name of consenting spouse: SARAH GORDON — 1(b) Social security number: 123-45-7890		
2 If the consent is effective for gifts made in a previous quarter(s) of the calendar year and no return was filed for such previous quarter(s) (see instructions) and such gifts are being reported on this return (see instructions), write the previous quarter(s) ending (month and year) in addition to the current quarter ending (month and year).		
3 Were you married during the *entire* calendar quarter(s)?	✓	
4 If the answer to 3 is "No," check whether ☐ married ☐ divorced or ☐ widowed, and give date (see instructions) ▶		
5 Will a gift tax return for this calendar quarter(s) be filed by your spouse?	✓	

6 **Consent of Spouse**—I consent to have the gifts made by me and by my spouse to third parties during the calendar quarter(s) considered as made one-half by each of us. We are both aware of the joint and several liability for tax created by the execution of this consent.

Consenting Spouse's signature ▶ *Sarah Gordon* Date ▶ 4/5/83

Computation of Tax

Line	Description		Amount
1	Enter the amount from Schedule A, line 25	1	120,000
2	Enter the amount from Schedule B, line 3	2	247,000
3	Total taxable gifts (add amounts on lines 1 and 2)	3	367,000
4	Tax computed on amount on line 3 (see Table A in separate instructions)	4	110,580
5	Tax computed on amount on line 2 (see Table A in separate instructions)	5	69,840
6	Balance (subtract amount on line 5 from amount on line 4)	6	40,740
7	Enter the amount of unified credit from Table B (see instructions)	7	62,800
8	Enter the amount of unified credit against gift tax allowable for all prior quarters	8	38,000
9	Balance (subtract amount on line 8 from amount on line 7)	9	24,800
10	Enter 20% of the amount allowed as specific exemption after September 8, 1976	10	
11	Balance (subtract amount on line 10 from amount on line 9)	11	24,800
12	Unified credit (enter the smaller of amount on line 6 or amount on line 11)	12	24,800
13	Credit for foreign gift taxes (see instructions)	13	
14	Total (add amounts on line 12 and line 13)	14	24,800
15	Tax due (subtract amount on line 14 from amount on line 6) (see instructions)	15	15,940

Please attach Check or Money Order here

Please attach the necessary supplemental documents; see instructions.

Under penalties of perjury, I declare that I have examined this return, including any accompanying schedules and statements, and to the best of my knowledge and belief it is true, correct, and complete. Declaration of preparer (other than donor) is based on all information of which preparer has any knowledge.

Donor's signature ▶ *Aaron Gordon* Date ▶ 4/5/83

Preparer's signature (other than donor) ▶ Date ▶

Preparer's address (other than donor) ▶

FIGURE 13-2. Aaron Gordon's Form 709 (Page 2)

Schedule A — Computation of Taxable Gifts

Item number	Donee's name and address and description of gift. If the gift was made by means of a trust, enter trust's identifying number below and attach a copy of the trust instrument	Donor's adjusted basis of gift	Date of gift	Value at date of gift
1	AARON GORDON 1 TUMBLEWEED DRIVE CLINTON NJ 08881 RANCH, CLINTON, NJ PRICE RECEIVED NET GIFT	$15,000	2/1/82	$280,000 20,000 $260,000

	Line	Amount	Line	Amount
1 Total gifts of donor (see instructions)			1	$260,000
2 One-half of items .... attributable to spouse (see instructions)			2	130,000
3 Balance (subtract amount on line 2 from amount on line 1)			3	130,000
4 Gifts of spouse to be included (from line 2 of spouse's return—see instructions)			4	
5 Total gifts (add amounts on lines 3 and 4)			5	130,000
6 Total exclusions not exceeding $3,000 for the calendar year for each donee (except gifts of future interests)			6	10,000
7 Total included amount of gifts (subtract amount on line 6 from amount on line 5)			7	120,000
Deductions (see instructions):				
8 Gift of qualified interests to spouse for this period (before annual exclusion, based on items .... from Schedule A)	8			
9 Annual exclusion attributable to gifts on line 8	9			
10 Net amount (subtract amount on line 9 from amount on line 8)	10			
11 First $100,000 marital deduction	11	$100,000		
12 Marital deduction for prior periods after December 31, 1976	12			
13 Balance of first $100,000 marital deduction available (subtract amount on line 12 from amount on line 11. If less than zero, enter zero)	13			
14 Excess over first $100,000 marital deduction (if total of amount on line 10 plus amount on line 12 is $100,000 or less, enter zero. Otherwise, enter amount on line 8 less amount on line 13)	14			
15 Excess over first $100,000 for prior periods (after December 31, 1976)	15			
16 Total excess over first $100,000 (add amounts on lines 14 and 15)	16			
17 Second $100,000	17	$100,000		
18 Gifts qualifying for additional marital deduction (subtract amount on line 17 from amount on line 16. If less than zero, enter zero)	18			
19 Enter 50% of amount on line 18	19			
20 Enter 50% of amount on line 8 but not more than amount on line 10	20			
21 Enter the smaller of the amount on line 10 or the amount on line 13	21			
22 Marital deduction (if amount on line 18 is zero, enter amount from line 21. Otherwise, enter amount from line 21 plus the smaller of the amounts on line 19 or line 20)	22			
23 Charitable, public, and similar gifts (based on items ...., less exclusions)	23			
24 Total deductions (add amounts on lines 22 and 23)			24	
25 Amount of taxable gifts (subtract amount on line 24 from amount on line 7)			25	$120,000

Schedule B Did you (the donor) file gift tax returns for prior periods? (If "Yes," follow instructions in completing Schedule B below.) ☐ Yes ☐ No

(a) Calendar years (prior to 1971) and calendar quarters (1971 and subsequent years)	(b) Internal Revenue office where prior return was filed	(c) Amount of unified credit against gift tax for periods after December 31, 1976	(d) Amount of specific exemption for prior periods ending before January 1, 1977	(e) Amount of taxable gifts
JUNE, 1979	HOLTSVILLE, NY	$38,000		$247,000

	Line	(d)	Line	(e)
1 Totals for prior periods (without adjustment for reduced specific exemption)	1			$247,000
2 Amount, if any, by which total specific exemption, line 1, column (d), is more than $30,000			2	
3 Total amount of taxable gifts for prior periods (add amount, column (e), line 1, and amount, if any, line 2)			3	$247,000

(If more space is needed, attach additional sheets of same size.)

☆ U.S. GOVERNMENT PRINTING OFFICE : 1981—O-313-393

FIGURE 13-3. Sarah Gordon's Form 709 (Page 1)

Form **709** (Rev. December 1980) Department of the Treasury Internal Revenue Service

United States Quarterly Gift Tax Return

(Section 6019 of the Internal Revenue Code) (For gifts made after December 31, 1976)
Calendar quarter(s) ending ☐ March, ☐ June, ☐ September, ☑ December, 1982
For "Privacy Act" notification, see the Instructions for Form 1040.

Donor's first name and middle initial	Donor's last name	Social security number
SARAH	GORDON	123-45-7890
Address (number and street)		Residence (domicile)
324 PARTRIDGE RUN		USA
City, State, and ZIP code		Citizenship
MOUNTAINSIDE NJ 07092		USA

	Yes	No
If you (the donor) filed a previous Form 709, has your address changed since the last Form 709 was filed?		
A Gifts by husband or wife to third parties.—Do you consent to have the gifts by you and by your spouse to third parties during the calendar quarter(s) considered as made one-half by each of you? (See instructions.)	✓	
(If the answer is "Yes," the following information must be furnished and your spouse is to sign the consent shown below. If the answer is "No," skip lines 1–6 and go to Schedule A.)		
1(a) Name of consenting spouse: AARON GORDON — 1(b) Social security number: 137-30-5585		
2 If the consent is effective for gifts made in a previous quarter(s) of the calendar year and no return was filed for such previous quarter(s) (see instructions) and such gifts are being reported on this return (see instructions), write the previous quarter(s) ending (month and year) in addition to the current quarter ending (month and year).		
3 Were you married during the *entire* calendar quarter(s)?	✓	
4 If the answer to 3 is "No," check whether ☐ married ☐ divorced or ☐ widowed, and give date (see instructions) ▶		
5 Will a gift tax return for this calendar quarter(s) be filed by your spouse?	✓	

6 **Consent of Spouse**—I consent to have the gifts made by me and by my spouse to third parties during the calendar quarter(s) considered as made one-half by each of us. We are both aware of the joint and several liability for tax created by the execution of this consent.

Consenting Spouse's signature ▶ Aaron Gordon **Date** ▶ 4/5/83

Computation of Tax

	Line	Amount
1 Enter the amount from Schedule A, line 25	1	120,000
2 Enter the amount from Schedule B, line 3	2	
3 Total taxable gifts (add amounts on lines 1 and 2)	3	120,000
4 Tax computed on amount on line 3 (see Table A in separate instructions)	4	29,800
5 Tax computed on amount on line 2 (see Table A in separate instructions)	5	
6 Balance (subtract amount on line 5 from amount on line 4)	6	29,800
7 Enter the amount of unified credit from Table B (see instructions)	7	62,800
8 Enter the amount of unified credit against gift tax allowable for all prior quarters	8	
9 Balance (subtract amount on line 8 from amount on line 7)	9	62,800
10 Enter 20% of the amount allowed as specific exemption after September 8, 1976	10	
11 Balance (subtract amount on line 10 from amount on line 9)	11	62,800
12 Unified credit (enter the smaller of amount on line 6 or amount on line 11)	12	29,800
13 Credit for foreign gift taxes (see instructions)	13	
14 Total (add amounts on line 12 and line 13)	14	29,800
15 Tax due (subtract amount on line 14 from amount on line 6) (see instructions)	15	NONE

Please attach the necessary supplemental documents; see instructions.

Under penalties of perjury, I declare that I have examined this return, including any accompanying schedules and statements, and to the best of my knowledge and belief it is true, correct, and complete. Declaration of preparer (other than donor) is based on all information of which preparer has any knowledge.

Donor's signature ▶ Sarah Gordon Date ▶ 4/5/83

Preparer's signature (other than donor) ▶ Date ▶

Preparer's address (other than donor) ▶

Please attach Check or Money Order here

FIGURE 13-4. Sarah Gordon's Form 709 (Page 2)

Schedule A Computation of Taxable Gifts

Item number	Donee's name and address and description of gift. If the gift was made by means of a trust, enter trust's identifying number below and attach a copy of the trust instrument	Donor's adjusted basis of gift	Date of gift	Value at date of gift
1				

1 Total gifts of donor (see instructions)	1		
2 One-half of items .... attributable to spouse (see instructions)	2		
3 Balance (subtract amount on line 2 from amount on line 1)	3		
4 Gifts of spouse to be included (from line 2 of spouse's return—see instructions)	4		130,000
5 Total gifts (add amounts on lines 3 and 4)	5		130,000
6 Total exclusions not exceeding $3,000 for the calendar year for each donee (except gifts of future interests)	6		10,000
7 Total included amount of gifts (subtract amount on line 6 from amount on line 5)	7		120,000
Deductions (see instructions):			
8 Gift of qualified interests to spouse for this period (before annual exclusion, based on items .... from Schedule A)	8		
9 Annual exclusion attributable to gifts on line 8	9		
10 Net amount (subtract amount on line 9 from amount on line 8)	10		
11 First $100,000 marital deduction	11	$100,000	
12 Marital deduction for prior periods after December 31, 1976	12		
13 Balance of first $100,000 marital deduction available (subtract amount on line 12 from amount on line 11. If less than zero, enter zero)	13		
14 Excess over first $100,000 marital deduction (if total of amount on line 10 plus amount on line 12 is $100,000 or less, enter zero. Otherwise, enter amount on line 8 less amount on line 13)	14		
15 Excess over first $100,000 for prior periods (after December 31, 1976)	15		
16 Total excess over first $100,000 (add amounts on lines 14 and 15)	16		
17 Second $100,000	17	$100,000	
18 Gifts qualifying for additional marital deduction (subtract amount on line 17 from amount on line 16. If less than zero, enter zero)	18		
19 Enter 50% of amount on line 18	19		
20 Enter 50% of amount on line 8 but not more than amount on line 10	20		
21 Enter the smaller of the amount on line 10 or the amount on line 13	21		
22 Marital deduction (if amount on line 18 is zero, enter amount from line 21. Otherwise, enter amount from line 21 plus the smaller of the amounts on line 19 or line 20)	22		
23 Charitable, public, and similar gifts (based on items ...., less exclusions)	23		
24 Total deductions (add amounts on lines 22 and 23)	24		
25 Amount of taxable gifts (subtract amount on line 24 from amount on line 7)	25		120,000

Schedule B Did you (the donor) file gift tax returns for prior periods? (If "Yes," follow instructions in completing Schedule B below.) ☐ Yes ☐ No

(a) Calendar years (prior to 1971) and calendar quarters (1971 and subsequent years)	(b) Internal Revenue office where prior return was filed	(c) Amount of unified credit against gift tax for periods after December 31, 1976	(d) Amount of specific exemption for prior periods ending before January 1, 1977	(e) Amount of taxable gifts

1 Totals for prior periods (without adjustment for reduced specific exemption)	1	
2 Amount, if any, by which total specific exemption, line 1, column (d), is more than $30,000	2	
3 Total amount of taxable gifts for prior periods (add amount, column (e), line 1, and amount, if any, line 2)	3	

(If more space is needed, attach additional sheets of same size.)

☆ U.S. GOVERNMENT PRINTING OFFICE : 1981—O-313-393

However, if Aaron and wife elect to split the gift, Aaron's gift tax return would be:

Current gift ($260,000 × 0.50)		$130,000
Less: Annual exclusion		− 10,000
Current taxable gift		$120,000
Total prior taxable gifts		+247,000
Basis for tax		$367,000
Tax on $367,000		$110,580
Less: Unified credit	$ 47,000	
Previous gift taxes paid	+ 31,840	− 94,640
Gift tax payable		$ 15,940

And Aaron's wife's gift tax return would be:

Current gift ($260,000 × 0.50)	$130,000
Less: Annual exclusion	− 10,000
Current taxable gift	$120,000
Total prior taxable gifts	–0–
Basis for tax	$120,000
Tax on $120,000	$ 29,800
Less: Unified credit	− 62,800
Gift tax payable	$ –0–

13-09.2 Tax Hint

The reduced tax liability, as a result of gift splitting, is caused by three factors:

1. The progressive tax structure is mitigated by having two taxpayers.
2. There are two $10,000 annual exclusion, instead of one.
3. Two unified credits may be used instead of one.

In gift and estate planning (Chapter 14), one spouse often has a significant estate, and one has a modest estate. The unified credit of the spouse with a modest estate may never be fully utilized. The gift splitting election helps to insure that both unified credits will be more effectively used to reduce the gift and estate taxes of the married couple.

PLANNING APPLICATIONS 13-10

Giving gifts to those who would otherwise inherit the property someday serves two tax planning purposes:

1. Income-producing property can be given to those in a lower federal income tax bracket. This transfer reduces the income tax paid on the income and therefore increases the total assets in the "family."
2. The estate tax is based on the fair market value of all the assets owned by the deceased (Chapter 14). So amounts given as gifts after December 31, 1976 are added back to the estate, but in most cases only the fair market value of the gift, *at the date of the gift,* is added back. Subsequent appreciation escaped the gift tax. The gift taxes paid also serve to reduce the taxable estate.

Although the effects on the estate tax are discussed more fully in Chapter 14, an example of how these tax savings can increase total assets within the family follows.

Example 13-10.1

Barney Colin has an estate of $5,000,000. He intends to give $1,000,000 to his children, "someday." He is a 50% incremental bracket taxpayer, and the $1,000,000 is earning income at 10% per year compounded annually. He feels that the asset will grow at a compounded rate of 5% per year in addition to earning 10% of its value. If he keeps the $1,000,000 asset and dies in five years:

Start of			$1,000,000
Year 1	Income ($1,000,000 @ 10%)	$100,000	
	Tax ($100,000 @ 50%)	– (50,000)	50,000
	Appreciation ($1,000,000 @ 5%)		+ 50,000
Year 2			$1,100,000
	Income ($1,100,000 @ 10%)	$110,000	
	Tax ($110,000 @ 50%)	– (55,000)	55,000
	Appreciation ($1,100,000 @ 5%)		+ 55,000
Year 3			$1,210,000
	Income ($1,210,000 @ 10%)	$121,000	
	Tax ($121,000 @ 50%)	– (60,500)	60,500
	Appreciation ($1,210,000 @ 5%)		+ 60,500
Year 4			$1,331,000
	Income ($1,331,000 @ 10%)	$133,100	
	Tax ($133,100 @ 50%)	– (66,550)	66,550
	Appreciation ($1,331,000 @ 5%)		+ 66,550
Year 5			$1,464,100
	Income ($1,464,100 @ 10%)	$146,410	
	Tax ($146,410 @ 50%)	– (73,205)	73,205
	Appreciation ($1,464,100 @ 5%)		+ 73,205
Estate value at death			$1,610,510
Estate tax (assuming 50% maximum)			– 805,255
Amount remaining for children			$ 805,255

On the other hand, if Barney gives the $1,000,000 to the children now, whose average incremental tax bracket is 35%, the remaining asset would be:

Beginning asset value		$1,000,000
Appreciation, 5% compounded annually		305,255
Income: Year 1	$100,000	
Year 2	110,000	
Year 3	121,000	
Year 4	133,100	
Year 5	+ 146,410	
	$610,510	

Tax ($610,510 × 35%)	(213,678)	+ 396,832
Asset value at end of 5 years		$1,702,087
Estate tax on $1,000,000 @ 50%		− 500,000
Amount remaining for children		$1,202,087
Amount remaining with no gift		− 805,255
Net savings		$ 396,832

The net savings is comprised of:

1. $305,255 appreciation not taxed in the estate @ 50%		$ 152,628
2. Federal income taxes:		
Paid by father ($610,510 @ 50%)	$305,255	
Paid by children ($610,510 @ 35%)	−213,678	91,577
3. Estate tax paid on income retained from investment		
Gross income	$610,510	
Income tax paid	−305,255	
Net in the estate	$305,255	
$305,255 × 50%		+ 152,627
Net savings from gift		$ 396,832

The savings would actually be higher than $396,832, since Barney would have to use other assets of his estate to pay the gift tax. That amount would be excluded from the estate and provide an additional savings in estate taxes.

14
ESTATE TAXES

STRUCTURE OF THE TAX

14-01

1. A taxpayer's death gives rise to several important tax events.

1. A new taxpayer is created—The Estate of ———.
2. Presuming the deceased is a calendar year taxpayer, a final return is filed for the period of January 1 to the date of death. If the deceased was married, the spouse can file a joint return for the year of death.
3. The estate files Form 1041, reporting income and expenses since death. Any item of income received by the estate is taxed in the same manner as if it had been received by the deceased. If items of income pass directly to a beneficiary because of the death of the taxpayer, the beneficiary must report the income element of such receipts in the same manner as the deceased would have.
4. The estate must also file an estate tax return. The tax is

based on the fair market value, net of certain debts and expenses, of *all* the property of the deceased, wherever it is located.

14-01.1 Computing the Tax

To compute the tax, the market value of all taxable gifts made subsequent to December 31, 1976 must be included in the property of the deceased. What market value do you use?

1. The general rule is the market value at the date of the gift is used.
2. If the gift was made within three years of death and was a gift of life insurance or certain other assets in limited situations, the market value either at the date of death or the alternative valuation date is used. The executor may choose one of these two dates: the date of death or six months from the date of death (called the *alternative valuation date*).
3. If the alternative valuation date is chosen, and if property is sold or distributed by the estate during the 6-month period, then the market value at the date of disposition is used for the market value.

Any gift tax paid on an asset in number 2 above is added back to the estate. The effect of this addition, in combination with the use of the market value at either the date of death or alternative valuation date, is to compute the estate tax as if no gift were made.

As the last step in computing the estate tax, take as a credit against the tax liability any gift taxes paid on gifts added back to the estate, along with the unified credit (Table 13-1).

A simplified example of the tax computation follows. A more comprehensive example is given in 14-12.

Example 14-01.2

Market value of property owned by the deceased		$2,000,000
Plus: Taxable gift made three years or more prior to death		100,000
Market value of life insurance gift made within three years of death		50,000
Gift tax paid on $50,000 gift		+ 15,000
Gross assets in computation		$2,165,000
Less: Liabilities of the deceased	$400,000	
Expenses of the estate	+ 45,000	− 445,000
Basis for computation		$1,720,000
Tax on $1,720,000 from unified tables (Table 13-1)		$654,800
Less: Unified credit (in 1987)	$192,800	
Gift taxes paid on $100,000	23,800	
Gift taxes paid on $50,000	15,000	231,600
Estate tax payable		$ 423,200

PROPERTY INCLUDED IN THE ESTATE 14-02

What is included in the deceased's estate?

1. All property that the deceased had beneficial ownership in is included in the gross estate.
2. Property held in *joint tenant* registration with rights of survivorship (or *tenants by the entirety*) is included 50% in the estate of the deceased.
3. Property held and registered as *tenants in common* is included in the estate only in proportion to the deceased ownership.
4. *Community property* is included in the estate of proportion to the amount owned by the deceased under state law.
5. Any property to which the deceased had a general power of appointment (13-03) is included fully in the estate.

6. A major area for potential controversy is *life insurance proceeds.* If the deceased had *any* incident of ownership over the policy, the proceeds payable at death are included in the estate—even if the payment went directly to the beneficiary, without passing through the estate.
7. All other payments made to beneficiaries, over which the deceased had *any incident of ownership* is similarly included in the estate, including pension fund proceeds and income earned but not yet received.

14-02.1 **Tax Hint**

One of the easiest first steps of estate planning is to transfer all insurance policies out of the control of the insured. Since the gift tax would be based on the market value of the policy before death, there is normally no gift tax, or a very small tax to pay. The insured could then make gifts of the future premiums if they were needed.

The key is to *give up* ownership of the policy. The two major factors of ownership are: (1) being able to change the beneficiary, and (2) being able to borrow against the policy. Have the ownership of the policy confirmed in writing by the insurance company, so there is no doubt when it comes time to prove the facts.

14-02.2 **Tax Hint**

Beginning in 1987, each taxpayer is entitled to the unified credit of $192,800. In other words, the first $600,000 of taxable estate is exempt from taxes, because the estate tax on $600,000 is exactly $192,800. See Table 13-1 for the credit and resulting exclusion for the years 1982 to 1986.

Single income-producing families often have the problem that the non-income producer does not have $600,000 in assets to fully utilize the unified credit and the marital deduction. This difficulty can be overcome by having the spouse with a large estate make gifts to the other spouse.

There is no limit on the amount of gifts that may be made between husband and wife, and no gift tax will be incurred. In addition, property held as joint tenants with rights of survivorship or as tenants by the entirety will be considered 50% owned by each.

THE EFFECTS OF LIFETIME GIFTS 14-03

To compute the estate tax, you have to add back to the estate those lifetime gifts that were made after December 31, 1976.

1. Gifts of life insurance and certain other assets under some conditions made within three years of the date of death must be added back to the estate on a basis as if no gift had been made.
2. Other gifts made after December 31, 1976 must be added back at the fair market value as of the date of the gift if a gift tax return had to be filed. The $10,000 excludible portion of the gift is not added back.

Retained Rights of Use or Income 14-03.1

Property transferred by a deceased can be included in the estate on the same basis as if it had not been transferred at all, *if the deceased retained certain rights to the property*. As an example, if the deceased retained a life interest in the income from the property, the property would be included in the estate as if the deceased had not transferred it. Similarly, if the deceased retained the right to determine who would receive the income or enjoyment from the property, it would be considered as if he or she still owned it.

On the other hand, if grantors of irrevocable trusts retain no economic interest in the property, it is generally not included in their estates. Irrevocable trusts, however, constitute an area of highly technical "tax traps" that are too often settled in court. The problems arise when grantors retain "some" control over the assets in the trust, such as the right to vote stock. Clearly, when grantors hold the right to determine whether the income will be accumulated or retained in the trust, the assets are included in the estate. Due to these pitfalls, taxpayers should enter into trust agreements only with the aid of competent legal and tax counsel. Further, if the power to alter or amend a trust is revoked within three years of death, it is considered to have still been in effect at the date of death.

Even limits on the powers of grantors normally do not keep the property from being included in the estate. For example, even if grantors cannot change the trusts to benefit themselves, they may have nonetheless retained enough power over the trust to include the trust property in their estate.

14-03.2 Transfers Taking Effect at Death

At times property is *contingently transferred*. This sort of transfer can occur under two circumstances:

1. The *final title passes only if the transferee survives the transferor*. If the reversionary interest of the deceased exceed 5% of the value of the property, then the full value of the property is included in the estate. It is not necessary that the instrument of transfer include the potential repossession of the property by the deceased. A reversionary interest existing under local law would cause the assets to be added to the estate for the computation of the estate tax. Obviously, local legal counsel is required when such a possibility exists.
2. *The transferee retains a reversionary interest in the property*. If the transfer of property is solely contingent on the transferee surviving the transferor, then the property is included in the estate of the transferor. But if the transfer is *also* contingent on the occurrence of another event, such as the passage of time, the property may be excluded from the estate. Such an additional event, however, must be real and measurable to be recognized by the IRS.

Uniform Gifts to Minors Act 14-03.3

The Uniform Gifts to Minors Act is in effect in all fifty states and the District of Columbia. It allows for the transfer of assets to a minor without the creation of a trust agreement. If, however, the donor of the gift is also the custodian under the act, then the full amount of the assets are included in the donor's estate. The reason is that the donor retains certain controls over the assets when acting as custodian. These controls are enough, in most cases, to include the assets in the donor's estate.

Tax hint 14-03.3A

When using the Uniform Gifts to Minors Act, it is always wiser to appoint a third party custodian. A third party appointment makes it quite a bit easier to prove that the donor has relinquished all the rights of ownership. Such a custodian should normally not be the spouse of the donor, but some adverse party who will clearly protect the rights of the minor child over the rights of the donor.

GENERATION-SKIPPING TRANSFERS 14-04

Prior to 1976, families could make arrangements so that they would have to pay the transfer tax (either gift or estate) only once every several generations. The grandfather (grantor) would set up a trust, with his son or daughter (the father or mother of the grantor's grandchild) as the *income beneficiary.* The beneficiary of the *corpus* of the trust was the grandchild of the grantor. In this manner, the assets of the trust would pass to the grandchild upon his or her parent's death, and a generation was "skipped."

In 1976, the generation-skipping transfer tax was established. The tax is imposed on the trust, not on the estate of any of the parties. The tax becomes payable at the earlier of:

1. the termination of the intervening interest (the parent's death),
2. distribution to the grandchild.

The parent is considered to be a "deemed transferor." In other words, the parent is deemed to have transferred the property received from the grandparent to the grandchild.

Based on the unified gift and estate tax tables, the tax is figured by adding the trust assets to the next highest incremental tax bracket that the deemed transferor's estate would have been in.

There is an exemption from the tax of $250,000 per deemed transferor. So if the grantor has three children, each of whom has children, the exclusion from the tax would be $750,000 in property transferred through generation skipping trusts.

14-04.1 Tax Hint

Despite the new tax, generation-skipping transfers still offer an excellent estate planning tool. The $250,000 exclusion from the tax reduces the grantor's estate tax from the highest incremental bracket. For large families, significant amounts can still escape the transfer tax through one or more generations.

The concept can be even more helpful when the grantor's children are established, when the ultimate beneficiary is the grantor's great-grandchildren, and when the deemed transferors are the grandchildren. Since there are often more grandchildren than children, there may be more $250,000 exclusions.

14-05 LIFE INSURANCE AND PENSION PROCEEDS

Life insurance proceeds are generally included in the gross estate, unless *both* of the following conditions exist:

1. The deceased possessed no incidents of ownership in the policy at death or for the three-year period preceding death.

2. The proceeds were not payable to the deceased or to the estate.

What about other payments made on account of the death of the taxpayer? As a general rule, they are included in the gross estate of the deceased—including the present value of annuities paid to survivors. But this rule has many exceptions, and some of the more important ones are discussed in this section.

Refund Plan Annuities 14-05.1

Some annuity plans call not only for payments until the death of the beneficiary, but also for a partial refund of the premiums paid if the beneficiary dies before a given date. If either the beneficiary of the deceased or the estate receives the refund payment in a lump sum, that amount is included in the gross estate. If the refund payments are taken as an annuity, then the discounted present value of the annuity is included in the estate. But the value of an annuity received by a widow(er), in the amount of the deceased employee's salary, is not included in the estate of the deceased if one of the requirements under the plan was that the deceased be employed at the time of his/her death.

Employee Benefit Plans 14-05.2

Excluded from the estate are payments from a qualified plan that relate to contributions made by the employer *and* that the deceased was *not* entitled to withdraw before death. The exception is as follows: If the payment from a deceased employee's pension plan is made in a lump sum, *and* if the beneficiary elects the favorable 10-year averaging method (09-05), then the entire amount is included in the estate.

Amounts that relate to employee contributions, as well as amounts that the employee was entitled to withdraw from the plan, are included in the gross estate.

14-06 TAX BASED ON MARKET VALUE

The estate tax is based on the fair market value of assets possessed by the deceased. *Fair market value* is normally considered to be what a willing buyer would pay and what a willing seller would accept, if neither is compelled to complete the transaction. But, the IRS may determine market value for you. If so, the burden of proof to show that the IRS is incorrect rests with the executor of the estate. The IRS must provide the information and computations of its determinations of market value.

The special rules regarding certain assets are discussed in this section.

14-06.1 Real Property

Most real property, covered by the general rule, is valued at its *best use.* In other words, the property's current use does not matter; the presumption is that a buyer would pay the highest price based on the property's best use.

Real property being used for a farm or for a closely held business may be an exception to the rule. For the exception to come into play, the objective of the owner must be to retain the property in the family and in the family's business. There are numerous requirements for the lower "actual" use market value to be used, some of the more important of which are:

1. At least 25% of the gross estate, as well as 50% of the net estate after expenses, is comprised of the farm or closely held business.
2. The property must pass to a qualified heir, such as a child, spouse, or other close relative.

3. The property must have been used by the taxpayer or by the family as a farm or closely held business for at least 5 of the 8 years preceding the death of the taxpayer.
4. The property continues to be used for at least 10 years by the heir in its original use.

The maximum reduction in market value from best use to actual use is $750,000 ($600,000 in 1981 and $700,000 in 1982).

The IRS normally places a lien on the property for the difference between the tax that would have been paid based on "best use" and the tax that was paid on actual use. If the property is disposed of, or if it is converted to a different use, by the heir within 10 years, the IRS claims the additional tax. If the property is disposed of or converted between 10 and 15 years after the death of the taxpayer, the amount of tax forfeited is prorated based on the number of years held.

Stocks and Bonds 14-06.2

Determining the market value on publicly traded *stocks and bonds* is relatively straightforward. If a sale takes place on the date of death (or on the alternate valuation date), then the mean between the high and low for the day is the market value. If no sale takes place on the valuation date, then use a weighted average price for the sales that occurred close to the valuation date. Lacking actual sales information, the mean between the bid and the ask may be used.

Series EE bonds and *mutual fund shares* are valued at their redemption prices.

A *closely held business* interest presents a more difficult problem. The value of a closely held business is the value of *all* its assets, including goodwill, less the liabilities of the business. The goodwill portion includes what a willing buyer would pay for the income-producing capabilities of the business.

14-06.2A **Tax hint**

For a closely held business, a cross-buyout agreement is often a solution to the estate tax valuation problem and to the business disposition problem when one of the stockholders dies. Annually, the stockholders agree on what their shares are worth. They further agree that the corporation *must* buy those shares from the estate of any stockholder at that price. Since the agreement is made by adverse parties, protecting the interests of both their business and their families, the IRS generally recognizes the values set. Such an agreement can be (and usually is) funded, in full or in part, by life insurance. The corporation is generally the beneficiary of the life insurance, which provides the funds to buy back the stock.

Competent legal counsel is required when you enter into such an agreement. First, and most important, each of the parties needs to be sure the agreement adequately protects his or her heirs. Second, the wording of the contract must be designed to insure that the proceeds of the life insurance are not taxable to the corporation.

The premiums on such a life insurance policy are not deductible for income tax purposes by the corporation.

14-06.3 Annuities

Annuities that terminate at the death of the taxpayer are obviously worthless and have no value in the estate. But annuities or other reversionary interests that pass to the heirs have value—normally the discounted present value of future payments. Regulation 20.2031-10 sets out the tables for computing the discounted present value.

If the payments are to be made to an heir who is known to be in poor health, or who dies before the filing of the estate tax return, the shorter actual period may be used.

DEDUCTIONS FROM THE TAXABLE ESTATE 14-07

In computing the net taxable estate, you are allowed certain deductions from the market value of the assets owned at death:

1. funeral expenses paid by the estate,
2. liabilities of the deceased paid by the estate,
3. claims against assets in the estate that are assumed by the beneficiary,
4. administration expenses of the estate,
5. losses sustained by the estate (unless they are deducted on the income tax return of the estate),
6. transfers to charitable organizations,
7. the marital deduction (14-08), and

Income taxes on income received after death are not deductible in computing the estate tax.

The rules for which charitable contributions qualify for the deduction are the same as the rules for charitable contributions that are exempt from the gift tax (13-08).

THE MARITAL DEDUCTION 14-08

An unlimited deduction from the gross estate is allowed for property passing to the surviving spouse.

Terminable Interest 14-08.1

The estate tax marital deduction may be lost if the property passing to the surviving spouse is subject to termination during the spouse's life. This rule prevents the use of the marital deduction to shield property going indirectly to a third party. As an example, the wife might inherit the property for one year, at which time it passes to a third party.

If the terminable interest is based on the life of the spouse, then the property may still qualify for the marital deduction. As an example, the wife receives the income from the property (payable at least annually), and upon her death the property passes to a third party or to other parties according to the will of the wife.

Between these two extremes is a multitude of contractual possibilities, which may or may not qualify for the marital deduction.

14-08.2 Tax Hint

If the amount of the allowable marital deduction is limited by the amount passing to the surviving spouse, how much should be left to the surviving spouse to take maximum advantage of this deduction? A difficult estate planning question!

Three objectives should be kept in mind:

1. full use of the lifetime credits of both spouses,
2. maximum deferral of the payment of gift and estate taxes, and
3. reduction of the incremental gift and estate tax rates.

The simplest answer is to leave 100% of the estate not covered by the lifetime credit to the surviving spouse. Doing so accomplishes maximum deferral of taxes. However, it will insure that, when the surviving spouse dies, the maximum incremental tax will be paid.

Obviously, the desires of the parties, their ages and the size of the potential estate must be analyzed to reach the "best" answer for attaining these conflicting objectives.

14-09 CREDITS AGAINST ESTATE TAX LIABILITY

All estates are allowed a unified credit of $192,800 (14-01). Also allowed as a credit is the gift taxes paid by the deceased during his or her lifetime. Certain other credits against the estate tax are described in this section.

State Taxes 14-09.1

A credit is allowed for the state inheritance and estate taxes paid by the estate. The credit may not be for the full amount paid, since the amount of the allowable credit is limited by the amount of the taxable estate. (See Table 14-1).

TABLE 14-1. Maximum Allowable State Tax Credits

Adjusted taxable estate more than—*	*But not more than—*	*Maximum Credit on amount in col. (A)*	*Rate of Credit on excess of amount in col. (A)*
(A)	(B)	(C)	(D)
$ 40,000	90,000		0.8%
90,000	140,000	400	1.6%
140,000	240,000	1,200	2.4%
240,000	440,000	3,600	3.2%
440,000	640,000	10,000	4.0%
640,000	840,000	18,000	4.8%
840,000	1,040,000	27,600	5.6%
1,040,000	1,540,000	38,800	6.4%
1,540,000	2,040,000	70,800	7.2%
2,040,000	2,540,000	106,800	8.0%
2,540,000	3,040,000	146,800	8.8%
3,040,000	3,540,000	190,800	9.6%
3,540,000	4,040,000	238,800	10.4%
4,040,000	5,040,000	290,800	11.2%
5,040,000	6,040,000	402,800	12.0%
6,040,000	7,040,000	522,800	12.8%
7,040,000	8,040,000	650,800	13.6%
8,040,000	9,040,000	786,800	14.4%
9,040,000	10,040,000	930,800	15.2%
10,040,000		1,082,800	16.0%

*Adjusted taxable estate means the taxable estate reduced by $60,000.

14-09.2 Foreign Taxes

A credit is allowed for all or part of foreign estate taxes paid. The amount of the foreign tax credit allowable is limited in several ways. In effect, the maximum credit that may be taken is equivalent to the U.S. estate tax that would have been paid had the property not been subject to the foreign tax.

Foreign estate taxes payable to certain countries may not be allowed at all. The President has the discretion to disallow any country's taxes as a credit if they do not allow U.S. estate tax as a credit in figuring their local estate taxes.

14-09.3 Prior Transfers

When part of an estate is comprised of property that has been subjected to either estate tax or to the generation-skipping transfer tax within 10 years, a credit may be allowed to alleviate the effects of double taxation. If the credit is allowed, only a portion of that credit is usable based on the following time table:

Years Since Acquisition	*Percentage Allowed*
0–2	100%
2–4	80%
4–6	60%
6–8	40%
8–10	20%

The amount of the credit is based on the valuation used in the estate of the prior deceased.

The computation of the credit is rather complex. But the net result is that the credit is the lower of:

1. the amount of tax that the estate of the prior deceased paid on the property, or

2. the amount of additional tax that the current deceased's estate would have paid on the property.

TAXABILITY OF DISTRIBUTIONS TO THE BENEFICIARIES 14-10

Beneficiaries of the deceased may receive their property (or money) either directly from the payer or from the estate. In either case, "Is this income taxable?" To the extent that payments are received that would have been taxable to the deceased, had he or she lived, *someone* must pay income tax on that amount.

If the beneficiaries receive property *from the estate,* the estate has already paid any income taxes required, and the amount received is exempt from federal income tax. In some states, the beneficiaries may have a state inheritance tax liability.

If the amount is received directly *from the payer,* such as the proceeds of a pension plan, the beneficiary must pay income taxes on the portion of the receipts that would have been taxable to the deceased (09-09.4 and 09-09.5). The beneficiary may receive an adjustment of basis for estate tax paid as it relates to the distribution received.

FILING AND PAYING ESTATE TAXES 14-11

The discussion in this section, more than any other, is presented for information's sake only. The filing of an estate tax return should be undertaken by an attorney fully qualified to handle such matters. The penalties for failure to file properly and to pay taxes in a timely manner can be severe.

An estate tax return (Form 706) is due 9 months after the date of death. Normally extensions are granted for at least 6 months, as are the requirements for paying the tax.

Special installment plans are available for estates containing significant amounts of farm property or closely held businesses. These installment plans can be entered into for periods of up to 15 years and at favorable interest rates. The objective of the installment programs is to preserve the assets of the deceased and to avoid forced sales. The executor of the estate must apply for such a plan. If the plan is granted, it is normally terminated upon the disposition of the related property.

14-11.1 Flower Bonds

Certain issues of U.S. government bonds (called "flower bonds") may be used to pay estate taxes. The bonds are honored at par value, and they must be reported in the estate tax return at par value. The bonds are low-yielding bonds, and they can generally be purchased at a discount from face.

To be usable for payment of estate taxes, the bonds must have been owned by the deceased prior to death. Since the bonds, even after consideration of the discount, yield less than other government bonds, rarely does a taxpayer own them except in contemplation of death.

14-12 ILLUSTRATIVE ESTATE TAX RETURN

Facts

Name of the deceased: John Begone
Date of death: June 6, 1987
Beneficiaries:
- Church: $70,000
- Wife: property and cash of $1,000,000
- Children: remainder

Assets:
- Home, registered joint tenants with rights of survivorship, 100% of cost was contributed by John, market value $165,000.
- Savings account, registered in John's name, $94,500.

Savings account, registered joint tenants with rights of survivorship, each contributed 50%, $111,000.

Insurance policy, payable to his wife who had all the incidences of ownership, $150,000.

Insurance policy, payable to his wife who paid the premiums; John had the right to change the beneficiary, $225,000.

Common stock, registered in joint tenants with rights of survivorship, market value $45,000; John contributed 2/3, his wife 1/3.

General power of appointment from John's father's estate, amount of assets $1,255,000.

Stamp collection, market value $285,000.

Liabilities:

Home mortgage, $45,000.

Expenses:

Funeral $17,250

Estate administration: $26,250

State death taxes: $36,300

Reportable gifts:

$67,500 in 1980 to his son.

Computation of Estate Tax 14-12.1

Home		$ 82,500
Personal savings		94,500
50% of joint savings acount		55,500
Insurance policy which John could change the beneficiary		225,000
Common stock		22,500
Property over which John had a general power of appointment		1,255,000
Stamp collection		285,000
Lifetime reportable gifts		+ 67,500
		$2,087,500
Less: Home mortgage	$45,000	
Funeral expenses	17,250	
Estate administration	+26,250	− 88,500
Adjusted Gross Estate		$1,999,000

Marital deduction	−1,000,000
	$ 999,000
Less: Charitable contribution	− 70,000
Taxable estate	$ 929,000
Tax on $929,000	$ 318,110
Less: Unified credit	− 192,800
	$ 125,310
Less: State tax credit	− 29,224
Amount payable	$ 96,086

APPENDIX

PARAGRAPH	REFERENCE
01-04	Sec 6012(a)
01-04.1	Sec 6017, Reg 1.61-3(a), Sec 6012(a)(1)(C)(iv), Sec 6012(a)(8)
01-04.2	Reg 301.6501(c)-1(c)
01-05.1	Reg 1.61-1(a)
01-05.1A	Reg 1.61-1(b)(2)
01-05.1B	Reg 1.61-1(a)
01-05.2A	Sec 62
01-05.2B	Sec 170, Sec 164(a)(1), Sec 163(a), Reg 1.164-1(a)(5), RevRul 72-463
01-05.2C	Sec 63(d), Sec 63(c)
01-06.a	Sec 6013, Sec 143(a)(1), Reg 1.143-1(b), H. David Boyter 74 TC 72, RevRul 76-255
01-06.2A	Sec 2(a)
01-06.2B	Sec 2(b)
01-06.2C	Sec 2(b)(2)(C)
01-06.2D	Sec 2(b)(1)(B)
01-07.1	Sec 151(b)
01-07.2	Sec 151(c)
01-07.3	Sec 151(d)
01-07.3A	Sec 151(d)(3)
01-08	Sec 151(e), Sec 152
01-08.1	Sec 152(a)
01-08.1B	Reg 1.152-1(a)(2)(ii)
01-08.1C	RevRul 64-222
01-08.1D	Reg 1.152-3
01-08.1E	Reg 1.152-1(c)
01-08.2	Sec 152(a)
01-08.2A	Reg 1.152-2(c)(1)
01-08.2B	Sec 152(a)(9), Reg 1.152-1(b)
01-08.3	Sec 151(e)(1)(A)
01-08.3A	Reg 1.151-2(a)
01-08.3A	IRS Publication 17 (revised 11/80) Page 19
01-08.3B	Reg 1.152-1(c), Sec 63(e)(1)(D), Sec 63(e)(2)

PARAGRAPH	REFERENCE
01-08.4	Sec 151(e)(2), RevRul 65-34
01-08.5	Sec 152(b)(3), Reg 1.152-2(a)(2)
01-09	Sec 1
01-09.1	Sec 63(e)(1)(A)
01-09.3	1980 Form 1940 Instructions, page 12
01-11	Sec 7201
02-02	Reg 1.61-7
02-02.2	Sec 128 (Effective 1/1/85)
02-02.3	Reg. 1.103 1, Sec103(b)
02-02.3A	Sec 103(c)
02-02.3B	Sec 103(b)(2), Sec 103(b)(4)
02-02.3C	U.S. Code Title 48
02-02.5	RevRul 73-112, RevRul 80-143
02-02.6	Collector v Day 1971 Supreme Court
02-03	Sec 101(a)
02-03.2	RevRul 61-134
02-03.3	Sec 101(c)
02-03.3B	Sec 101(d)
02-03.4	Cohen 39 TC 1055, Sec 1035
02-04	Sec 72(e)(1)(B), Sec 72(e)(2)
02-04.2	Sec 72(h)
02-04.4	Reg 1.1035-1(b)
02-05	Reg 1.72-4
02-05.2	Reg 1.72-4
02-05.3	Reg 1.72-6
02-05.4	Reg 1.72-6(a)(ii)
02-06.1	Sec 104(a)(3)
02-06.2	Sec 104(a)(1)
02-06.3	Reg 1.105-2, Sec 105(h)
02-06.4	Sec 105(d)
02-07	Reg 1.102-1(a)
02-07.2	Reg 1.102-1(b)
02-07.3	Sec 74(a), Reg 1.74-1(b), Sec 117

Abbreviations used:

Sec	Internal Revenue Code
Reg	Federal Regulation
TC	Tax Court
AFTR	American Federal Tax Report
AFTR2d	American Federal Tax Report, Second Series
RevRul	Revenue Ruling
US	United States Reports

PARAGRAPH	REFERENCE
02-08	RevRul 70-217, RevRul 70-341, RevRul 71-425, Reg 1.85-1
02-09	Sec 116(c)(1), Sec 316(b)(1), Sec 301, Sec 316
02-09.1	Reg 1.301-1
02-09.2	Reg 1.301-1(b)
02-10	Sec 301(c)
02-10.2	Sec 346
02-11	Sec 305
02-11.1	Reg 1.307-1
02-11.2	Reg 1.305-3(c)
02-11.4	Sec 305(b), Sec 305(c)
02-12.2	Reg 1.307-1, Reg 1.307-2
02-12.4	Reg 1.307-1
02-12.4B	Reg 1.1223-1(f)
02-12.5	Reg 1.307-1, Reg 1.1223-1(e)
02-12.7	General Counsel's Memoranda # 13275 & 13414
02-13	Sec 691(a)
02-13.2	Reg 1.691(c)-1
02-14	Sec 243(a)(1)
02-14.3	Sec 245, Reg 1.244-1, Reg 1.244-2
02-14.4	Sec 246
02-14.5	Reg 1.246-3(d), Reg 1.246-3(e), Reg 1.236-3(c)(3)
02-14.6	RevRul 60-177
02-14.7	Reg 1.246-3(d)(2)
02-15	Reg 1.61-14, Raytheon 32 AFTR 1155
02-16	**Sec 911**
03-01	Reg 1.61-1 to Reg 1.61-15, RevRul 55-2, Eubank 311 US 122, Horst 311 US 112, RevRul 72-312
03-02	Reg 1.61-2
03-03	Reg 1.61-11, Reg 1.72-8
03-03.1	Sec 72(d)
03-03.2	Reg 1.101-2
03-03.3	Sec 402(e), Sec 403(a)(2)
03-03.4	Sec 402(a)(5)(D)(i)(II), Sec 403(a)(4), Sec 403(b)(8), Sec 408(d)(3)(A)
03-04.1	Sec 79
03-04.2	RevRul 64-328, RevRul 66-110, RevRul 67-154
03-04.3	Sec 127
03-04.4	Sec 119, Kowalski 40 AFTR2d 77-6128, Office Decision 514
03-04.5	Reg 1.61-2(d)(2), Reg 1.83-1
03-05	Sec 83
03-06.1	Sec 423
03-06.2	Reg 1.61-15, Reg 1.421-6
03-07	Reg 1.61-2(d)(2)
03-07.2	Reg 1.301-1(j)
03-08	Sec 61(a)(4), Sec 101(c), Sec 101(d), RevRul 72-77
03-08.1	Sec 454(b), Sec 1232(a)(3)
03-08.2	Sec 1232(a)(3)
03-08.3	Sec 454, Sec 1037(a)
03-08.4	Reg 1.61-7(d), RevRul 72-224
03-08.5	Reg 1.61-7(c)
03-08.6	Reg 1.1232-1, Reg 1.1232-3
03-08.7	RevRul 80-143
03-08.8	Reg 1.171-1, Reg 1.171-2
03-09	Sec 61(a)(5), Sec 61(a)(6), Reg 1.109-1, Reg 1.1241-1
03-10	Reg 1.102-1(a), Reg 1.61-12, Reg 1.016-7, Sec 108
03-11	Sec 61(a)-8, Sec 979, Reg 1.71
03-12.1	Davis 9 AFTR2d 1625, Section 2516
03-12.2	Reg 1.71-1(d)(3)
04-02	Sec 212, Reg 1.1001-1
04-02.2	Sec 165(g), Reg 1.165-4
04-03	Sec 1012
04-04	Reg 1.1012-1(a), Reg 1.61-1(a)
04-05	Sec 1015(a)
04-05.1	Sec 1015(d)(1)(A)
04-06	Sec 1014(a)
04-07	Sec 356
04-07.1	Sec 355, Sec 1036, Reg 1.1036-1(a), Sec 1016
04-07.2	Sec 351
04-07-3	Sec 1035, Sec 1031
04-07.4	Sec 1031
04-07.5	Sec 1031(b)
04-08	Reg 1.61-6
04-08.1	RevRul 68-528
04-08.2	Reg 1.307-1, Reg 1.307-2
04-08.4B	Reg 1.1012-1(c)
04-09	Sec 174
04-10	Sec 1033

PARAGRAPH	REFERENCE
04-11	Sec 1034, Sec 121
04-11.1	Sec 1034
04-11.2	Sec 121
04-12	Sec 165, Sec 167, Reg 1.165-3(a)(1)
04-13	Sec 267(a)(1), Sec 267(d), Reg 1.1239-1, RevRul 72-225
05-01	Reg 1.1221-1, Sec 1221(1), Sec 1236
05-02	Sec 1222, Sec 1223, Sec 1231, Sec 1235
05-02.1	RevRul 70-598, San Joaquin Fruit 297 US 406
05-02.2	Reg 1.1233-1(e)
05-02.3	Reg 1.1223-1
05-02.4	RevRul 70-344, RevRul 72-381
05-03-2A	Reg 1.1234-1(b), Sec 1234
05-03.2B	Sec 1234
05-03.3C	Sec 1234
05-03.4	Sec 1233(b), Sec 1233(c)
05-04	Sec 1222, Sec 1201, Sec 1202
05-05	Sec 1222, Sec 1211
05-05.3	Sec 1212
05-05.4	RevRul 62-42
05-06.3	Sec 582
05-07.2	Sec 1233(b)
05-07.4A	Reg 1.1233-1(e)
05-08	Sec 852 to Sec 855, Sec 116
05-09	Sec 1091
05-09.2	Hamlin Exec. 24 AFTR 36, RevRul 58-210
05-09.3	Reg 1.1091-1(a)
05-10	Sec 1092, Sec 263(g) Sec 1256 (a), Sec 1212(c)
05-11	Sec 1232(a)(4)
06-02.1	RevRul 70-474, Harsaghy 2 TC 484, Sec 162(a)(2), RevRul 73-529, RevRul 54-147
06-03	Lincoln Electric 38 AFTR 411, Walsh 12 AFTR 1456, Heininger 320 US 467
06-03.1	Reg 1.162-2, Sec 280A
06-04.1	**Sec 280A Bolton 77TC No. 8**
06-05.1	Sec 263, Reg 1.167(a)(3), Sec 248
06-05.2	Sec 41
06-05.3	Reg 1.265-1, Sec 162, Gale 13 TC 661
06-05.4	Sec 162(c), Sec 162(f), Sec 162(g)
06-06.1	Sec 401(a)(1)
06-06.1A	Sec 401(a)(7)
06-06.1B	Sec 401(a)(3)
06-06.1C	Sec 401(h)
06-06.1D	Sec 401(a)(4)
06-06.2	Sec 414(j)
06-06.3	Reg 1.401-1(b)
06-06.4	Reg 1.401-1(b)
06-06.5	Sec 414(j)
06-06.6	Sec 401(c), Sec 401(a), Sec 401(d)
06-06.7	Sec 408
06-06.8	Sec 408(j), Sec 408(1)
06-06.9	Sec 408(d)(3)
06-07.1	Sec 263
06-07.2	Burwig TC memorandum, Houston Chronicle 32 AFTR2d 73-5312-A RevRul 69-511
06-08	Reg 1.262-1
06-09	Reg 1.162-2, Correll 389 US 299
06-09.1	Revenue Procedure 80-7, Revenue Procedure 80-32, Reg 1.162-17, Reg 1.274-5, Reg 1.170A-1(g), Sec 213(e)(1)(B)
06-09.3	Sec 274(h)
06-09.4	Sec 274
06-10	Reg 1.162-1, Reg 1.274-2(d)(3), Reg 1.274-2(d)(4)
06-10.1	Sec 274
06-11	Sec 82, Sec 217
06-12	Reg 1.162-5
06-13	Sec 172
07-01	Sec 163(a), Sec 483
07-02.1	Sec 163(d)(1)
07-02.2	Reg 1.265-2
07-02.3	Reg 1.264-2
07-03.1	Reg 1.164-2
07-03.2	Reg 1.64-1
07-03.3	Sec 162, Sec 212
07-03.4	Sec 901 to Sec 908

PARAGRAPH	REFERENCE
07-04	Sec 170
07-04.1	Reg 1.170A-1(b), Sec 170(a)(2), Reg 1.170A-11(b), Reg 1.170A-1(c)(2), Revenue Procedure 80-7, Revenue Procedure 80-32, 1980 Form 1040 instructions, page 18
07-04.2	Reg 1.170A-4
07-04.4	Reg 1.1011-2
07-04.5	Reg 1.170A-6
07-04.6	Reg 1.170A-7(b)
07-04.7	Sec 170(f)(3)(B)(ii)
07-05	Sec 170(b)
07-06	Reg 1.170A-10, Reg 1.170A-11
07-07	Sec 213, RevRul 76-332, RevRul 79-162
07-07.2	RevRul 56-18, Sec 104(a)
07-08	Sec 165(c), Reg 1.165-7, Sec 104(a), Reg 1.165-11
07-08.2	Reg 1.165-7
07-09	Sec 162, Sec 212
07-10	**Sec 221**
08-01	Sec 167, Reg 1.167(a)-3, Reg 1.167(a)-10(b)
08-02	Reg 1.167(a)
08-02.1	Reg 1.167(a)-4, Sec 178
08-03	Reg 1.167(a)-10(a), Reg 1.167 (b)-0(a), Reg 1.167(g)-1 Reg 1.167(a)-5
08-03.2	Reg 1.167(f)-1
08-04	Sec 168
08-05	Sec 179
08-05.4	Sec 48(a)(8)
08-06	Sec 611
08-06.1	Reg 1.1611-1(b)
08-06.2	Sec 614
08-06.3	Reg 1.612-3, Proposed Reg 1.613A-7(f)
08-07.1	Reg 1.611-2
08-07.2	Sec 613(b)(1)(B) to Sec 613(b)(7), Reg 1.613-2, Sec 613A, Reg 1.613-4
08-08.1	Sec 617
08-08.2	Sec 616(a)
08-08.3	Reg 1.612-4, Reg 1.703-1(b)
08-09	Sec 451, Sec 175, Sec 182, RevRul 75-150, Reg 1.162-12, Sec 464
08-10	Sec 4986 to Sec 4997
08-11	Sec 183, Reg 1.183-1

PARAGRAPH	REFERENCE
08-12	Sec 166
08-12.4	Sec 165(g)
08-12.6	Sec 166(d)
08-13	Sec 174
09-01	Sec 1301 to Sec 1305
09-02	Sec 56 to Sec 58
09-03	Sec 55 to Sec 58
09-04	Sec 402
09-08.1	Sec 41
09-08.2	Sec 37
09-08.3	Sec 44A
09-08.4	Sec 901 to Sec 906
09-08.5	Sec 40, Sec 50
09-08.6	Sec 44B
09-08.7	Sec 44C, Sec 51
09-08.9	Sec 39, Sec 6420, Sec 6421, Sec 6424, Sec 6427
09-08.11	Sec 43
09-09	Sec 1(e), Sec 641, Sec 651, Sec 643(b), Sec 661, Sec 662, Sec 663
09-10	Sec 671 to Sec 678
09-11	Sec 666, Sec 667
09-12.2	Sec 584
09-12.3	Reg 301.7701-4
10-01	Sec 3401 to Sec 3403, Sec 6671, Sec 6672, Sec 1401 to Sec 1403, Sec 3501 to Sec 3506
10-01.1	Reg 31.3401(c)-1
10-02	Sec 6015, Sec 6073, Sec 6153, Sec 6654
10-02.1	Sec 6154
10-03	Sec 471
10-04	Sec 471, Sec 472
10-05	Reg 1.446-1
10-06	See references paragraph 03-01
10-07	Sec 163(d)(4)(A)
10-08	Sec 441, Sec 442
10-09.1	Reg 1.61-8
10-09.2	Moorman 26 TC 666, RevRul 53-234
10-09.3	Kahler 18 TC 31, Fischer 14 TC 792
10-09.4	Reg 1.1232-1, Reg 1.1232-3A
10-09.5	Reg 1.454-1(b)
10-10	RevRul 70-344, RevRul 72-381

PARAGRAPH	REFERENCE
10-11.1	Reg 301.6511(a)(1)
10-11.2	Reg 1.461-1(a)(1), RevRul 78-38
10-11.3	Sec 465
10-11.4	Sec 461(g)
10-12	Sec 453, Sec 453B
10-12.2	Sec 483
10-12.3	Sec 453B
10-13	Reg 1.453-6
11-01.1	Sec 6698
11-02	Reg 1.701-1, Reg 1.704-1
11-02.2	Sec 704, Sec 761(c)
11-02.4	Reg 1.704-1(b)(2)
11-02.5	Revenue Procedure 74-17
11-03	Sec 703(a)
11-04	Sec 704(e)
11-05	Sec 706
11-06	Sec 707
11-06.2	Reg 1.721-1
11-06.3	Sec 267(a)(2)
11-07	Sec 722, Sec 742
11-08	Sec 704, Sec 732 to Sec 735
11-09	Sec 736
12-01	Reg 301.7701-2
12-02.1	Sec 11(b)
12-02.2	Sec 1201(a)
12-02.3	Sec 1211(a), Sec 1212(a)
12-02.5	Reg 1.441-1(a)(3)
12-03	RevRul 55-234, Molin Properties 319 US 436, Chandler 27 AFTR 1291, Dean 35 TC 1083
12-05	Sec 170(b)(2), Sec 170(d)(2)
12-05.1B	Reg 1.162-15
12-05.2	Sec 248, Reg 1.248-1(b)(3)
12-06.1	Sec 1032
12-06.2	Reg 1.61-12(c)(3)
12-06.3	Sec 249
12-07.1	Sec 333
12-07.2	Sec 337
12-07.3	Sec 368
12-07.4	Sec 368(a)(1)(D)
12-07.5	Sec 341
12-07.6	Sec 306
12-08	Sec 531 to Sec 537
12-09	Sec 1371 to 1379
12-09.2	Sec 1378
12-09.3	Sec 1375
12-09.6	Sec 1371(a)
12-11	Sec 1561, Sec 1563
12-12	Sec 541 to Sec 547
12-13	Sec 851 to Sec 860
12-14.1	Sec 172(b)(1)(F)
12-14.2	Sec 585, Sec 593
12-14.3	Sec 582(c)(1)
12-15	Sec 801 to Sec 820
12-17	Sec 991 to 997
13-01	Sec 2502, Sec 2505
13-02	Sec 2501, Sec 2511, Sec 2522, Sec 2515, Sec 2503, Reg 25.2512-8, Merrill 324 US 308
13-03	Sec 2514
13-04	Roester 2 TC 298, Reg 25.2515-1
13-05	Sec 2035, Sec 2012
13-06	Sec 2512
13-07	Sec 2503, Sec 2523
13-08	Sec 2501, Sec 2522
13-09	Sec 2502
14-01	Reg 1.6012-3, Reg 1.6013-1(d), Reg 1.6012-5, Sec 2033
14-01.1	Sec 2035, Sec 2032, Sec 2001
14-02	Sec 2033, Sec 2040, Sec 351 (Revenue Act of 1948), Sec 2041, Sec 2042
14-03	Sec 2035
14-03.1	Sec 2036
14-03.2	Sec 2037
14-03.3	RevRul 70-348, Stuit 54 TC 580
14-04	Sec 2601 to Sec 2603, Sec 2611 to Sec 2614
14-05	Sec 2042, RevRul 68-334
14-05.1	Sec 2031, Fusz 46 TC 214
14-05.2	Reg 20.2039-1, RevRul 67-37
14-06	Reg 20.2031-1(b), Kinney's Est. 17 AFTR 81
14-06.1	Sec 1014(a), Sec 2032A, Sec 6324B
14-06.2	Sec 2031, RevRul 68-269
14-07	Sec 2053, Sec 2055, Sec 2057
14-08	Sec 2056, Reg 20.2056(c)-1, Sec 2031
14-08.1	Reg 20.2056(b)
14-09.1	Sec 2011
14-09.2	Sec 2014
14-09.3	Sec 2013
14-11	Sec 6018, Sec 6075(a), Sec 2002, Sec 2003, Sec 6166
14-11.1	Bankers Trust Co. (Ellis) 7 AFTR2d 1691

INDEX

C

D

E

J

K

L

M

N

O

P

Q

R

S

T

U

V

W

Y Z